Beyond the PhD

Prof Kenneth K Mwenda
PhD, LLD, DSc(Econ)

Beyond the PhD

International and State Recognition in Global Thought Leadership

VOLUME 2

Mereo Books

2nd Floor, 6-8 Dyer Street, Cirencester, Gloucestershire, GL7 2PF
An imprint of Memoirs Books. www.mereobooks.com
and www.memoirsbooks.co.uk

Beyond the PhD
ISBN: 978-1-9191788-6-8

First published in Great Britain in 2025
by Mereo Books, an imprint of Memoirs Books.

Copyright ©2025

Prof Kenneth K Mwenda has asserted his right under the Copyright Designs and Patents Act 1988 to be identified as the author of this work.

A CIP catalogue record for this book is available from the British Library.
This book is sold subject to the condition that it shall not by way of trade or otherwise be lent, resold, hired out or otherwise circulated without the publisher's prior consent in any form of binding or cover, other than that in which it is published and without a similar condition, including this condition being imposed on the subsequent purchaser.

The address for Memoirs Books can be found at www.mereobooks.com

Mereo Books Ltd. Reg. No. 12157152

Typeset in 11/17pt Garamond by Wiltshire Associates.
Printed and bound in Great Britain

TABLE OF CONTENTS

Chapter 9	My path to academia	1
Chapter 10	The Oxford Years	31
Chapter 11	The Yorkshire Years	82
Chapter 12	The Warwickshire Years	95
Chapter 13	Moving from England to the US	106
Chapter 14	Ambidexterity in global thought leadership	154
Chapter 15	Beyond the PhD	190
Chapter 16	Father, husband and scholar	216
Chapter 17	International and State Recognition of Global Thought-Leadership	274
Chapter 18	Leadership and Lifelong Learning	286
Chapter 19	The momentous Oxford gala dinner held in my honor	328
Chapter 20	Conclusion	358

Preface

In a monotheistic religion such as Christianity, there are often two types of prayers. One is for thanking the Deity and the other is for asking the Deity for His providence. So, if you are a Christian and believe in God, then we can safely say that there is a time for thanking God and a time for asking God for His providence. Now, which one of the two types of prayers do you often throw at God, and why? As believers, we all need to examine ourselves and our attitude towards God. Are we selfish and egocentric in our prayers? Do we also pray for others or is it just about ourselves and our wants? Don't you think God notices these things? God is not a hospital or bank for you to turn to only when you are besieged with problems. Normalize thanking God, even when all is going well for you. Because if you cannot thank God, you are less likely to thank your fellow human beings who have been there for you. And so, in this autobiography, I proceed with a deep sense of eternal gratitude to God Jehovah Almighty, my Heavenly Father, for everything that He has done and made possible for me even when the road ahead did not always look quite promising, but He came through and paved a way. It is for this reason that I share my story.

That you have lived an impactful life globally is the very reason you cannot conceal or hide the story of your life. A star will not shine if it is hidden underneath the bed, for it was not meant to be there but up in the skies for mankind to see or admire. Your extraordinary life is meant to inspire and motivate others. Distinguished people and notable dignitaries, including Chief Justices, central bank governors, eminent Professors, Vice-Chancellors and Chancellors of top universities, leading businessmen and women, diplomats and parliamentarians as well as many other government and corporate executives, both in your home country and abroad, cannot just gather at the highest level to honor you at elaborate luncheons and dinners dedicated exclusively to recognize your global thought-leadership and impressive scholarly work, unless there is something worth paying attention to about your name. So, I do not take these rare momentous experiences lightly. They are all blessings from the Heavenly Father, God Jehovah Almighty.

Indeed, it is not every day, for example, that the world's best university, the University of Oxford, gets to confer on you the highest honor that any Oxford college can confer on an eminently qualified and distinguished individual. And it is not every day that you would find some of the most distinguished professors at Oxford as well as several distinguished Oxford alumni, Oxford administrators and friends of Oxford gathered at a special gala dinner held exclusively in your honor to celebrate your indelible and edifying global thought-leadership. To me, all these are blessings from God. And I am truly humbled. I am arguably only the second black African since the year 1314 when my alma mater college in Oxford, Exeter College, was established to receive this highest honor at Oxford's Exeter College. So I consider myself blessed.

It is also not an ordinary occurrence that various universities where one teaches host luncheons in your honor whenever you visit them to celebrate your scholarly contributions. I do not take all this lightly. Neither is it an ordinary accomplishment for two sitting governments and Heads of State to honor you for your outstanding scholarly work and distinguished global thought-leadership, in addition to a revered foreign Head of State asking for you to provide his country with professional technical advice. Indeed, I have advised several other States and governments across many regions of the world on various legal, institutional and policy reforms. Closely related to this, I have often been sought after, as a global thought-leader, and invited to appear in numerous print and broadcast media programs, including the *New York Times* (USA), *Voice of America* (VOA, USA), *CCTV* (USA), *The Times* (UK), the British Broadcasting Corporation (BBC, UK), and Sky TV (UK). And so, my public intellectualism has continued to transcend national boundaries, extending into the frontiers of knowledge at the global and international levels.

Further, not every scholar's name makes it into the official government or State gazette in their home country or elsewhere in recognition of their outstanding scholarly achievements and eminent global thought-leadership. So, again, I do not take anything for granted. Honors have come both from home and abroad. And some of my former students continue to serve or have served at the highest levels of government in various countries around the world. Among them are a Chief Justice, Supreme Court Judges, Constitutional Court judges, Court of Appeal judges, High Court judges, Attorneys-General, several cabinet ministers, an ambassador and many more. My other former students are now Professors, Deans and Vice-Chancellors at leading universities in their home countries, while some occupy top positions in international organizations. Indeed, it has been an extraordinary life well lived. And I am ever grateful to my Heavenly Father, God Jehovah Almighty, as well as to all those through whom He has made it possible. I hope this, my story, will help to inspire others.

I am mindful, however, that some folks with something inspiring to talk or write about choose to hide their life story, insisting that they are private people or that they would like to remain private. Various reasons could help to explain the inclination of such people towards the alleged 'privacy', which in many cases is simply 'secrecy'. Folks who are too superstitious tend to be quite secretive. They believe in hiding everything about their private or professional lives. Others, especially those that have a checkered past, want to lie low to avoid any detection. But some sections of the public often mistake such maneuvers for humility. There is a difference between humility and concealment. By parity of reasoning, there is a difference between confidence and arrogance. People who are overly sensitive, for example, can easily mistake someone's confidence for arrogance simply because that person's confidence rubs them up the wrong way. Yet it is their own insecurities that are at play.

Also, in life, there are folks who, with nothing of substance to write home about except for hot air, are too loud and try too hard to be noticed. Yet the facts on the ground do not match their talk. If you are going to tell your life story, the truth should match the talk. People who know something about your background will even implore you to say something. Indeed, many people have approached me, asking me when I will write my autobiography. The writing of this book took longer than expected due to some competing academic and professional engagements, but I have finally delivered my life story. I am, however, mindful that some people could have expected me to talk about, say, any presidential ambitions I hold. Others would want me to revisit my first experience with snow when I first arrived in Europe close to four decades ago. It is always one thing or another, insisting on asking why you did not talk about this or that, or why you decided to include ABC, and not XYZ. Almost everyone has something that they expect you to say or write about. Others already know the kinds of things they expect you to say and how you should say them. Then there are those who will try to judge you based on your garb, as if your designer clothes can adversely affect your intellectual faculties. But remember that your autobiography is your life story, not theirs. Some people might want you to include them in your life story, but you can't please everybody. You just have to tell your life story as you, not for others.

As a global thought-leader and public intellectual, your life story is already a public book. You simply have to bring the book to your audience. Many people want to read it. The story does not belong to you alone. The impact of your life story has benefited many people near and far, so your story must be shared. That your story has touched the lives of many people around the world is a compelling reason why it must be shared, especially that it will continue to inspire many more. Through God, you owe that responsibility to humanity. As a leader, you are a role model that many people look up to. So, you have the moral responsibility, through your life story, to provide authentic leadership, even to people who have not met you but follow you and your works closely. Otherwise, it would be a grave injustice to deny people a glimpse into your extraordinary life. Many people have been inspired by your works and life story. And many others will continue to be inspired. Together, they are a part of your story. Therefore, you must tell your story, and nobody can tell it better than you yourself.

Neglecting to tell the story of an impactful life, I contend, is unfortunate if one has indeed lived such a life. It is like asking someone to deliver a distinguished lecture on your behalf when you are available to speak. The audience expects to hear from you, not from your delegate or surrogate. What comes from the horse's mouth is often treated more seriously than any hearsay from a third-party. But if you choose to retreat from this responsibility of telling your life story, your truth might get distorted one day by naysayers, haters and superficial cynics. So, if today you have a chance to tell your story, then do it right. Tell your story yourself, since you know it best.

It is a truism that some leaders are an enigma. Many people out there want to know what drives or motivates you to reach the heights that you have reached professionally and academically. People want to know how and where you grew up. They also want to learn something about the schools you attended so that they too can be inspired. Some young people have dreams modeled around your life story. They want to understand your career choices or decisions and how you approached them, as well as how they have impacted your professional and academic life. People are eager to hear from you. So, tell your story not only because your life has impacted the lives of many others in a positive and progress way, but also because, as a leader, you owe society that moral responsibility. You must tell your story not only because posterity will one day look back to see what your generation accomplished and left behind for them, but also because those in the present times deserve a chance to learn from chapters in your life. Indeed, you must tell your story not because you just want to be heard, but rather because you inspire many people around the world and your name is a household name both in the Global North and Global South, especially among those who follow leading African intellectuals.

Further, remember that your family members, friends, professional colleagues, mentees, students, former students, followers and other members of the public want to hear from you about your life story. You cannot allow them to sit and wait on gossip about it. Such a thing would not only be doing yourself a disservice but also dishonoring your legacy. Although oral tradition is still an acceptable method of transmitting knowledge to posterity, documenting one's life story is a more reliable method of avoiding any distortions or the misrepresentation of facts by others.

In this autobiography, I have endeavored to document facts as accurately and objectively as I can. Understandably, not everyone will agree with me on everything. But what I have stated is nothing but my truth as it stands. I am also awake to the political realities inherent in certain dogmas that are often veiled as objective critiques but are simply a charade of misconceived anecdotal conjectures. For some parochial cynics, the value of some of my ideas might not sit well with them. For others who have not yet been initiated globally, the ideas might not register immediately until they get initiated.

The perspectives that I have shared in this autobiography cannot be reduced to a monolithic cultural perspective, for they are global and universal in scope and scale, as opposed to parochial and insular perspectives. So the reader is invited to take off the local lens of, say, a monolithic Zambian or African cultural perspective, to look at issues from a more global and heterogenous perspective. It is that transition which many people struggle with. Ever wondered why some celebrities in Hollywood will ask members of the public for privacy if, say, some news was to break out about a scandal or some development affecting the concerned celebrity's personal or professional life? Other celebrities will show up at a social event just for a few minutes and then leave, claiming that they are off to another engagement even if there is no such other engagement. It is all about managing expectations. Something that is too common can easily lose value and become cheap, especially because we know that familiarity often breeds contempt. Rarity is a virtue. Some folks can visit you in hospital, that is, if, as a celebrity, you are ill, just to take a glimpse at how bad you are looking so that they can broadcast to the whole world. Others can pretend to commiserate with you when things are not going too well for you, say, in your marriage, work, or business, but all they want is gossip. You can pre-empt such people by asking them to buy and read a copy of your autobiography if they have any burning questions to ask you.

It is my sincere hope that this autobiography will also serve as a useful contemporary and historical guide to the generations of the Mwenda family to come so that they may know who their ancestors were and where they came from. As one Pan-African activist, journalist and entrepreneur, Marcus Garvey, once wrote: "A people without knowledge of their past history, origin, and culture is like a tree without roots." In a work of this kind, I am mindful that I owe my gratitude to many people. Indeed, it is not without difficulty that I record my indebtedness to all the people that I owe my gratitude. If I omit or forget to mention anyone, please forgive me.

Let me start by thanking the Good Lord, God Jehovah Almighty, and my dearest parents, Mr. Joseph T Mwenda and Mrs. Esther M Mwenda. To God, our Heavenly Father, His mercy endures forever. The fear of the Lord is the beginning of wisdom. To my dearest parents, though you have crossed over, your fatherly and motherly love endures forever. Your words of wisdom will forever remain indelible in my heart, edifying my thoughts and aspirations. I thank you for everything.

My thanks also go to my lovely wife, Dr Judith Mvula-Mwenda, and my adorable son, Joseph. They have been my rock. I cannot thank them enough. I am grateful for their patience, understanding and support, as I worked tirelessly long hours in the night and on weekends to bring this book to fruition. Further, I would like to thank my many friends, colleagues, mentors and mentees across the world, whose names are too numerous to mention, for their inspiring camaraderie and warm support.

Finally, I would like to express my gratitude to my siblings and other extended family members not only for their familial support and encouragement, but also for sharing some helpful information on the various genealogical aspects of the Mwenda family tree. Other sources on possible origins of the people from the region where I hail from in Luapula Province of Zambia included academic colleagues and reliable contacts in and from the neighboring countries of the Democratic Republic of Congo, Tanzania, Kenya, Uganda, Rwanda and Burundi. I remain ever grateful to all of them.

The interpretations and conclusions expressed in this book are entirely those of the author.

They do not represent the views of any institution, organization or other individual. All the facts presented in this book are as at the date of publication of the book.

Kenneth K Mwenda, PhD, LLD, DSc (Econ)
Washington DC
March 28, 2025

CHAPTER 9

My path to academia

By the end of 1991, I was done with the Law Practice Institute (LPI), now known as the Zambia Institute of Advanced Legal Education (ZIALE). I was ready to move to my next challenge in life. As noted in the previous chapter, Chapter 8, I was called to the Zambian Bar in December 1991 as the overall best graduating student, having also been one of the only two students out of a class of almost thirty to have passed all the mid-year exams in my LPI cohort. I got admitted to the Bar with an unquestionably impressive record.

In the picture below, taken shortly after I was sworn in as an Advocate of the High Court for the Republic of Zambia (AHCZ) by the then Chief Justice of Supreme Court for the Republic of Zambia, Hon Mr Chief Justice Annel Silungwe, I can be seen standing in the third row from the back. I am the third person in that row from the left side of the picture.

As a qualified Zambian lawyer, though based in the diaspora, I have remained in touch with some senior judges back home in Zambia. For example, at one time when Hon Ms Justice Lombe Chibesakunda was serving as the Acting Chief Justice of the Supreme Court for the Republic of Zambia I was in touch with her and was resourceful to her office on a major judicial ruling that the Supreme Court was working on. Similarly, I have collaborated professionally with Hon Ms Justice Florence N. M. Mumba who also served as a leading Supreme Court judge in Zambia. I co-authored a scholarly journal article with Hon Ms Justice Florence N. M. Mumba when she was based in the Hague as a judge on the Appeals Chamber of the International Criminal Tribunal for the former Yugoslavia and the International Criminal Tribunal for Rwanda (ICTY/ICTR). The said article was published in the George Washington University International Law Review in the

US. Further, I was in regular contact with yet another prominent Zambian Supreme Court judge, Hon Mr Sandson S Silomba (now deceased), who was one of my Master of Laws (LLM) degree students at the University of Warwick in the UK in the 1990s. I co-authored a scholarly journal article with Hon Mr Justice Sandson S. Silomba in the Stellenbosch Law Review at the University of Stellenbosch in South Africa. In the picture below, I can be seen donating some of my scholarly books to Hon Ms Chief Justice Irene Mambilima (now deceased), the successor to Hon Ms Chief Justice Lombe Chibesakunda, when we met at the World Bank in Washington DC. Similarly, I have donated several books to the University of Zambia (UNZA) Main Campus Library using my own financial resources. We do it for the love of the country.

In 1990, as a graduating law student at the University of Zambia (UNZA), that is, prior to going to LPI, I graduated as one of the best two law students and won the Law Association of Zambia (LAZ) Best Student in Jurisprudence Award. The other top graduating law student was an Asian colleague by the name of Zunaid Coovadia. Shortly after we graduated from UNZA, Zunaid is said to have moved to South Africa to pursue his calling as a religious leader in Islam. He left Zambia and did not attend LPI. He had made it clear that his interest was not in practicing law. Indeed, the two of us had something in common. I was also not very interested in practicing law, especially at the local level in Zambia. I only went to LPI to fulfil the 'scriptures' of what by statute is known as becoming a 'qualified lawyer' before I returned to academia.

From the UNZA Law School graduating class of 1990, I became the first to earn a PhD when in 2001 I obtained the Warwick PhD in Law. Two years later, in 2003, one of my former classmates at UNZA Law School, Dr Iris C. Mwanza, also earned her PhD. Hers was a PhD in International Relations from Johns Hopkins University School of Advanced International Studies in Washington DC, USA. So, from that UNZA Law School class, only the two of us ended up with PhDs. It is not too bad a record. Other UNZA Law School graduating classes have not produced a single PhD but can only boast of producing such political appointees as State Counsel. Otherwise, I have always been a pioneer, leading and charting the path for others to follow, starting from my childhood days. Even among my high school peers who completed Form 5 (Grade 12) in 1985 at Luanshya Boys' Secondary School in Zambia, I got into Oxford and later obtained a British PhD from a leading British university before anyone else earned his PhD. A few others have since followed my PhD footsteps and earned their PhDs back home in Africa.

Right from my law school days at UNZA, I had always admired an academic life, as well as the professional life of working for the United Nations or the World Bank. That was what I wanted to be. Apart from my apprenticeship as a Bar admission student in Zambia, when I practiced law at a law firm called Jacques and Partners, I never really had much interest in practicing law in Zambia. I chose instead to practice law at the highest international level when I became the first Zambian lawyer to ever practice law within the Bretton Woods institutions. I served for close to a decade as Senior Counsel in the World Bank's Legal Vice-Presidency before serving as Senior Counsel in the World Bank's Integrity Vice-Presidency. In addition, I chose, as a leading scholar, to join academia and have since produced several top-notch judges for the judiciary in my home country, Zambia, as well as in other countries around the world.

Interestingly, many colleagues in the legal profession in Zambia who have often looked down on academia continue to appear before some of my former law students who are now judges in the Zambian courts of law. In life, each of us has a path ordered by God. You just have to know your calling. For example, there are people who want to get into the academic space but don't just have what it takes to be a scholar of international repute. When I joined academia at the University of Zambia (UNZA) in 1991, only the brightest graduating students at UNZA would be retained as Staff Development Fellows (SDFs) to prepare them for an academic life. You could not enter academia at UNZA back then if you were just an average student or did not graduate among the crème de la crème. I can safely say that many who later in life somehow managed to join academia after starting off with less impressive academic backgrounds have not had much success as prolific researchers and writers. If anything, most of them do not even have an impressive scholarly publication record. It often shows. Even if you try to force matters, it will eventually show that the domain you are in might not really be your calling. And that is why some people cannot even complete their PhD studies, or they end up simply abandoning those doctoral studies.

In my youthful days in Zambia, I used to read a lot of autobiographies and biographies of prominent West African and East African authors. They inspired me. Most of those profiles were impressive, filled with PhD holders from top universities in Europe and America. Some of them had even taught at leading universities in Europe or America while others had worked for the United Nations, the World Bank or the International Monetary Fund (IMF). That was what I wanted to be. I wanted to reach similar heights and even excel beyond. I never entertained the thought of running a small law firm locally in Lusaka or on the Copperbelt region of Zambia. That was too small a vision for me. I had bigger dreams. My vision was to get to major global and international heights, and I knew that academia would provide me with a platform to attain those goals, but it would require a lot of discipline and sacrifice.

At the time, the economy in Zambia was not doing so well. When I joined academia as a Staff Development Fellow (SDF) and Tutor at UNZA in 1991, I was earning one-third of what my friends and former classmates at LPI were making in law firms. It required character to avoid being moved by the temptation of making more money. I was not bothered by those financial differentials. For, I knew the difference between money and knowledge. My academic record has always been beyond reproach, and I knew exactly what I wanted. At one point, my salary as an SDF even fell below the stipend or allowances of undergraduate students at UNZA who were sponsored by the Zambian Government Bursaries Committee. But my vision was bigger than fighting over small monies. So, I weathered the storm.

While growing up in Zambia, many children had their parents tell them that, during their time in school, they (*i.e.* the parents) were the smartest of the lot in class. Most parents would tell their children stories of how they were the best students in school. Culturally, our elders, like elders in many other foreign cultures, do not like to expose their intellectual insecurities. And so, many of them would come up with all sorts of stories about their intellectual prowess in their youthful days. Even parents who had fared poorly in life would tell the same stories, and their children would believe them. No parent would ever say that he or she was a dull student or would perform badly in school. Rather, they would all assure their children that they were the academic stars in school.

Admittedly, some parents habitually tell 'small sweet lies' to inspire their children, especially where such parents have nothing to show for their lives or have no real success story to point at. But telling lies can backfire. It can mislead your children, especially where you give your children an impression that you are wealthy, and yet are only using perks from your workplace to impress your children (*e.g.* having your children driven around in a personal-to-holder company vehicle by your driver, where your employer pays for your children's education abroad, staying in a company mansion, going on foreign trips paid for by your employer, and so forth). Many children get shocked when they lose a parent only to discover that their father died owing many people money and left behind nothing except several other children fathered illegitimately outside marriage. That's the danger of faking it.

But as we all grow older, we begin to question the fairytales of our parents. If every parent was the best student, then who came second, third, fourth, fifth, sixth, or even the worst? Surely they all could not have been the best student in class. It reminds me of how a number of my Zambian Bemba and Lozi friends like to claim that they hail from some royal family. Surely, how can that be? You all can't be royalty. And by a stretch of imagination, if, say, you were all royalty, then who are the sons and daughters of the messengers and guards at the royal palace? Put simply, as we say in Bemba,

"Teti bonse mube abana Ba Mfumu. We muntu niwe mwana kapasao, ati 'Na fuma ku bu fumu!'" ("You all cannot come from the royal family. Some of you are just children of guards or messengers at the royal palace yet claim to be children of the King or Paramount Chief.")

When I was a graduate student in England, I met a number of Nigerian friends who claimed that 'deya fada' (their father) was a chief back home in Nigeria. How can that be? Look, you are struggling in London, barely making ends meet, and yet are saying that your father is a chief in Lagos? It doesn't add up. The moral of the story is that life often teaches us that you cultivate traces of excellence in whatever you are doing from early childhood. Rarely does it happen that you become a star without a record of excellence in your childhood. Sometimes it can happen, but it rarely does. So, today, when I tell my son, nephews and nieces that I was a top student, they can see for themselves my impeccable track record. I don't need to lift up my hands to be noticed. I win with my hands down.

Academia is not a profession for the desperate. You do not join academia simply because you lost parliamentary elections and now need a job to make ends meet, or you have been kicked out of your corporate executive position and now don't know what to do. It has become fashionable in many parts of Africa for anyone with a postgraduate degree who is unemployed to try out academia as a means of livelihood to sustain themselves, especially at some lesser-known private universities. Many such individuals also moonlight as consultants, entrepreneurs, pastors or farmers on the side. Also, retirees from the civil service as well as those who have lost jobs try to shelter from the storm of economic hardship by moonlighting as lecturers or professors in little-known local private universities. But academia is not a profession for the desperate. Rather, it is a profession for the brightest and the committed.

When I joined academia in 1991, it was quite prestigious to teach at the nation's top university, the University of Zambia (UNZA). You could not be hired to teach at UNZA if, say, you did not graduate for your first degree with a distinction (first class) or strong merit (stronger upper second class), notwithstanding that you also hold a Masters degree from a decent British or American university. It was that competitive. Your first degree mattered before people could even look at your Masters degree. You had to prove yourself as a budding scholar. A credit (lower second class) or bare pass (third class) degree was simply not enough. It was even worse if you had no first degree and then sprung up from nowhere with a Masters degree or PhD and some professional qualifications earned prior to your Masters degree or PhD. You wouldn't cut it.

I was hired as a full-time academic at UNZA by one of the most erudite legal scholars to have come out of Zambia, the then Dean of UNZA Law School, Professor Lawrence Shimba, who later served as Minister of Foreign Affairs for the Republic of Zambia in the MMD Government. Professor Shimba also taught me in my first and final years of law school. He taught me constitutional law in first year of law school, a course he taught jointly with Professor Robert Kent, a Visiting Professor of Law from Cornell University in the USA and a former Dean of UNZA Law School. Professor Shimba also taught me Jurisprudence in my final year of UNZA Law School. So, he knew my intellectual capabilities very well. I was the only one hired from my LPI and UNZA classes as SDF. The University of Zambia Staff Development Fellowship (SDF) Program was established in 1969 as a capacity-building program for UNZA to build a steady pipeline of indigenous Zambian academic staff. The SDF program was started a few years after the country attained political independence, and the program would attract and retain the best brains among the students graduating from UNZA. SDFs would be hired to lead undergraduate student tutorials while they worked on their Masters degree programs locally at UNZA or as they prepared to go abroad to obtain their Masters degree at leading universities before returning back to UNZA to teach as lecturers. Upon obtaining your Masters degree, you would be promoted from SDF to Lecturer III. So, the SDF track was an elite and prestigious academic path to enter academia in Zambia. Often, if you did not join academia through the SDF path, some folks among the academics at UNZA would look at you with suspicion, wondering how you found yourself teaching there. The SDF route was the ideal way of entering academia in Zambia. Anything else was considered less inspiring. It often indicated that you were not smart enough to enter academia through the front door but had to be sneaked in through the window or the back door. You had to prove yourself by coming in through the front door, which was the prestigious SDF route, as opposed to the less inspiring back door paths of, say, part-time lecturer, Graduate Teaching Assistantships (GTAs) or Graduate Research Assistantships (GRAs). By parity of reasoning, even some notable international organizations have their elite and prestigious hiring programs such as the Young Professionals Program (YPP), which attract the crème de la crème, as opposed to entering those organizations as a consultant or intern and then hustling your way up into a fixed-term or regular appointment. That's just how it is.

When I joined UNZA as SDF in 1991, the Law School had a vibrant academic community. Professor Lawrence Shimba was the Dean. He was preceded by a number of other law deans before I got to UNZA. At the time, a number of academic staff at UNZA Law School were out on study leave abroad for their PhDs though there was also a critical mass that had already obtained their PhDs and returned to teach at UNZA.

The two senior lecturers I found on the faculty of UNZA Law School were Dr Fred Ng'andu and Dr Beatrice M. Kamuwanga. Professor Chuma Himonga, who was at the time also a senior lecturer at UNZA, had just left Zambia for an academic stint in Germany before she moved to South Africa at the University of Cape Town as a law professor. Dr. John Mulwila, another senior lecturer, was no longer lecturing at UNZA. He had moved into private law practice. Dr Anthony C. Mulimbwa was around. Dr Joshua Kanganja too was no longer lecturing at UNZA and had taken up a senior position in government. Dr Remmy Mushota had also left the university by then and had gone into politics. Professor Alfred Chanda was out at Yale University Law School in the USA working on his law doctorate, the JSD. Hon Professor Justice Margaret Munalula had just joined UNZA as a law lecturer after working for the Development Bank of Zambia (DBZ) in Lusaka. At the time, she had not yet gone for her law doctoral studies for the JSD at the University of Notre Dame in the US. Dr Chaloka Beyani was completing his law doctorate, the DPhil, at the University of Oxford in England. Dr Ngosa Simbyakula had just returned to Zambia in August 1990 after completing his law doctorate, the SJD, at the University of Wisconsin in Madison, Wisconsin, USA. Then, that same year when I joined UNZA Law Faculty as SDF (1991), Dr Tukiya Kankasa-Mabula had just defended her PhD in Law thesis at Queen Mary and Westfield College, University of London, and was preparing to return to UNZA.

A few years year before I joined UNZA as SDF, the current Chief Justice, Hon Dr Chief Justice Mumba Malila, had just returned to Zambia after completing his Master of Laws (LLM) degree program at the University of Cambridge. Then, as I was preparing to leave for Oxford in 1992, the current Deputy Chief Justice, Hon Mr Deputy Chief Justice Michael Musonda, arrived in Zambia from Oxford. He found me as an SDF at UNZA Law School, busy preparing to leave for Oxford. He gave me some helpful pointers as to what to expect at Oxford. He had just completed his graduate studies at Kings College, University of London, for his Master of Laws (LLM) degree program, and then went on for further studies at the University of Oxford for his two-year Master of Philosophy (MPhil) degree program in Management Studies.

At UNZA Law Faculty, I also found Hon Dr Justice Winnie Mwenda. At the time, she had not obtained her PhD yet and had just joined UNZA Law School as a lecturer shortly before I arrived. A couple of years or so before I joined UNZA Law Faculty as SDF, Professor Evance Kalula and Professor David Ailola had just gotten their law doctorates, the PhD, from the University of Warwick in England. However, they both took up academic appointments at the University of Lesotho after completing their PhD studies. Later, Professor Kalula moved to South Africa's premier university, the University of Cape Town (UCT), and Professor Ailola moved to another leading university in South Africa, the University of Western Cape. Professor Ailola also taught at the University of South Africa after leaving the University of Western Cape. Then, Professor Michelo K Hansungule was out in Graz, Vienna, studying for his law doctorate, the PhD, at the University of Graz. Dr Enoch M. Simaluwani was in London studying for his law doctorate, the PhD, at the School of Oriental and African Studies (SOAS), University of London. Professor Kalombo T. Mwansa was also in London finishing up his law doctoral studies for his PhD at SOAS, University of London.

There were other academic staff who I never found at UNZA Law School and who I never got to meet. They were at the time already abroad working on their law doctoral studies. They include Dr Chad Kawamba, who was studying for his law doctorate, the PhD, at SOAS, University of London; Dr Munira Mwalimu, who was studying for her law doctorate, the SJD, at Georgetown University in Washington DC; Dr Charles Mwalimu, who was also studying for his law doctorate, the SJD, at Georgetown University in Washington DC; and, Dr Wakefield C. Simapungula, who was studying for his law doctorate, the PhD, at Cardiff University in Cardiff, Wales. Others like Professor Liyoka Kakula, who completed his law doctorate, the SJD, in 1982 at the University of Wisconsin in Madison, Wisconsin, USA, had already moved into the diaspora and were teaching at leading universities in South Africa or elsewhere outside Zambia. Then, Professor Mpazi W. Sinjela and Professor Isaak I. Dore, who both completed their law doctorates, the JSD, at Yale University Law School in 1978 had joined the United Nations after completing their JSD studies. Professor Dore returned to academia a year later as a law professor in the US while Professor Sinjela remained with the UN until his retirement but has since returned to academia in Zambia. When I joined

UNZA Law School as SDF, other leading scholars such as Professor Muna B. Ndulo and Professor Patrick M. Mvunga were no longer at UNZA and had taken up international careers with the United Nations (UN). Professor Ndulo was in Vienna, Austria, with the UN Office of Legal Affairs that deals with International Trade Law, while Professor Mvunga was in Addis Ababa, Ethiopia, with the United Nations Economic Commission for Africa (UNECA).

On my arrival at UNZA as SDF, I was assigned to teach Contract Law to students in the first year of Law School. Zambia is a common law jurisdiction, meaning that the English common law has a great bearing on the Zambian legal system. The class that I taught at UNZA Law School in 1991/92 has arguably produced the largest number of judges for the judiciary in Zambia. I am so proud of them. In fact, one of the students from that class, Frederick Mudenda, even became the Dean of UNZA Law School. So, I can proudly say that, among things, I have produced for Zambia some notable judges as well as a dean of Zambia's leading law school, UNZA Law School.

At UNZA, while serving as an SDF, my employment contract included terms that the university would provide me with residential housing accommodation. Often UNZA would house its SDFs at Marshlands, a residential gated community across the university that was at the time reserved almost exclusively for UNZA dons who had just returned from abroad after their Masters or PhD studies, or SDFs who were studying locally at UNZA for their Masters degrees or were about to leave for graduate studies abroad. But each time I went to check for the availability of housing accommodation at Marshlands, I was told by one of the officers there that there was no vacant apartment. So, I ended up staying at my elder sister's place in Kabulonga residential area for a few months and would commute daily to UNZA by bus. It was so frustrating. But I never gave up.

A colleague of mine who was also an SDF was given an apartment at Marshlands while I was kept on the waiting list. I wondered why. Then I got to learn that the man assigning the apartments was from the same province as my SDF colleague. I could not believe it. The man offered me to take up a dilapidated and rundown apartment on the ground floor of some unsafe apartment block in Handsworth Court, a few miles from Marshlands. I went to inspect the place. It was uninhabitable.

Although I was desperate to get my own residential accommodation, I could not take up his offer. The place was not safe. There was no fence around the block of apartments, and all I could see through the bedroom window was a thicket facing an adjacent township that was notorious for high crime rates. So, I politely declined to take up the offer and insisted that I would wait until there was suitable housing at Marshlands.

Then, one day, by a stroke of luck, the man responsible for allocating apartments at Marshlands fell sick and someone else was acting on his behalf. When I showed up to check on the availability of housing accommodation, the man who was acting greeted me with an unassuming warm and welcoming smile before he mentioned that he had seen me frequenting Marshlands to chase up on my housing issue. The man opened his logbook to check on the availability of housing. He then asked for my name to track progress, if any. I told him my full names. My last name is found in many parts of Zambia, but certainly not in his boss' home area. So, it is possible that his boss was able to tell that I am not from his region and thus chose to discriminate against me deliberately.

As we were chatting, the man who was acting on behalf of his sick boss asked me where I hailed from in Zambia. I told him that my parents were both Ushi from Luapula Province. He raised his head, smiled, and said, "Ba Mwenda, chine fye? Nga mwa li landile. Ta pa fishe apa. Accommodation epo ili." ("Mr Mwenda, for real? You should have said. There is no problem here. I have a vacant apartment for you.")

Coincidentally, the man was also from Luapula. It appeared that he had noticed that his boss, a man from the north-western part of Zambia, had been playing me arguably because my name gave me away as it was not a typical north-western name. Indeed, his boss had given housing accommodation to two of my SDF colleagues from north-western, yet he was making it difficult for me. Here, I need to clarify something before I am misunderstood. It is important to stress that I do not see the support I received in getting housing accommodation at Marshlands as a reverse tribal act. Rather, it was genuine bona fide resolution of injustice and a demonstration of affirmative action to redress what appeared to be some nuance of tribal prejudice. I had suffered enough, walking long distances daily to 'beg' for housing accommodation which should have been given to me soon after I started work. That is how I moved to live at Marshlands.

The following week the north-western man returned from sick leave and found that I had already been allocated an apartment at Marshlands and had even moved in. There was nothing he could do or say. He would just look down sheepishly with guilt each time he saw me. He definitely knew that what he had been doing was not right.

I stayed at Marshlands for a year while teaching at UNZA and before leaving for graduate studies abroad. When I joined UNZA as SDF, I was told that there were no scholarships available for me to study abroad and I would have to pursue my Masters degree locally at UNZA. I was disappointed, but remained focused. I started working on my local Masters degree program entirely by thesis. My research was interdisciplinary and focused on the political economy of law in Zambia, especially the regulation of foreign direct investment. My Masters degree thesis supervisor was Dr Mwangala B Kamuwanga, then a Senior Lecturer at UNZA Law School. I made great progress on my work. My supervisor had approved not only my research proposal but also three chapters of my thesis. However, I was stuck midway because of the bureaucracy at UNZA. The University had a very rigid system of requiring a research proposal for graduate studies to be submitted to, and subjected to, the whims of a Graduate Studies Committee, comprising academics from various disciplines that had nothing to do with your discipline or area of study. Surely, how much value was an engineering, social work, metallurgy or agriculture science lecturer going to add to a research proposal in the field of law? These were the people who would sit on the said committee to vet and approve research proposals from various schools.

So, my supervisor and I were stuck and could not proceed. We had to wait for the Graduate Studies Committee to meet and approve my research proposal before we could proceed. Sadly, the committee rarely met. Through the one year I spent at UNZA as an SDF, the committee only met once. So, I could not make any meaningful progress. It was frustrating. But, to overcome the frustration, I started working quietly and concurrently on some private studies for an Advanced Diploma in Management Studies with the Institute of Commerce (IoC) in England. I applied to IoC to be exempted from their coursework since I had a law degree from UNZA and bar admission as well as my two University of London 'A' Levels and the Group Diploma in Law from London Chamber of Commerce and Industry (LCCI). My request was approved, and I was granted exemptions from all IoC coursework. However, to qualify for the IoC Advanced Diploma in

Management Studies, I was asked to write a dissertation on a topic in the field of management. The dissertation was going to be assessed for the award of the said IoC qualification as well as for grant of the IoC senior-most membership status of Fellow of the Institute of Commerce.

At the time, I was not earning much, though I had some modest savings from my earnings. I had to find additional monies somewhere for me to pay for the IoC program. I ran to my elder sister, Catherine, to ask for financial help. She assisted me with a contribution, and I remain ever grateful. But, I still needed a bit more cash to meet all the fees for the entire IoC program. I looked around at UNZA Law School. The current Chief Justice of the Supreme Court for the Republic of Zambia, Hon Dr Justice Mumba Malila, was then a lecturer at UNZA Law School. I was a first-year student at UNZA when Chief Justice Malila was a fourth-year law student. So, I knew of him when we were both undergraduate students at UNZA and before he went abroad for his graduate studies. I went to Mumba and asked him for a loan to be paid back as soon as I got my salary. He trusted me and assisted me. I remain ever grateful. I promised him that I would pay him back as soon as I got my next salary. I proceeded to pay for my IoC Advanced Diploma in Management Studies. Also, I remain ever grateful to one of the secretaries at UNZA Law School who was so nice and kind to me, and helped with the typing of the IoC dissertation. I would give her my handwritten draft chapters and she would type them for me. At the time, there were no computers, but only typewriters.

I wrote my IoC dissertation on corporate law. When I finished writing, I took the final document to the Dean of the School of Law at UNZA, Professor Shimba, for authentication and signature. The document needed to be certified before I could submit it for examination in the UK. Professor Shimba held the dissertation in his hands, skimmed through the pages, and then asked me, "When did you write this?"

I explained to Professor Shimba that since I had a bit of free time on my hands due to the delays of the UNZA Graduate Studies Committee in approving the research proposal of my UNZA Masters degree thesis, notwithstanding that my supervisor and I had made so much progress, I embarked on the IoC program. Professor Shimba shook his head in disbelief about the bureaucracy and red-tape at UNZA, and said, "This place, I just don't understand! You have written a great piece of work. Congratulations!"

Professor Shimba proceeded to sign off the document. A few months went by as I waited for the results from the IoC. In the meantime, the very day I got my next salary from UNZA, I walked down to Chief Justice Malila's then residence at Canada Court within UNZA premises. I knocked on the front door. Chief Justice Malila opened the door. He was surprised to see me standing at his doorstep and wondered what I was up to. I smiled and said to him, "Thank you so much for your help, Mumba. I had promised to make good the money that I had borrowed as soon as I got paid. I have kept my promise. Here is the money. Many thanks again, my brother."

Frankly speaking, I am one person who is seriously honest when it comes to issues of money because I am not moved or excited by money. I rarely borrow, unless it is for something serious, urgent and meaningful. Usually, I would rather dig into my savings, if I have to, or wait until I have money, to get what I want. Money is just a means to an end. By contrast, I am moved by sound intellect. Put simply, for those who easily get excited over money and power, be reminded that, "Ta tu tina aba maka nelyo aba mpiya. Tu tina aba mano." ("We prioritize brains over brawn or money."

Generally, I dislike dishonest behaviors when it comes to financial dealings or transactions. So I went back to Chief Justice Malila to thank him and return his money without waiting for him to remind me. He did not have to chase me around to get his money back. A lot of people have a habit of not honoring their word in paying off their debts. You don't need to behave that way, especially as a lawyer. You have to be beyond reproach when it comes to issues of money. It is a disgrace for a person to embezzle other people's money, including client's money. Your attitude will often determine your altitude in life. Swindling people out of money and conning your way around will never take you anywhere. Learn to be honest.

People shouldn't have to remind you that you owe them money. The onus is on you to take yourself to the person you owe money to and pay it back. And that is exactly what I did. People will have nothing but respect for you if they know that you can keep your word and are truly honest in your dealings. Respect is earned, not demanded. You cannot earn someone's respect if you are not honest and trustworthy. So, do not act like you forgot that someone gave you shelter when you had no place to stay, gave you a ride to work or school and saved you from walking long distances on a dusty road, guided you academically or professionally to be where you are today, bought you the kind of gifts that you yourself can never buy him or her, helped you with your studies so that you make it in life, or provided you with some finances, clothes, shoes, perfumes or food when nobody else would help you. Learn to be grateful.

I'm going to say this one more time: do not act like you forgot that someone was there for you and that he or she did for you what you yourself would probably not have done for him or her if that person were in your shoes. For one who is well-cultivated and well-mannered, gratitude is not optional. It speaks to your levels of civility and integrity. Otherwise, some people are just a 'flight risk' and will try to hide or flee if they see someone that they owe money to approaching. We just have to learn to be more honest.

Many years later, when I was serving as Senior Counsel in the Legal Vice-Presidency of the World Bank, Chief Justice Malila was visiting Washington DC on a business trip under the auspices of the African Union Commission on Human and Peoples' Rights. Chief Justice Malila paid a courtesy call on me at the World Bank. At the time, he had gone back to academia at the University of Zambia (UNZA) School of Law after serving as Attorney-General for the Republic of Zambia. We sat in my office at the World Bank in Washington DC, reminiscing about the good old days of academia in Zambia. Chief Justice Malila then mentioned to me that he was working on his PhD in Law. I asked him where he was pursuing his doctoral studies. He informed that he was studying locally in Zambia at the University of Zambia. Knowing how slow things can be back home in Zambia, I encouraged Chief Justice Malila to consider switching for his doctoral studies to the University of Pretoria, where I was at the time serving concurrent with my position at the World Bank as Extraordinary Professor of Law. I also mentioned that one of his colleagues from his graduate student days at the University of Cambridge in the UK, where they both pursued their Master of Laws (LLM) degree program in the late 1980s, was now a Full Professor of Law at the University of Pretoria and always asked me about him. After some years, when I had even forgotten about the discussion that I had in my office with Chief Justice Malila, I saw congratulatory messages flying everywhere on social media that Chief Justice Malila had obtained his PhD in Law from the University of Pretoria. I was pleased to learn that he had taken my advice. It took me back to our meeting in my office at the World Bank. That's what friends are for. You look out for each other, encourage each other, and give each other support and positive advice.

Now, back to my IoC Advanced Diploma in Management Studies in 1991/92 when I was teaching at UNZA. After waiting for my exam results for some months, the results were finally in. I had aced it. I passed my dissertation without corrections to earn the Advanced Diploma in Management Studies from IoC and was also granted the highest membership of Fellow of the Institute of Commerce in England. All this was happening whilst I was an SDF at UNZA working on my local UNZA Masters degree program in law. I am one person who is always open to multi-tasking, and I do so ambidextrously while attending to the immediate demands of today and envisioning the emerging trends of a changing landscape of tomorrow. I will tell you soon how this ambidextrous approach has paid off. For now, suffice it to say, never put all your eggs in one basket.

Frustrated with the slow pace and bureaucracy of the Graduate Studies Committee at UNZA, I started looking for scholarships to take me abroad for my graduate studies. In the meantime, I did not abandon my UNZA graduate studies. Rather, I opted to push in both directions, ambidextrously. Until you get a full scholarship, it would be foolishly unwise to abandon the local Masters degree program. I made several scholarship applications and would only get partial scholarships from a number of leading British universities such as the University of Leicester and the University of London. And there was nobody to help me with some bridging finance to cover the remainder of the costs for a Masters degree program in the United Kingdom.

I wrote to Zambia's State-owned mining company, ZCCM, to ask them to help me with the bridging finance and that I become bonded to them on the completion of my graduate studies abroad so that I could then serve as a Law Lecturer at their Accountancy Training College in Chingola. At the time, ZCCM was spending a lot of money on sponsoring some Zambian students to pursue undergraduate degree studies in the UK and the US. My case, I thought, was straightforward since ZCCM would only have to meet me halfway and for only nine months, as opposed to the undergraduates that they were funding for three to four years. Interestingly, I got no positive feedback from ZCCM. I'd guess I knew nobody in the top ranks there. I turned to Meridien Bank in Zambia. I never even heard back from them, and a few years later Meridien Bank became defunct. The moral of the story is that it is not easy to get things done on merit. Those who excel on merit alone are few, but I can proudly say that I am one of them. I knew nobody to pull strings for me or put in a good word, but that did not deter me. I kept looking for various possible options for a way forward.

Before joining UNZA as SDF at the Law Faculty, I had gotten an offer from the Ministry of Higher Education to serve as a Law Lecturer at Evelyn Hone College. I had reached out to the

Ministry of Higher Education and received a favorable response, but then UNZA invited me back as an SDF. So, I opted to go to UNZA. At no time did I regret my decision to go back to UNZA, notwithstanding the challenges that I was facing.

One afternoon, as I was walking from the UNZA bus stop to my apartment at Marshlands, I ran into an old friend from my high school days at Luanshya Boys' Secondary School. He was a few years behind me in high school, and we had both been cadets. His name is Kenworth Siajunza. His elder brother, Shento, was my intake mate, though Shento was at Roan Antelope Secondary School (RASS) and later moved to Mpelembe Secondary School in Kitwe, where he became the Head Boy. I had in my hands plastic bags loaded with groceries. I had gone to pick up some groceries in town and passed through Soweto market behind Lusaka city center. I had just alighted from a bus at UNZA bus station, with plastic bags in my hands filled with some chicken, mincemeat and T-bone steak as well as some greens. Kenworth recognized me as I was approaching him from the opposite direction on the sidewalk near what was then known as the 'Basic Center' across UNZA's Great East Road Campus. We both stopped and greeted each other. Kenworth said, "Mdala, so what are you up to these days? It's been a while."

I replied saying that I was back at UNZA as a Staff Development Fellow and pursuing my Masters degree program there whilst teaching in the Law School. He quickly chimed in and said, "Have you seen today's newspaper? There is a scholarship that has been advertised. The Rhodes Scholarship. Check it out."

I promised Kenworth that I would do the needful. After we parted, I followed up and got myself a copy of the newspaper. If I had not met Kenworth that day, I probably would have missed the Rhodes Scholarship opportunity for that year. God brings people in your path for a reason. And I am ever grateful to my good brother Kenworth for mentioning that opportunity to me. Not everyone will share helpful information even if they have access to it. The tendency to hide or conceal information is very common. It is like a pandemic. But Kenworth was above board. He was selfless and generous with the information about the Rhodes Scholarship, and for that, I am ever grateful to him. I am one person who never takes things for granted. In life, you should never feel entitled. The world owes you nothing! So do not belittle any type of help you get from people. No help is too small. When you needed help, you were acting humbly. Now that you have that help you want to act as if you have forgotten. Only foolish people behave that way. And it is not an uncommon phenomenon.

After buying a copy of the newspaper, I sat down in my apartment at Marshlands to read the requirements of the Rhodes Scholarship. I kept ticking the boxes and my confidence kept growing. At the time, the internet did not exist, and there were no smartphones or tablets, nor social media. So, if you missed a copy of the newspaper, or someone did not send you a letter through 'snail mail', the only other option would be to get the information, like I did, through word of mouth. It was tough. But we survived and made it.

So that is how I started preparing to apply for the Rhodes Scholarship. I lined up all my references. I reached out to my uncle, Professor Mwelwa C Musambachime, who was a Professor of African History at UNZA, for a reference. He was always there for me, and I remain ever grateful. I also reached out to one of my former lecturers, Dr Anthony C Mulimbwa, another wonderful gentleman, for a second reference. Dr. Mulimbwa was such a fine gentleman. In his presence, you felt valued. I think I got the third reference from a gentleman by the name of Mr Luke Muleya who was an SDF when I was in my final year of undergraduate law studies, but had since completed his local Masters degree program at UNZA and was now serving as a law lecturer. I made sure that I went for the most reliable people for my references, and they all wrote good and honest references. I remain ever indebted to them.

I had a tight deadline to beat. Unfortunately, that week, I picked up a bout of malaria. I was feeling very weak, but I could not give up. I walked all the way from Marshlands to the Institute of African Studies of the University of Zambia, somewhere near Chamba Valley in the direction of Kaunda Square township, to submit my Rhodes Scholarship application forms to the then Secretary of the Rhodes Scholarship Selection Committee for Zambia, Professor Oliver S Saasa. He was at the time the Director of the UNZA Institute for African Studies. It was a very hot day as I walked in the scorching sub-Sahara sun. It was around noon, and I was really feeling weak, exhausted and dehydrated, but I had to do what had to be done.

I tried to be strong and hide how I was feeling when Professor Saasa came to meet me in the reception office to collect the forms. He welcomed me warmly and was very nice and courteous. Professor Saasa had taught me in my first year at UNZA, and I was one of the best students in the course, ADS100. Had it not been for my pursuing law, I would have probably pursued a major in

Development Studies and ended up denying someone a spot as SDF in Development Studies. Aside from law, I was equally good in the social sciences, including Political Science.

I handed Professor Saasa my Rhodes Scholarship application forms. We chatted briefly and he walked me out before I headed back to my apartment at Marshlands. Many a youth today would have asked Professor Saasa for an extension of the deadline on the grounds that they were sick. In fact, many of today's youths would have expected Professor Saasa and the other distinguished members of the Rhodes Scholarship Selection Committee to accommodate them past the deadline, claiming that they had been ill. But I did not do that. Rather, I walked a long way in the scorching sun of sub-Sahara Africa while dealing with malaria. A determined person has no time for excuses. He or she will climb any mountain or obstacle you put in from him or her to get to his or her goal or destination.

I got back to my apartment and took another bath before making myself some coffee and relaxing in bed. I was exhausted. But I was also glad that I had submitted my Rhodes Scholarship application forms in time and before the deadline. The idea of asking for an extension did not cross my mind. In my time, we were raised not to give excuses, especially to people in authority who are much older than you. You just had to get the work done. How you did it was your own problem.

A few weeks after I submitted my Rhodes Scholarship application, I got a letter to say that I had been shortlisted for the scholarship interviews. I had been praying all along for this, and I continued to pray that God should see me through it all successfully. I had no one out there to push for me but God. My parents were both retired civil servants, but I knew my God was not retired. He was still working.

I kept the news about getting shortlisted for the Rhodes Scholarship interviews quietly to myself. I did not want to announce anything, just in case I ended up not getting the scholarship. I continued praying while preparing for the interviews. I knew that my God was with me. What I did not know was when He would answer my prayers. It was my God, my faith in Him, the talents that God has given me, and the values upon which I was raised by my parents that kept me going. In life, sometimes there will be people who will doubt you or will be cynical about your efforts and chances of making it. The Nobel Laureate and acclaimed physicist Professor Albert Einstein is widely reported to have said, "Great spirits have always encountered violent opposition from mediocre minds."

The more you pray, the more you are likely to face opposition. Do not be surprised, for the ancient serpent will not rest if he sees you praying and getting closer to God. He will do everything to try to draw you away from God and Jesus Christ. Temptations will come your way. Challenges will also confront you so that you begin to doubt the Power of God. Do not be surprised. Remember always that prayer is a declaration of war against the ancient serpent and all those he was won over. They will fight you. You will not understand where it is all coming from, but it is the Spirit of God in you that troubles their demons. So, have the power of discernment. The story of Job in the Bible and the forty days of fasting in the desert by our Lord Jesus Christ are both instructive. If Jesus Christ, the Son of God, could be tempted by the ancient serpent, you too will be tempted.

Some folks will even say that you are too ambitious. Others will bear false witness against you just to discredit you, but there are also those who will believe in you as well as those who are honest with the truth and know your true worth and that you can make it. God never forsakes or abandons those who believe in Him.

A fable is told of four young men gathered for a drink at some local pub. They were busy talking ill of a supposedly mutual friend of theirs. Each one of the four would throw some shade and negativity in the conversation. An elderly man seated nearby listened quietly as the four young men continued to denigrate their mutual friend, who was not even present to defend himself. Suddenly, two young beautiful ladies joined them. The hate from the four guys continued. Then, innocently, one of the two ladies said that she knew the guy that they were all attacking and that he was actually a very nice guy who had even helped her personally with her career. That infuriated the guys further. The four of them tried to recruit both ladies into hating their supposedly mutual friend. Then the old man seated nearby cleared his throat to get their attention and politely addressed the four young men. "Gentlemen, sorry for the intrusion. I know it is none of my business. But I am a priest. I am here waiting for the young man you are talking about. I know him. But do not worry, I will not tell him a word. I am a priest and am sworn to the oath of confidentiality. I just want to understand you. How well do you know the guy?"

They all went quiet. There was silence. The gal who had been trying to correct the four haters asked them all to respond to the priest. Two of them had never even met the person they were criticizing and had just been recruited into hating someone they did not even know. The other two had both benefitted from the guy they were attacking. In fact, he had helped them before and was now doing far much better than them in life. The priest could sense that it was out of malice and envy that the four were talking ill of their 'friend'. The priest prodded further. "It's okay," he said. "You can trust me. Please feel free to speak."

As the priest was speaking, the guy they were talking about showed up in his latest Mercedes Benz. Unaware of what was going on, he greeted everyone warmly. Pointing to two of the four haters, the guy said to the priest, "Father, these are my two friends I was talking about when I had said that even though they are Pentecostals, and I am Catholic, we are still very good friends. In fact, when we were together at university, I would often share with them some of the money that my parents would send me because they had no one from their families to support them financially."

The priest smiled warmly, and then turned to the two haters, saying: "Nice to meet you gentlemen. So, I am interested to know, what did you give your friend in return for showing you kindness and generosity during your university days? As you know, every good deed deserves another in return."

One of the haters foolishly tried to be clever by quoting Matthew 6:3-4 in Bible, saying:

"But when you give to the needy, do not let your left hand know what your right hand is doing, so that your giving may be in secret. And your Father who sees in secret will reward you."

The priest smiled and said, "My son, I hear you. But always remember the Ten Commandments in the Bible. One of them says, 'Thou shalt not take the name of the Lord thy God in vain' (Exodus 20:7), meaning that, among other things, Scriptures must only be quoted for the prophetic truth, not for personal convenience. Another Commandment says, 'Thou shalt not bear false witness against thy neighbor' (Exodus 20:16), meaning speak only the truth about others, not falsehoods. Thirdly, and equally important, 'Thou shalt not covet (Exodus 20:17)', meaning that you will not be so jealous of something someone else has that you want it desperately and thus end up failing to put God first."

The four haters were quiet. Then the priest said to everyone, "My children, always remember what our Lord and Savior Jesus Christ said in Mark 12:30-31. He said: 'And you must love the Lord your God with all your heart, all your soul, all your mind, and all your strength'. The second is equally important: 'Love your neighbor as yourself'. No other commandment is greater than these."

The moral of the story is that some people who say bad things about someone are people who have been helped by the same person they are badmouthing. It is often the people you have helped who will say bad things about you because they want to be like you but can't. Envy begins to consume them because of their jealousy. Like a jilted lover, these people become bitter over your success. But a wise man or woman knows that it is unwise to disparage or try to bring down or compete against someone who has helped you just because you are envious of what that person has, notwithstanding any petty disagreement or differences you may have had with him or her. If that person is no longer beneficial or useful to you, at least try to be silent and walk away quietly or simply respect the moments when the person helped and supported you. Do not act like you have forgotten.

Generally, there are cultures where it is common for people to celebrate a friend or colleague's challenges in life or setbacks. In such cultures, the same people that often celebrate and broadcast failure will remain mute with malice, and much to their chagrin, of course, if the person succeeds or makes it. Put simply, some cultures, especially where there is a lot of poverty, tend to celebrate and broadcast failure so that you all become afraid of trying and remain in the same bucket of crabs with nobody ever trying to get out. By contrast, in other cultures, especially where there is greater economic prosperity, people generally tend to celebrate and broadcast success more openly because they too want to get out of the bucket of crabs and are thus looking for successful role models to inspire them, or to emulate or learn from.

And so, I understood some notorious cultural elements in my native country, Zambia, as I prepared for the Rhodes Scholarship interview. I remember that some of the candidates I competed with for the Rhodes Scholarship were my fellow SDFs at the University of Zambia (UNZA). It was tough. But I had extra ammunition and artillery that many other candidates were not aware of. They simply assumed that we all came to the interviews with only a top-class first degree, except for one candidate who had just obtained his Masters degree from the University of Cambridge a couple of years or so before he was shortlisted for the Rhodes Scholarship. To me, that Cambridge guy was the only apparent threat. And he is still a very good friend of mine.

When I walked into the interview room and noticed that a good number of the panelists were either UNZA professors or former UNZA dons, I felt somewhat reassured of objectivity and fairness. These were all serious intellectuals, with high integrity. Among them was a Catholic priest who was also a professor at UNZA. I weighed my prospects, noting that my friend from Cambridge who had started off as an SDF at UNZA had since left academia for the private sector. I wondered if there would be any good reason for the Rhodes Scholarship selection committee to give the scholarship to my friend since he had left academia for the private sector. I wondered whether it would be a good and noble idea for the Rhodes Scholarship selection committee to invest in someone from the private sector, leaving out those of us who were with the public sector and in a critical area that was in need of capacity-building.

Looking at the composition of the interviewing panel, I knew that my goal would be to stick to my academic aspirations as a Staff Development Fellow (SDF) at UNZA, showing the panel why I deserved to get the scholarship so that I could return to UNZA after completing my graduate studies abroad to contribute to higher education in Zambia. I maintained that line of thought.

The interviewing panel was pleasantly impressed with my resourcefulness when it came to my qualifications. The interviewers wondered where I had found the time and energy to get my University of London 'A' Levels and my London Chamber of Commerce and Industry (LCCI) Group Diploma in Law as well as my Fellowship and Advanced Diploma in Management Studies from the British Institute of Commerce, in addition, of course, to my UNZA law degree and Bar admission qualification. I was, without doubt, way ahead of the other candidates. The interviewers asked me several questions about, *inter alia*, my leadership skills, my sportsmanship, my commitment to academia, and how I managed to prioritize my time to achieve so much unlike many other young people my age.

Professor Oliver S. Saasa, the then Secretary of the Rhodes Scholarship Selection Committee for Zambia, was among the interviewing panel members, together with Mr David Phiri, a renowned corporate executive and one of the first Zambians to study at Oxford. Mr Phiri, as Chairperson of the Rhodes Scholarship Selection Committee, chaired the interviews. Other members were Dr Bwalya Ng'andu, who was predecessor of Professor Saasa as Secretary of the Rhodes Scholarship Selection Committee for Zambia and who later became Zambia's Minister of Finance, Ambassador Ms Gwendolene Koni, a notable diplomat and political figure in Zambia, and Professor Fr Michael Kelly, a Jesuit Catholic Priest from Ireland, who had been teaching at UNZA for many decades. Incidentally, Professor Fr Michael Kelly was recently awarded posthumously UNZA's first ever Higher Doctorate degree.

Looking back at the interview, I have come to fulfil everything that I said in that interview. I assured the interviewing panel of my unwavering commitment to academia and thought leadership. Also, I assured them with my interests in sports. As I write, I am now a certified football coach. I also spoke a bit about my faith, although it was not a requirement for selection. As I write, I am still a committed Catholic. You will know a person by his or her consistency.

After the interview, I went back to my apartment at Marshlands. I somewhat felt good about the whole interview process and had allowed myself to just speak freely and naturally during the interview. I spoke no rehearsed words. I simply spoke from my heart and kept to the truth. There was nothing to hide or pretend about. My record was there for all to see.

A week later, I was in my office at UNZA when one of the secretaries came looking for me. She said there was someone to see me. I asked who it was. And she said, "Professor Saasa is looking for you."

I was not expecting Professor Saasa to come in person to look for me. I thought that maybe he just wanted to ask for one or two additional documents in support of my application. I walked towards the Law School Dean's office, where I met him. That day, I was wearing a khaki denim shirt and pair of trousers. Professor Saasa greeted me and proceeded to ask: "How were the interviews?"

I responded politely, saying: "Quite challenging actually."

He smiled, handed me a sealed big brown envelope and said: "You will find this even more challenging. Please get back to me before Friday this week."

I said thank you, and we shook hands before he left. I went back to my office, closed the door behind me and opened the envelope steadily. There was the news! I had been selected as the sole Rhodes Scholar-Elect for Zambia for 1991/92. I could not believe it. I am ever grateful to Professor Oliver S. Saasa and the other eminent and distinguished interview panel members who conducted the interviews for the Rhodes Scholarship that year for believing in me and giving me a chance. They made the right decision. Over the years, I have come to learn that, in life, things earned on merit are not like things lobbied for or hustled for. Neither are they like what you get through relatives, cronyism, patronage, favoritism, white privilege, tribalism, ethnic bias, or such shenanigans as schmoozing or sucking up to folks in power, commonly known as 'networking' or 'connections.' Such shenanigans are nothing but pitiful versions of mediocrity masquerading as meritocracy.

In my entire life, I have not had to rely on someone to pull strings for me or use my father's name to get around. I have earned everything on merit. I have always stood on my own two feet as a man. I have never earned anything from or through dubious, unscrupulous, questionable, unethical or corrupt means. There are people who will temporarily get ahead of you in life, not because they are good at what they do, but because they have someone to help them get through the door or to twist arms so that they can be allowed in. But sooner or later, the mask will fall off and you will know them for who they are. Once that godfather or godmother is gone, they become exposed because there is no one to protect them or cover up for them.

For me, all my accomplishments and achievements have come in a transparent manner and on merit, not through deals struck behind closed doors or favors exchanged underneath the table. I have never had to know someone in the system to get through the door or for things to work for me. I have simply had to rely on the skills, competences, credentials and qualifications that God has given me. Even where I have been recommended for an opportunity or position, it was because I was well qualified, not because I was related to someone, played golf with the top dogs, or joined a certain political party or some dark secret society where certain deals are cut. As such, my record is beyond reproach. At the end of the day, it is about integrity, authenticity and honesty. You have to be able to stand up and look at yourself in the mirror to check who you truly are. Ultimately, it is about the prophetic truth, not otherwise. And I am proud of that.

When I got the news that I had been selected as a Rhodes Scholar-Elect for Zambia, I never shared the update with anyone. I simply pretended that Professor Saasa had come to see me on a normal work-related matter since he was also with the University of Zambia as Director of the Institute of African Studies.

After work hours, I went back to my apartment at Marshlands and started going through the paperwork contained in the package that Professor Saasa brought me. Looking back now, among the other candidates that I beat for the Rhodes Scholarship is a friend who was a year behind me in law School at UNZA and who is now a State Counsel as well as a former President of the Law Association of Zambia (LAZ). The other candidates included two ladies, namely, a colleague who is currently an Associate Professor of Geography at UNZA, and was at the time, like me, an SDF at UNZA, and a colleague who was my First Grade classmate in primary school in Livingstone, Zambia, and who later got a different scholarship when I was in my second year of graduate studies at Oxford to also come to Oxford. Then, much later, my State Counsel friend won a different scholarship to attend one of the constituent bodies of the University of London for his Masters of Laws (LLM) degree. Closely related to that, and while I was in my second year of graduate studies at Oxford, my other colleague, the Associate Professor at UNZA, also got another scholarship to go for her Masters degree at one of the constituent bodies of the University of London.

After I was selected as a Rhodes Scholar-Elect, I kept my cards close to my chest. While some of my SDF colleagues who had various kinds of scholarships to go to the UK and elsewhere would be busy talking about their flight details and travel plans, I simply kept my cool. At one point, I remember walking from work at UNZA to Marshlands in the company of two of my SDF colleagues. One of them was preparing to go to Cardiff while the other was scheduled to travel to Lancaster. They were both busy talking about their flight arrangements. I simply kept quiet. I would have felt bad if I had nothing in my kitty. My friends celebrated too early. I let them enjoy the moment. It was as if I was not there when the conversation was taking place. As we say in Ichi-Copperbelt, "Ilyashi lya mu ndeke, uwa njinga ta iposa mo." ("A discussion on flying the world by those who habitually enjoy the affluence of air travel is not for folks who habitually travel on a cheap bicycle.")

I was the guy in the adage above who could be assumed to travel frequently on a bicycle, while they, as they thought of themselves, were cut out for the plane. But my humble consolation, drawn from the analogy of sound intellect versus a big job title, was that: "Ta tu tina aba tu fulo. Tu tina aba mano. Utu fulo tu la pwa, but amano ta ya pwa." ("Someone can have a big job title today, but it will come to an end sooner or later. However, your sound intellect is yours for life. Wise people respect sound intellect over a job title or position.")

In their minds, my two colleagues must have reasoned that I would be confined to Zambia working on my local Masters degree program at UNZA while their destinations were lands afar in a place where it snows every year. Little did they know that I was headed to a more prestigious university and on a more prestigious scholarship. I just maintained my cool.

Not even my siblings knew that I was preparing to leave for Oxford until my mother spilt the beans. I had shared with my parents in good confidence the news about my upcoming trip, but my mother could not contain herself with excitement and ended up telling some of my siblings. Later that year, the Rhodes Scholarship Selection Committee also informed my dean, Professor Shimba. The dean met me in the corridors at UNZA and congratulated me. He added that there were one or two other Zambians studying at Oxford who could help me settle down once I got to Oxford. He gave me their names. It was not as if I had been hiding the news of my Rhodes Scholarship from the dean. Rather, I was not quite sure how he would react given that I was already pursuing a local Masters degree program at UNZA. So, I figured that it was best that the dean should find out from the formal channels through the Rhodes Scholarship Selection Committee. That way, I could let him know that I was waiting for the Rhodes Scholarship Selection Committee to inform him first before I could provide him with fuller details.

As the date of my going abroad was approaching, I wrote to my sponsors at Rhodes House in Oxford to ask them kindly to send me my air ticket ahead of time. They had been informed earlier by the Secretary of the Rhodes Scholarship Selection Committee for Zambia that I had been selected for the scholarship. So I was already in contact with them. I wanted to really make sure that I had the air ticket in my hands, fearing that maybe something could go wrong if I delayed in getting it. My sponsors sent me the air ticket months ahead of my departure. Also, I got my British student permit endorsed in my Zambian passport since I did not need to get a British visa as a Zambian national travelling to the UK on a Zambian passport. All I needed was a simple student permit.

Further, I had my medical exams done at the University of Zambia Teaching Hospital (UTH). A friend of mine, Bonny Chikonde, who was a year ahead of me in high school at Luanshya Boys' Secondary School was quite helpful in arranging for my medicals. UTH would have long queues if you wanted to do your medicals, unless you knew someone there.

Earlier, as I sought to secure an appointment to have my medicals done at UTH, I reached out to a friend's elder sister from Luanshya who was working in one of the labs at UTH. The lady was a few years ahead of me at UNZA and had studied biochemistry for her first degree before she later upgraded to become a medical doctor. But she was very cold and unhelpful. Luckily, my friend Bonny, who was a clinical officer at UTH, took me to a doctor he knew and lined me up for the medicals. I had all my medical exams, including x-rays and blood work done, and everything was fine.

I remember that day when I was going for my medicals. On the way I met a colleague from my UNZA days, Dubois. We met somewhere near Ministry of Foreign Affairs and Cabinet Office. Dubois was working with the Ministry of Finance which is located not too far from where we met. He informed me that he had also won a scholarship and was preparing to go for his Masters degree in the UK at the University of Birmingham. That same day, he too had been getting his medicals done.

A week later, Dubois was involved in a terrible road accident and lost his life. He and his workmates had been travelling to Livingstone by bus for a conference. The bus reportedly veered off the road and hit a tree, and Dubois died on the spot. He never made it for his postgraduate studies in the UK. It was a tragic loss. He was such a nice guy.

At UNZA, word was beginning to spread quickly among my SDF colleagues that I was going to Oxford as a Rhodes Scholar. Others were going places like Ethiopia and Kenya. My colleagues who had been talking about their travel plans to the UK were silent. I could tell that they had thought that they were a step ahead, only to find that I was miles ahead. Life is not a race or a competition, but if you want to outpace me, just wait until I get on the racing track.

I was admitted to Exeter College at the University of Oxford. That is where I was headed to, and not elsewhere in the UK. At Oxford, you need two different admissions when applying to be a student. The first admission relates to college admission, while the second relates to faculty or department admission. I also got admission to the Oxford Law Faculty to read for the two-year graduate Bachelor of Civil Law (BCL) degree program, now structured as a one-year BCL and a sequential one-year Master of Philosophy degree in law (MPhil in Law). It was a clean and straightforward admission to a highly competitive program for which many people's applications are rejected. There was no need for any additional references or checks. I was admitted directly and at first attempt.

However, when I got my admission letter to study for the Oxford BCL degree, I was a little confused because of the nomenclature associated with titles of some Oxford degrees. I thought that Oxford had a Masters of Laws (LLM) degree program because that is what you find at many other universities worldwide. To me, anything with the word 'Bachelors' in the title sounded like an undergraduate degree. So I started thinking that I did not have to do another Bachelors degree since I already had a Bachelor of Laws (LLB) degree from UNZA. Admittedly, some Irish universities have an undergraduate law degree titled, 'BCL', but that Irish BCL is not the same thing as the Oxford BCL which is an intensely rigorous graduate degree. My thinking was that every Masters degree had to have the word 'Masters' in its title. Indeed, that is what we were used to in Zambia. But I was wrong. Oxford showed me another worldview.

But before my 'discovery' of the prestige of the Oxford BCL degree, I wrote to Exeter College for clarification on the standing of the said degree. Exeter College wrote back to me explaining that the nomenclature associated with titles of some Oxford degrees can at times be confusing to someone who is not familiar with the Oxford system. That letter from Exeter College went on to confirm that the BCL is arguably the most rigorous and most prestigious taught Masters degree program in law in the entire English-speaking world. I took the letter to Professor Saasa to ensure that it was okay that I pursue the BCL degree, especially as I was preparing to be a lecturer at UNZA. Professor Saasa assured me that all was well. I must admit that, until then, I had never heard of the Oxford BCL degree because no Zambian had ever earned one from Oxford. The Zambian Rhodes Scholar who went to Oxford a couple of years before I got selected as a Rhodes Scholar, Elias Chipimo Jr, was the first Zambian to pursue the Oxford BCL degree program, though he had not yet graduated from Oxford by the time I was admitted. He was still a BCL student at the time. Generally, admission to Oxford's prestigious BCL degree program is very competitive. Many applicants get rejected. However, in my case, I did not face any challenges when being considered for admission to the Oxford BCL degree program, arguably because of the additional qualifications I had already earned from top British institutions, in addition to my UNZA law degree. I was admitted directly and without any difficulties. For, I was already equal to the task in my own cognizance.

CHAPTER 10

The Oxford Years

When you have been to a prestigious school such as Oxford, you often take it for granted without realizing that others would give an arm and a leg just to get admitted there. Many who have been to good schools such as Harvard, Yale, Cambridge or Stanford still admire Oxford. The Oxford aura is simply unmatchable. I remember meeting one young and overly ambitious Ugandan lady in Washington DC. She told me that she was a lawyer from Uganda. My natural unconscious bias made me assume that she must have studied at Makerere University which is arguably the oldest and most prestigious university in Uganda. When I asked her if she was at Makerere, she got upset and said: "Makerere is not the only university in Uganda!"

I wondered why she had reacted with so much emotion and anger. I apologized and proceeded to ask her where she had studied law. Suddenly, she lowered her voice and murmured what sounded like the name of some unknown university. Very often, people don't tell you the full story, especially folks who think that full disclosure can hurt their standing. Rather, they will only tell you half the story, focusing on what they want you to hear. But, for me, that you are a lawyer does not tell us the full story. Tell us which law school you graduated from and how you fared in law school, especially if you pride yourself as a brilliant lawyer or intellectual. Some people can come to you bragging that they have a Masters degree or PhD without mentioning where they got that Masters degree or PhD from. Can you please tell us where you got your so-called Masters degree or PhD from? We want to know. Otherwise, if you catch us on a bad day, we might even ask you to tell us how you fared in your undergraduate degree program, that is, if you even had a first degree before embarking on that Masters or PhD degree you are making so much noise about.

Of course, folks with questionable and dodgy credentials easily get offended with such questions. But, it matters where you got your education from and how many years you spent at university. There is no need to get upset if you have nothing to hide. You can't wing it. Just tell us. And don't lower your voice when talking.

The year was 1992, and the month was September. I flew out of Lusaka, Zambia, on Tuesday, September 29, 1992, at 19:05 hours Zambian time, and arrived in London, Great Britain, at Heathrow Airport's Terminal 4 early the next morning (Greenwich Mean Time (GMT)) on Wednesday, September 30. When I was leaving Lusaka, I was accompanied to Lusaka International Airport by my parents. They came to see me off. I was leaving Zambia for the United Kingdom not for a few days, weeks or months, but, rather, for a number of years. I was on my way to pursue postgraduate studies at the oldest university in the English-speaking world and the world's most respected, the University of Oxford. I was going there to take up what many consider to be the world's most prestigious scholarship, the Rhodes Scholarship. And I was heading to Oxford to pursue what is widely considered the world's most rigorous and most prestigious taught Masters degree program in the entire common law world, the two-year Oxford BCL (Bachelor of Civil Law) degree.

It was the first time that I had travelled out of Africa before I had even visited all the many countries highlighted at the beginning of Chapter 1. I did not know what to expect. I was excited, of course, by an opportunity to see England and to study at Oxford. I was flying with British Airways directly from Lusaka to London's Heathrow Airport and arriving at Terminal 4. I had heard so much about London and Heathrow Airport, and so much about the University of Oxford. So, I was looking forward to seeing all these places. Good disco music was coming out of London back then. Fashion and style were coming out of London, too. You name it, it was all there in London.

In those days, going abroad was not as common as it is today. If anything, only a handful of my peers from my student days at UNZA, LPI or high school had been to England. Even for those few, many only managed to go through their parents or guardians, especially if, say, your father, uncle or auntie was posted to a diplomatic post, or had gone abroad for college or university studies and had taken his family along with him. Some would go abroad to babysit their relative's child or children. Now there is nothing wrong with that. We are just trying to spell out the different routes to town. Otherwise, a great many of my peers back then had not even been to nearby places such as Johannesburg or Cape Town in South Africa. England, as some Zambians understood it back then, was mainly for the 'apa mwamba kids' (rich kids) whose parents were heading some State-owned enterprises in Zambia and could thus afford to use corporate perks for executives to send their children abroad to university or high school. Others who went abroad for university education were ZCCM-sponsored students, especially if your father or uncle held a managerial or corporate executive leadership position in ZCCM. Some folks who found themselves in England had relatives working for the national airline, Zambia Airways, and would thus get the heavily subsidized air tickets that were periodically sold to employees of the airline and their family members.

Before I left Zambia for England, I contacted my cousin Mutamba Bwalya, who was at the time pursuing his accountancy professional studies in London. He had moved to England a few years before I got there. I informed Mutamba of my travel plans. In those days, there was no email or social media platform to reach out to someone instantaneously. Everything had to be done through snail mail. I wrote to Mutamba and waited for his reply. I provided him with my itinerary so that he could meet me at Terminal 4 of Heathrow Airport.

I had one challenge before leaving Zambia. I needed to organize a bit of cash for me to move from London to Oxford and for my first few days before I got my student stipend payment from my sponsors in Oxford. My sponsors in Oxford were going to provide me with a cheque once I got to Oxford, but I needed a bit of cash to move from London to Oxford and for a few snacks along the way. I checked with my employer, the University of Zambia (UNZA), if they could assist me. I was told that since I was not travelling on a scholarship provided or secured by UNZA, they could not assist me, notwithstanding that I was still their employee. Basically, I was on my own. So, I had to think outside the box.

At the time, there were no bureaux de change in Zambia, as we know them today. Foreign exchange in Zambia was heavily controlled by the central bank, the Bank of Zambia. You could only get US dollars or British Pounds Sterling from the central bank. No commercial bank would sell foreign currency. And only people travelling for medical treatment outside Zambia or going abroad for school would be allowed to buy foreign currency from the central bank. It was tough. As a result, the US dollar and other convertible international currencies would also trade on the black market, but the exchange rate on the black market for the US dollar was quite unfriendly. So I was stuck, because I did not have enough local currency to buy a few US dollars from the central bank even though I was going to school.

The other people I thought would help me out in Zambia could not come through for me. I had turned to a close family member for support. He promised to give me the local Zambian Kwacha to buy US$1,000 from the central bank and said he would then get about US$930 of that money so that he could offload the same on the black market and make his profits, leaving me with only US$30. It was a raw deal. I knew that on his own he could not access that money from the central bank. Luckily, a good Samaritan, an old friend of mine, stepped in to assist me instead. The good Samaritan helped me to get US$1,000, of which he gave me US$300 and took the remaining US$700. It was a kind and generous deal. He really helped me because he was going to make a bit of a loss when offloading his take on the black market, but he didn't mind. He trusted me and was only helping me since he knew me very well. I am ever thankful to that dear friend of mine. In Bemba, we say, "Ukwangala kwa chila ulupwa." ('It is not always that blood is thicker than water. Sometimes, a genuinely good and kind friend can help you where you own blood neglects or fails to help you.")

I was now ready to board my British Airways flight from Lusaka to London. I was the first of my parents' children to travel abroad to a western country. Apart from my father, nobody else in the family had been abroad. So, I inspired not only my siblings, but also some close relatives and friends to travel the world and see for themselves. Dressed in a grey suit with a briefcase in my hand, I said goodbye to my parents and proceeded to the boarding gate at Lusaka's International Airport. Before leaving Zambia, my father had given me some helpful advice on life and living abroad since he had spent some time in Canada as a university student. His guidance was very helpful, and he was very candid. He did not mince his words or beat about the bush. He spoke especially about not getting oneself into mischief that would compromise my moral integrity for short-term gratification. I knew what he meant. I carried those words with me. He also encouraged me to continue going to church and believing in God.

I arrived at Terminal 4 of Heathrow Airport in London in the wee hours of Wednesday, September 30. It must have been around 05:30am. It was misty and dark. All the passengers on the flight started disembarking and heading to the customs and immigration section. At the time, if you were a Zambian national travelling on a Zambian passport, you did not need a British visa to enter the UK. All I needed to enter the UK was a British student permit. While in Zambia, I had heard stories of some Africans, including some Zambians, who had been sent back to Africa and denied entry into the UK at Heathrow Airport because either their immigration paperwork was not in order, or they were found in violation of some British immigration laws. But thankfully, I did not have to worry about such things. I was legitimate.

The British immigration officer attending to me asked me what I had come to do in the UK. I explained to him confidently and politely that I was a Rhodes Scholar headed to Oxford. He looked at my passport and paperwork before congratulating me, saying that I was going to a very prestigious school. He then proceeded to stamp my passport with the usual immigration clearance date stamp and welcomed me to the UK. I was good to go. I proceeded to pick up my luggage from the baggage carousel before heading out to 'Arrivals' where I found my cousin Mutamba waiting for me. I had landed in 'Engy', as we used to call England.

The weather in London was grey and cloudy, and it was raining. I was so glad that my cousin was there to help me settle down. I remain ever grateful. Had he not been there, it would have been a bit of a challenge for me to settle down. Mutamba welcomed me and informed me that we were going to take the 'tube' to his place in London. I had no idea what the 'tube' was all about. Later, I found out that it was simply the underground train. So, we took the tube and changed trains at a few stations. It was wet and cold. When we got to Mutamba's place, I took a bath to freshen up a bit before grabbing some breakfast. Thereafter, we proceeded to Oxford. We took the intercity train from Victoria Station in London to Oxford Station on Park End Street in Oxford. The train started off on time. There were no delays or unnecessary waits, even though there were some empty seats in the carriages. We took a fast train and I saw Reading on the way before we got to Oxford. Mutamba was really helpful.

From Oxford station, Mutamba and I took one of the famous black cabs, basically hackney carriages, to Rhodes House, where we were welcomed by Ms Sally Colgan, one of the main administrative officers. She was so gracious to us and took me to meet Professor Sir Anthony Kenny, who was the warden of Rhodes House at the time. I felt at home. Immediately, I fell in love with Oxford. The people there were so nice, welcoming and friendly. I was handed my stipend cheque and given some paperwork to read up on.

When Mutamba and I left Rhodes House, we went to my college, Exeter College, where I was given information regarding my graduate student accommodation. I was going to be staying in Exeter House, a college residence exclusively for graduate students. Mutamba and I took another black cab to Exeter House. We arrived at 239 Iffley Road, the address of Exeter House, which was a lovely big house with about 32 single rooms. The elderly ladies responsible for maintaining and managing the place took me around the house and asked me to choose my student room. I opted for a spacious room that was located on the first floor near the laundry room.

Now that I had everything sorted out, Mutamba and I took the train back London. I spent a couple of days at Mutamba's place in order to familiarize myself a bit with London before returning to Oxford at the weekend. To get back to Oxford, I took the Oxford Tube at Victoria Station, which is actually a coach service, since it was more economical to take a luxury coach than the train even though the coach was equally comfortable. I boarded the Oxford Tube from Victoria Station in London to Gloucester Green Station in Oxford. It was a smooth and comfortable ride on the coach, but one thing caught my attention. The Oxford Tube left on time, even though there were a lot of empty seats. In Zambia, most buses will not start off until all the seats are taken, causing inconvenience to those passengers who had boarded early to get where they were going in time. The bus driver would simply ask everyone to wait until the bus was full before you start off. Very rarely would you find a bus driver adhering strictly to time. Some buses back home in Zambia can have a set departure time, but adherence to time is often a problem. But here I was in Engy on a nice luxury coach with only a handful of passengers and several empty seats, yet the bus started off on time.

There were no delays or unnecessary waiting. We left London on time and arrived in Oxford within about 45 to 50 minutes.

In my first few days in Oxford, I was not quite settled. I wanted to switch universities to go the University of Warwick, which had offered me admission to a one-year Master of Laws (LLM) degree program, followed by an additional two years of research that could enable me to develop my LLM thesis into a PhD thesis. For me, that was a great deal, and I was excited about it. I thought the Warwick offer was better, as both the Warwick LLM and PhD could be covered by my three-year Rhodes Scholarship. So I made an appointment to see the Warden of Rhodes House in Oxford, Professor Sir Anthony Kenny, to seek his views. I took with me the Warwick admission letter and spiritedly presented it to Sir Kenny. He read the letter, looked at me and smiled. Sir Kenny then said calmly with a smile, "Your friends fight to get into Oxford, and you want to leave Oxford?"

I knew right there and then that something was not right with what I was proposing. For me, coming straight out of Africa at a time when the internet had not even been discovered, I had limited exposure. Back home in Zambia, a PhD was all that mattered in the end. My modest thinking at the time was that why should I waste two years in Oxford studying for a degree called a 'Bachelor' of something when I could go to Warwick and become a 'Dr' in the three years of my Rhodes Scholarship. I was wrong. Oxford is Oxford. It's not Warwick, even though Warwick is also a prestigious university and ranks consistently in the top ten of the best British universities. And the Oxford BCL is simply miles apart from other law degrees. But there I was. I had my foot inside Oxford, yet, out of naivety, I was trying to leave.

Fortunately, given the good and sound advice offered by Sir Kenny, I reluctantly stayed on in Oxford. Looking back now, Sir Kenny was right. Oxford is Oxford. He saved me from making an irresponsible decision to leave.

As fate would have it, after graduating from Oxford in 1994 and getting my MBA from Hull in 1995, God not only took me to the same University of Warwick that I had wanted to go to in 1992, but He also elevated that Warwick offer to a full-time lectureship or Assistant Professorship in Law. God had to take me through Oxford first. Without Oxford, I might not have been able to attract the interest of an elevated Warwick offer. We just have to be patient with God. He knows what we need and at what point in our lives. And through the elevated offer from Warwick, I was able to pursue my Warwick PhD studies while serving as a full-time Law Lecturer at the said University of

Warwick. In Chapter 3 of this book, I touched briefly on the path leading to my Warwick PhD. Let me now provide below some fuller context and insights.

I noted in Chapter 3 that shortly after I joined the University of Warwick, I looked at the graduate studies handbook and guidelines. I noticed in those guidelines, first, that there was provision for an academic staff member at the University of Warwick to pursue a PhD free of charge. Secondly, I realized that there was provision for someone to develop his or her Masters degree thesis into a PhD thesis. These two guidelines were quite appealing to me. As noted in Chapter 3, a full-time academic at the University of Warwick could pursue a PhD at that very university for free. Many other universities have similar incentives for their academic staff. So, I opted to develop my Oxford BCL thesis into a Warwick PhD thesis.

Put simply, a good part of the work for my Warwick PhD thesis was carried out and completed at the University of Oxford as my Oxford BCL thesis. Yes, the Warwick PhD guidelines, like similar PhD guidelines at many other leading universities, allow for the development of a Masters degree thesis into a PhD thesis. Even the University of Oxford has similar provisions for law graduate students to transfer to the DPhil (PhD) in Law status after successfully completing their Master of Philosophy (MPhil) in Law thesis. At Warwick, I was also attracted to the idea of pursuing the Warwick PhD because, as a full-time academic at that university, I did not have to pay any tuition fees, except for a modest examination fee for the PhD viva voce. This deal was too good to be true.

But before I could register for the Warwick PhD, one of my senior colleagues at the University of Warwick, who was an Oxford graduate himself, wondered why I needed to pursue a PhD since I already had the Oxford BCL. He had a point. I really did not need to get a PhD given that I already had the Oxford BCL. But then, I could not explain to him that where I come from in Africa a number of people will not buy into such arguments since they look at a PhD as the ultimate qualification. You are either a 'Dr' or you are not. Explaining to folks how academically rigorous the Oxford BCL is, in comparison, say, to a PhD, would be pursuing a red herring. Many people will think that you are simply trying to justify your own inadequacies. Even in the US where I live now, I would have had to deal with similar challenges. The terminal degree that is widely known in the US and everywhere else is a PhD, notwithstanding that the Oxford BCL has a strong reputation as the most prestigious and rigorous taught postgraduate law degree in the entire English-speaking world.

And so, in the summer of 1996, I embarked on my Warwick PhD journey. In less than two years, that is, by mid-1998, I was done with the first draft of my Warwick PhD thesis which was immediately accepted for publication into a scholarly book by a leading academic publisher. As a full-time academic at the University of Warwick, I was not required to have a PhD supervisor, though in lieu of a supervisor the Warwick PhD guidelines required me to have an Advisor who would simply 'oversee' that the PhD project was going well. Professor Hugh Beale was appointed as my PhD Advisor, though I worked independently for the most part. At a later stage, Professor Upendra Baxi and Professor John McEldowney played advisory roles in the absence of Professor Beale. I am ever grateful to all the three.

I have provided below three pictures taken when I was graduating for my PhD at the University of Warwick on Friday, January 12, 2001. The first picture is with the then Dean of the School of Law, Professor Mike McConville, who hired me as a Law Lecturer when I joined Warwick Law School. Mike was such a great scholar, administrator and fine human being. I am ever grateful for his kind support, camaraderie and true friendship.

In the picture below, I am with Professor John McEldowney, another great scholar and a wonderful human being.

In the picture shown here, I am standing at the entrance to the graduation hall at the University of Warwick, with the American Star-Spangled Banner and the British Union Jack displayed in the background, signifying my transatlantic journey in the world of erudition.

I must add that one other dimension that got me to pursue the Warwick PhD after getting my Oxford BCL was that I was not sure if I would remain in the UK or return to Africa. So I had to equip myself with what Africa expected of me. In Africa, we love titles. And the 'Dr' title has a special place in our societies, forcing some politicians and pastors to start purchasing phony doctoral degrees from unaccredited schools and diploma mills.

I look back at the Oxfordshire years with great nostalgia. I have studied and taught at many prestigious universities in three continents, namely, Europe, North America and Africa, but none of them compares to Oxford. A few other universities get close, but Oxford is Oxford. With the Oxford experience comes Oxford thinking, characterized by critical thinking and logical reasoning. In my humble view, Oxford was and remains miles apart from the rest. The rigor of the Oxford tutorial system is unparalleled. On the BCL, for example, if you did not read thoroughly and understand in great detail the recommended cases, journal articles and scholarly books on the reading list, you would end up looking like you are studying law for the first time. At the University of Zambia (UNZA), by contrast, like at many other universities around the world, one could get away with good lecture notes and just reading one or two casebooks, a few journal articles and a few textbooks on a particular field of law. At Oxford, it was different. You could not just rely on lecture notes and a few additional sources. And you would not only get different reading lists for your tutorials, lectures, and seminars from different tutors, lecturers and professors, but were also expected to do your own research and come up with additional materials that would deepen your critical understanding of the law. As an Oxford BCL student, I would go deeper into the law reports themselves, dissecting the reasoning of each judge in a particular case as well as traversing a wide range of sources that included several scholarly journal articles. There was hardly any time to rest or relax.

At UNZA, by contrast, I rarely read from the library. I had most of the books I needed in my room. If I needed to go to the library, it was to borrow an additional book and then retreat to my room to read. Put simply, I would simply borrow the book from the library and read it from my room, but at Oxford it was different. You had to immerse yourself in those law reports that you could not carry with you to your room. Also, just reading the headnote or summary at the beginning of a full-text law report on a principle of law established by a case was not enough. You had to read everything. For, you would be quizzed in tutorials to explain, for example, why a particular judge said what he or she said, or the reasoning behind the dissenting judgements of Judges XYZ and ABC, and if you agree with either or both of them. And if you said you agreed or disagreed with either or both of them, you were also expected to explain why and to provide your reasoning. It was not enough to say 'I concur' and then fall asleep. It meant you had to read widely and know your stuff. Otherwise, your ignorance would be exposed in the tutorials. And the tutorials were quite intense. There was nowhere to run or hide. It would be one or two graduate students only before one tutor for a full hour. Now, imagine that you have not read your work and the other student has done all his or her reading and keeps coming up with thoughtful contributions whilst you are just seated there looking lost! It can be a deeply embarrassing moment, especially for a minority student. Such situations had to be avoided at all costs by going to class fully prepared.

In many cases, the tutor will have written widely in the course he or she is taking you in. So, there was no room for waffling or trying to play clever by throwing big words around or fishing for speculative arguments. You either knew your stuff or you did not. And to succeed, you had no option but to read widely and deeply before class so that you had sensible things to say.

I remember that there were some scholarly books that I read over and over from the beginning to the end. I even got to know what was on which page and in which chapter or paragraph by heart. I just had to. Most of the professors, lecturers and tutors were the authors of the top books that were highly recommended in the field they were teaching. And you know what that means – they were experts in their respective fields. A professor or lecturer would walk in class and give you a reading list of about 200 cases for the component of the course that he or she was going to teach. Another one would come in for his or her component of the course and give you another 200 cases to read. At first, it was confusing and overwhelming. I wondered if these guys did not realize that we were already given enough to read by other lecturers or professors. In the meantime, your tutor in college would also hand you his or her reading list of about 300 sources to read. As students, we would simply run with the ball. That was Oxford. There was no time to complain that the reading materials were too much. Seminars would also have their own reading materials. So, you were thrown into the deep end to swim with the sharks out there. Almost all the students admitted to the BCL were among the brightest from wherever they came from in the English-speaking world. Many had graduated with Distinctions or First Class for their undergraduate law degrees, so you can imagine the intensity of the competition. One was pitted against the best of the best. It was intense, but quite intellectually stimulating and enriching too.

In the first year of my two-year BCL degree program, there were only three black students on the program, namely, a Ghanaian friend of mine who is now practicing law in New York, Samuel G Owusu Esq (who was at Keble College), a distinguished Jamaican law professor, Professor Tracy S Robinson (who was at Balliol College), now based at the University of the West Indies in Jamaica and has taught at a number of leading US law schools, and I. Sam took the one-year variant of the BCL. Tracy and I took the two-year variant. After the first year, Sam graduated and moved to the US for further graduated studies at the University of Michigan at Ann Arbor. Tracy and I remained behind for the second year of the BCL. The structure of the one-year BCL comprised four taught courses while that of the two-year BCL involved seven taught courses or five taught courses with a 25,000-word thesis. I went for the option of five taught courses and a 25,000-word thesis. Today, that BCL thesis stands as separate degree in Oxford and is known as the Master of Philosophy in Law (MPhil in Law) degree. I think Tracy also went for the BCL thesis option. For the five taught courses for the two-year BCL, I took Public International Law (which was mainly Law of the Sea), Law of Trusts, Remedies in Contract and Tort (also known as Economic Analysis of Law), Corporate Insolvency Law, and Corporate Finance Law. Then my BCL thesis was on securities regulation and privatization. Professor Ian Brownlie, DPhil, DCL, who was Chichele Professor of Public International Law and a Fellow of All Souls College at the University of Oxford, took us in lectures and seminars in public international law.

Every morning, I would get on my bike in the cold winter to ride quietly from my graduate student residence at Exeter House on Iffley Road to the Oxford Law Faculty building or All Souls College for lectures and seminars in public international law. I would repeat the rides in the Hilary and Trinity terms. Looking back, it all seems like yesterday. I would park my bike at my college, Exeter College, and then walk down Turl Street to All Souls College on High Street for my graduate seminars in public international law. The seminars would be held on Saturday mornings from around 08:30am to around 11:30pm, and Professor Brownlie would chair them. The depth of erudition on those BCL seminars was like nothing pedagogical that I have ever experienced in the entire 40-50 years of my academic life. You had to be extremely well-prepared to avoid getting exposed. His lectures, too, were very illuminating and would be held at the Law Faculty building during working days of the week.

I recall that in one of my seminar presentations on the United Nations Convention on the Law of the Sea 1982, I thought I had scored a touchdown, having studied all night before the seminar, when Prof Brownlie thoughtfully guided me on the relevance of weaving together a mosaic of conventional international law, customary international law and State practice. All the three pieces had to come together nicely. Suddenly, it dawned on me that what seemed to be an almost impeccable presentation had room for improvement. Those BCL lectures and seminars cast a new light on my understanding of public international law. I had studied public international law in the final year of my first professional law degree, but it was not as insightful as the Oxford BCL experience. At Oxford, it all seemed totally new and very illuminating. It was an honor to study under such a fine legal scholar as Prof Brownlie. His reputation always preceded him.

In the law of trusts, I had a number of lecturers and professors who taught me, including Professor Ann Kennedy and Professor Susan Bright. My tutor in the law of trusts was Professor Simon Gardner at Lincoln College, right next to Exeter College. Professor Gardner had written extensively in property law and trusts and had published a great book on the law of trusts. His tutorials had so much depth. After the tutorials, you came out well immersed in the material, though you also had to be well-prepared when going to his tutorials. Professor Donald Harris, then a Senior Research Fellow at Balliol College, taught me Remedies in Contract and Tort. He would occasionally invite some economic scholars to add a perspective of quantitative economics to the economic analysis of law. Don had a warm and fatherly personality. His seminars and lectures were so informative. He had written what is arguably the standard textbook in remedies in contract and tort in the United Kingdom.

Professor Dan Prentice, who was also my BCL thesis supervisor, took me in Corporate Finance Law. Professor Prentice was at the time serving as the Allen & Overy Professor of Corporate Law at the University of Oxford (the first Chair in corporate law in the UK) and a Fellow of Pembroke College. Other lecturers in corporate finance law included Professor Paul Davis, who later became the Allen & Overy Professor of Corporate Law at the University of Oxford after initially moving from Oxford to London School of Economics and Political Science (LSE) as the Cassel Professor of Commercial Law, and Professor Fidelis Oditah, a Nigerian and a British legal scholar who was at the time serving as a Fellow and Tutor in Law at Merton College and the Travers Smith Braithwaite Lecturer in Corporate Finance Law at the University of Oxford. In corporate insolvency law, Prof

Roy Goode, the then Norton Rose Professor of English Law at the University of Oxford, was the main course convener, accompanied by Professor Oditah and Professor Prentice. In my humble view, no other English legal scholar has written more than Professor Roy Goode in the field of corporate insolvency law. His works alone occupy a whole library shelf. Both the corporate finance law and corporate insolvency law seminars and lectures were so illuminating. They had depth. The critical analyses of legal issues as well as pertinent aspects of the law would make your jaw drop if you had not read or prepared before class.

In my college, Exeter College, I found two college law tutors and fellows, namely, Professor Sandra Fredman, a South African-British legal scholar, and Professor Benedict Kingsbury, a New Zealand national who had just completed his PhD (DPhil). Professor Kingsbury later moved to the US as a Professor of Law at Duke University Law School before joining New York University (NYU) Law School where he serves as the Vice Dean of Global Programs and the Murry and Ida Becker Professor of Law as well as the Director of the Institute for International Law and Justice. Exeter College assigned me a mentor in Professor Fredman to help me settle down quickly and adapt to studies at Oxford. I also benefitted from the guidance and encouragement of Dr Michael Hart, a fellow of Exeter College and a university lecturer in politics.

When I arrived at Oxford, I got to learn that a BCL student from East Africa had just failed his BCL exams while the other African student on the BCL degree program, a Zambian, Elias Chipimo Jr, had passed. I was happy to hear that the Zambian had passed, but sad to learn about the East African student who failed. The latter even had a Master of Laws (LLM) degree already from a top Canadian university, Queen's University at Kingston in Canada, before embarking on the Oxford BCL News about the East African guy's challenges with the Oxford BCL sent chills down my spine. I started thinking, if a guy with an LLM can flunk the BCL, what does that tell you? I thought to myself, does it mean that one of the two of us black students on the BCL, that is, Tracy or I, will have to go down?

With that thought, there was no resting. I read the books nonstop. Towards the end of the first year, I saw the same East African guy who had had trouble with the BCL return to Oxford to re-sit his BCL exams, and he passed this time around. In fact, a few years later, he went back to Oxford to pursue his doctoral studies (DPhil in Law) and obtained this successfully and without any problems. It shows that in life you just have to remain focused, work hard and persevere. At the time when the East African guy went back to Oxford for the DPhil in Law, I had already graduated from Oxford and was teaching at the University of Warwick.

Back at Oxford, after two years of intense studying for the two-year postgraduate BCL degree program, both Tracy and I passed the BCL exams. So no black BCL student failed in my cohort, although another East African student who was admitted to the BCL program when Tracy and I were in our second year of the BCL was not able to complete the program. When Tracy and I graduated, she moved to the US for further graduate studies at the best US law school, the University of Yale Law School, where I also got an offer and fully-funded fellowship a few years later but declined the Yale offer to join instead the World Bank. From Oxford, I moved to Yorkshire in England to pursue a Master of Business Administration (MBA) degree at the University of Hull, as I had a year left on my Rhodes Scholarship. I was not going to throw away that third year. At the time, there was no business school in Oxford. Oxford University's Templeton College was only offering a two-year Master of Philosophy (MPhil) degree in Management Studies and a one-year Master of Science (MSc) degree in Industrial and Labor Relations. Said Business School at the University of Oxford,

as we know it today, was not in existence. It was only established in 1996 when I was already teaching at the University of Warwick. So, in 1994, after graduating from Oxford, I went for the MBA at the University of Hull. I wanted to get a General Management MBA that would complement my Oxford BCL and give me a broader set of managerial and leadership skills, as opposed to a narrowly focused or too specialized MBA degree program. And Hull had that program.

In the picture shown here, I am with my learned brother and friend Professor Henry Fadamiro, a fellow Rhodes Scholar in my time at Oxford (who was at Green College). We reunited in Washington DC, USA, after several decades from our Oxford matriculation and graduation days. Henry and I were in the same cohort as Rhodes Scholars at Oxford. In

1992, Henry was the sole Rhodes Scholar from Nigeria matriculating at Oxford. I was also the sole Rhodes Scholar from Zambia matriculating at Oxford. Henry read for a DPhil (PhD) in Biology. He currently serves as Full Professor of Entomology and is the Associate Vice President for Strategic Initiatives at Texas A&M University in the US. He has also previously served as a researcher at the International Institute of Tropical Agriculture, Ibadan, Nigeria as well as at Iowa State University, the University of Minnesota, and Minnesota Department of Agriculture. Professor Fadamiro taught for many years at Auburn University in the US before he joined Texas A&M University.

Other Rhodes Scholars in my 1992 cohort at Oxford included U.S. Senator Cory A Booker (who was at the Queen's College), a Rhodes Scholar from the U.S. (selected from the State of New Jersey after graduating from Stanford University in California) and former U.S. Assistant Secretary for the U.S. Department of Health and Human Services who is also former Governor of the State of Louisiana, Governor Piyush Robert (Bobby) Jindal (who was at New College, and selected from the State of Louisiana after graduating from Brown University). On the official government website of the Secretary of State of Louisiana, Governor Jindal is said to have "...graduated with honors in biology and public policy. Following his graduation from Brown he attended Oxford University in England as a Rhodes Scholar, having turned down admissions to medical and law schools at both Harvard and Yale." As Rhodes Scholars, we seem to be spoilt for choice and can afford to turn down lucrative offers from some of the most coveted schools that others can only dream of.

There is just something about Rhodes Scholars. Perhaps, we are indeed spoilt for choice. As noted earlier, I also turned down a fully-funded fellowship at Yale University Law School, the best law school in the US that beats even Harvard University Law School. I was admitted to Yale Law School with a fully-funded fellowship, but chose instead to go to the World Bank in Washington DC.

My decision to turn down Yale Law School was made a bit easier because I had by then already graduated from the University of Oxford as a Rhodes Scholar and taught law at one of the top ten British universities, the University of Warwick. So I proceeded to join the World Bank under its highly competitive and prestigious Young Professionals Program (YPP). The 1998 World Bank YPP cohort comprised about 32 YPs. Three of us, Dr Vera Songwe from Cameroon, Dr Modibo K Camara from Mali, and myself from Zambia, were the black Africans on the cohort. There were also two Arab-Africans from Tanzania and Sudan, respectively, but they had been living in the US for some time. Many years later, my colleague, Dr Vera Songwe, headed the United Nations Economic Commission for Africa (UNECA) at the level of Under-Secretary-General.

At Oxford, the photo below captures my 1992 Rhodes Scholars class.. I, however, missed the photoshoot session for that class photo, as I overslept after the heavy jetlag from my long fight from Zambia. So, I ended up joining the 1993 Rhodes Scholars class for a class photoshoot. Back then technology was not so advanced for someone to be photoshopped into an existing photo if you had missed out on the original photoshoot.

RHODES SCHOLARS 1992

Below is the 1993 Rhodes Scholars class photo where I appear, having missed the 1992 Rhodes Scholars class photo.

The University of Oxford has three academic terms, namely, Michaelmas (October to December), Hilary (January to March) and Trinity (April to June). There is no such thing as 'first term', 'second term', 'third term' or 'semester' at Oxford. Rather, it's Michaelmas, Hilary and Trinity. Each college has what is known as the Junior Common Room (JCR), the Middle Common Room (MCR) and the Senior Common Room (SCR). The JCR is a place within the college which is reserved as a hub for social activities and a meeting place for the undergraduate student body. Common rooms help to shape and define student life at Oxford. The MCR is a common room reserved for graduate students, whilst the SCR is reserved mainly for academics such as tutors, fellows, lecturers and professors. So, I was member of the MCR at Exeter College as a BCL student. In 2023, when I was elected as Honorary Fellow of Exeter College at Oxford by the Governing Council of the college, I was elevated to membership of the SCR. So, I am now a member of the SCR of Exeter College at the University of Oxford.

While studying at Oxford, it was customary for graduate students to get invitations from the college to join some members of the SCR for dinner in the college dining hall on some Fridays. As graduate students, many of us looked forward to those college dinner invitations. The dress code was always formal. Men had to wear a black tuxedo suit, a white shirt and white bowtie, with a black graduate student gown on top. The picture below helps to put things in perspective.

The discussions at the college dinner table in Oxford were always enlightening and edifying. You could have come to Oxford well-cultivated from your own cultural background, but the Oxford experience enhanced your social intelligence and your ability to conduct yourself with finesse. It was about the ways of a learned and enlightened gentleman or lady in a polite society and how to carry out polite conversation. For example, a member of the SCR would ask you about current affairs in your home country or elsewhere in the world. It was quite engaging. There was no talk of where to find a nightclub or some cute gals (i.e. nyash, bokossi, or wowowo) for the night. Such conversations were below the expected norm at the Oxford dinner table. Some SCR members would ask you, say, about how you are settling down in Oxford and how your studies are coming along. Others would touch on your doctoral research, or share with you what they are working on. We would also have some conversation around worldly travels, including different fine restaurants and wines in foreign countries, various cultural experiences around the globe and current affairs globally. It is called 'polite conversation'. At no time would you hear a crude joke or talk about whores, strippers and strip clubs, or hear someone laughing out loudly with his legs thrown in the air from hysterical laughter. Such uncouth conduct could offend the diners. All dinner conversations were in good measure and in fine taste. No ichi-Copperbel!

It may sound snobbish, but as an Oxford graduate, where are you likely to end up as a professional? You might as well start to prepare early enough so that when you graduate you do not end up a misfit, socially or culturally, in the higher echelons of the social strata. Your appreciation of fine wines, for example, would start from an evening of mulled wine at the MCR. Also, a sherry would often be customary before dinner, as you mingled with others, say, at a Rhodes House dinner. I cannot think of any other academic environment outside the Oxbridge circles that offers you this kind of preparation. That is the difference between Oxford and many other leading universities in the English-speaking world. I don't think one can get such a holistic academic experience as at Oxbridge anywhere else in the world. Even your choice of tea mattered. You had to know something about some fine brands of tea.

Pub-crawling was popular among some undergraduates at Oxford. By contrast, many graduate students were less engaged in the pub-crawling culture, especially those who were older or came from different universities and cultures outside Oxford. Others were international students. When I arrived in 1992, I found a few Zambian students there. One of them was an undergraduate law student, Ms Sebako Siame, who is now a notable investment banker in London. Dr Chaloka Beyani, currently teaching at London School of Economics and Political Science (LSE), had just completed his PhD (DPhil) studies in law at Wolfson College in Oxford and taken up a postdoctoral research fellowship at his alma mater, Wolfson College, and the Refugee Studies Centre in Oxford. Dr Beyani attended Oxford as a Commonwealth Scholar. I also found Dr Monde Muyangwa, who, under the US President Joe Biden administration, served as the Assistant Administrator in the Bureau for Africa at USAID in Washington DC. Dr Muyangwa was at St Anthony's College in Oxford and had just commenced her PhD (DPhil) studies after completing her second Bachelors degree (a PPE – Politics, Philosophy, and Economics) at Oxford, following her first Bachelors degree earned from the University of Zambia (UNZA). Dr Muyangwa attended Oxford as a Rhodes Scholar.

Another Rhodes Scholar who was in Oxford when I arrived there was Ms Yoliswa Wendy Nkuhlu-Siyolwe who was at St. Anne's College. She was finalizing her Master of Letters (MLitt) degree thesis before taking up a corporate executive position in London, UK. Other Zambian Rhodes Scholars such as Mr Elias Chipimo Jr. and Hon Mr Deputy Chief Justice Michael Musonda had just completed their Oxford graduate studies and had returned to Zambia.

Later I got to know other Rhodes Scholars from Zambia who had passed through Oxford before my time, including Mr Chisanga Puta-Chekwe who was at Exeter College. Mr Puta-Chekwe has served as a leading corporate executive and public figure around the world. In 2009, he became the Deputy Minister for Citizenship and Immigration as well as Women's Issues in Ontario, Canada, and was also named in July 2013 the Deputy Minister for Seniors' Affairs, taking on additional responsibilities in Ontario, Canada, as Deputy Minister for international trade as well in 2014. There is also Professor Evance Kalula (who attended Balliol College) (currently serving as Emeritus Professor at the University of Cape Town (UCT) in South Africa who previously held a Professorial Chair in Law at the said UCT), Dr Remmy Mushota (who attended Exeter College) (a former academic at the University of Zambia (UNZA) who later became a Cabinet Minister in the Zambia Government), Dr Sebastian Kopulande (who was at Jesus College) (a leading corporate executive and former Permanent Secretary at State House under Zambia's President Frederick Chiluba who also later served as a Special Assistant to the President (Special Duties) under President Levy P. Mwanawasa), Professor Victor M. Mpepo (who was at Linacre College) (a former academic at UNZA who also later served as Professor of English Language and Linguistics at the University of Zululand in South Africa), Mr Nduba Namoonde (who was at University College) (leading a corporate executive in Zambia and the US), Ms Lucy Banda-Sichone (who was at Somerville College) (a leading gender and human rights lawyer and activist, who, in 1978, was selected as Zambia's first female Rhodes Scholar and is now the only female Rhodes Scholar to appear in a portrait at Oxford), and Mr Meebelo Mutukwa (who was at Lincoln College) (leading a corporate executive in Zambia).

In addition, I got to know Mr David Phiri (the first black African to gain a golf Blue at Oxford and a former Governor of the Central Bank of Zambia who also headed several other major organizations in Zambia and chaired several boards, in addition to serving at some point as Chairman of the Football Association of Zambia). In fact, before he passed on in January 2012, Mr David Phiri, one of Zambia's earliest graduates of the University of Oxford, sent me a wonderful Christmas card and message which I received in my office here at the World Bank in Washington DC. He died two days after I received it. It was if he wrote to say goodbye. He was an absolute gentleman. And I am ever grateful for his edifying and inspiring camaraderie. Earlier, when I was based in the UK and lecturing at the University of Warwick, I met his wife, an English lady, Mrs Ann Phiri, and visited her home in Oxford.

As a graduate student at Exeter College, the University of Oxford, I was staying at the college's graduate student residence, Exeter House, located on Iffley Road. I have provided below a picture of my parents, Mr Joseph T Mwenda and Mrs Esther M Mwenda, at Exeter House in Oxford, England. The picture was taken in the summer of 1996 when I invited my parents over from Zambia to spend summer with me in England. At the time, I was lecturing at the University of Warwick. My parents and I had taken a train from Coventry to Oxford when the said picture was taken.

As part of their visit to the UK, I wanted to share with my parents the academic journey that I had travelled in the UK, including memories of my graduate student days at the world's leading university, the University of Oxford. We toured Oxford city and the University of Oxford extensively, including visiting places such as Oxford Law Faculty, Rhodes House, Exeter College, the Sheldonian Theatre, the Radcliff Camera, the Carfax Tower, the Covered Market, shops and stores on High Street, historical buildings on Broad Street, the Magdalen Tower, the University of Oxford Botanic Garden, the Magdalen Rose Garden, the Bodleian Library, Magdalene College, Christ Church College and meadow, Merton College, New College, All Souls College, Trinity

College, the Bridge of Sighs, Balliol College, and many other places. I was happy that my parents could spend some time with me in England while they were still alive. You honor people while they are still alive, not when they are gone.

When I first arrived at Exeter House in 1992, as a Rhodes Scholar, I was told that there was another Zambian student who had just checked-in a few hours before I got there. I was happy to meet my colleague Mr John L Mulutula, a fellow UNZA product. John held additionally a Masters Degree in International Relations from Japan, and was an employee of the Zambian Ministry of Foreign Affairs. John came to Oxford to pursue a one-year graduate program (non-degree) in diplomatic studies. He and I were the only two black students at Exeter House that year (1992-93). All in all, the place housed about 32 graduate students. John and I were also the only two black graduate students in Exeter College. When John completed his program in 1993, I remained alone as the only black student at Exeter House, though I had many other friends from the UK and elsewhere. Exeter House was an international community. In college, I think I was also the only black graduate student, though it did not bother me at all. For me, my studies were my priority.

Before John left, we would sometimes hang out together in Oxford. We would at times be joined by another Zambian man, Mr Thomas Mabwe (who was at Wolfson College), a lecturer at UNZA who had come to Oxford to pursue his PhD (DPhil) in Development Studies. Mr Mabwe was also a graduate of UNZA, and held a Masters degree in Development Studies from the University of East Anglia in Norwich, England. It was always fun when the three of us would go out for a drink. Mr Mabwe was a humorous elderly brother. Oxford was never short of parties, and we would link up at such events. Sometimes we would attend African and Caribbean parties organized by the African and Caribbean students at Oxford Brookes University, the former polytechnic in Oxford city. The culture at Oxford Brookes was very different from the one obtaining at the main university in Oxford, the University of Oxford. There was definitely a stronger presence of black students and black culture there, and a good number of the Oxford Brookes students were not so much into the cycling and studious culture found at the University of Oxford. Rather, you would see student cars parked everywhere around and near the campus of Oxford Brookes.

Around mid-1993, Mr Mabwe travelled to Zambia for his doctoral field research. He never returned to Oxford to complete his DPhil studies but simply abandoned them, much to the disappointment of everyone, including his doctoral thesis supervisor. Mr Mabwe's supervisor tried everything to get him back to complete his DPhil studies in Oxford, without success.

In my second year in Oxford, I had a good friend from Road Town, Tortola, in the British Virgin Islands, who I would often hang out with. Her name was Monique Adams. She stayed off Cowley Road, and thus I would get on my bike to ride from my place on Iffley Road to Monique's place. It was a short ride of about 10 to 15 minutes. Also, I remember that one of my housemates, a white lady, reached out to me one day on behalf of a mutual friend of ours who was also staying at Exeter House. The mutual friend was a pretty and charming soft-spoken German lady. I was told that she liked me. I simply smiled and played it down. All I was thinking about was my schoolwork and what I had come to do in Oxford. I knew clearly that I was not in Oxford to look for gals. My mind was fixated on my academic work and ensuring that I did not disappointment myself academically on the BCL which was a very demanding degree program. And when I visited Zambia after my first year in Oxford, a number of my Zambian friends in Lusaka would ask me, since I was now based in the UK, if I had dated a white chick and how it felt. Jungle fever was real in the brothers. I could not believe it. But they kept pushing inquisitively: "Mdala, ufwile ule ba lya sana ba bugga ba pa Oxford." ("Man, you must be having a great time with the educated white ladies of Oxford.")

By then, my colleagues Mr John Mulutula and Mr Thomas Mabwe were no longer in Oxford. They had moved back to Zambia. I would say that dating in Oxford did not require a lot of money, but rather a lot of brains. You had to have something sensible and intelligent to talk about. Both guys and gals in Oxford would get on their bicycles to go out on a date, or they would simply walk or jump on a bus. There was nothing wrong with that. No gal would look down on you because you came by bus on a date or had no car. By contrast, back home in Zambia, you would be lucky if a gal ever talked to you if you showed up on a bicycle or a bus. The contrast between these two worlds was quite intriguing to me. I have come to learn that many folks from less wealthy nations often detest the idea of getting on a bicycle or bus as a mode of transport, while many folks from much wealthier nations have no problems with that. What does that tell you? In those societies where a large faction of the public is grappling with basic physiological needs or issues of safety on Maslow's Hierarchy of Needs, you expect to see relationships and dating motivated by somewhat unsophisticated needs for food, transport, water, electricity, shelter, sex, clothing, jobs, and assets. You are likely to find in such communities a ubiquitous presence of fortified security wall-fences around residential homes that look like a maximum-security prison wall-fence just to secure the homes from thieves. Indeed, people have to ensure that they are safe, can still breathe and remain alive.

By contrast, in societies where many people operate above physiological and safety needs, you are likely to see a different set of needs that motivate relationships and dating. In particular, you are likely to find needs such as love, esteem and self-actualization predicated not on what one can get economically out of the relationship for his or her own 'selfish' physiological needs but on a quest for self-esteem, confidence, love, respect of others, respect by others and inner fulfilment. So here I was among the some of the most learned men and women in the world riding on bicycles to go to school, on a date or shopping, yet some poor folks back home in Africa would have looked down on me if I had shown up on a bicycle as my mode of transport. Many folks back home in Africa believe that if you are educated you should own and drive a nice car, and not ride a bicycle as your means of transport. In a way, dating, say, a British doctoral student at Oxford who came from a traditional upper-class family tended to be far much less costly than dating a local gal in Zambia from a low-income background or township. On a dinner date in Oxford, topics such as the Oxford and Cambridge Boat Race or people's experiences with rowing or punting in Oxford would often come up, so you had to be well-versed in Oxbridge culture to hold your own. By contrast, back home in Zambia, an average local slay-queen is likely to talk about the latest smartphone that one of her friends has, thinking that you might fall for the trick and offer to get her one. Or she will be talking about the fancy car that her friend's 'blesser' or boyfriend drives, as if she owns one herself. And every time you take her out, she will expect you to pay for her meals and drinks, in addition to possibly giving her some money. Others will even ask you for money for their monthly home rentals, or want you to buy them a car, give them money to do their hair, buy them some groceries, give them money for nails, or help with paying their college or university fees. And if you are unlucky, some slay-queens might even tell you that they are feminists, yet the same people will be busy harassing you with a begging bowl in their hands.

But Oxford was different. Many British gals there were truly independent and would often pay for themselves if you went out on a date, unless you insisted that you would take care of the bill. Also, many an Oxford chick would not bring along a group of friends if you invited her out on a date, unlike what you see back home in Africa if you are dealing with some local university or college chick. I remember that, in Oxford, if you were invited to a friend's party, it was not polite to show up empty-handed without a gift or something for the host or hostess. Rather, it was courteous to give the host or hostess a bottle of wine. It was part of the etiquette, as opposed to the common practice back home in Zambia of some guys and slay-queens just showing up with several uninvited and hungry friends of theirs.

Indeed, travelling is knowledge. You learn a lot. And every experience is a learning moment. For example, throughout my two years in Oxford, I never saw or heard of a guy going to hustle for a free meal at a female friend's room because he had run out of money or was broke. Neither would a guy be asking a female friend who comes from a well-to-do family to get him this or that or loan him some money. People would stay in their lane and mind their own business.

When my colleagues Mr John Mulutula and Mr Thomas Mabwe went back to Zambia, I was left to wait for the arrival in Oxford of the Rhodes Scholar-Elect for Zambia who was selected after me in 1993. Unfortunately, he was not admitted to Oxford, notwithstanding that he graduated from a decent British university. I think he graduated from the University of Liverpool. The guy ended up going to the University of Manchester for his graduate studies as a Rhodes Scholar. We met briefly in Oxford when he came to Rhodes House on his way to Manchester. After that, I never heard much from him. Before, during and after my time in Oxford, there were a number of Rhodes Scholars from Zambia and elsewhere whose applications for admission to Oxford got rejected. Some got conditional offers of admission. Others would be put on a one-year postgraduate diploma, say, in development economics, before they could be admitted the following year to a Masters degree program in developments economics. There were also those who would graduate successfully from Oxford with a Masters degree, yet be denied admission to a second or third Oxford Masters degree program. Also, I had heard of a few Africans who failed some courses in Oxford and could not graduate.

Of those who were admitted to Oxford, there were a few who ended up leaving prematurely for one reason or another to switch to other British universities where they would eventually complete their studies. Oxford was very competitive. Some Rhodes Scholars who did not gain admission to Oxford ended up at other British universities before eventually finding their way back into Oxford after first obtaining a Masters degree from another British university. One would call such long-winded routing to Oxford a 'degree cleansing' strategy to improve one's chances of gaining admission to Oxford. Being selected as a Rhodes Scholar was no guarantee that you would be admitted to Oxford. That said, in 1993, one Zambian managed to gain admission to graduate studies at the University of Oxford on a scholarship other than the Rhodes Scholarship. She was Ms Mulima Kufekisa-Akapelwa, my former First Grade classmate in Livingstone, Zambia, and a fellow UNZA product. She came to read for a one-year Masters degree program, an MSc in Comparative Social Policy. Otherwise, the other Zambian who joined the Zambian community in Oxford in 1993, though he was not studying at the University of Oxford, but at Ruskin College, an independent small college within the city of Oxford, was Mr Martin Mweene, a journalist working for the Zambian Congress of Trade Union (ZCTU) in Kitwe.

Life at the University of Oxford centered mainly around scholarship and academics. It was an atmosphere of erudition. At weekends, I would sometimes get on my bike and take a tour of Oxford city. That bike took me many places. I remember one time going to pick up some groceries in the city center. It was on a workday around 18:00 hours (6pm) in the evenings. I parked my bike outside Westgate Shopping Mall in Oxford and walked into Sainsbury's, a supermarket and clothing store at the said mall. I was just about to pick up some apples from the shelf when I saw a pretty and fine-looking young lady, standing next to me, and clad in a fine dark woolen winter coat, trying to reach the same set of apples that I was trying get. We looked at each other, like Adam and Eve, and hesitated a bit. We both smiled. I let her get the apples. I greeted her and she greeted me back. We chatted a bit about shopping and the weather in Oxford before I asked for her name. She told me her name and said she was a student at Oxford Brookes University. On hearing her name, I knew she was from a Southern African country, but was not sure if it was Zambia, Zimbabwe, or Malawi, since her surname is found in all the three countries. I introduced myself and said I was from Zambia. She looked pleasantly surprised. She too was from Zambia. We laughed about it. We exchanged numbers and kept in touch from time to time, but Oxford was so busy that months would go by without seeing or hearing from someone.

One day I got on my bicycle and rode spiritedly off to pay her a surprise visit only to find her boyfriend home. I was not aware that she had a boyfriend since she had not mentioned one, but I knew that that was her apartment, not his place, because I had visited once. The guy welcomed me inside and offered me a drink. She was not around. As we chatted, we both discovered that our parents were good friends from way back in their youthful days in Mansa, Zambia. In fact, one of his first cousins or older brother had stayed for some time with my eldest brother, Kelvin, at Kelvin's penthouse apartment in downtown Lusaka, and I had met his other siblings and cousins through Kelvin. So the discussion became more about family, and I had to abort my mission. Otherwise, during the week, I would sometimes get my groceries from Asian stores on Cowley Road in Oxford since that was closer to my place on Iffley Road. In a number of the Asian stores, one could easily find cornmeal to prepare nshima.

Occasionally, I would go to play soccer with some of my BCL colleagues. I remember a game on which I featured for the Oxford BCL students when we played against the Cambridge LLM students at the University of Cambridge in Cambridge in 1993/94. I was then in my second year of the BCL at Oxford. Hon Mr George K Chisanga, a Member of Parliament in Zambia, who was my junior by a year in law school at the University of Zambia (UNZA), had just arrived in England for his LLM studies at the University of Cambridge, so he was on the Cambridge LLM team, together with a colleague from Kenya, Mr Duncan Kiara Mwenda, who is now a Chief Counsel in the Legal Vice-Presidency of the World Bank. On my Oxford BCL team, I was the only African. We gave Cambridge LLM team a good run for their money.

On some weekends, if I had some free time, I would stop by to see my Zambian colleague, Dr Chaloka Beyani, and his family in Oxford. Otherwise, I would head into London to see my cousin Mutamba. There were also times when I would spend some time with some of my fellow Rhodes Scholars like Professor Henry Fadamiro, who I have already mentioned above, and Dr Cyril Ruwende (who was at Green College), a medical doctor from Zimbabwe who completed his MSc degree before pursuing a DPhil (PhD) at Oxford. Cyril, Henry and I were all Rhodes Scholars in the same cohort. After graduating for his DPhil from Oxford, Cyril completed his medical residency and postdoctoral fellowship at Johns Hopkins University Medical School in Baltimore, Maryland, US, and is now US board-certified in cardiovascular disease and interventional cardiologist. Dr Ruwende practices as a cardiologist in Michigan, US, and previously served as a professor at the University of Michigan Medical School.

In the picture below, taken on June 26, 2024, I am with my good learned brother, Dr Ruwende, when he paid a courtesy call on me at the World Bank. The picture was taken in my office at the World Bank. Cyril and I had last seen each other in 1994 when I graduated from Oxford. So, this was our first reunion after thirty years.

In Oxford, my housemates at Exeter House and I would sometimes get together for a cheese and wine party. These were decent events, punctuated with civility and decorum. There would be no loud music or shouting at the top of your voice. Neither would fights break out, as was often the case when I was a student at the University of Zambia. The UNZA Students' Center was known for loud music and fights breaking out, but throughout my two years in Oxford, I never saw or witnessed any fight, nor even a drunk student hurling insults at other students. Neither did I see anyone spitting in public, or a drunk person peeing on or behind a tree. Indeed, I never saw anyone peeing on the streets or in the nearby bushes. It was all about decorum and edifying manners. Even in the US, the only few times I have seen someone park his car on the side of the highway and walk into a nearby bush to pee involved some Latino immigrants who were driving a handyman's van. I could not believe it each time it happened. You will never see such things in Oxford. Even the MCR parties at Exeter College were relatively quiet. There was nothing like a drunk student blacking out or shouting on top of his voice for more beers, saying: 'Iwe chikala, leta ubwalwa!' ('You dickheads, give me more beers!'). The only noise that you would hear occasionally in college was from some JCR parties, though it would be manageable noise.

I still have fond memories of those cheese and wine parties in Oxford. Your palate becomes accustomed to them. Occasionally, I do host cheese and wine parties as well as dinner events for my guests even here in the US, as can be seen in the pictures below.

And then, of course, I love eating out at fine restaurants.

Sometimes, you just can't help it. It is something your palate gets accustomed to once you acquire the fine taste.

My wife and son know me when it comes to eating out and going on vacations. I love treating them to fine dining at fine restaurants. If I don't give them that kind of experience, then who will? It is my responsibility as a responsible father and husband to give my family the best that I can.

Of course, we live within our means and have to plan. I take them on exotic vacations where you may even find famous Hollywood personalities. Exposure matters. It helps to build one's self-esteem and confidence. It may not be the only way to do this, but it is certainly one of the best ways to do so, especially once you realize that you can also go to such famed places and enjoy what others are enjoying. It is important to feel that you are also somebody, not just anybody or a nobody.

Before I left Zambia for England, my father would share with me inspirational stories about his university student days in Canada at the University of Toronto and the University of Saskatchewan. There was a sense of sophistication in his intellectual outlook to life. I learned a lot from my father. He was my greatest role model and hero. I did not have to search far for a role model – he was right there in our house!

I remember that I kept my father's university student ID from Canada in my wallet when I was a student at the University of Zambia. It inspired me to get somewhere in life. Some colleagues at UNZA would idolize certain friends of theirs whose fathers were, say, a cabinet minister. But not me. I found that to reveal a kind of inferiority complex. For me, it was good enough that my father went to good schools abroad (top universities in Canada). I knew that there was no need to be someone's henchman or to be impressed by a politician's son or daughter, especially that many politicians had never been to any man's university. From an early age, I knew who I was, and I knew where I was coming from. So my appreciation of cheese and wine parties in Oxford simply spoke to some of the learning I received from my parents.

As noted in Chapter 4, my mother had a fine collection of kitchenware and chinaware, including crystal dinnerware sets. She was a teacher by profession, with a focus on what was then known as 'home economics', so she would prepare fine meals and teach us good table manners. For me, Oxford simply reaffirmed my upbringing. And that explains my eclectic taste for fine wines, nice restaurants, and decent meals.

In the picture shown here, I was indulging in some organic salmon with lemon slices and cream cheese, taken together with olives and pickles, for breakfast at a hotel where I was staying in Vienna, Austria.

As I continue to travel around the world, my eclectic taste for palatable, savory and delectable food as well as my varied choices of fine wines is unmistakable. I have shared below some photos taken in some of the countries where I have been in different parts of the world.

The picture immediately below is what a fine entrée of steak au poivre looks like.

And if I may, the picture immediately below is what a fine dessert looks like.

Some pictures of a healthy assortment for a fine cheese and wine held in Washington DC, USA follow below.

As they say, good food keeps good company.

A fine mushroom soup like the one in the picture below, taken with a few slices of baguette, is one of my favorites for the hors d'oeuvres.

Eating out is something I often treat my lovely wife and adorable son to. I have simply perfected what my father taught me. Indeed, the way you were raised as a child can have a big influence on how you turn out in life. I grew up in a cultured home, with well-cultivated values. Manners and etiquette mattered. As noted earlier, nobody would take his or her plate of food to the living room and sit on the sofa to watch a movie on television; we all ate from the dining table. And we all knew that the living room is not a place for dining. My father always said: 'That is why there is what is known as a dining room and a dining table. You dine from there.' Indeed, you pick up certain values from your parents.

I have shared below some lovely two pictures from some of the family dinners with my wife, Dr J, and my son, Jojo.

As established already, when I am travelling the world with my family, I always make it a point to treat them to fine restaurants and food, as can be seen in the pictures below.

I remember one time when I threw a cheese and wine party at my place in Washington DC. I was still a bachelor then. I had invited over some friends, including a few Zambians. An African sister who was helping out with setting the table threw away my Cabrales cheese, thinking it had gone bad or was rotten. For her, the blueish spots and patches meant it was rotten, until her boyfriend explained to her that it was supposed to look like that. She was embarrassed. To lighten the situation, I changed the subject quickly and asked for glass of Merlot before retreating to talk to my other guests.

Otherwise, in Oxford, during our cheese and wine parties, networking was key, often with some light jazz playing in the background. I remember one British guy at Exeter House who had a strong interest in music. He claimed to have played for some jazz band in the UK. The guy had a rich collection of jazz CDs. I would sit down with him to compare notes on jazz. I would buy most of my jazz music in London and had built a rich collection of smooth jazz CDs. His collection was more of the old blues, whereas my collection was more contemporary smooth jazz, but we would compare notes from time to time.

I remember the guy asking me if I had ever thought of moving to the US after Oxford. I told him that, yeah, I was actually thinking along those lines. And here I am today. On other weekends, a few members of Exeter House would get together to play frisbee in a field across the road from Exeter House. Sunday morning was mainly church business. There was a Catholic Church nearby, Greyfriars, located along Iffley Road about a three to five-minute walk from Exeter House. It made things easier for me. I could therefore not afford to miss Sunday Mass, given that there was a Catholic Church right across the street from Exeter House. Sometimes I would go to church on Sundays with my good friend Ms Monique Adams, from the British Virgin Islands, who was studying at a private college in Oxford. She was not a Catholic but would join me for Mass. Put simply, I had no excuse for not going to church. God had put a Catholic church right in front of the house where I was staying. I would wake up every morning with the Catholic Church staring at me.

After my first year in Oxford, I applied and was selected for an internship program in South Africa. The program was exclusively for Rhodes Scholars, and I would spend my summer as an intern in

Cape Town. My colleague and fellow Rhodes Scholar Angus Morkel Stewart (who was at Corpus Christi College), a white South African Rhodes Scholar in my cohort, was helping to coordinate the placements. I was placed with the Legal Resources Centre in Green Market area in Cape Town, South Africa. I have not heard from Angus since he graduated from the one-year BCL in Oxford in 1993. However, I pleasantly learned a few years ago from the *Journal of the NSW Bar Association* that Angus was appointed to the Federal Court of Australia on February 25, 2019.

"Justice Stewart practised at the Bar in Sydney from 2011 to February 2019 and was appointed Senior Counsel in 2014. His practice at the Bar included public law and private law specialising in Admiralty/shipping and international trade, commercial disputes and arbitrations. Justice Stewart was appointed a Fellow of the Chartered Institute of Arbitrators (FCIArb) in 2014. Stewart J graduated from the University of Natal (BA LLB cum laude) and the University of Oxford (BCL first class) where he was a Rhodes Scholar (Natal 1992). From 1996 to 2010, he practised at the Bar in South Africa and was appointed Senior Counsel in 2006."[1]

Other South African Rhodes Scholars in my cohort that I was friends with included Dr Penny Kew (who was at Exeter College), a white South African veterinary doctor, with an MSc degree in Tropical Veterinary Medicine from Edinburgh University, who, as a Rhodes Scholar at Oxford, obtained a first-class Honours degree in English Language and Literature as well as an MSc degree in Comparative and International Education, and Mr Omphemetse Mooki (who was at the Queen's College), a graduate of Stanford University in the US with a degree earned in Immunology and Microbiology before coming to Oxford as a Rhodes Scholar. At Oxford, Omphemetse read for an MSc degree in Physiology (Microbiology). After Oxford, he trained as a lawyer at the University of Cape Town in South Africa and is now practicing law in South Africa. Admitted as a Senior Counsel at the South African Bar, Omphemetse has also been the Secretary of the Rhodes Scholarship for Botswana, Lesotho, Malawi, Namibia and Swaziland for a number of years. Then, from neighboring Zimbabwe, apart from Dr Cyril Ruwende, the Rhodes Scholar who I mentioned earlier as having been in my Rhodes Scholar cohort at Oxford, we also had a number of other Zimbabwean Rhodes Scholars who were either a cohort head or some light years ahead. They included Professor Arthur Mutambara, who completed a DPhil in Robotics and Mechatronics at Merton College and later

---

1 See *The Journal of the NSW Bar Association*, "Appointments," [2019] (Winter) Bar News, pp. 93-95, available Online at: <<https://www8.austlii.edu.au/au/journals/NSWBarAssocNews/2019/80.pdf>>, accessed January 31, 2024.

became one of the two Deputy Prime Ministers of Zimbabwe, Dr James Manyika, who completed a DPhil in artificial intelligence and robotics at Keble College and is now a senior partner emeritus at McKinsey & Company and serves concurrently as Senior Vice-President of Technology and Society at Google, and Dr Simukai Utete, who completed a DPhil in Engineering Science at Balliol College and was a Junior Research Fellow in Oxford for a while but now serves as the Academic Director at AIMS South Africa in South Africa. Then, from Kenya, Kenya's economist and columnist, Dr David Ndii, who completed a DPhil in Economics at St. Anthony's College, arrived as a Rhodes Scholar in Oxford in 1993 when I was in my second year of the Oxford BCL. David was a cohort behind me. A recent media report indicates that he now serves as the Chairperson of Kenyan President Ruto's Council of Economic Advisors (CEA).

In 1993, I travelled from Oxford to South Africa, with a stopover in Zambia for a few days. It was the first time I had traveled to South Africa. This trip took place shortly after South Africa attained independence from a minority apartheid regime. I was going as a Rhodes Scholar intern to join the Legal Resources Center in Cape Town. In Lusaka, I was introduced by my brother Kelvin to some fellas who would periodically travel to South Africa to buy secondhand cars that they would resell in Zambia. These chaps were basically street hustlers. They gave me the impression that a bus ride to South Africa was easy and smooth, and that I did not have to waste money buying an air ticket. So, together, three of them and I, we started off by bus to South Africa. Each one paid for his bus fare. We left Lusaka in the morning and got to Livingstone around 18:00hours. We found the Kazungula boarder in Livingstone between Zambia and Botswana closed. We were scheduled to transit through Botswana on our way to South Africa, so everyone on the bus had to sleep overnight in our bus seats, as we waited to cross Kazungula border the next morning. It was the first and only time ever in my life that I have had to sleep in a bus. It was so uncomfortable. I could not find sleep while seated.

We crossed the Zambezi River at Kazungula border on a pontoon. It was scary. There was no bridge at the time, and the river looked so deep. When we got to the other side of the river on the Botswana side of Kazungula border, it took almost four hours for the Botswana immigration officers to process our travel documents. By the time they were done, it was almost noon. From there, it was another long journey to Francistown and then eventually Gaborone. We travelled overnight.

This was now the second night on the bus. I could not believe what I was going through. In the meantime, one of the guys I was traveling with kept staring at my clothes. I somewhat stood out. I was dressed in smart casual, so my UK clothes looked too classy and expensive for the local Lusaka attire.

We got into Francistown around 05:00am. From there, we proceeded to Gaborone. We got into Gaborone around 07:30am. We rested a bit and proceeded into South Africa. We got to Johannesburg around 13:00 hours. From Johannesburg, we now had to connect to Cape Town. The fellas I was travelling with were all about implementing their own austerity plans and cost-saving measures. They suggested that we jump on a small mini-van bus known locally as a 'taxi'. There are several of these taxis that run between cities in South Africa.

We left the Rotunda Bus Terminal in Johannesburg around 15:00 hours. The driver was speeding, and it was scary. We travelled overnight, the third night on a bus. When we finally got to Cape Town the following morning around 06:00am, I went with the guys to a guest house in Cape Town where they were booked in. It was in some unsafe neighborhood in one of the townships. I got myself a room and took a shower. After taking a short nap, I woke up only to find that the fellas had already left the place for their business. They left no message for me, and there was no way to contact them since there were no cellphones at the time. I was all alone in a strange place. So I asked the receptionist to call the Legal Resources Center and let them know that I had arrived in Cape Town. And that was how I was picked up from the township. I never saw those Zambian car dealers ever again.

In Cape Town, I stayed in the Woodstock area, renting a room in a shared house. The main assignment that I was working on in my three months in Cape Town was on land and mineral rights of the people of Namaqualand. I worked closely with attorney Mr Henk Smith, who is now with Henk Smith and Associates in Cape Town, and attorney Mr Wallace Amos Mgoqi, who later served as Regional Land Claims Commissioner for the Western and Northern Cape Provinces and the Chief Land Claims Commissioner as well as the Acting Judge of the Land Claims Court. Henk, a graduate of the University of Warwick where I later taught and got my PhD from, was my immediate supervisor.

At the Legal Resources Center, I met and became good friends with a black South African brother, attorney Mr Chopologe Olckers Koikanyang. Chops, as we called him, was at the time finalizing his studies for a graduate law degree at the University of Western Cape (UWC) where I currently serve as Extraordinary Professor of Law. He was a very kind and generous brother. Chops would pick me up on weekends and we would have braais (barbecues) at his place. He made me understand some of the internal dynamics of the liberation movement in South Africa. When I left Cape Town, I lost contact with Chops but never forgot his kindness and warm camaraderie. A few years ago, I looked him up on the internet, and we have since reconnected after almost 30 years.

I am forever grateful to all my friends and colleagues at the Legal Resources Center in Cape Town for their warm hospitality and camaraderie when I served there as a Legal Intern in 1993. I was in South Africa at a critical time in race relations in that country, and I was dealing with issues concerning the human rights of colored people, a pretty sensitive topic back then when the vicissitudes of apartheid were still lingering on.

When I completed my Cape Town internship, I decided not to go back to Zambia by road. I bought a one-way air ticket from Johannesburg to Lusaka. For my return to the UK, I was going to fly from Lusaka. But from Cape Town to Johannesburg, I opted to take a luxury Greyhound coach overnight. That way, I would travel comfortably. The Greyhound was spacious and comfortable, and the flight from Johannesburg to Lusaka was only two hours. So within 24 hours, I was back home and safe in Zambia and ready to fly out to the UK for the second part of my two-year Oxford BCL.

Throughout the entire decade or so that I spent in England, my father would often write me letters on a regular basis. A month would hardly pass by without receiving a letter from my father. In some months, I would get one every fortnight. My father was good at communicating. He was also a good listener. Perhaps it was because he had studied educational psychology at university when he was in Canada, or it could just have been in his nature. All I know is that he always kept in touch and would update me on the politics, the economy and various developments back home in Zambia. At the time, internet or email was not in existence, not even social media. So, I was quite lonely. Having lived abroad for many years, my father could relate to what his son was going through, so he never gave up writing me those encouraging letters throughout his life when I was away from Zambia. I still have a collection of some of his letters. We corresponded continuously. My father became my pen-pal, and I always looked forward to receiving and reading his letters. I remain ever grateful for his thoughtfulness, kindness, and clairvoyance. Very few of my fellow African peers at the time in Oxford would receive letters regularly from their parents, so I was very lucky. I do not take my father's good communication skills for granted. My father was a very thoughtful man, filled with much parental love and empathy. His letters kept me going. By contrast, I did not hear much from my siblings or friends. My mother did write me a few letters, but it was my father who wrote the most. Those letters not only inspired me, but also made me feel loved, especially being young and far away from home.

From time to time, I would get some coins and run to a phonebooth to call my parents in Zambia. They had a landline at home in Luanshya, Zambia, and that made it easier to reach them directly, though it was expensive. So. I would place brief international calls.

Generally, my parents always took a keen interest in my studies and my father would ask me how they were coming along. The Oxford BCL was a very demanding course, but I was equal to the task, so I would reassure my father and tell him not to worry.

Let me add more ink to the narrative on the Oxford BCL, especially the two-year BCL, so as to place all this in context. The debate among many Oxonians and other interested parties, for example, on which course in Oxford between the BCL and the DPhil in Law is held in higher esteem continues to fill many blogs and social media pages. I have touched on my personal experience as an Oxford BCL graduate and what motivated me to pursue the Warwick PhD (*i.e.* the equivalent of the Oxford DPhil). Let us now take a more reasoned look at other attributes of the Oxford BCL.

The University of Oxford Law Faculty avers that 'the Oxford BCL has been a pivotal feature of Oxford's law provision since the sixteenth century,' and that 'this rich history has helped to maintain its status as the most highly regarded taught masters-level qualification in the common law world'.[2] On its website, the University of Oxford Law Faculty postulates as follows:

"The BCL is our world-renowned taught graduate course in law, designed to serve outstanding law students from *common law* backgrounds. As a Masters level degree, its academic standard is significantly higher than that required in a first law degree, such as a BA, LLB, or JD, and only those with outstanding first law degrees are admitted. Courses are not introductory, and students are

---

2 *Ibid.*

expected to analyze complex material critically and to make their own contribution to the debate.³

"The BCL aims to bring students into advanced intellectual engagement with some of the most difficult issues in law and legal theory, an engagement distinguished by rigour, depth and conceptual sophistication requiring immersion in law as an academic discipline as well as informed openness to neighboring disciplines. The BCL raises students to the highest level of professionalism in analysis and argument, equipping them intellectually for legal practice or work as a legal academic at the highest level, as well as for a wide range of other intellectually demanding roles."⁴

Historically, Oxford has had other graduate degrees with the title of 'bachelors', though, like the BCL, they are not undergraduate degrees. Examples include the two-year taught Bachelor of Philosophy (BPhil) degree in Philosophy and the now replaced two-year Bachelor of Letters (BLitt) degree. Both the BPhil and the BLitt, like the BCL, commanded the highest levels of intellectual and academic rigor.

Writing on the Oxford DPhil, Richard Lofthouse, in an article published on November 28, 2017, on the website of the University of Oxford, and titled, '100 Years of the DPhil,' submits: "The first person to supplicate for a DPhil (in 1919) was an Indian called Lakshman Sarup of Balliol; the first woman was Evelyn Mary Simpson (November 1922) — women having been admitted to the University two years earlier."⁵ In essence, this means that the BCL degree predates the DPhil in Law degree at Oxford, notwithstanding that 'the Doctor of Philosophy (DPhil) is the most prestigious of the Law Faculty's research degrees.' The distinction here lies in the fact that while the BCL is the most prestigious of the Law Faculty's taught degrees, the DPhil is the most prestigious of the Law Faculty's research degrees.

Interestingly, during graduation ceremonies at the University of Oxford, the order of precedence is such that the BCL graduating students are among the first, together with Higher Doctorates, if there are any graduating, to walk into the Sheldonian Theatre and have their degrees conferred while the DPhil students wait outside the Sheldonian Theatre. Only after the BCL degrees have been conferred do the DPhil graduating students then walk into the Sheldonian Theatre for theirs.

---

3 *Ibid.*

4 *Ibid.*

5 Richard Lofthouse, "100 Years of the DPhil," *University of Oxford: Oxford Alumni*, (November 28, 2017), available Online at: <<https://www.alumni.ox.ac.uk/quad/article/100-years-dphil>>, accessed on February 1, 2024.

The DPhil graduates are followed by Masters degree graduands. Put simply, as one BCL graduating student once told me in Oxford:

"I came to Oxford to study for the BCL. I came here to master the English common law at the most advanced level, that is, to get something that you can use to become a judge or professor here in England. The BCL involves intellectually rigorous taught courses on various aspects of the English common law delivered through critically insightful lectures, seminars and tutorials. I did not come to Oxford to sit alone or by myself in the library, doctoring some kind of philosophy, say, on African customary law or witchcraft and the law among some tribal people. Of what relevance would that be to me if, say, I wanted to work in England? I came here to master the English common law, not to philosophize on African, Latino or Asian law."

In the US, similar cynical views are expressed by some American lawyers who hold the Juris Doctor (JD) degree regarding the value of the Doctor of Juridical Science (SJD/JSD) degree which is mainly offered to foreigner-trained lawyers in the US, although the JD is not at the same echelon as the Oxford BCL degree. It would appear that in many countries and cultures where academic titles matter more than what you studied, the DPhil or SJD has an edge over the BCL or JD. But in countries and cultures were titles matter less, the BCL or JD is self-sustaining on its own and does not require a DPhil or SJD to support or complement it, as the case may be. Hence, many old English professors who graduated from Oxford back in the day with a BCL rarely took the DPhil. The Oxford BCL was seen as the gold standard. Some of those old professors would, after developing a substantial body of published scholarly work, simply supplicate for the Higher Doctorate degree of Doctor of Civil Law (DCL) at Oxford or for its equivalent at another university. A higher doctorate is, indeed, a much more prestigious research degree than a DPhil. And higher doctorates rank substantially higher than a DPhil.

Before I close this chapter, let me turn to two notable incidents from my Oxford experience. The first episode occurred about 17 years after I had graduated from Oxford. By then, I had already taught at the University of Warwick in England and was working at the World Bank. I was on my way from Washington DC to Eastern Europe for work and decided to make a stopover in Oxford.

There I ran into a tutor I knew from my student days at Oxford. I had not seen him for almost 17 years since I had graduated from Oxford. The tutor asked me what I was up to, given that we had not seen each other for almost two decades. I explained politely that I was now based in Washington DC at the World Bank. He then mentioned the name of a former Oxford DPhil (PhD) student whose doctoral thesis that same tutor had supervised a few years ago. I recognized the name and said to the Oxford tutor, "Oh, I know her. So, she was your DPhil student?"

To my surprise, after admitting that that is indeed a recent former student of his at Oxford, the tutor then asked me, "So, is she your senior at the World Bank?"

I was shocked at that ostensibly biased and prejudiced assumption. Whether it was unconscious bias or not, I just could not believe the underling prejudice in that Oxford tutor's question. Why assume that someone who was not even at Oxford when I was there 17 years ago would be my senior today? Why not assume that I was her senior and say, "So are you her senior?" Was it because my workmate was white, whilst I was a black man? Are whites meant to enjoy the privilege of seniority over blacks just because of their race? Surely, it would have made more sense had the Oxford tutor assumed that I was the senior, since I went to Oxford and the World Bank much earlier than the white lady that the Oxford tutor was referring to. I wondered why the Oxford tutor asked me such an unintelligent question. Why would someone assume that a person who only joined the World Bank a few years after completing her DPhil studies would suddenly become your senior, especially given that I had graduated from Oxford and joined the World Bank many years before her? Besides, I had even taught at the University of Warwick in the UK before joining the World Bank. And the Oxford tutor knew all this fully well. I thought to myself, 'When will this thing of assuming that a black person can never be smarter than a white person ever end?' But I kept my cool and responded politely, saying: "I am a Senior Specialist while she is only a Specialist. She only joined the World Bank yesterday."

When I returned to Washington DC from my World Bank mission in Eastern Europe, I sat down to write a note to the Oxford tutor, thanking him for sparing time to meet up with me when I stopped over in Oxford. I included a copy of my full curriculum vitae (CV) as well as a copy of one of my books published by the World Bank. Sometimes, you have to set the record straight for some people to know their place. And I did just that.

The second episode, which is more pleasant than the one highlighted above, occurred around 2022. In 2008, more than a decade after I had graduated from the University of Oxford, I had decided to get myself a University of Oxford alumni ring. Many people underestimate the value of university memorabilia. That Oxford ring has stood me good over the years in many places where I have been. Indeed, I have not had to make lengthy and laborious introductions of myself, regarding, for example, who I am or how I found myself a seat at the table. A university alumni ring has a signaling effect. It can protect you from being hit by other 'motorists' when they see your 'signal', especially those who are insecure, ambitious, and overzealous, and are only too eager to overtake others.

It is a truism that your university alumni ring can speak for you. For me, I can confirm that my Oxford alumni ring, like a pair of alumni cufflinks, or an alumni tie or lapel pin, has given me some good introductions. Those who understand the power of immutable brands can relate. That is why some corporate executives with fine taste will spend money on a quality pen such as a Montblanc or a Caran d'Ache Astrograph Fountain Pen. Likewise, many wealthy folks will don designer clothes to help them navigate the business world with comparative ease. Impressions matter. People often treat you as they see you. Unless there is a sudden structural change, it takes time to give people a different impression. Put simply, the impression you make regarding how you present yourself is just as important as your substance. After all, even Catholic Bishops, Cardinals and the Pope wear rings. But to an observer who lacks understanding, he or she will think that a university alumni ring is just a waste of money. On the contrary, a university alumni ring can help you with networking, for it signals your identity. It can also help to minimize or ward off unconscious bias from those who cherish racist or sexist stereotypes. Some people will assume that because you are a black person or female then you are not good enough and are not supposed to be where you are. Those who subscribe to such an ideology, especially white supremacists and male chauvinists, often think that if you are not a white person then you do not belong. For them, it is all about maintaining white privilege for white folks, especially male white folks. Almost always, if you are not white and are a person of color, they will want to know how you got yourself a seat at the table.

Institutional racism is real. I have seen it and experienced it both in America and Britain. Even in South Africa and the Middle East, I have seen it. Bigotry is not something we can gloss over and pretend that it does not exist. Sometimes racism is not just from white supremacists. It can also come from other races, including Asians, Arabs and Latinos. Some of them work like cartels and can be very racist, and a good number of them want to be associated more closely with white people and will do everything to try to assimilate into white culture even if it means marrying a white person solely for that purpose.

A racist, like a tribalist, is a small-minded and primitive person. For them, a black person is seen as a distraction to their agenda, just in case the white folks prefer him or her to them. It is thus not uncommon for these middle shades of race to try to dim the light of some black folks, especially in the corporate world. You cannot delude yourself by thinking that your work will speak for you. It rarely plays out that way. Life out there is not a level playing field and never has been. Some racist or tribalist folks will try to find faults in your work no matter how good it is, and if they have to sacrifice or throw someone under the bus, it will most definitely be you, unless maybe you are married to one of their sisters or brothers, or you keep sucking up to them.

Sadly, even some black folks of mixed-race as well as those with a light complexion tend to behave the same way towards their fellow blacks who happen to have a darker skin complexion. This inferiority complex about whiteness is perplexing. It has even permeated some places of worship among the faithful. So instead of engaging in emotive outbursts in the workplace and attracting the 'tag' of an angry black man or woman, you can leverage your university alumni ring, or other similar university memorabilia, to signal to such bigots that you have earned your place and respect meritoriously in society.

Admittedly, in some extreme cases, a university alumni ring itself can offend some bigots and bring you problems, for it can attract envy and jealousy, especially from the insecure. But the cost of offending a bigot cannot outweigh the benefits of the ring.

We should not confuse this type of a ring with a wedding or engagement ring, because anyone can get married. Neither should we confuse a university alumni ring with rings worn by some members of a royal family, or a dress or style ring. Some rings are worn simply for fashion or symbolism associated with a cult or secret society. Others are worn to depict membership of a club. Shown here are two pictures of my University of Oxford alumni ring.

One summer weekend in 2023, while on a beach vacation with my family in the US, I dropped my alumni ring into the salty ocean water. I felt power leave me. I searched for the ring but could not find it. I was so upset with myself. I felt like a posh car that was suddenly losing battery-power, with the engine about to turn off. My priceless Oxford ring was gone. I thought about how much money I had spent on that ring. My body felt weak, as if some power had just left me.

I went back to my hotel room, feeling low. My wife and son knew that something was wrong. They came over to comfort me, but I was so frustrated with myself for having gotten into the water with my Oxford alumni ring on my finger.

After a while, I recollected myself and thought: 'Why am I worrying? That ring was for my Oxford BCL degree, but now I am Honorary Fellow at Oxford. Perhaps, it is time to upgrade to a new Oxford ring that captures my new status as an Honorary Fellow.' So I pulled myself together. When we got home from our family vacation, I ordered myself a new Oxford ring to reflect my Oxford Honorary Fellow status. Indeed, had I not lost that Oxford BCL class ring maybe I would not have upgraded to a new ring for my Oxford Honorary Fellow status. A picture of my new Oxford ring follows below. The moral of the story is that sometimes God allows us to lose something in order for us to be elevated to a new position.

Like the epic standing of a Higher Doctorate in many Commonwealth universities, or a Nobel Prize, an Honorary Fellowship at many an Oxford college can best be described as the Holy Grail of the Oxford collegiate system.

CHAPTER 11

The Yorkshire Years

Law alone is not enough. At some point, you might need more than just the law. It was not fashionable back then for a Zambian lawyer to study anything other than law, especially as law has always been offered as an undergraduate degree program in Zambia and many other Commonwealth countries, including the United Kingdom, Australia and New Zealand.

Before I went to Business School in the United Kingdom, I had not heard of any Zambian lawyer with a Master of Business Administration (MBA) degree. Some Zambian Rhodes Scholars before my time at Oxford, for example, who were also lawyers, had taken other Oxford degrees outside law, but these were not MBA degrees. Rather, they were degrees such as the Honours Bachelor of Arts degree in Philosophy, Politics and Economics (PPE) and the Master of Philosophy degree (MPhil) in Management Studies. When I was in Oxford, as noted in Chapter 10, there was no Said Business School, but I wanted to augment my Oxford corporate law specialization on the two-year Oxford BCL degree program with an MBA in order to give myself a holistic grounding in both corporate law and management. Indeed, law alone is not enough, especially if you plan to work in, or lead, multidisciplinary and interdisciplinary teams. You should be able to speak the language of other professionals outside the legal fraternity, especially the language of colleagues from disciplines such as economics and finance. And an MBA is a perfect bridge for that.

After sitting and passing my two-year BCL exams at Oxford, I was exhausted from the intensity of the Oxford degree program. I was not too sure if I should go back to Zambia to teach at UNZA or utilize the third year of my Rhodes Scholarship for another postgraduate degree in Oxford or elsewhere. I remember my Zambian housemate at Exeter House in Oxford, Mr John Mulutula, telling me: "Ken, you are still young, my brother. Don't rush back to Zambia. Just stay on here in the UK and make use of that third year of the Rhodes Scholarship. Those guys back home will frustrate you if you try to rush back to Zambia so quickly. The people promising you this and that will just disappear on you the moment you try to reach out to them for help. So, do not listen to them."

Mr Mulutula was right, and I thank him for such candid and honest advice. It would have been a big mistake if I had not stayed on in the UK for the third year of my Rhodes Scholarship. I say so because some of my colleagues who had deferred their third year got caught up in other things in their home countries and never got back to Oxford or another British university for the third year. So I decided to stay on in the UK for my third year of the Rhodes Scholarship. In the meantime, one of the senior officers at UNZA's Staff Development Office in Lusaka was busy asking me to get him a fridge from the UK, thinking I would be going back to Zambia after my two-year Oxford BCL. The man promised to refund me the cost of the fridge upon my arrival. He even promised to help me get a PhD scholarship as soon as I got back home in Zambia. But I knew that there was no way he would organize me a PhD scholarship if he could not help me when I was looking for a Masters degree scholarship whilst I was in Zambia. Besides, I was not sponsored by UNZA to Oxford. So, why would he think that I would be returning to Zambia immediately given that I had a three-year scholarship? I got the Rhodes Scholarship independently of UNZA, so I was under no obligation to go back to UNZA, at least, until I was done with what I wanted to do.

UNZA had a long waiting list of academics waiting to get institutional support for PhD scholarships. Returning to UNZA right after my Oxford BCL would have meant joining that queue, and it would have taken ages for my turn to come. Put simply, the man was not being honest about the PhD scholarship cajolery. He simply wanted me to help him to get what he wanted from abroad. So I ignored his request, and started applying to different business schools in the United Kingdom to pursue an MBA degree program for the third year of my Rhodes Scholarship since there was no Business School in Oxford.

I looked up the University of Cambridge MBA program, but the apparent duration of the program at the time was discouraging. I looked up other MBA programs in the UK, and a good number of them had specializations tailored towards, say finance or human resource management. I wanted an MBA that would give me a holistic perspective on general management. I looked up the

Cranfield University MBA, but the quantitative emphasis was discouraging. At the time, Cranfield University was known as the Cranfield Institute of Technology and had a great reputation for producing top engineering graduates in England. I also applied to the University of Hull. I had heard that there were a few Zambians in Hull, and that one of them was a lawyer. So, I figured that it would not be a bad idea moving up to Yorkshire, though it was not because I wanted to pick up a Yorkshire accent. Far from it. When I looked at the various MBA programs that were being offered at the University of Hull at the time, I found what I was looking for. Hull had four variants of the MBA degree program. There was the popular General Management MBA degree program, then there was an MBA in Financial Management as well as the MBA in Information Systems and Technology, in addition to the Executive MBA.

Later, after graduating from the University of Hull, I learned that an additional variant of the Hull MBA, focusing mainly on human resources management, was being offered in London in collaboration with a London-based academic institution that was hosting that MBA degree program. So, some London-based individuals could get the Hull MBA from London without having set foot on the campus of the University of Hull. By contrast, I went to Hull full-time and opted for the General Management MBA. This MBA degree program was in line with what I wanted. Also, I had a year of funding left on my Rhodes Scholarship. So I was spoilt for choice. Money was not an issue. It was just a question of me letting my sponsors know what I wanted to study and where. I had to make my choices quickly. Time was not on my side, as I was making my MBA applications during the summer.

Upon getting an offer letter from the University of Hull to pursue the General Management MBA, I quickly informed the Warden of Rhodes House, Professor Sir Anthony Kenny. This time around, he was supportive of my decision and approved the request. I was now ready to leave Oxford for Hull. The University of Hull is where Zambia's first Rhodes Scholar, Dr Wilkinson Kunda, elected as a Rhodes Scholar for Zambia in 1974, obtained his PhD in 1986, focusing on applied mathematics, fluid dynamics and thermodynamics. Dr Kunda also taught at the University of Zambia (UNZA) for many years. He held additionally a first degree from UNZA and a Master of Science (MSc) degree from Aston University in Birmingham, England.

I arrived in Kingston upon Hull in August 1994. Some of my luggage from Oxford was delayed, so I travelled back to Oxford by train to collect all my personal belongings. I left behind a bicycle and asked a friend of mine to sell it on my behalf and then deposit a cheque in my bank account. In Oxford, I had accumulated quite a number of books and other personal items that I could not transport without hiring a car or making a couple of trips between Oxford and Hull. Like my stay at Exeter House in Oxford, in Hull I moved into a graduate student residence, on 80 Cranbrook Avenue. Most of the houses on Cranbrook Avenue located close to the University of Hull were occupied by university students. I was housed at no. 80 Cranbrook Avenue, in a five-bedroom house for graduate students. The two bedrooms downstairs were occupied by two oriental students, both studying fisheries-related graduate degree programs. I took one of the rooms upstairs, with a good view of the roadside. It was a spacious room. The remaining two rooms upstairs were taken up by an Arab friend, Nashet, who was pursuing a masters degree in electronics engineering, and a South African brother, Isaac, who was pursuing his second masters degree in chemistry.

In the picture here, taken in 2014 when I went back to the University of Hull after almost 20 years to receive the Higher Doctorate degree of Doctor Science in Economics (DSc(Econ)), I can be seen reminscing on the good old days, standing in front of the main entrance of 80 Cranbrook Avenue. Indeed, it was good to be back in Hull after almost two decades.

I first arrived at 80 Cranbrook Avenue in the summer of 1994. On arrival at the University of Hull, I went straight to register for my General MBA degree program at the Business School. Recently, the Business School shared the following statement:

"Hull University Business School has been ranked in one of the top two per cent in the world after securing prestigious re-accreditation from the Association of MBAs (AMBA). Accreditation from AMBA, one of the world's leading authorities on post-graduate business education, represents the highest standard of achievement in post-graduate business education."[6]

I took the following courses on the University of Hull General MBA: (a) Introduction to Management Thought; (b) Total Quality Management; (c) Human Resource Management; (d) Financial Management; (e) Global Marketing and International Trade; (f) Management of Information Technology; (g) Project Management; (h) Strategic Management and Business Policy; (i) Marketing Management; (j) Creative Problem Solving; (k) Financial Analysis; and, (l) Entrepreneurship, Innovation and Change. I also had to write a 12,500 to 15,000 words MBA dissertation. I wrote my dissertation of the regulation of foreign investment in Zambia.

I remember some of my professors on the University of Hull General MBA degree program. Professor Robert L Flood, a leading scholar in systems thinking and management, took us in Creative Problem Solving and Total Quality Management. Bob Flood, as we often called him, was a widely published and highly regarded academic in the UK, especially on total quality management (TQM) as well as systems thinking and management. His books won several esteemed awards.

Professor Paul Keys took us in Project Management. Another academic that I remember is Professor Ranko Jelic, who is now Professor of Finance at the University of Sussex Business School. Ranko took us in Financial Management. At the time, he had just been appointed as a lecturer (Assistant Professor) at the University of Hull Business School and was also working on his PhD at Hull. Professor Richard Briston, who was Professor of Accounting and Finance and Dean of the Faculty of Social Sciences at the University of Hull, supervised my MBA dissertation. As MBA students, a lot of us also benefitted from the able guidance of the MBA course coordinator, Mr Louis Fong. Louis was such a gentleman.

---

6 University of Hull Business School, "Hull University Business School receives prestigious AMBA re-accreditation," *News*, (February 5, 2021), available Online at: <<https://www.hull.ac.uk/work-with-us/more/media-centre/news/2021/hull-university-business-school-receives-prestigious-amba-re-accreditation>>, accessed on February 12, 2024.

Academic life in Hull was quite different from Oxford. Oxford was very intense, while Hull was less competitive. Although the workload on the Hull MBA was volumnious, it was not as intense as the Oxford BCL. And the quality of students on the Oxford BCL and the Hull MBA was not the same. The Oxford BCL would only take in the crème de la crème. In fact, I remember that most of my MBA classmates at Hull could not believe that I had been to Oxford. They thought I was just bluffing. For them, Oxford was beyond reach and unamiginable, especially for an African like myself. A good number of my MBA classmates had come to the UK for the first time in their lives, so our points of reference were quite different.

A month or so into my MBA program, I travelled back to Oxford to attend the graduation ceremony for my two-year BCL degree. Afterwards, I returned to Hull and took with me a video of the Oxford graduation ceremony. The following week on a Monday, during lunch break, as everyone in class was waiting for the next lecture to start, I pulled out the Oxford graduation video-cassette and started playing it on the video-player that was available in the lecture room. When it started playing, everyone was shocked. There was silence. Even those who were pretending not to notice what I was doing started watching. A few minutes later, our lecturer walked in and then stopped halfway through the door. He joined us in watching the Oxford graduation video. He then looked at me, smiled and said, "Congratulations, Kenneth! So, you went to Oxford, right? What are you doing here? This is impressive."

My MBA classmates now understood. They realised that what might not have been possible for them could be possible for someone else. From that time onwards, they understood why I would often get top grades on my MBA modules. The MBA class was cosmopolitan. We had several international students. Some students came from the Middle East, continental Europe, East Asia, South Asia, and Latin America, while others came from various parts of Africa as well as from the UK itself. Some names I remember from that MBA class include Ms Jennifer Mueni Nzoka (Kenyan), Ms Ifoema Obi (Nigerian), Ms Similolu Adeyinka (Nigerian), Ms Mabatho Seeiso (Lesotho national), Mr Gideon Dlamini (Estwatini national), Mr Felix Adeyanju (Nigerian), Ms Tlamelo Sikwane (South African), and Chris Stone (British). Gideon became a cabinet minister at some point in the Government of the Kingdom of Eswatini.

At some point during my studies, the university arranged for the MBA class to travel to the Netherlands for a study tour. We travelled overnight from Hull to Rotterdam by ferry. The ferry was huge and had a disco inside. We got to Rotterdam the following morning, and proceeded to board a luxury coach into Amsterdam. It was a smooth ride and we were in Amsterdam within about an hour and a half. The Netherlands was a learning experience for all of us. We saw folks smoking weed freely in public. Smoking or purchasing weed there was legal. It was a big cultural shock for everyone amongst us. Walking through the Red District area, we could see folks emerging from some sex boutique while wiping off sweat from their face after receiving a 'good service'. Prostitution too was legal. Another cultural shock. Prostitution was not seen as a big deal and something wrong, as in the conservative societies that most of us came from. Nobody was trying to hide or operate clandestinely when getting relief from the services offered by prostitutes. It was out there in the open and you could get whatever you wanted to as long as you paid for it.

I also got the opportunity to see the University of Amsterdam. I sensed a strong culture of roller-skating by some youths. Cycling too was popular in Amsterdam. Many years later, after I had moved to the US, I would often fly to the Netherlands and other parts of Europe.

At the University of Hull, I had met two Zambians who were pursuing other variants of the MBA degree program. Mr Valentine Mwanza, who later became a lecturer at the University of Zambia (UNZA), was pursuing an MBA in Financial Management. Dr Alice Shemi, a senior lecturer at Copperbelt University, was pursuing an MBA in Information Systems. Later, after we had all graduated from Hull, Dr Shemi obtained a PhD at the University of Salford in the UK in Information Systems and taught at the University of Swaziland and the University of Botswana, among other universities. Other Zambians, like Ms Mwansa Kaluya and Ms Daphne Kapilikisha, had just graduated for their Masters degrees a year or so before I got to Hull. There were also some undergraduate students at Hull from Zambia who included Mr Niza Siwila, Ms Kyansenga Vundamina-Chitoshi, and Ms Namwinga Sichula. Otherwise, within the city of Hull, the other Zambians that I met included the Chitolo family, the Mwantemba family and the Vumbrai family. I remember that Ms Mwansa Kaluya would occasionally invite my South African housemate and me to her home for some lovely African meals. She was such a pleasant big sister. And from time to time, she would drop by our house to check on us. Then, Mr Mwantemba would annually host and deejay at Zambia's Independence Day parties.

In Hull, one famous nightclub patronized by many students at the University of Hull back then was called "LA". As graduate students, we would hit the club at weekends to let off steam after much indulgence in our books during the week. I also used to host cheese and wine parties at the residence where I was staying. The events would start off as a cheese and wine get together before someone would demand that I play some Congolese Rhumba music so that they could dance. Who was I to say no? Give the people what they want. However, unlike Oxford where some parties hosted by international students, say, at the neighboring Oxford Brookes University students would also have some international students from the main university, in Hull, I never saw or experienced that kind of ambience. Throughout my stay in Kingston Upon Hull I never got to interact with or attend a social event hosted by students from the neighboring University of Humberside.

On Sunday mornings, I would often get up early, take a shower and grab breakfast in readiness for Sunday Mass at Our Lady of Lourdes and St Peter Chanel Parish on Cottingham Road in Hull. This was the main Catholic Church near the University of Hull. The church was a short five-minute walk from where I used to live. Like St. Edmund and St. Frideswide, the Roman Catholic Church (Greyfriars) near Exeter House where I lived in Oxford, Our Lady of Lourdes and St Peter Chanel Parish was within easy reach. I could even see the church from the window of my bedroom, so I had no excuse not to go to church. For some reason, I have always found myself residing in places not too far from a Catholic Church. Even when I moved to the US, my place in the north-west of Washington DC was only about a five to eight-minute walk to a nearby Catholic Church, St. Stephen Martyr Catholic Church. And when I moved to Virginia, again I was staying not too far from a Catholic Church, Saint Rita Catholic Church in Alexandria, Virginia. The church was only a twelve to fifteen minute-walk from my house. In Maryland too, I found myself residing only about a short eight to ten-minute drive to St. Mary's Catholic Church in Rockville, Maryland.

When I visited the University of Hull in 2014 to receive my Higher Doctorate degree of Doctor of Science in Economics (DSc (Econ)), I noticed that the building that now houses Hull University Business School was part of a smaller neighboring university which was then known as the University of Humberside. That university was located right next to the University of Hull. That university was previously a polytechnic until 1992 when it was elevated to the status of a university and named the University of Humberside. Some of its buildings on Cottingham Road now house the Hull-York Medical School. In January 1996, the University of Humberside was renamed the

University of Lincolnshire and Humberside. Then in October 2001, the University of Lincolnshire and Humberside changed its name to the University of Lincoln and moved its main campus from Hull to Lincoln the following year in 2002. In the picture below, I can be seen standing in front of the main building of Hull University Business School after receiving the DSc (Econ) degree in the summer of 2014.

I have fond memories of my days in Hull. The city has some spectacular views of the Humber Bridge, a 2.22 km (1.38 miles; 2,430 yd; 7,300 ft) single-span road suspension bridge. It is indeed one of the most beautiful bridges in England, and a walk at the Hull marina on Saturday afternoons was simply gorgeous. Hull, which has one of Yorkshire's waterfronts, has an array of lovely galleries, cafes, and shopping places. On some weekends, I would go into the city center to do some shopping.

When I was an MBA student at the Hull University Business School from 1994 to late 1995, all the university's MBA programs were run from a separate building on campus which now houses business consultancy enterprises. So, there was a whole building on campus, with modern infrastructure, dedicated mainly to the various MBA programs. However, unlike Oxford, Hull was not so much a city where you found university students or professors biking to or on campus. As Hull graduate students, my colleagues and I would simply hop on a bus or take a cab if we wanted to go into town or elsewhere. The culture was, indeed, quite different from Oxford.

On other weekends, I would take the train from Hull via Doncaster or Sheffield into King's Cross Station in London to see my cousin Mutamba. My childhood friend from high school days, Mr Masanguza Thole, had also moved to London from Zambia at the time, so I would catch up with either or both of them from time to time. Also, I used to buy most of my jazz CDs in London. There was one particular store that had a good supply of smooth jazz and R&B music from the US. I would make sure to stop by that place before heading back to Yorkshire.

While in Hull, I got to visit other places in Yorkshire and nearby places, including cities such as Leeds and York. I remember visiting York with some of my MBA classmates and getting Regina Belle's CD, titled 'Passion,' just when it came out. Of the female soul and R&B vocalists at the time, Regina Belle and Anita Baker were prominent in my CD collection. I would get some of Anita Baker's music in London. I remember when she released the CD 'Rhythm of Love'. I was in London at the time and I could not pass up the opportunity to get myself the CD. It was a time of good music. Luther Vandross had just released his CD 'Songs'. Everyone who appreciated fine music had to have that one among his or her top collection of CDs. The Hull years were the years of Blackstreet, Keith Washington, Keith Sweat, Brandy, Monica, Boyz II Men, Jagged Edge, Jodeci, 112, Bell Biv DeVoe, En Vogue, TLC, Shai, Dru Hill, Mint Condition, Tony Rich, Whitney Houston, Toni Braxton, Babyface, Tevin Campbell, Lisa Fischer, R Kelly, Gerald Levert, Michael Jackson, Janet Jackson, Prince, George Howard, Grover Washington Jr, George Benson, Vanessa Williams, Kenny G, Pieces of a Dream, Earl Klugh, George Duke, Joe Sample, Walter Beasley, Najee, Marion Meadows, Freddie Jackson, Bob James, David Sanborn, Nelson Rangell and many more. They were simply years of musical genius and a great cultural experience.

As I was winding up my MBA degree studies, I started exploring prospects for pursuing PhD studies in the UK or simply getting a law lectureship. After all, I reasoned, some of my Oxford BCL colleagues had gotten prestigious teaching posts at top universities in the UK, so why wouldn't I? I never once doubted myself. So, I started applying for academic jobs in the UK. I remember a Zambian colleague in the UK telling me that some of our mutual friends within the Zambian community in the diaspora were saying that I was being too ambitious to think I could teach at a white man's university. I forgave those cynics because in their narrow minds a white man is superior to a black man and cannot therefore be taught by a black man. These naysayers were saying that I should go back to Zambia to teach at UNZA, and stop dreaming about teaching at a British university, but I am not a man who is distracted by counterproductive noise.

Interestingly, my South African housemate too kept asking a Zambian colleague if the Bachelors' degree that I came with from the University of Oxford would be accepted by UK universities for me to hold a lecturing position in the UK. My housemate and I both came from the academic track. He had taught at the University of Fort Hare in South Africa and was pursuing a second Masters degree in Chemistry at Hull. His first Masters degree, also in chemistry, was from South Africa. I had also taught at UNZA, though I had been in the UK much longer and had already studied at another leading British university. From that perspective, I had better informed insights into the British system of higher education. But what surprised me most was that my South African housemate avoided asking me directly, even though we were housemates, and chose to ask instead our mutual Zambian friend. When the Zambian man shared the story, I simply smiled and said, "Our brother is new to the UK. He has no clue regarding the nomenclature associated with Oxford degrees."

I kept applying for lecturing positions in the UK and would get shortlisted. That gave me confidence and hope that I could crack it. In the meantime, some Zambian friends were busy telling me that unless I married a white British woman to get myself British nationality, it was going to be difficult for me to work in the UK since I was a foreigner with a foreign passport. Others were suggesting to me that I should go into a 'marriage of convenience' with a British white woman to help me fit in quickly and get my British citizenship. I ignored their misleading and misguided advice. That is not who I am. They had no idea how much fuel I had in my intellectual tank. I knew I could drive long distances intellectually without worrying about any of what they were saying. So, I applied for a lecturing position at the University of Warwick. I was called for interviews by Warwick Law School and travelled to Coventry. I was interviewed and hired by the University of Warwick as a Zambian with a Zambian passport. I did not have to marry a British woman to get a

British passport and work in England. I worked in the United Kingdom on a Zambian passport. In life, if you have earned your respect, what might appear impossible to other will be possible for you.

No other Zambian lawyer had achieved what I had achieved in the UK when I took up the job at the University of Warwick, one of the top 10 British universities. I was only 26 years old when I was hired as a Law Lecturer (Assistant Professor of Law) there, becoming the first Zambian lawyer to hold a full-time lecturing position at a top British university.

I remember how it went after I got back from the job interview at the University of Warwick. I was tired from the long train ride from Coventry back to Hull. I decided to take a bath before grabbing some dinner. As I was bathing, the house phone rang. It must have been around 6:30pm. My South African housemate took the call and came running upstairs. He knocked on the bathroom door and said that someone by the name of Professor McConville wanted to speak with me. I knew immediately who it was. It was the Dean of the Law School at the University of Warwick. I got out of the water, wrapped a towel around my waist and grabbed the phone. And for sure, it was Professor Mike McConville.

Mike greeted me and asked how I had found the interviews. He then conveyed the great news that the interviewing panel had been impressed by my performance and credentials, and that I was being offered one of the two positions that Warwick Law School was hiring for. I had to control my excitement. I remained composed, and accepted the offer calmly. Mike also stressed that one of the two people I had asked to provide the Law School with a reference letter had not done so. I knew immediately who it was before Mike even mentioned the name. It was a Zambian colleague who had earlier written one of the references for my MBA application at the University of Hull. I am ever grateful for his MBA reference but was disappointed that he probably did not want to push for me any higher than that. I am often a very trusting person and had trusted my colleague, thinking that we were cool as brothers until the incident of the Warwick job offer. I then realized that I might not have been a threat when I was applying for the Hull MBA degree program, but now that I was trying to become a university lecturer at a top British university I had become a threat. Yet, naively, I kept trusting my colleague until I was told by Warwick Law School that he had not come through for me.

I figured that the most likely rationale for this lack of support from a compatriot was because I was going for something bigger than what he had. Rarely is one too busy to write such an important reference letter nor does one forget to do the needful. But when you are young and naïve, as I was back then, you tend to think that everyone is working along similar lines as you. You are thus likely to be slow to suspect any uncalled for issues until perhaps one day you are woken up by a surprise phone call from a colleague, calling you just to inform you that he had also been offered an academic job similar to yours. Only then does it dawn that someone is either trying to compete with you or has not been very happy with your academic strides. So, in the end, I decided to ask the supervisor of my Hull MBA dissertation, Professor Richard Briston, to write me the Warwick reference letter. That's how I finally clinched the job deal at the University of Warwick. Later, the Zambian colleague who had disappointed me emailed me saying that he had also written a reference, but it was too late. I had already found someone else to do it.

As I spoke with Professor McConville on the phone that evening, he informed me that I was going to receive some documentation in the mail in a few days' time. When I got off that phone call, I went back to my bath without informing my South African housemate. The news was too good to be shared immediately. I needed to soak myself in warm bathwater to savor the moment before I could break the good news.

When I broke the news to my South African housemate, he could not believe it. I could see the shock in his eyes. It was not his fault that he had underestimated my credentials. He was new to the UK and the British education system and thus did not fully grasp the subtle nuances of how things work there. The Zambian skeptics and naysayers too were silent. And that is how I moved to Warwickshire.

CHAPTER 12

The Warwickshire Years

Although Coventry's position as part of Warwickshire changed in 1972, pursuant to the British Local Government Act 1972 which integrated Coventry into the West Midlands, I will refer to my time at the University of Warwick as the Warwickshire Years, not the West Midlands Years, given that the University of Warwick is located on the outskirts of Coventry between the West Midlands and Warwickshire. In fact, the University of Warwick is not too far from Shakespeare's home in Stratford-upon-Avon. The distance is only about 11 miles or 20 minutes.

Against this background, let us now take a deep dive into the Warwickshire Years. After accepting the offer to serve as a Law Lecturer (Assistant Professor of Law) at the University of Warwick in Coventry, England, I had to leave England for Zambia for a few weeks to await the issue of the work permit that would enable me to work in England, since I was not a British national. I bought my air ticket to Zambia and asked some movers to load my personal items for air freighting from Hull, where I was at the time, to Zambia. The movers came over and did the necessary. Unfortunately, my music system went missing from the cargo when in Zambia. I tried to follow up with the Zambian company and offices that were handling the freight services at Kenneth Kaunda International Airport, but all I would get were unreasonable excuses or promises. They had stolen my music system. I know it was not stolen at the UK end but at the Zambian end, because the UK paperwork showed that all my personal items were loaded on the cargo plane, but I saw no paperwork from the Zambian freight company for what was received. So, to me, that lack of transparency from the

Zambian freight company and airport cargo handlers leads only to one conclusion – it was the Zambians who stole my music system. That is the price of doing business in some parts of the world. I was neither compensated for the loss of my musical system nor given an apology.

Be that as it may, I stayed in Zambia to await my British work permit. A week or so after my arrival in Zambia, my sister Catherine, whose address I was using, called me to say that there was a letter for me from the Home Office Department in the United Kingdom. I knew what it was. I rushed over to pick up the letter. I opened the letter, and there, before my eyes, was my British work permit. I was ready to head back to England and commence my duties as Assistant Professor of Law at the University of Warwick.

When I arrived back in England, I thought my employers would arrange for my transport from the airport in London to Coventry and for my housing in Coventry in the same manner as we often do in Africa when we are receiving European, American or Asian expatriates coming to work in Africa, but there was no one waiting for me at the airport. I was on my own. It was a learning experience. I wondered why in Africa many companies or employers send drivers to pick up Westerners and Asians travelling to Africa for various assignments and engagements. Why can't these people simply jump in a taxi from the airport, as we do when get to their countries? Could it be that Africa is not safe or that its broken-down systems make it unsafe to leave our guests on their own? Or is it just the 'ubuntu' in us Africans that motivates us to be extra nice to our visitors?

Anyhow, I landed back in England at London Gatwick Airport and took the tube into central London, where I connected from by train to Coventry. When I got to Coventry, I had to find myself a bed and breakfast place while I searched around for housing. Eventually, I found an apartment in the Canley area which is not too far from the University of Warwick. The place was a fifteen to twenty-minute walk to the university campus.

The Warwickshire years gave me a solid foundation on which I built my academic life as a scholar. The experience of teaching at a leading British university such as the University of Warwick was different from that of teaching at UNZA. It is one thing to study at a top university and another thing to teach there. When you are a student, your experience is limited to that of a student. You do not get the see or experience what an academician does, namely, setting and marking exams, preparing for and delivering lectures, leading seminars, and guiding tutorials, in addition to being involved in administrative tasks such as screening and selecting prospective students for admission to degree programs and participating in various administrative committees of the faculty and the university as well as publishing scholarly work. As a student your experience is quite limited, whether you are at PhD level or Masters degree level. Most of the Zambian academics I knew back home had only experienced the student side of life of a university in the Global North. They had never been on the other side of the aisle as academicians in a top Global North university. By contrast, I had seen both sides. I had been both a student and an academician at leading universities both in the Global North and the Global South. And that duality of experiences is important in the shaping of one's global perspectives on higher education.

At the University of Warwick, I taught both on the undergraduate and postgraduate law degree programs. On the Bachelor of Laws (LLB) degree program, I taught, among other courses, Public International Law, English Law of Trusts and Commercial Law. I remember one unfortunate incident with a white faculty colleague who took issue over the fact that they had been informed by a student that I had dismissed or taken lightly in my tutorials some of the course materials that they had introduced the students to during lectures. A bald and semi-mature white male student, who always wore a mischievous demeanor and never looked me in the eye, went behind my back to snitch to the white faculty colleague, saying that I had informed the students in the tutorials not to worry much about the material introduced in the lecture and to focus instead on the more traditional and doctrinal material of the course. The white faculty colleague was mad at me. But, of course, I was right. This person was bringing speculative things into the course which were not found in any leading or major published scholarship in the field. I had studied that course at the highest level on the Oxford BCL, and there were no such things as they were trying to make up, notwithstanding the subtle differences between the Warwick 'law in context' approach and the Oxford 'black-letter law' approach. I would guess that maybe they took offence mainly because I was black and had just joined the faculty, while this person was white and had been around for a while. Inflated egos can sometimes get in the way, especially if we have a skewed sense of our own superiority.

On the Masters of Law (LLM) degree programs, I taught courses on both the LLM in International Economic Law and the LLM in Law and Development. In addition, I supervised and examined several dozens of LLM dissertations. Among the many students I taught at the University of Warwick Law School were three Zambian ladies and one Zambian gentleman. The Zambian man was Hon Mr. Justice Sandson Silomba, who later became a Supreme Court Judge in Zambia. At the time, he was a High Court judge. At Warwick, he was pursuing an LLM in International Economic Law. Then the three Zambian ladies that I taught at Warwick were Ms Lydia Sameta-Chilumba, Ms Amanda Khozi-Mukwashi, and Ms Natasha Chiumya-Machila. After Warwick, they all did very well and excelled in their respective careers. At Warwick, Lydia and Amanda were both on the LLM degree programs, albeit in different cohorts. I also supervised their LLM dissertations. In Zambia, they were both only a year behind me in our undergraduate student days at the University of Zambia Law School, but at Warwick, I was on the other side of the aisle. Then Natasha was an undergraduate student pursuing her Bachelor of Laws (LLB) degree program at the University of Warwick. Natasha's father, Mr Patrick Chiumya, a former Director at UNECA, remained a good colleague even when I moved to the World Bank in Washington DC.

When I was lecturing at the University of Warwick, the *Independent*, a leading British daily newspaper, published an article on September 29, 1997, titled, 'Dictator takes his place in lecture hall,' regarding Sierra Leone's former president, Valentine Strasser, who had just lost power and was trying to get into the University of Warwick as an undergraduate law student. The university campus was filled with disquiet and discomfort about prospects for Captain Strasser becoming a law student at the university. The said *Independent* media article posited:

"Human rights observers say that Captain Valentine Strasser, the former West African military dictator, has never been one to show much regard for legal process. But yesterday a man who, according to Amnesty International, presided over the 'torture, ill-treatment and execution' of captured or suspected insurgents in Sierra Leone, joined undergraduates at Warwick University for the first lectures in his law degree course."[7]

The *Independent* article went on to say:

"Captain Strasser, 32, whose studies are being paid for by the United Nations, seized power in a military coup in 1992, but was himself overthrown four years later and forced into exile in Guinea."[8]

Before Captain Strasser could be admitted as a law student to the University of Warwick, the Law

---

[7] I. Burrell, "Dictator takes his place in lecture hall," *Independent* (September 29, 1997), available Online at: <<https://www.independent.co.uk/news/dictator-takes-his-place-in-lecture-hall-1241985.html>>, accessed on February 18, 2024.

[8] *Ibid*.

School at Warwick decided to convene a meeting of law faculty members to discuss and deliberate the way forward and the implications, especially because the matter was getting extensive coverage in the media. Indeed, there was a possible element of reputational risk if the Law School did not handle the matter well. So, the faculty meeting was an excellent way of getting broader consultation among concerned academic staff, as part of the decision-making process.

The matter was handled exceptionally well and very professionally by Warwick Law School. I attended that meeting, the only black African faculty member in the Law School at the time. My voice, I reasoned, if I was going to speak, would not be premised on race issues, but on the merits of giving someone a second chance in life. Some members of the law faculty argued strongly and passionately against the admission of Captain Strasser, citing gross violations of human rights when he was in power. I waited to hear some of the submissions before I made my own. I spoke strongly in favor of giving Captain Strasser a second chance as part of the process of reformation and reconciliation. Others also spoke in the favor of admitting him. In the end, Captain Strasser was admitted to Warwick Law School, though he only stayed at Warwick for a year 'after his scholarship from the United Nations development project expired.'[9]

I met Captain Strasser on the campus of the University of Warwick on a number of times. He also came to my office a few times in the company of a Nigerian student who was also studying law. Captain Strasser had a calm demeanor and never spoke much. He struck me as a reserved guy and someone who was trying to do something good with his life, having realized that he no longer had power and was simply an ordinary citizen. These stories, and many others, remain some of my fondest memories of the Warwickshire years.

While lecturing at Warwick, I remember travelling to London for an event at the Zambian High Commission. I met a Zambian government official at the Zambian High Commission in London who had travelled from Zambia to England on a business-related trip. When I introduced myself as 'Kenneth Mwenda', he looked at me with some attitude and said, "Which Mwenda is this?"

---

9 K. Perry, "Sierra Leone ex-dictator living in UK," The Guardian, (May 26, 2000), available Online at: << https://www.theguardian.com/world/2000/may/27/sierraleone1>>, accessed on February 18, 2024.

From his demeanor, I could tell that he was trying to assess my social rank – that is, whether I came from some aristocratic family back home in Zambia or was related to one. I knew exactly what he was trying to get at. I smiled politely and responded as follows: "The Mwenda who is the first Zambian lawyer to ever hold a full-time lectureship at one of the top 10 British universities where your current boss, the President of Zambia, is actually one of our graduate students. I am sure you have heard of this Mwenda who you are now meeting for the first time."

My sarcasm was intentional and deliberate. I wanted the man to understand that I did not need to be related to the people that he thought mattered for me to earn my respect. I needed no external validation. I had earned my respect already in my own cognisance. Indeed, I needed no one to validate my name. I was already playing at the international level in a competitive professional league in the United Kingdom such that it did not make sense to be asking me if I was related to some local name in a small domestic league as the Zambian market. You don't expect someone playing professional football for Manchester City, Liverpool or Arsenal in the United Kingdom to be validated by some Zambian local footballer at Kabwe Warriors or Roan United footbal club. It doesn't work like that. If anything, it is the other way round, that is the Zambian local player should be the one seeking validation from the guy playing in the competitive British premier league. Of course, I could tell that the man lacked exposure and was thinking that the so-called big names of Zambia still count when you are abroad. They don't. Nobody out there knows Ba Kantwa or Ba Chite. Leave those things in Zambia. Out there in the diaspora, you have to prove yourself. Your father's name does not matter. If anything, even as university students in the United Kingdom, those of us who were on well-funded scholarships lived a more comfortable life than a number of the sons and daughters of the so-called elites or aristocrats of Zambia who were privately funded by their parents. The decline in the value of the Kwacha against the British pound sterling often showed on the worried faces of privately-funded students whose parents would at times struggle to raise money to send to their children abroad. Such is life. But for people who do not know or understand these things, they might think naively that their local heroes in Lusaka also count as heroes in London or New York.

In Chapter 3, I metioned my parents' visit to England. They spent the summer of 1996 with me when I was lecturing at the University of Warwick. The then Dean of the School of Law at the University of Warwick, Professor Mike McConville, asked to have lunch with my parents. It was very kind and generous of Mike to extend the lunch invitation to my parents. They had lunch together, and my parents were most grateful for the warm hospitality that they received from my Dean. I also took my parents around the university campus where they met a number of my colleagues and students. My mother, in particular, was quite intrigued to find that her son, an African child that she had raised in Africa, was teaching white children their own law and in their own country. She was having difficulty processing that. I remember that one of the administrative secretaries in the School of Law at Warwick, assigned to work with me, came to meet my parents in my office. She greeted my parents and they chatted a bit before she left. As soon as she closed the door behind her, my mother whispered to me in delight, saying, "Kaoma mwana wandi, na ba aba sungu niwe boss wabo? Ine, nati limbi bana be sukulu fye?" ("Kaoma, my son, even this white lady reports to you? I thought that maybe your job is just confined to teaching university students who, understandably, include white students.")

I smiled and replied calmly, saying, "You have seen for yourself, Mum. Nothing is impossible with God and a good education."

I could understand where my mother was coming from. During the harsh colonial days in Africa, the time in which she and my father grew up, it was unfathomable for a black person to lead, manage or teach white people. It was totally unthinkable. Luckily, my father had travelled abroad after Zambia attained political independence in 1964. My father, as established already, went to Canada for his university studies before I even went to university in Zambia. So, he was not surprised, as he was quite familiar with how things play out if you are highly educated, irrespective of your race.

On Sundays and on some working days in the week, I would attend Catholic Mass at the Catholic chaplaincy on the campus of the University of Warwick. The location of the chaplaincy was convenient for me, especially as I lived only a few minutes away from the university campus. So, when my parents were visiting England, we would attend Mass together every Sunday at the university chaplaincy. Again, as in Oxfordshire and Yorkshire, in Warwickshire I found myself living not too far from a Catholic Church. I had no excuse really not to go to church.

One thing has, however, remained with me. My Christian faith is not about Christianity being a white man's faith. Far from it. If anything, Christianity is not any racial group's faith. It simply became associated with 'whiteness' because many European and North American white slave-traders and slaveowners used the Bible selfishly to mislead, misguide and indoctrinate those that they dominated. Christianity was often misused and abused by those who practiced such evils as slavery, apartheid and colonialism. Otherwise, Christianity itself is not a part of those despicable evils, nor is it a white man's religion, especially given that it originated from the Middle East. The God of the Christians today is the God of my African ancestors. My people simply expressed themselves differently in their faith. But they too knew and accepted that there is a God who would carry them through each and every day.

Shown here are two pictures taken in church at St. Stephen Martyr Catholic Church in Washington DC on Ash Wednesday 2024, a date that also happened to be Valentine's Day (Wednesday, February 14, 2024). Ash Wednesday Mass that day was scheduled to start at 12:10pm. So, during the lunch hour, I walked briskly from the office to the church to attend Mass. I knew that although it was Valentine's Day, all manner of Valentine's Day celebrations could wait.

I got to church in time and sat at the back, even though I had arrived early enough to get a front row seat. Indeed, there were many empty front row seats in church when I arrived. For me, one should never express oneself as a perfect Christian, especially if you are honest with yourself. If anything, an honest person will often feel as if he or she is not good or worthy enough to sit close to the altar. Your conscience just tells you to own up and take a seat at the back, not in the front row. As a Christian, you learn that a holier than thou approach is nothing but selfish sin of self-deceit, so you submit yourself as a sinner. For we are all works in progress.

That day, some young people walked into church late and left as soon as they had the ashes imprinted on their

forehead and before Mass was over. We cannot judge anyone, but, as humans, we are simply left to wonder. Maybe, one day, when they get older, they will understand and learn to be patient.

At the University of Warwick, I had many friends and colleagues among faculty members from different parts of the world. In particular, I would be remiss if I did not mention the edifying camaraderie of my good brother and friend from Cameroon, Professor Zacharie Tamainot-Telto, who is a professor in the School of Engineering at the University of Warwick. Zacharie is such a gentleman. We shared many academic experiences together and have remained in touch. Some of the Zambian colleagues and friends that I was close to in Coventry included Ms Susan Sitemba, Hon Mr Justice Silomba, Mr Themba Munalula, and Mr Sylvester Munyenyembe. In fact, my parents met Ms Susan Sitemba and Mr and Mrs Munyenyembe when they visited Warwickshire. Ms Sitemba, popularly known as 'Auntie Sue', has always been like my big sister. She is never short of fun. She hosted my parents to a lovely African meal at her residence in Coventry and has since been a close friend of my elder sister, Catherine, who she had interacted with briefly during their years of compulsory military service for post-secondary school graduates in Zambia. They reconnected through me. When my wife and I were getting married in the US, Ms Sitemba was the graceful matron of honor at our wedding. She flew in from England for our wedding in Washington DC, together with my good friend, Mr Kelvin Nkonda and his dear wife, also based in England. I am ever grateful to all of them for their unwavering support. The wedding was held on a luxury yacht in Washington DC, while sailing on the Potomac River.

In Warwickshire, the Munyenyembes also hosted my parents to dinner at their home. Coventry had a small but neat Zambian community. Ms Sitemba was working in the banking sector and about to embark on her PhD studies. Mr Munalula was pursuing his Masters degree program at Warwick, together with Judge Silomba who was an uncle to Mr Munyenyembe. The latter was teaching and working on his PhD studies. These were the Zambians that I interacted with mainly in Coventry. They were people who not only valued and appreciated education, but also respected knowledge.

On some weekends, I would go into Birmingham from Coventry to do some shopping for my wardrobe as well as for some weekend outings. Birmingham is a bigger city and has a lot more to offer in terms of fashion and style as well as nightlife. Coventry had one nightclub in the city centere, but it did not match much of what Birmingham had to offer. And Birmingham is only a short drive of about 20 to 30 minutes away from Coventry. Even closer to my place in Coventry was Birmingham International Airport. So, my residence in Coventry was conveniently located between London and Birmingham, with Oxford somewhere midway on this triangular axis. I, however, preferred residing in Coventry to residing in Birmingham much the same way I preferred Oxford to London. Even in the US, I prefer Washington DC to cities such as New York, Chicago or Los Angeles. In South Africa too, I prefer Pretoria and Cape Town to Johannesburg. There is a certain sense of quiet and tranquility, away from the daily hustle and bustle of the bigger and busier cities, that you find in these lesser populated and lesser congested cities.

In my third year of lecturing at the Unversity of Warwick, I started exploring prospects for moving to the US. My plan was to continue with my academic career in the US. However, to transition into the US legal academy, I figured that it would help me to start with something like a Harry A. Bigelow Teaching Fellowship at the University of Chicago Law School. I read about the requirements of that fellowship. I knew that I was more than equal to the task. However, I was also required to send my application package together with supporting references. I turned to a Zambian academic colleague to assist me with a reference, but he did not come through. It was déjà vu. Otherwise, I would not have known that my Zambian colleague had not come through if he was to send the reference directly to the University of Chicago Law School.

I followed up on the pending reference only to receive it past the deadline. I mentioned to him that I could not proceed with my application because I had not received the reference before the deadline. The guy then asked me to send him back the reference letter unsealed. He insisted that I should not open the envelope to read the reference. I wondered why. After a day or two, I got a reminder from him to send him back the reference unsealed, leaving me wondering what was contained in the reference for him to insist that I should not open the letter. I obliged and did as he requested, but that lack of transparency was an awakening call. It destroyed the goodwill and trust that was there between us, as brothers. So, on my next application, I dropped that Zambian colleague for people to help me with references. It was obvious that there was a problem.

I then applied to go to Yale Unversity Law School and used other references. I was admitted to Yale without difficulty and given a fully-funded fellowship. My strategy was to move later from Yale into a professorship or professorial appointment at another top US university. However, as established already, before I could move from Warwick to Yale, the doors at the World Bank opened. I had always wanted to work for the United Nations or a major UN agency. The World

Bank is indeed a UN specialized agency, which was what I had been dreaming of. So, why go to Yale when what you have been dreaming of is right at your doorstep? The window of opportunity opens only once. If it shuts, you might not get a second chance. So, I decided to turn down Yale University Law School, the best law school in the US, and go to the World Bank. That is how I moved to Washington DC and left England for the US in September 1998.

CHAPTER 13

Moving from England to the US

Prior to moving to the US, I had studied, lived and worked in England for almost a decade. There was nothing left for me to prove or see in England. But I do appreciate what England gave me as much as I appreciate what Africa gave me and what the US has given me. However, I needed to get new experiences and broader perspectives beyond Africa and the United Kingdom. I was looking for some novel and stimulating challenges professionally, socially and personally. My name is Mwenda, and, as mentioned earlier, in many Eastern and Southern African Bantu languages, the name means a traveler. So, I travelled or flew from England to the US, moving from academia in England to work for the World Bank in the US. I arrived in the US in September 1998. I must admit that it took a while for me to adjust from how things are done in England to the way things are done in the US. Shortly after I arrived in the US, I stopped by the Zambian Embassy in Washington DC to pay a courtesy call on the Zambian Ambassador. One of the senior officers at the embassy who came to meet me asked me, "The Ambassador would like to know if there is a problem."

I smiled and said, "There is no problem. I simply came to pay a courtesy call on His Excellency and to let him know that I am a Zambian professional who recently relocated from England to the US, and that I am with the World Bank."

I'd guess that many Zambian Embassy folks were used to meeting only Zambians beleaguered with personal problems of one kind or another. It might have appeared strange to them that someone could have no personal problem, and show up to just say hello. I was told that the Ambassador was busy and could not see me that day. The following week, the Ambassador flew to Zambia. However, immediately upon his return, he asked me to stop over at the Zambian Embassy to see him. I don't know what had happened. Suddenly, he was not too busy. There was a change of heart. My thinking was that he could have been briefed in Lusaka about me by one or two of his seniors in the Movement for Multi-party Democracy (MMD) Government. I say so because he was just too eager to meet me after he returned from Zambia. Indeed, both at the Minister and Permanent Secretary levels at the Ministry of Foreign Affairs in Zambia, the people who had occupied those positions around that time had worked with me previously when we all taught at the University of Zambia (UNZA) Law School. So, they were my academic colleagues, and they knew me very well.

When it came to settling down in the US, it did not help matters much that a Zambian friend who I was close to during our graduate student days in England was now a diplomat at the Zambian Embassy in Washington DC. Upon my arrival in Washington DC, I reached out to him, hoping that he would help me with settling down, as I was new to Washington. I was not asking him for money, but I don't know what he was thinking to somewhat distance himself. I was simply touching base as a friend. Maybe he mistakenly thought I would ask him for money, forgetting that I had my own money and my own accommodation. Or maybe he was just too busy or had moved on. So, I was all alone trying to find my way in a new city and new country. The good part, though, was that my finances were solid, and I could get whatever I needed or wanted. Money was not an issue. In fact, I was staying at a hotel that was fully paid for, so I had nothing to worry about.

Culturally, I found that the UK and the US were worlds apart. In England, I could get almost anywhere I wanted to go by cab or other forms of public transport. Buses there run frequently. By contrast, in the US, buses are not as frequent as in the UK and some places are simply not accessible by public transport. One just has to drive. I found that in the US, especially in the Washington DC, Maryland and Virginia area (the 'DMV'), there wasn't a strong culture of high-income earning folks commuting by public transport during the week. On weekends, it was worse. Many people preferred driving in their own cars to using public transport. It was very different from England. Even many students in the US would jump into their cars and drive off. And if you wanted to go out at night or were coming from somewhere, cabs, especially in Washington DC, would rarely stop for you if you were a black man waving them down on the streets. Many cab drivers would rather pick up a white or Asian man, fearing that a black man could possibly attack them. I began to understand the racial dynamics of the US. It was frustrating. I was also missing England somewhat and even contemplated going back to the UK. But as time went on, I started adjusting to the American way of life and to settle down in the US.

Before I joined the World Bank, I had not met, heard of or read about any Zambian professional working at the World Bank in Washington DC. At the time, I was only 29 years old, so I had no point of reference or benchmark to emulate. It was a road less travelled. Sometimes, you have to go where there is no path to leave a trail for others to follow. I was breaking new ground for other Zambian professionals to follow. The same thing happened when I was in England. I was only 26 years old when I took up my position as a law professor at the University of Warwick. Again, I had not met, heard of or read about any Zambian academic who had held or was holding a full-time Law Lectureship at any of the leading British universities, so I was basically breaking new ground. I was doing things at a young age that would catch the attention and interest of any progressive. Indeed, I was doing the right things and pitching the right notes that any parent, or prospective parent-in-law, would like to see in a son or son-in-law. Put simply, I stood out.

There were not many Zambians in my age group, be it in England or the US, who were doing or had done most of the pioneering and ground-breaking things that I was doing at the international stage. I was not even 30 years old, but I was already at the World Bank and had even taught at a prestigious European university. I was setting records for my home country and doing things that a good number of my peers could only dream of. Naturally, I was attracting a lot of attention from many quarters, but I did not let that get to my head. My joining the World Bank in Washington DC opened doors for many other young Zambian professionals to gather courage to apply for professional jobs at the World Bank in Washington DC. Other Zambians who were locally recruited in World Bank country offices in Africa were motivated by my story to try out career opportunities at the World Bank headquarters in Washington DC. I was hired as internationally recruited staff at the World Bank headquarters in Washington DC straight from a top academic job in Great Britain. I was not hired locally in Zambia. In a nutshell, I helped to demystify the World Bank to many Zambian colleagues who started joining the Bank in Washington DC after me, and I mentored and coached a number of them as they aspired to join the World Bank. Others mimicked my career path in academia before they too joined the World Bank. And that's fine, because a leader inspires others to follow. Also, I helped with references for many young Zambian professionals for strategic university and job placements, as some of them worked towards joining the World Bank and others attended graduate school in preparation for careers there. Furthermore, I took some compatriots under my wing, sheltering them from stormy weather. Others came to the World Bank on secondment directly from the Zambia Government under my leadership.

I also gave strategic opportunities to some compatriots for visibility within and beyond Washington to help them in their career progression. In academia too, I facilitated some external academic appointments of some Zambian professionals working at the World Bank. Further, where there was room, I would invite a compatriot to come and sit with me on a publication or institutional committee. Tribe did not matter. Those who fit the descriptions I have a given here include several compatriots who are originally from Zambia's Northern and Muchinga provinces as well as those from Southern, Western and Northwestern provinces, in addition to some from Luapula, Central and Eastern provinces. To me, it did not matter whether you were Tonga, Lozi, Luvale, Kaonde, Chokwe, Lunda, Lenje, Lamba, Soli, Lala, Bemba, Bisa, Ngoni, Nsenga, Tumbuka, Ushi, Ng'umbo, Chishinga, Tabwa, Namwanga, Mambwe or whatever. I am above the pettiness of parochial tribal shenanigans. Through my broad networks in academia, as noted above, I even recommended some compatriots at the World Bank who are not from my tribe for external appointments for professorships. After all, this is what a true leader does. He or she inspires others. To that extent, I have played my part.

Generally, many Zambians just sit and wait to be appointed to some lofty job and thus have not had an impactful presence at the international level in the own cognizance, with the exception, of course, of a few impressive cases such as those of Lottie Mwale in boxing circles, Kalusha Bwalya and Barbra Banda in football circles and Dr Kenneth Kaunda in international politics. A job title per se is not an achievement, no matter how grandiose it might appear. Tell us and show us what you have really achieved beyond your job title. Otherwise, many Zambians have simply not been effective trendsetters internationally. They rarely shine globally through impactful engagements or pioneering initiatives carried out on their own. Rather, they will wait until they see someone else break new ground before they start to emulate or mimic him or her. Their self-doubt and lack of confidence is quite apparent. Generally speaking, a good number of my countrymen and women are followers rather than leaders. They like to imitate or mimic, but not to pioneer or initiate. For example, the practice of early morning jogging in Lusaka did not gain much prominence until a few years ago when a few prominent Lusaka socialites and political elites started jogging in the wee hours of the morning. Only then did other folks in Lusaka start mimicking that. Another example is farming and playing golf. If the rich are playing golf or going into farming, most of the wannabes will try it out too. When a few Lusaka socialites and political elites started buying land in the outskirts of Lusaka to set up semi-commercial farms, many wannabes started following the trend. Now almost everyone talks about owning a piece of land for some kind of farming in Lusaka. It is the same thing with playing golf, which is often associated with elitism. Now almost every wannabe in Lusaka claims to be into playing golf. People can't come up with their own ideas. They would rather simply copy what someone else is doing.

When I joined the World Bank in 1998, I found only one black Zambian professional staff member at the World Bank. Her name is Dr Shimwaayi Muntemba and she holds a PhD from the University of California at Los Angeles in the US. Dr Muntemba had previously taught at UNZA many years before my time there, so many people in my age-group and below had not heard of her. When I joined the World Bank, she was not too far from retirement, so many people in my age-group and below could only relate to my story since my career path was more contemporary and visible to them. The other two Zambian professionals that I found at the World Bank were of Asian and Caucasian ethnicity, and were in strategic managerial and leadership roles that somewhat made them inaccessible. I never got a chance to meet any of them while they were in Washington DC. Otherwise, the remainder of the black Zambians were non-professional staff in administrative and support roles.

Across the street in Washington DC, at the International Monetary Fund (IMF), the Zambian professional staff that I found included Dr Justin B. Zulu, who holds a PhD in Economics from the University of Colorado in the US. Dr Zulu once served as a Special Assistant to President Kenneth Kaunda (the then Head of State of Zambia) from 1970 to 1971, as well as Adviser to an Executive Director of IMF in Washington DC from 1971 to 1974 before serving as Alternate Executive Director at the IMF from 1974 to 1976, and then transitioning into mainstream IMF professional staff in 1976 as Deputy Director and then from 1976 to 1984 as Director of the IMF African Department. Dr Zulu also served as Director of Monetary and Exchange Affairs at the IMF. Another Zambian professional that I found at the IMF is my good brother and friend, Mr George M Kabwe, who holds a Bachelors degree in Electronics and Computer Engineering from the University of Birmingham in England and an MBA in Finance from the Wharton School at the University of Pennsylvania in the US, in addition to his professional credential as a Fellow of the Institute of Chartered Accountants in England and Wales. George retired from the IMF in mid-2025. His last position before retiring from the IMF was as Assistant Director in the IMF Finance Department. When I arrived in Washington DC in 1998, George had only been at the IMF for about a year. He joined the IMF as an international hire from an international accounting and audit firm, having worked both in England and elsewhere in the US. I also found Ms Inutu Lukonga, who joined the IMF as an international hire in 1993. Before joining the IMF, Ms Lukonga served as Deputy Director of Research at the Bank of Zambia and then proceeded for her PhD studies in Economics at the University of Sussex in England. Then, there were few other Zambians in support roles at the IMF.

A few blocks from the World Bank and IMF, I found Ms Dolika Banda at the International Finance Corporation (IFC). She had just joined IFC as an international hire in Washington DC in 1996, a couple of years before I arrived at the World Bank. Dolika, who holds both a Bachelors degree in International Business and Marketing and a Masters degree in International Business and Banking from Schiller International University in France, in addition to a Higher National Diploma in Business and Finance from Anglia Ruskin University in England, was the only Zambian professional working at the IFC in Washington DC when I arrived at the World Bank. Before Dolika retired, she served briefly as a Director at IFC. The remaining of the few Zambians at the IFC in Washington DC were mainly in non-professional administrative and support roles.

At the World Bank, my first 6 to 8 months rotational assignment as a Young Professional under the World Bank Young Professionals Program (YPP) was in the current Development Finance Vice-Presidency (DFi) of the World Bank. My work there focused on World Bank-administered trust funds (TFs) and Recipient country-executed TFs. I was involved in developing and reviewing TF policies as well as TF operational procedures. I had a great manager, Ms Dale Hill. She was a white American lady and a graduate of Princeton University in the US. The Director was Mr Geoffrey Lamb, an Irish national of South African origin. Geoff was later promoted to Vice-President of the same Vice-Presidency. He succeeded Mr Motoo Kusakabe from Japan who was our Vice-President. At the time, DFi was known as the World Bank Resource Mobilization and Co-Financing (RMC) Vice-Presidency.

Also, in RMC, I worked on the simplification, effectiveness and successful implementation of the policy agenda for World Bank TFs. Building on that work, I have since led the preparation and implementation of several World Bank-administered TFs as well as provided policy and legal advice to several World Bank operational teams on TFs. For example, I served as the World Bank Task Team Leader (TTL) of a major World Bank Development Grant Facility (DGF) TF for Capacity-Building in International Trade and Investment Law in Africa. As an experienced World Bank TTL, I have been involved in the design and implementation of different types of TFs for various World Bank lending operations. While in RMC, I also worked on, *inter alia*, cost recovery and disclosure policies of World Bank-administered TFs, as well as provided several Project teams with valuable operational guidance on pertinent issues affecting the possible application of World Bank environmental and social safeguard policies to World Bank-administered TFs.

Further, I have been involved in the design and execution of both Recipient country-executed TFs and World Bank-executed TFs as well as in analyzing and identifying cross-cutting issues in Regional, Global Practice Groups and Donor-Specific TF portfolios. For example, I worked on TFs from various perspectives as a TTL, extending to my respective work assignments as World Bank Senior Projects Officer in the World Bank Europe and Central Asia Vice-Presidency (ECA), followed by my respective roles as World Bank Senior Counsel in the World Bank Legal Vice-Presidency and World Bank Senior Counsel in the World Bank Integrity Vice-Presidency. In addition, I have worked in RMC on mechanisms to increase the International Development Association's (IDA) ability to mobilize resources for poverty alleviation as well as on IDA replenishments, including financing for development and leveraging private sector partnerships.

My second 6 to 8 months rotational assignment as a World Bank Young Professional was in what was then known as the Poverty Reduction and Economic Management Vice-Presidency (PREM) of the World Bank. My director in PREM was Dr Cheryl W Gray, a white American lady with a PhD in Public Policy from Harvard University. In PREM, I worked mainly on governance and anti-corruption projects as well as on privatization and tax reform issues. Among the countries that I worked on are the Philippines and Ghana. In the early 2000s, I travelled on World Bank mission to Ghana to support work there on Ghana's National Institutional Reform Programme for the transformation of the Ghana Institute of Management and Public Administration (GIMPA) into a self-financing institution. That was my first World Bank operational mission.

My third 6 to 8 months rotational assignment as a World Bank Young Professional was in the Legal Vice-Presidency of the World Bank, becoming the first Zambian lawyer to work in the Bretton Woods institutions, and, thus, paving the way for a few other Zambian lawyers to follow. When I joined the World Bank Legal Vice-Presidency (LEG) on October 1, 1999, there was no known history in LEG of any other Young Professional having worked there. I was arguably the first Young Professional to have worked in LEG. From the time I joined LEG in 1999 until 2022, no other Young Professional had worked as a lawyer in LEG. After more than two decades, LEG finally hired in 2022 a young East African female lawyer as a Young Professional. Interestingly, the young lady's PhD thesis (2022) written at Trinity College Dublin in the University of Dublin (Ireland), like my PhD thesis (2000) written partly at the University of Oxford and the other part at the University of Warwick (England), is also on capital markets. Twenty-two years after I wrote my PhD thesis, which focused on the prospects for developing buoyant securities markets in Eastern and Southern Africa through the integration of securities markets and the promotion of cross-border trading and multiple listing of securities, the young lady's PhD thesis at the University of Dublin examined the issue of making cross-border securities markets work for Africa and the question of whether or not the integration of markets is the solution. A great coincidence there!

When I joined LEG, I remember meeting the then Senior Vice-President and General Counsel of the World Bank, an erudite and distinguished Egyptian thought-leader and diplomat, Dr Ibrahim F.I. Shihata, just before he retired. We met at an LEG Christmas party held at the New Zealand Embassy in Washington DC. I did not know who Dr Shihata was, though I had read and heard about him. That evening, I sat next to him without realizing who he was. We were chatting comfortably until I saw one of my supervisors in LEG kneeling before Dr Shihata when asking him if he could get him something to eat or drink. The man said meekly, "Mr Shihata, sir, can I get you something to eat or drink?"

Immediately, I recognized who was sitting next to me. I recognized the name from his voluminous body of scholarship which was widely referenced in academia and elsewhere. And I thought to myself, "Oh, so this is the man! Okay, let me seize this moment and opportunity to talk to him on a one-on-one."

As we spoke, Dr Shihata asked me for my nationality. I told him I was Zambian. I did not want to say much to avoid making a fool out of myself by dishing out too much information. I was coming from England and had not yet caught up with the American idea of the elevator pitch (*i.e.* self-promotion). I was wearing a West African boubou, uncharacteristic of many lawyers who often want to wear a tuxedo suit at dinner parties or an expensive dark suit with a white shirt and fancy cufflinks.

Dr Shihata asked me about my educational and professional backgrounds. After I provided a summary, he said to me, "You have an impressive background with admirable achievements, yet you look so simple and humble."

I was, of course, flattered, especially because the compliments were coming from an intellectual luminary of his gigantic scholarly stature. However, I did not want to show my excitement. I maintained my cool and remained calm, as I replied, "Thank you, sir."

Dr Shihata shared with me some highlights of his indelible work at the World Bank as Senior Vice-President and General Counsel, including his contribution to a complex project on Zambia where he provided some valuable legal guidance to the Board of World Bank Executive Directors. It was a very enriching, illuminating and inspiring experience. Dr Shihata was highly respected and well-regarded internationally, both in academia and international development circles. I met him again a few times before he finally retired from the World Bank. Each time we met he always remembered me.

In LEG, I started off in the advisory services unit that dealt with private and financial sector development (LEGPS). My manager in LEGPS was Mr Douglas Webb. He was from New Zealand. I worked mainly on capital markets, privatization, bankruptcy, banking regulation and corporate governance issues. The work covered contemporary issues for law reform and development in countries in Eastern Europe and Central Asia, Latin America and the Caribbean Islands, East Asia and the Pacific Islands, Middle East and North Africa, and South Asia as well as Sub-Sahara Africa. I spent a year in LEGPS before rotating to my next assignment in LEG. I moved to an operational unit which covered countries in East Asia and the Pacific Islands (LEGEA), focusing on the transactional work of World Bank lending operations, including drafting, amending, and negotiating major

World Bank legal agreements with the client countries of the World Bank as well as providing legal guidance to World Bank operational teams on the preparation and implementation of World Bank projects as well as on the various World Bank lending operational policies and procedures.

It was in LEGEA that I got my first experience as a World Bank country lawyer negotiating a World Bank-financed project. The assignment involved two World Bank-supported projects in the mining and gas sectors of Papua New Guinea. I prepared the legal agreements, led the negotiations and was present at the Board of the World Bank Executive Directors when the projects were being approved. Also, I was present to guide the authorized signatories of the World Bank and the Government of Papua New Guinea in signing the legal agreements of the two projects.

After about a year in LEGEA, I decided move to a World Bank Regional Vice-Presidency, the Europe and Central Asia Vice-Presidency (ECA-VPU). There I served as Senior Projects Officer, focusing on private and financial sector development in Eastern European and Central Asian countries. The unit in ECA-VPU was known as ECSPF, meaning Europe and Central Asia Private and Financial Sector Development Unit. My director was Mr Paul Siegelbaum, who had served previously in LEG before becoming the director of ECSPF. Paul hired me in ECSPF. Truly, I cannot thank him enough. My manager was Mr Alex Fleming.

One memorable World Bank mission that I undertook while I worked in ECSPF was in another region, namely, North Africa. In 2001, I was invited by the Libyan Government to provide advisory services on the setting up of an African stock exchange. I was all alone on that World Bank mission, as I was approached directly on the basis of my technical expertise, though I had to operate vicariously through my employers, the World Bank. The Libyan Government authorities made it clear that they wanted nobody else from the World Bank but me to provide the advisory services, as they had seen my scholarly writing on the development of stock markets in Africa. The incident attracted some envy, of course, as I remember some elderly Caucasian European lady in the unit passing some cynical remarks about Col Gaddafi and his projects in Africa. That lady was equally hostile to me. I could not understand why. Anyhow, she died not too long after I joined the unit.

The Libyan Government authorities informed me that they had seen my published scholarly writing on African stock markets, some of which has been cited widely in working papers of the International Monetary Fund (IMF). I told them that I would have to check with my director before I could take up the assignment. I went and informed my director, Paul, about the invitation, which came through from the office of the World Bank Executive Director. Paul was supportive. He advised me to prepare a concept note and then get it peer-reviewed before I could proceed. I did the needful and the concept was peer-reviewed and cleared, so I was ready to head out to Libya. Some Caucasian friends of mine in the US were worried for me. They were basing their fears, of course, on media propaganda about Col Muammar Gaddafi. But I am an African and knew that Col Gaddafi was a Pan-Africanist, so I had nothing to worry about.

When I landed in Libya, I was given first class VIP treatment at the airport by the Libyan government authorities who were waiting for me. It was the first time I had travelled to Tripoli. The government authorities informed me that I was a 'Guest of the Brother Leader'. I did not know who the Brother Leader was until one of the officials told me that that was the title by which Col. Gaddafi, liked to be called. During my stay in Libya, I was privileged to have had a couple of one-on-one meetings with Col. Gaddafi. I was intrigued and humbled by his kind and patient demeanor as I presented my technical paper before him. In Libya, they looked after me very well, especially as I was designated officially as a Guest of the Head of State. It was at a time when the African Union was being born. I was later provided with a presidential jet to fly me from Tripoli to Sirte, where the African Heads of State were meeting.

After the meeting of Heads of State in Sirte, as we were all preparing to fly back to Tripoli, I met a number of African Heads of State at the airport. They had all travelled to Libya to attend the meeting leading to the establishment of the African Union. Among them was Zambia's first Republican President, Dr. Kenneth Kaunda. I saw Dr Kaunda, the founding father of the Nation of Zambia, seated among the eminent dignitaries at the end of the red carpet, but security was tight, and I couldn't get through to him. However, I gathered some courage and told the Libyan security officials to let me through so that I could say hello to my very good friend President Kaunda. I told them to ask him about me and to let him know that it was his good friend and namesake from Zambia, Kenneth, knowing that Dr Kaunda would never say no to meeting a fellow Zambian.

For sure, to their surprise, Dr Kaunda confirmed to them that he was my friend and asked security to let me through. I walked down the red carpet to the amusement of everyone and we embraced and chatted for a few minutes. When I first told this story to my wife, she never believed me until I shared it again when we had dinner with Dr Kaunda in Maryland, US. And Dr Kaunda, looking at my wife, smiled and said, "It's true. We are very good friends."

What a gentleman Dr Kaunda was!

Dinner in Maryland, USA, with the first President of Zambia, Dr Kenneth Kaunda

When flying back from Sirte to Tripoli, Dr Kaunda and I were given the same presidential jet by the Brother Leader. For the first time, I could feel 'power' around me. Even when I first arrived in Libya from the US, I was given VIP treatment at the Libyan airport by the receiving government officials. From the airport in Tripoli to the hotel where I was booked up, I was given a VIP motorcade with sirens and all, just like a head of state. I could not believe it. An innocent African boy being spoilt!

There were security motorbikes in front of the motorcade clearing the way as I was being driven to the hotel. I was lost for words and full of gratitude. Not even in Zambia have I ever been accorded such a dignified reception. I could not believe that it was the same me, the simple African boy, because normally when one is on a World Bank mission you simply jump on a cab or taxi from the airport to the hotel, unless you have made your own prior arrangements for pick up. But the Libyan experience was different. They chose to treat me with utmost respect and courtesy. I was told repeatedly by the authorities that I was a Guest of the Brother Leader. All security clearance protocols were done in a VIP manner. When I think of the time Dr. Kaunda and I shared the presidential jet from Sirte to Tripoli, I just wish there had been smartphones to take some selfies, especially with the pretty young ladies that formed the presidential security detail of the Brother Leader standing in the background. Dr Kaunda was given a seat in the First Class cabin of the presidential jet, while I took a seat in the Business Class cabin, but my seat still felt presidential. I had no regrets. This was clearly a league of Big Boys!

I reminisce with fond memories now of that Libyan mission. Prior to that trip, I had made an earlier trip to Libya where I had two long meetings with the Brother Leader himself. The first meeting was in a building that looked like a national library. I sat facing the door, thinking that the Brother Leader would enter the meeting room through the main door, only to see the bookshelf-like structure in front of me turn around 180 degrees and open. Then he walked in calmly and patiently. I was taken by surprise.

The second meeting I had with him was in a large and modern tent. On both occasions, he wore the traditional West African boubou with a crest of the African map on the chest, and on both occasions, the meetings did not start as scheduled. The meetings would be rescheduled, and you would be told to stay put in your hotel room without giving you any update on the rescheduled time for the meeting. Then, as you waited patiently, the phone would ring, and you would be asked to leave immediately with security.

In Libya, I also paid a courtesy call on the Zambian MMD Government officials that had accompanied the Zambian president to the Sirte meeting of Heads of State. We were all staying in the same hotel. At the time, the Zambian Minister of Foreign Affairs was Hon. Mr Kelly Walubita. He was so nice to me and very welcoming. I was happy to meet him. I also recognized Hon Dr Ngosa Simbyakula, the then Permanent Secretary in the Ministry of Foreign Affairs, who I taught with at the University of Zambia (UNZA) Law School before I left Zambia for Oxford. It was nice to reconnect. We had a good chat.

One or two of the other folks in their entourage were behaving somewhat weirdly, posturing as if they were big boys while pacing up and down, as they spoke on those old cellphones of the time. Yet they had just escorted the Zambian president, H.E. President Frederick T Chiluba, to the meetings of Heads of State, whereas I was actually a Guest of the Brother Leader himself. There is a big difference between escorting someone from your country and being invited, as I was, as a special guest of the host President himself. But I don't know what those compatriots were thinking by posturing to me as if they were very important people. Maybe they thought that I was a stranded Zambian student in Libya who would ask them for money. If only they knew, they would have been a little bit more sober and humble.

While in ECSPF, I travelled extensively and frequently to many countries in Eastern Europe and Central Asia. I was hardly in Washington DC, but frequently in the air on my way to various World Bank missions. Often, I would either be connecting to different destinations at major international airports, grabbing a quick meal or a fine wine here and there in the business or first-class lounge at international airports. I would at times be checking in and out of hotels or held up in meetings with senior government officials in some Eastern European or Central Asian countries. I remember the September 11 2001 terrorist attacks in the US which saw three planes taken over, diverted by terrorists and crashed into the Twin Towers and the Pentagon. I had just returned from Eastern Europe the previous weekend and was in my office at the World Bank in Washington DC when the incidents started unfolding. It was so scary, especially as I was not too far from the Pentagon.

During the time I spent in ECSPF, I also remember meeting Mr Anderson K Mazoka, the founding president of Zambia's ruling party, the United Party for National Development (UPND).

One of Mr Mazoka's daughters, Mrs Mutinta Mazoka-M'membe, who is a family friend of my wife and I, called me up from Atlanta, Georgia, asking if I could meet up with her father, who was coming to Washington DC for some meetings. I agreed and we firmed up a date and time. I met up with Mr Mazoka and hosted him to a lunch at the World Bank. It was just the two of us, as this was a private meeting. He came alone, giving us enough time to discuss in greater detail. We had fruitful discussions and he shared with me his vision for UPND and Zambia. He had a well-articulated and thought-out vision. We had a good uninterrupted two hours of cordial and intellectually stimulating dialog. This was before the current politics that have now come to Zambia.

I then introduced Mr Mazoka to some good friends at the International Monetary Fund (IMF) and asked them to come over and meet him. They all came immediately. It was a fruitful and productive engagement. After the meetings, I saw him off. Again, it was just the two of us. He was a visionary leader. I am ever grateful to my good learned sister, Mrs Mutinta Mazoka-M'membe, for arranging the meeting, and to her father, Mr Anderson K Mazoka, for coming to meet me in person and for sharing his vision for Zambia.

In my work in Eastern European and Central Asian countries, I focused mainly on projects pertaining to private and financial sector development, including privatization, the development of capital markets, banking regulation and supervision, Financial Sector Assessment Programs (FSAPs carried out jointly with International Monetary Fund (IMF) staff), Investment Climate Assessments (ICAs), corporate governance, unified financial services regulation, pension funds and insurance regulation, micro-finance regulation, access to finance, mortgage lending, and many other issues pertaining to private and financial sector development. This experience was most useful to me, as I have an interdisciplinary background in law, economic policy and business administration.

Among some of the notable assignments that I worked on when I was in the Europe and Central Asia Vice-Presidency of the World Bank were the joint World Bank and International Monetary Fund (IMF) Financial Sector Assessments (FSAP) of Bulgaria, Slovenia and Guyana, respectively. They were very informative. I also won a research grant from the World Bank to conduct a study on financial services regulation, focusing on the emerging trend of a single mega unified regulator that regulates the entire financial sector. To carry out activities under this grant, I traveled extensively to Hungary, Iceland, Bulgaria, Romania, Poland, Estonia, Latvia, Lithuania and Canada, examining the experiences of these countries in developing the institutional and regulatory frameworks for financial services regulation. In addition, I worked on World Bank-supported financial and private sector development projects in Tajikistan, Moldova, Serbia and Albania. I remember travelling to Tirana, Albania, and finding some folks on the streets roasting corn or cobs of maize on a small charcoal brazier like in Africa. I even saw some stray dogs there. It made me understand that there is poverty everywhere in the world, including in Europe, and that poverty is a global phenomenon. In Belgrade, Serbia, I hardly saw a black person in the city center throughout my stay there. I was in Belgrade for about two weeks. It left me wondering. In Ljubljana, Slovenia, I only saw one African person, a young Tanzanian student pursuing his university studies there. We stopped to greet each other. We chatted a bit and the young man told me that he was from Tanzania. He looked happy to see a fellow African so far away from home.

Then, in Reykjavík, Iceland, I saw an interesting African fella. He had a lot of 'attitude', trying to behave as if he was a native Icelandic person. I figured out quickly which part of Africa he could have come from by his demeanor. This is not a stereotype, but simply an aspect of culture. Some arrogance is a cultural thing and can easily be attributed to certain cultural traits, or dominant values and norms, depending on where you come from. There are certain cultures where people have a dominant and visible arrogance. You don't have to search far to find it. The chap was with a white woman, busy pretending not to have seen me, so I just let him be. I could tell that he was trying hard to fit in. I would not be surprised if he had come to Europe as a stowaway, hiding in one of those boats that try to smuggle desperate Africans into Europe.

During my years as a bachelor in Washington DC, I lived in a centrally located affluent neighborhood of north-west Washington DC, right next to the famous John F. Kennedy Center for the Performing Arts and the Watergate Hotel. My place was a five-minute walk to the World Bank. I would traverse the campus of George Washington University (GWU) to get to my place. I could even go home for lunch if I wanted to do. The location of my apartment was very convenient. As a result, I often used to host professional Zambian colleagues working for various government institutions in Lusaka to drinks and dinner each time they would come for meetings at the World Bank or IMF in Washington DC. I would host them for drinks at my place and even take them out to dinner in the evening, all that at own expense, thinking that every one of us appreciated the 'One Zambia One Nation' philosophy of the Kaunda days. Indeed, there were not many indigenous Zambian professionals working at the World Bank at the time. It was just Dr Shimwaayi Muntemba and I.

What surprised me each time I visited Zambia was that I would not hear again from most of the people I hosted to drinks and dinners in Washington DC. None of them would be there for me except one particular family who have always treated me to a fine reception and meal at their farm in the State House Lodge area. That family has always been there for me and even hosted a major event in my honor to celebrate and recognize my unparalleled scholarly accomplishments at their farm. The rest of my Zambian compatriots would know I was visiting Lusaka but would be nowhere to be seen. I would even bump into some of them in Lusaka, but they would never offer the reciprocal hospitality that I often afforded them in Washington DC. Yet, each time they were in Washington DC, they would expect me to be there for them and even to drive some of them around to shopping malls for their shopping. I realized that the culture of 'using people' is ingrained in our psyche as a people, so I stopped hosting my compatriots from Zambia. After all, it was not my job to be friendly and nice to people who hardly appreciated my hospitality. My home became a private place reserved only for myself and a very few selected guests, especially after I got married.

In one of the cold winters of the early 2000s, I had travelled to Moscow, Russia, for World Bank work. It was so cold that we in the World Bank team could not leave the hotel and stayed indoors. Luckily, all our meetings were to be held indoors. We were running workshops on anti-money laundering training, and I was at the time the key coordinator for anti-money laundering work for the Europe and Central Asia Regional Vice-Presidency of the World Bank. I had been to many other parts of Eastern Europe, including Hungary, Poland, Romania, Georgia, Bulgaria, Estonia, Latvia, Lithuania, Georgia, Slovenia, Slovakia, and Serbia, but it was not as cold as Moscow. Moscow was really cold. I then understood why most of the electricity supply cables in Moscow are not connected to poles above the ground, as we see in many other countries, but are placed safely under underground. Those cold and harsh winters, especially if there is a snowstorm, or in situations, say, of a hurricane or tornado, can sometimes knock out the power lines or bring down the poles to which the electricity cables are connected, and that could endanger human life. Indeed, I have seen incidents happen where poles to which electricity supply cables were connected were brought down by a hurricane or tornado. Also, placing electricity supply cables underground reduces the risk of damage caused by the theft of cables, sabotage, and illegal connections. Further, laying the cables underground reduces the risks of fire as well as the risks associated with the emission of electromagnetic fields to nearby areas.

While in Moscow, I tried to step outside the hotel to get a few items at a nearby convenience store, but my ears were almost freezing. It was so cold. I ran back inside the hotel. The local folks would walk around freely, as they were clad in the appropriate winter gear. Many wore thick woolen and leather hats that covered their ears. It was December, and right in the thick of winter.

I must say that wherever I travel to, I try to pay a courtesy call on the Zambian Ambassador or High Commissioner. So, I was thinking of touching base with the Zambian Embassy in Moscow. When I lived and worked in England in the 1990s, the Zambian High Commissioner there was His Excellency Mr Love Mtesa. He was such a fine gentleman and a seasoned diplomat, and we were often in touch. I can only thank him for his authentic leadership and fatherly inspiration.

When I moved to the US, I remember the good and cordial ties with His Excellency Ambassador Mr Lazarous Kapambwe, when he was the Permanent Representative of Zambia to the United Nations (UN) in New York, US. On a number of occasions, I would pay him a courtesy call when I would be visiting the UN for some business meetings. In the picture below, I can be seen leading a 30-member World Bank team for some meetings and knowledge-exchange engagements at the United Nations headquarters in New York, US.

This photo was taken during a short break when non-permanent members of the United Nations Security Council were being elected.

Her Excellency Ambassador Dr Mwaba Kasese, who succeeded Ambassador Kapambwe as the Permanent Representative of Zambia to the UN in New York, US, was equally welcoming. I enjoyed similar warm and cordial ties with her office. In fact, at one time, when I was gunning for a senior executive position in a UN-specialized agency to serve as General Counsel and Senior Vice-President, my good friend and brother His Excellency Ambassador Dr Chibamba Kanyama, who is currently serving as Zambia's Ambassador to the US, and was at that time working at the IMF in Washington DC, reached out on my behalf to the then Secretary to the Cabinet in Zambia, Hon Dr Ronald Msiska, for the Zambian Government to endorse and support my candidacy. Hon Dr Msiska, a real gentleman and a fine diplomat who had served in the UN before, and with whom I had previously corresponded, albeit briefly, was more than willing to support my candidacy. He immediately asked Ambassador Dr Kasese at the UN in New York to write and send in a strong recommendation and government endorsement of my candidacy, and Dr Kasese did so. She even blind-copied me on the correspondence so as to keep me posted.

In the meantime, I had also asked one of my former law students at UNZA who was at the time serving as a senior diplomat in the foreign service to put in a second endorsement. He did promise me that he would assist, but I doubt he did. I never saw or heard anything from him on that topic after we spoke. Perhaps, he was now feeling too big. People change. And some people have short memories. I am, however, so grateful to Hon Dr Roland Msiska, Her Excellency Ambassador Dr Mwaba Kasese, and His Excellency Ambassador Dr Chibamba Kanyama, for their unwavering support. They all came through for me when one of my boys from UNZA failed me.

When I was in Moscow, I decided to pay a courtesy call on the Zambian Ambassador to Russia. I went up to my hotel room and called the Zambian Embassy in Moscow, asking if, as a Zambian national, I could stop over at the Zambian Embassy for a courtesy call on the Ambassador. The Zambian Ambassador, His Excellency General G. Francis Sibamba, was more than happy to hear from me. He sent his driver to pick me up from the hotel. My other World Bank team-members were shocked that I had connections in Moscow and was getting VIP treatment from diplomatic circles. I looked at them, smiled and said, "Yes, we came here together, but guys, c'mon, we're not at the same level. I will see you later."

I was welcomed at the residence of the Zambian Ambassador to Russia. He had also invited over some Zambian students who were studying in Moscow to come and meet me. While speaking with

General Sibamba and his wife, I discovered that his wife was the elder sister of my eldest brother's close friend, Professor Njunga Mulikita. My eldest brother Kelvin was a close friend of Professor Njunga Mulikita, starting from their undergraduate student days together at the University of Zambia (UNZA) in the late 1970s.

As the evening progressed, there were more positive developments. One of the Zambian postgraduate students who came to meet me was a young man by the name of Evans Mushota Kabaso (now Dr Mushota Kabaso). He was at the time pursuing his Masters degree in Moscow. Mushota recognized me and said to me, "Big man, how are you? It's been a while. Do you remember me?"

I hesitated a bit, as I tried to place him where we could have met him. I then said to him,

"Please forgive me. Age is catching up. Kindly help me to remember our last meeting."

Mushota explained to me that two of his elder brothers, Higgins and Mwape, used to play youth football with me when he was a small boy. Indeed, Higgins and Mwape were my childhood friends before their father got transferred to work in Mumbwa, a town in Central Province of Zambia, and the family left Luanshya. By the way, Mushota later went on to get a PhD from the University of Southampton in the England, so I will address him appropriately as Dr Mushota Kabaso.

Dr Kabaso then followed up with another question: "So, how's the family, mdala?"

I smiled and said, "I am not married. I am still single."

Then, he said lightheartedly, "I will introduce you to my cousin. She is a fine young lady."

I asked him what his cousin did for a living, and added, "At my level, it must be someone who has gone to school, preferably, holds at least a Masters degree or a PhD from a decent university. If not, then it must be someone with not only a first degree but a professional doctorate, such as a medical doctor. You know I am sapiosexual."

Dr Kabaso smiled and said, "She actually just graduated from UNZA Medical School as a medical doctor and is currently completing her medical residency (internship) at the University Teaching Hospital (UTH) in Lusaka."

I asked Dr Kabaso a few questions to make sure that I had the facts right and that we were on the same page. The feedback was encouraging. To cut the long story short, that is how I met my wife. I did not meet her in Lusaka, Luanshya or any part of Zambia. No, I was first introduced to her and her professional standing in the field of medicine when I was in Moscow, Russia. That was how it started. I am moved by substance, not form. I always separate wheat from the chaff. Indeed, it was not like one of those mundane local introductions at a local eating or drinking place in Lusaka; far from it. It was in Moscow, Russia, at the residence of the Zambian Ambassador to Russia where I first heard of my wife. Her name was mooted to me at the Ambassador's residence as we all dined and wined that evening. My extensive international travels thus helped me to meet my wife through her cousin in Moscow, Russia.

I am ever grateful to His Excellency General Francis Sibamba and his dear wife, Mrs Sibamba, for providing me with an enabling environment to meet someone who would then introduce me to my dearest wife, Dr Judith Mvula-Mwenda. I believe God always brings people in your life for a reason.

A year after I got married, that is, in 2003, I lost my father. I was working in the ECSPF Department at the World Bank at the time. I was devastated, as I was very close to him and was his favorite child. My father knew that I always worked so hard to honor and uphold the family name. I may not be perfect, but would always strive to do good, choosing to see things through the eyes of the heart. In most families, there are children who bring honor and those who sometimes bring shame or embarrassment. In my case, I would always strive to do good and bring honor to the family.

When I lost my father, I made sure that I covered most of my father's funeral expenses instead of claiming that I had spent so much on air tickets for my wife and me as well as for my young brother, Eugene, to travel to Zambia, and thus had run out of money. Similarly, when I lost my mother two decades later, I made sure that I covered most of her funeral expenses before I even got on the plane to fly to Zambia. Our Christian faith is often tested when it comes to money. When I lost my other siblings, Kelvin and Francis, again much of the financial responsibility fell on me. I have heard stories of some families where people can be quite frugal, always claiming that they have no money or that their money is held up somewhere as they wait for a cheque payment to clear, so that other family members can take over the funeral expenses. It's shameful. I am one person who does not shy away from responsibility. In our African culture, it is deeply irresponsible and shameful behavior to be frugal at a funeral or to corruptly and inappropriately embezzle funds donated by some mourners for the funeral. A wise man knows that you should never expect or wait for outsiders to handle matters that are your responsibility as a family.

On the evening of August 13, 2003, I travelled to Zambia with my wife when I received news that my father had suffered a second stroke and was critically ill. The prognosis was not good. I could not wait. The inevitable appeared obvious. And I could not leave my dearest wife behind. I also had to buy another round-trip air ticket for my immediate younger brother, Eugene, who was an MBA student at Cardiff University in the United Kingdom, so that he too could travel to Zambia immediately. Otherwise, Eugene, on his own, would not have made it to Zambia. I had to step in. When you are in the diaspora, unlike back home in Africa where relatives and friends often chip in to help you out financially if you have a family bereavement, it is wise not to expect other people from outside the family to shoulder your financial burdens. The onus is on you and your family. I was able to demonstrate that am responsible enough as a man to take of my own and those close to me. In life, you always have to be ready to attend to emergencies. So, I bought all the three emergency round-trip air-tickets to Zambia for my wife, myself and Eugene, in addition, of course, to dealing with the heavy funeral expenses during and after the funeral in Zambia. It is always a decent thing to plan your financial affairs and not to bother other people with requests for financial contributions when you are faced with such an emergency. While unsolicited support is welcome, it is wise to avoid any kind of solicitation.

When my father died, my wife and I had only been married for a year. I had a huge wedding bill to attend to, but luckily I had planned for our elegant and classy yacht wedding. Also, I had just put my wife in graduate school for her MBA degree studies soon after our wedding. I could have easily used these two arguments as an excuse to ask other people to help me financially with the funeral expenses of my father's funeral, but I did not. I am a man. I was not raised like that. I was raised by my parents to be a responsible son, so I had to honor my father as a responsible son and man would do. By parity of reasoning, it is not in dispute that some people will have limited or no financial means, and that different people are faced with different financial situations. There is no contest there. But if you have the means and then choose to be frugal or to act like a miser, yours is nothing but irresponsible behavior. Generally, the idea of soliciting finances from people can be embarrassing, especially if you are not short of financial means. It is often an indication of irresponsible behavior on the part of the party soliciting funds for funeral expenses unless it can be shown or proven otherwise.

My wife and I arrived in Lusaka, Zambia, via South Africa, the following day and were picked up at the airport in Lusaka by a close family friend of my other older brother, Dennis, since the whole family was already in Luanshya attending Dad's funeral. Eugene arrived in Zambia from England a couple or so hours before we got to Zambia. Hon Mr Gaston Sichilima, who was a Deputy Minister in the Zambian Government at the time, was waiting for my wife and me at Kenneth Kauda International Airport in Lusaka.

When we left Washington DC, my father was still in a coma. The situation was quite bad. But when we landed in Lusaka, I noticed from the somber mood of Hon Mr Sichilima, who is usually a jovial person, that something was not right. He ushered my wife and me to the VIP lounge at the airport in Lusaka and then broke the news that we had lost Dad earlier in the day while we were en route to Zambia. The news was too much to bear. I did not know how to react. The shock was a bit too much. I did not expect it to happen so fast.

I remained quiet for a while. I had told my mother on the phone when I called her from Washington DC to let Dad know that I was about to start off for Zambia, even though I knew he was in a coma. I was hoping against hope that he would wait for me, but by the time I got to Zambia, he was gone that same day, on August 14, 2003.

There was silence in the VIP room. I thanked Hon Mr Sichilima for being there for us. He offered to let my wife and me spend a night at his residence in Lusaka and then we all proceeded together to Luanshya the following day, August 15, for the funeral.

We started off for Lunashya, as planned, in the early hours of the morning. I am ever grateful to Hon Mr Sichilima for being there for us. He had his official government vehicle with the Zambian flag installed, with the driver following all protocols as we journeyed from Lusaka to the Copperbelt. We arrived in Lunashya in the evening. Everyone was waiting for us. I was broken. A few days before my father passed on, I had been speaking with him on the phone and promising him that I would see him in a couple of weeks or so when I travel to Zambia for summer vacation, not knowing that that was the last time I would ever hear from him.

When travelling to Zambia, I had carried sufficient cash to ensure that all funeral expenses were taken care of mainly from my end without bothering or soliciting funds from outsiders. And everything went as planned. Unfortunately, the day we were putting my father to rest, August 16, 2003, I got an email from Washington DC informing me that my director at the World Bank, Mr Paul Siegelbaum, had also died. It was a sudden, unexpected death. I was told he had collapsed while playing tennis. So, I lost both my father and my director at work in the space of three days. Things were never the same in ECSPF after Paul passed away. His shoes were too big to fill.

In December 2004, I left ECSPF to rejoin the World Bank's Legal Vice-Presidency (LEG) as Senior Counsel in the then newly developed unit that covered knowledge management (LEGKM). Within the first three months of my rejoining LEG, I produced a manuscript of a book for the World Bank Legal Vice-Presidency. The book dealt with contemporary legal, policy and institutional aspects of private and financial sector development. It was the first book ever to be written by a LEG lawyer on private and financial sector development under the World Bank Legal Vice-Presidency's flagship book series, 'Law, Justice and Development Series.' The manuscript of the book had to undergo rigorous peer-review by two seasoned reviewers who were both my seniors in LEG. The work was unanimously accepted by the reviewers and approved by the editorial board of the World Bank Law, Justice and Development Series for publication as a book. It was published the following year, 2006, under the title: K.K. Mwenda, *Legal Aspects of Financial Services Regulation and the Concept of a Unified Regulator*, (Washington DC: The World Bank, 2006).

I always thank the Good Lord Jehovah Almighty for this gift of writing. What seems impossible to others is something that I am able to do with comparative ease. In fact, in that very year, 2006, I had two other books published, and all three books were monographs and not co-authored. I was the sole author of all three. These books are not compendiums of cases, statutes or treaties, nor is any of them a collection of contributions from various authors. I remember one seasoned colleague in LEG saying to me, 'I have never come across anyone who has published three books in one year! This is just unbelievable.'

When I first joined the Legal Vice-Presidency of the World Bank (LEG) in 1999, that is, after spending a year as a Young Professional in the World Bank's Resource Mobilization and Co-Financing Vice-Presidency and the World Bank's Poverty Reduction and Economic Management Vice-Presidency, I found in LEG an inspiring intellectual luminary, Dr Ibrahim Shihata, who had served as Senior Vice-President and General Counsel of the World Bank from 1983 to 1998 and as Secretary General of the International Centre for Settlement of Investment Disputes (ICSID) from 1983 to 2000. I recalled earlier in the book sitting next to Dr Shihata at an LEG Christmas party held at the New Zealand Embassy in Washington DC. Dr Shihata was an unassuming man, with an insightful and open mind. This was a man who was very highly respected at the World Bank and beyond, and he remains arguably one of the most highly regarded General Counsels to have headed the Legal Vice-Presidency of the World Bank. I had heard of Dr Shihata whilst I was in academia in the United Kingdom. The man was so well read and widely published too. He held a Doctor of Juridical Science (SJD) degree from Harvard Law School. Dr Shihata was truly an intellectual giant. Without doubt, he was the most published lawyer at the World Bank in his time. Dr Shihata retired and left the World Bank not too long after I joined the LEG. He went on to take up a professorial chair at the University of Dundee in Scotland.

By the time I was leaving the Legal Vice-Presidency of the World Bank in 2012 to move to another World Bank Vice-Presidency, that is, the Integrity Vice-Presidency (INT), I had, like Dr Shihata, become the most published lawyer in the entire Legal Vice-Presidency of the World Bank. I recall one particular incident when one of the Chief Counsels in LEG came to my office to see me on what I thought was a business-related matter. I had no idea what it was. After we chatted a bit, the Chief Counsel asked me politely if it was okay for him to close the door behind me so that we could chat privately. I had no objections. Then he opened up to me and said, "Kenneth, I know you write very well. I need a huge favor, my brother. I am applying for a big position and need your support with a well-written application letter. Can you help me with preparing one?"

It was a very humbling request and experience. All along I thought that nobody was paying attention to my prolific scholarly writing, but I was wrong. They were following me. I assured him of my full support and proceeded to assist accordingly. And he got the job. Thereafter, a number of colleagues in LEG would approach me quietly to help them write up personal documents in support of their career progression. Word had gone around that if anyone needed to get a document well written, all they had to do was go to Kenneth. At some point, I was invited quietly to write a major keynote speech for one General Counsel at the World Bank that was later published as a journal article. My scholarly writing in academia was visible. It is not something that I could hide. Even the World Bank was benefitting from that talent. In 2008, while serving as Senior Counsel in the Legal Vice-Presidency of the World Bank (LEG), I was conferred upon by Rhodes University, a leading South African university, the coveted and prestigious Higher Doctorate degree of Doctor of Laws (LLD), in recognition of the substantial body of my published scholarly work. As Senior Counsel in LEG, I also served as peer-reviewer of eight major World Bank Insolvency-Creditor Rights Assessments (ICR-ROSC). These were ICR-ROSCs for Thailand, South Africa, Ghana, Kenya, Zambia, Kyrgyz Republic, Jordan and Tanzania, respectively. In addition, I carried out single-handedly the ICR-ROSC of Uganda.

I remember flying to Uganda in 2005. I flew with Lufthansa Airlines from Washington DC to Frankfurt, Germany. From Frankfurt, I connected to Entebbe, Uganda, with Lufthansa again. The Washington DC-Frankfurt leg was Business Class while the Frankfurt-Entebbe leg was First Class. I got an upgrade to First Class in Frankfurt using my frequent traveler points.

As I boarded the plane, I saw an elderly lady in the First Class cabin in the company of a very good-looking young lady who was carrying a baby. I had no idea who they were. I decided strategically to chat with the old lady, who was seated across the aisle and not too far from my seat, to avoid the young lady thinking that I was trying to be 'funny' with her, but I knew that through the old lady I would eventually greet the young lady and her baby as well.

So I began with cordial greetings and polite conversation with the old lady. She said she was travelling with her daughter and granddaughter. So, of course, I had to greet them too. The old lady never said who she was but asked me if I was Ugandan. I told her I was from Zambia. I also mentioned a few names of close friends in Uganda whose names were in the public domain. She recognized some of the names as we chatted. As we approached Entebbe, two African guys who sat behind me tapped me on the shoulder and said, "Are you with the First Family?"

The two men were part of the security detail of the First Family. It was then that I realized that the old lady I was talking to was Hon Mrs Janet Museveni. I quickly informed the men that I was just a simple guy travelling on my own.

I remained calm as the pilot made an announcement upon landing that all passengers had to remain seated in their seats as the First Family disembarked. I politely said goodbye to her without any panic. I think the First Lady understood that I was an innocent foreigner who did not recognize her and the family until the announcement was made by the pilot.

Suffice it to say I had a good mission in Uganda and visited many places, including Jinja, the second largest town after Kampala in Uganda, the Uganda Martyrs Catholic Shrine, Namugongo, and the source of the Nile River close to Lake Victoria in Jinja. I also enjoyed some lovely tilapia in Jinja. It is a common delicacy there.

At the World Bank, before transferring from the Legal Vice-Presidency (LEG) to the Integrity Vice-Presidency (INT), I switched from working with the LEGKM team to working with an operational unit that focused on World Bank lending projects in the Middle East and South Asia (LEGMS). My manager in LEGMS was Mr Hans Juergen Gruss, a German lawyer. Later, LEGMS was renamed LEGEM to cover countries in Eastern Europe and Central Asia as well as those in the Middle East. I worked as the senior country lawyer for Kyrgyzstan, Tajikistan, Uzbekistan and Jordan, in addition to giving support to colleagues working for several other countries. I remember trying out some horse meat at a dinner in Bishkek city when I travelled to Kyrgyzstan.

I would often make my stopovers in Frankfurt, Munich or Bremen in Germany, or I would go via Vienna in Austria, before taking my connection flights to and from Eastern Europe or Central Asia. Occasionally, I would go via Paris, France, or Geneva, Switzerland. Amsterdam in the Netherlands or London UK were other popular stopovers before taking my connection flights.

I have shared below some pictures taken on one of my many trips to Amman, Jordan. When visiting Amman, I always took time to visit the Baptism Site of our Lord Jesus Christ at Bethany beyond the Jordan. The Baptism site is where our Lord Jesus Christ is reported to have been baptized by his cousin, John the Baptist. The place is on the banks of the Jordan River, as you go past the place in the desert where the Prophet Elijah is said to have been taken up to Heaven on a chariot of fire. The whole area is where John the Baptist is said to have spent much of his life. At the Baptism site, I once stood at a place that the tour guide informed me was the exact spot where Jesus Christ was baptized, trying to imagine the unimaginable. I was thinking that maybe I would hear the Voice from up on high and see the Holy Spirit descend in the form of a white dove, but nay. I waited and waited, to no avail. Perhaps I was being delusional. I must say though that I was so excited to be in that place, notwithstanding that Israel also has a place it calls the Baptism site.

Below is a picture of the signpost on the road to the Baptism site in Amman, Jordan, followed by a picture of where the tour guide pointed me as the actual spot where the baptism took place.

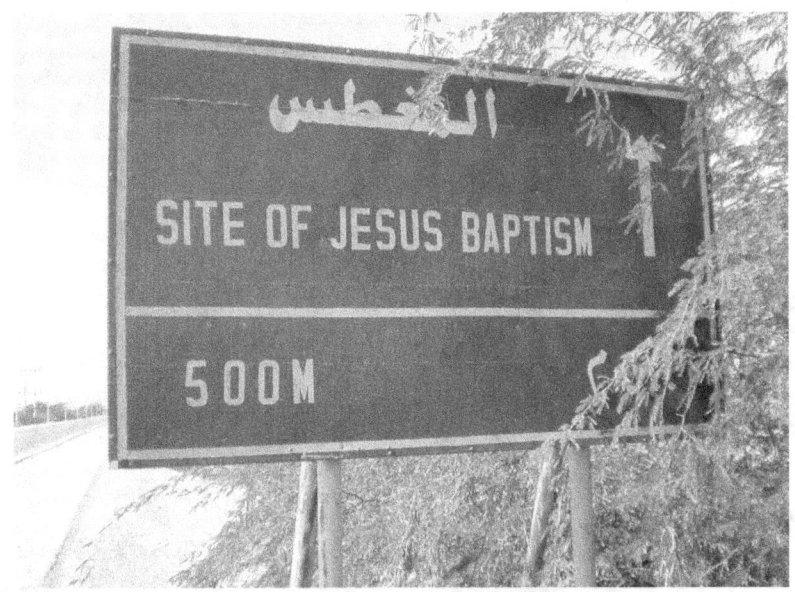

In the picture below, I am standing on the banks of the Jordan River on the Jordanian side after washing my face in the river. Across the river is of the State of Israel. The Jordan River forms the border between Israel and Jordan.

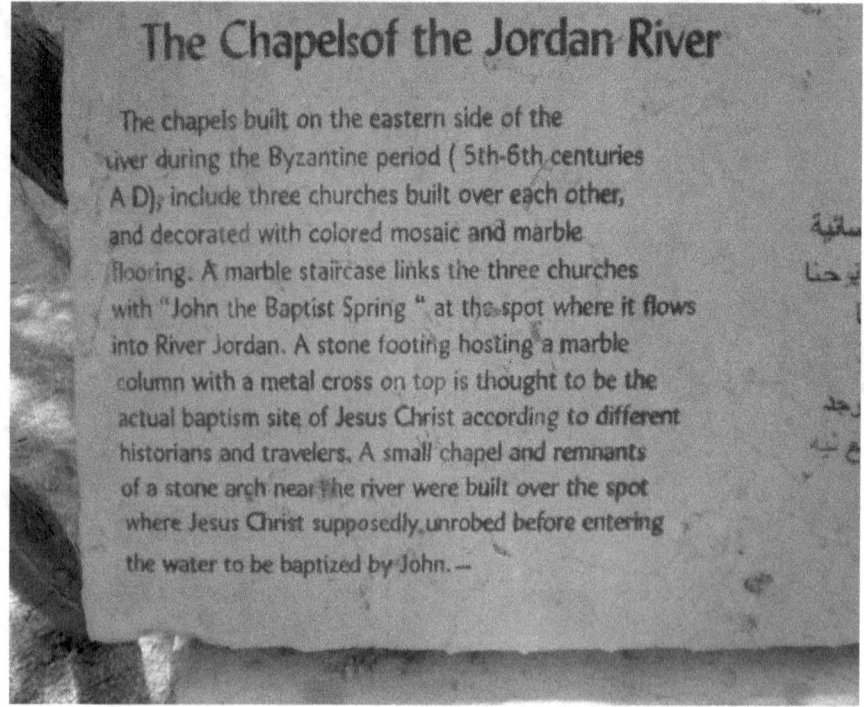

In Jordan, I would also visit the famous Dead Sea mentioned in the Bible. The Dead Sea is a landlocked salt lake whose main tributary is the Jordan River. Its shores are the lowest land-based elevation on Earth. The Dead Sea is also the deepest hypersaline lake in the world.

As Senior Counsel in LEGMS and LEGEM, my work focused mainly on the transactional work of World Bank lending operations, including drafting, amending and negotiating major legal agreements with the client countries of the World Bank as well as providing legal guidance to operational teams on the preparation and implementation of World Bank projects, as well as on the various World Bank lending operational policies and procedures. The sectors and issues covered under the various projects ranged from road construction and other infrastructure, and dam construction and safety to land resettlement as well as environment and social impact assessments, public health, energy, education, higher education, financial sector development, private sector development, mining, agriculture, livestock, telecommunications and many more. Aside from working on investment lending operations, I also covered development policy lending operations, prepared several co-financing operations of the World Bank and task-managed some trust funds.

In early 2012, I decided to move from LEG to INT in the same capacity as Senior Counsel.

In INT, I provided real-time advisory services to World Bank operational staff on integrity risks and preventive measures to address them in the context of the design and implementation of high-risk World Bank operations. I also conducted integrity reviews at the sector, country, project or instrument levels based on INT's investigative information, as part of project preparation or supervision and INT Preventive Services Unit's (PSU's) analytic work. Further, I helped to develop diagnostic tools for World Bank staff and stakeholders in World Bank client countries to better detect and prevent integrity risks. Additionally, I not only developed and delivered training and capacity-building programs, in coordination with other World Bank units, for World Bank staff and partners focused on fraud detection and risk mitigation, but also supported the implementation of the World Bank's Governance and Anti-Corruption (GAC) Agenda in collaboration with operational colleagues in World Bank regional and sector units. Additionally, I led policy dialog for major World Bank anti-corruption initiatives, including carrying out substantial legal, regulatory and compliance work for the prevention of fraud and corruption in several World Bank-funded projects in countries such as Senegal, Malawi, Niger, Mozambique, Cameroon, Guinea, Ethiopia, Sudan, Burundi, Uganda, Congo, Seychelles and Nigeria.

The Vice-President of INT at the time was a South African, Mr Leonard F McCarthy. He and I connected well, and he appreciated my potential and expertise. I remember in 2012 when I lost my eldest brother, Kelvin, I sent an email to inform senior management in my VPU (INT), and only Leonard replied. I did not hear from the others. Ordinarily, one would expect some empathy, but only Leonard came through. So I was left wondering. Leonard told me not to worry, but by then I had already started looking to move.

To put my MBA skills to work, I took up a leadership role in 2013 to head the World Bank Group Voice Secondment Program (VSP). The VSP is a capacity-building initiative of the World Bank Board of Executive Director aimed at strengthening the capacity of key governmental focal agencies of World Bank client countries in their knowledge of World Bank operational policies, procedures and processes so as to strengthen their dialog and relationship with World Bank operational teams as well as with the offices of the World Bank Executive Directors. The picture below was taken when I was welcoming a cohort of the VSP Secondees to the World Bank in Washington DC, USA.

Some VSP alumni have gone on to occupy senior government positions. For example, in Gabon, a VSP alumnus, Hon Ms Justine Judith Lekogo, served as Deputy Minister of Finance of Gabon after graduating from the VSP and is now a member of the Gabonese National Assembly and a Senator in the transitional parliament of Gabon where she serves as 'third rapporteur for the Finance Commission for budget and public accounts.' In Georgia, Hon Ms Ekaterine Guntsadze, another VSP alumnus, serves as the Deputy Minister of Finance. In Bangladesh, too, Mr Delwar Hossain, also a VSP alumnus, is now the Joint Secretary of the Economic Relations Division in the Ministry of Finance. In the picture below, the then Deputy Minister of Finance of Gabon, Hon Ms Justine Judith Lekogo, stopped by my office at the World Bank in Washington DC for a courtesy call.

Below are some pictures taken with my VSP Secretariat colleagues and some recent cohorts of VSP Secondees at the World Bank.

2025 VSP Cohort 20

At the World Bank, I have also served previously on an intermittent basis as Acting Director of the Corporate Affairs and Administration Division (SECCA) in the Corporate Secretariat Vice-Presidency. The pictures below, starting with my Versace badge holder, were taken on arrival at the United Nations (UN) headquarters in New York, US, when I was leading a 30-member VSP delegation from the World Bank in Washington DC to the UN.

In the picture below, the VSP delegation from the World Bank is being addressed by His Excellency Ambassador Lazarous Kapambwe, who served as the sixty-seventh President of the United Nations Economic and Social Council (UN-ECOSOC) as well as the Ambassador and Permanent Representative of the Republic of Zambia to the United Nations in New York, US.

Below is a picture of His Excellency Ambassador Mr Kapambwe and I at the conclusion of the presentation on the work of UN-ECOSOC.

As the manager and executive head of the World Bank Voice Secondment Program (VSP) in Washington DC, US, I lead and manage the VSP Secretariat as well as the Program itself, with approximately 35 professionals reporting to me under the Program and the Secretariat. As the team-lead, I provide executive leadership in program development and delivery of the VSP, focusing on designing, developing, directing and managing all aspects of the program, including:

1. formulating program policies and business processes based on the business criteria agreed upon by the World Bank Board of Executive Directors, and further developing implementation plans and actions to implement said policies and processes;

2. preparing annual work plans and managing resources using inputs from all respective parties;

3. ensuring that the budget is appropriately allocated as well as effectively monitored and timely reported;

4. providing executive leadership in the identification, selection and placement of candidates under the VSP;

5. coordinating with the World Bank Executive Directors' offices and the World Bank regional units in the identification, selection and placement of candidates under the VSP;
6. coordinating the identification of productive terms of reference for the Secondees in the World Bank's operational units;
7. developing a clear work program, including a mission assignment for each Secondee; and
8. organizing, coordinating and supervising various phases of the capacity-building initiative and ensuring the finalization of the secondment assignment of each selected government official, as well as signing the legal and recruitment documents, including providing candidates with pertinent and necessary information, and implementing the appointment process.

Further, as head of the VSP, I am responsible for:

(9) providing leadership in capacity-building, knowledge agenda, learning and development;
(10) carrying out quality assurance, program monitoring and evaluation;
(11) carrying out outreach, public relations and information management activities; and
(12) carrying out such administrative tasks as designing, planning and supervising the contracting and monitoring of effective implementation of the logistical arrangements for Secondees and the efficient management of assignment benefits as well as supervising and planning the work program of all staff in the Secretariat of the VSP.

Among the key milestones of the VSP under my leadership are the development and implementation of a major diversity, inclusion and equity strategy that was approved by the World Bank Board of Executive Directors to give equal opportunities to men and women to participate in the VSP as well as the bringing on board of participants from low- and middle-income countries that have had the least number of participation, especially candidates from Fragile and Conflict-Affected States (FCS) and Small Island Developing States (SIDS).

The pictures below were taken at some of the VSP events in Washington DC, celebrating the accomplishments and contributions of several VSP host team members and the VSP cohorts.

PROF KENNETH K MWENDA

A smile in the middle of work, as seen below, can make a difference in a world where we are all busy with our everyday engagements.

Leadership requires you to connect with people, as can be seen in the picture below.

In the two pictures below, I can be seen relaxed at one of my yacht parties in Washington DC, US, while sailing away on the Potomac River. It's that happy moment when you inform your guests that they can drink as much as they want because all drinks are on you.

Concurrent with my role as head of the World Bank Voice Secondment Program (VSP), I also head the Disclosure of Interests (DOI) program for the World Bank Board of Executive Directors, a governance tool that deals with business risks and compliance risks of Board officials, including pertinent aspects of monitoring and reporting. In this role, I lead, *inter alia*, the development and implementation of a DOI strategy for managing business and compliance risks of Board officials as well as manage the confidentiality aspects of the DOI program.

But then, one might be tempted to ask, with all this global experience that I have accumulated over the years internationally, why don't I help out my country back home? Let us take a more reasoned look. First, I did mention earlier in this book some philanthropic work that I do with an educational institution run by some Franciscan Catholic nuns in Zambia. Secondly, when I was lecturing at the University of Warwick in the UK, the Zambian Government, through the Securities and Exchange Commission (SEC), which was then headed by Ambassador Mr Mumba Kapumpa, flew me from the UK to Zambia to help them with work on reforming the laws on securities regulation in Zambia.

Thirdly, when I moved to the World Bank, SEC again flew me to Zambia, but this time from South Africa, where I was giving some lectures. I travelled to Zambia to give a SEC Master Class on securities regulation. Fourthly, I mentioned the case of many young Africans that I have continued to mentor, coach and teach over the years at various academic institutions worldwide. I have also secured scholarships and job placements for a number of them. Fifthly, I did mention my service to the academic community in Africa, specifically, both in terms of research and teaching.

Sixthly, I remember in my early years as a lawyer at the World Bank in Washington DC when I was involved in the preparation of a conference on international trade law. We were trying to line up possible speakers at the event. A name of one of my lecturers in First Year at the University of Zambia (UNZA) came to mind. It was Professor Oliver S. Saasa. Professor Saasa had also served as the Secretary of the Rhodes Scholarship Selection Committee for Zambia when I was selected as a Rhodes Scholar for Zambia. I remembered that he was always well-prepared for his lectures at UNZA and never missed a class. He struck me as a diligent, professional and well-organized scholar, and I knew that he was the kind of person I could recommend and who would do Zambia proud, especially as he had done some commendable scholarly work in the field of regional integration in the Southern Africa Development Community (SADC) and the Common Market for Eastern and Southern Africa (COMESA).

I recommended Professor Saasa together with that of another leading Zambian scholar, Professor Gerry Nkombo Muuka, who was then a Professor of Management at Murray State University in Kentucky, US. We were honored at the World Bank in Washington DC to have both Professor Saasa and Professor Muuka give their remarkable presentations, and I am ever grateful to both of them for having accepted the invitations and for having done Zambia proud.

Finally, on a somewhat disappointing note, I must say that you cannot force yourself on a people unless they are willing to welcome you. A few years ago, the CEO of a key government institution in Zambia surprised me with a pleasant email. It was indeed kind of him to reach out, and I am ever grateful. He emailed me to say that the government institution that he was heading needed my expertise to help them with some technical work that they were carrying out. I called him up and we spoke. I was to be seconded to that government institution as his advisor for a period of about two years. The CEO then said that I should kindly get in touch with one of the members of his senior management team who I mistakenly thought was a good friend and would magnanimously do the needful to finalize the arrangement. But I was wrong. All I can say here is that, as Voltaire once said, "Lord, protect me from my friends; I can take care of my enemies." For we often know who our enemies are and how they are busy scheming all manner of shenanigans behind our backs, but we do not know who our true friends are, or those who, among the so-called 'friends', may betray us. And so, we need God's protection from those 'friends' whose hearts we do not know fully well before they betray us.

My thinking was that the deal at that government institution was sealed and that all that was remaining was the logistics and formalities. Unfortunately, Voltaire was right. I needed God's protection from someone I thought was a friend. In the end, it is the country, Zambia, that loses out on the exceptional skills of its best people out there in the diaspora simply because of unnecessary personalization of issues.

On March 23, 2024, one of my mentees shared with me via WhatsApp an interesting post from social media, with a caption of his own, which brought back memories of the government institution story that I have shared above. I have reproduced below the social media post shared by my mentee.

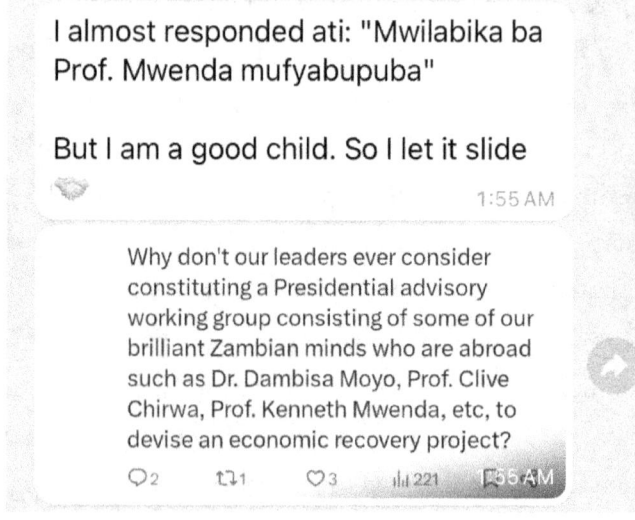

The dialog above speaks to some of the issues and challenges that many diasporans face each time we think of engaging in productive work back home. Yes, we are willing to help, and let it be known that not everyone from the diaspora comes with an 'I know it all' attitude. The locals must be open-minded enough not to feel threatened or intimidated. They must be willing and ready to receive or welcome their own. But, as Bob Marley once sang in his song *Survival:*

Some people put the best outside...
A good man is never honoured (survivors)
In his own country (Black survival)
Nothing change, nothing strange (survivors)
Nothing change, nothing strange (Black survivors)
We got to survive, you all! (survivors).

CHAPTER 14

Ambidexterity in global thought leadership

Once a scholar, always a scholar. You can deviate, take a detour, go on sabbatical, take leave with or without pay, get appointed to some lofty position, or simply sojourn at some place along the way, but the underlying fulcrum of who you are is that you are a scholar. It never leaves you, unless you were not a scholar from the very beginning. The global character of your thought leadership as a scholar cannot and will not remain a secret forever. Hiding your God-given talent is like denying who you are. There is nothing wrong in being different. For, we are all not cut from the same cloth and cannot therefore be the same. After all, there is strengthen in diversity, inclusion and equity. Society is not, and has never been, homogenous. Rather, it is heterogenous. Any attempt at fashioning society into some monolithic or uniform worldview only invites group think and dogmatism. Indeed, group think often results from excessive conformity to the values and norms of those who have the power to influence the ideology of members of a group, team or society. One has to step back a bit and take a bird's eye view of things to appreciate the value of objectivity over subjectivity. And an ambidextrous approach, as I contend, allows you to use both your left and right hands without feeling inadequate on either side. This is a metaphor for the life I have lived and the approach I have taken.

The dualism and ambivalence inherent in ambidexterity is a strength, not a weakness. To be able to do two things at the same time and to execute for the moment while anticipating tomorrow often speaks to a great vision. It also speaks to greater capabilities than those of someone who can only do one thing at a time. Ambidexterity is not the same thing as multi-tasking. Rather, it invites you to deal with the present while envisioning the future. This is an approach that I have embraced professionally without fear or apology. I am who I am.

Even though I am an international development practitioner, I am also a scholar, thought-leader and public intellectual. My thought leadership cannot, and should not, suffer just because of my busy schedule as a practitioner. I simply have to apportion my time appropriately to drive in different lanes at different times. There is time to drive in the High Occupancy Vehicle (HOV) lane and time to avoid the HOV lane. If anything, as I submit, to be effective as a well-rounded practitioner, a person can do well to leverage his or her knowledge skills as well. For, there is nothing as practical as a good theory. Indeed, there is strength in drawing synergies from both sides of the aisle. To that end, on June 26, 2022, the *Sunday Mail* newspaper of Zambia published the article reproduced here.

Marrying theory and practice, I have maintained a dual career in academia and international development practice. There is a symbiotic relationship between the two. One simply has to find the right balance. In a world that is constantly challenged by emerging technologies such as artificial intelligence, the field of practice can best cope with the pace of change by twinning with the knowledge world.

As the media article above demonstrates, my international development practice has benefitted from my global thought leadership as much as my international development practice has helped to inform my global thought leadership. While engaged in a busy professional career at the World Bank, I have also held concurrently over the years a number of senior academic appointments at various leading universities. Closely related to this,

---

Mwenda: Law professor extraordinaire

VIOLET MENGO

WASHINGTON DC-based Zambia's renowned legal luminary, Professor Kenneth Mwenda, has been appointed to the prestigious academic rank of extraordinary Professor of Law in the Department of Mercantile and Labour Law at the University of Western Cape in Cape Town, South Africa.

A man of firsts, Prof Mwenda continues to serve concurrently as the executive head of the World Bank Voice Secondment Programme (VSP) in Washington DC, USA.

In 1998 he became the first Zambian to join the World Bank under the Young Professionals Programme (YPP), and other Zambians have since followed in his footsteps.

Prof Mwenda notes: "Sometimes, you have to go where there is no trail and chart the path for others to follow. It is an honour to serve at the highest level."

In 2009 Prof Mwenda became the first Zambian legal scholar to be appointed to the rank of Extraordinary Professor of Law when the University of Pretoria in South Africa appointed him to that rank.

Later, he served again as Extraordinary Professor of Law at the same university, the University of Pretoria.

Prof Mwenda has taught law in three continents, namely Europe, North America and Africa.

In the US, he has served as Adjunct Professor of Law at American University Washington College of Law (WCL) in Washington DC.

In 1995, at the age of only 26 years, he became the first Zambian legal scholar to be appointed to a full-time Law Lectureship at one of the top 10 British universities, the University of Warwick.

Truly a man of firsts, Prof Mwenda remains the only Zambian legal scholar to have been honoured for his exceptionally outstanding scholarly work by two successive Zambian governments, the MMD government under President Rupiah Banda that appointed him as Honorary Tourism Ambassador for Zambia, and the PF government under President Edgar Lungu that conferred on him the Presidential Insignia of Meritorious Achievement (PIMA).

Prof Mwenda has also received national honours from the then Governor of the Bank of Zambia, Dr Caleb Fundanga, at a ceremony officiated by the then Chief Justice of Zambia, Ernest Sakala (rtd), and attended by the then Deputy Chief Justice of Zambia, Lombe Chibesakunda, and many other eminent persons and distinguished scholars.

Prof Mwenda has also served as Visiting Full Professor of Law at a number of leading universities in Europe and South Africa, including the University of Miskolc in Hungary and the University of Cape Town.

He is author of 27 scholarly books in addition to more than 100 articles in leading academic journals worldwide.

Prof Mwenda is a Rhodes Scholar and alumnus of the University of Oxford and Harvard University John F Kennedy School of Government.

He is a recipient of a prestigious scholarly award from Yale University Law School. Prof Mwenda is an avid learner and has attended many other leading universities, including MIT, Stanford, INSEAD, London Business School, Northwestern, Cornell, and Georgetown.

He is a soccer enthusiast. Prof Mwenda recently became the first Zambian to obtain top professional soccer coaching credentials from Barcelona Football Club Coaching Academy, a leading soccer coaching academy in the world.

In 2008 and 2014, respectively, after a rigorous and thorough examination of Prof Mwenda's selected scholarly books and peer-refereed journal articles by two leading universities in South Africa and the United Kingdom, namely Rhodes University and the University of Hull, Prof Mwenda was admitted to the rarely awarded Higher Doctorate degrees of Doctor of Laws (Rhodes, LLD, 2008) and Doctor of Science in Economics (Hull, DSc (Econ), 2014).

Until 2019, there was no other known legal scholar in the entire English-speaking world with two Higher Doctorates in two different disciplines.

In 2008, Prof Mwenda became the first and only Zambian academician to be ever conferred upon a higher doctorate degree in any academic discipline.

He broke his own record when he received his second higher doctorate, the DSc (Econ).

Prof Mwenda also holds a PhD in Securities Regulation from the University of Warwick.

At the World Bank, Prof Mwenda has served for a decade as Senior Counsel in the Legal Vice-Presidency, as well as Senior Counsel in the World Bank's Integrity Vice-Presidency, before taking up his current managerial role as head of the VSP. A highly sought-after thought-leader, Prof Mwenda has been interviewed and quoted by numerous print and broadcast media, including the New York Times (USA), the Voice of America (VOA, USA), CCTV (USA), the Times (UK), the British Broadcasting Corporation (BBC, UK), and Sky TV (UK).

I have maintained a sustained scholarly publications record and have supervised and examined several PhD dissertations at a number of leading universities around the world.

In 1996, while teaching at the University of Warwick in England, I took leave to serve as a Visiting Full Professor of Law at the University of Miskolc in Hungary. I flew from London to Budapest and then took a train from Budapest to Miskolc. It was a great experience. Budapest, as the capital city of Hungary, was, of course, more cosmopolitan than Miskolc, which is the fourth largest city in Hungary. That said, the University of Miskolc is the largest university in the northern part of Hungary.

When I got to Miskolc, I was well received by my hosts at the University of Miskolc. I gave lectures in the English law of Trusts and Public International Law. After my professorial engagement in Hungary, I took a train from Bishkek back to Budapest enroute to Bucharest, Romania. The train I took from Budapest to Bucharest was coming from Poland. I boarded the train in Budapest and was booked in a carriage where I found a young white lady about my age. She was travelling alone and was also headed to Bucharest. There were just the two of us in the carriage. The carriage had two extended seats on either side on which each one would stretch down to sleep, and a door for privacy. The young white lady was cool and nice. She greeted me and we chatted briefly. I then put my luggage in the luggage area of the train carriage before sitting down to relax.

It was an overnight trip, and there were just the two of us in the carriage, a black man and a white woman. It did not even cross my mind that this would be a source of concern for the security folks on the train. I wondered why the guards kept checking our carriage every fifteen to twenty minutes, asking the white lady if everything was okay. Somehow, my subconscious informed me that the security guards, who were all white men, of course, could not trust a black man left alone with a white woman in a secluded train carriage. But I just ignored them and kept my cool until we got to Bucharest the following morning around 11:00am.

It was the first time I had travelled to Hungary and Romania, though I later got to visit both countries again a number of times after I joined the World Bank. Also, I got to visit Warsaw, Poland, after joining the World Bank, carrying out some work there on financial services regulation.

In Bucharest, Romania, I got to see the presidential palace that President Nicolae Ceaușescu, the deposed Romanian communist politician and statesman, had built before he was overthrown in a revolution in 1989. The hotel where I was staying was not too far from there. I also visited the leading universities both in Budapest and Bucharest. Wherever I travel to, the places that are a priority on my to-do-list include visiting top universities, major cathedrals, national libraries, national museums, major government buildings and fine restaurants. That's just me. I have below and on the next pages some pictorial insights into my eclectic taste of finesse.

I know other folks could have different priorities that might include things I consider less edifying, especially things such as nightclubs, pubs, casinos, brothels, strip-clubs, prostitutes, and nightlife. Those items are never on my to-do list. For me, simply show me where the top universities, major cathedrals, national libraries, national museums, major government buildings and fine restaurants are. That is all I need.

Aside from the aforesaid European academic experience, my US academic experience includes my appointment in 2010 as Adjunct Professor of Law at American University Washington College of Law (WCL) while serving in the full-time employ of the World Bank. I taught international financial law and development at the American University, a fairly decent and well-ranked university located in the heart of Washington DC. I always wanted to augment my European academic experience of teaching at top European universities with teaching at some top American universities. And so, this was a perfect opportunity for me. In addition, in 2024, I was appointed to the prestigious Archibald McDougall Visiting Professorship in International Law at the University of Western Virginia Law School in Morgantown, West Virginia.

This visiting professorship was my second major academic appointment at a leading US law school, in addition, of course, to the many guest lectures and keynote addresses that I have given at such leading US universities as Duke University Law School in Durham, North Carolina; George

Washington University (GWU) Law School in Washington DC; Howard University Law School in Washington DC; the University of South Florida in Tampa, Florida; and Bridgewater College in Bridgewater, Virginia.

On the African continent, the University of Cape Town (UCT) Graduate School of Business, arguably the best university and best business school on the African content, appointed me in May 2024 as Honorary Full Professor. I remain eternally grateful to my colleagues at UCT Graduate School of Business, especially Dr Mundia Kabinga, my good learned brother and friend, who is a Senior Lecturer at the said Graduate School of Business.

Prior to my appointment as Honorary Full Professor at UCT Graduate School of Business, I served in 2010 as Visiting Full Professor of Law at the University of Cape Town (UCT) Faculty of Law. Then, on June 1, 2022, I was appointed Extraordinary Professor of Law in the Faculty of Law at the University of Western Cape (UWC) in Cape Town, South Africa. Prior to that, I had been teaching at the same university as a visiting law professor since 2008. Below is a picture taken in 2019 at UWC with Professor Riekie Wandrag, standing on my right, and the Dean of UWC Faculty of Law, Professor Jacques de Ville, to my immediate left. On the far left is Professor Patricia Lenaghan. I am ever grateful to all the three for their edifying camaraderie, collegiality and kind support. Professor Riekie Wandrag, in particular, has been extremely helpful in my professional and academic endeavors over the years. I can't thank her enough.

Below is a picture of the Master of Laws (LLM) degree class in International Trade and Investment Law that I taught at UWC in 2020 just before the COVID-19 pandemic broke out.

In the first picture below, I can be seen engaging with some faculty members during my academic visit to UWC in 2020. In the second picture below, I can be seen with the Dean of the Law Faculty at UWC, Professor Jacques de Ville, at a cocktail reception hosted in my honor to welcome me to UWC Law Faculty.

In the picture below, I am with the Head of Department of the Mercantile and Labor Department at the UWC Faculty of Law, Professor Riekie Wandrag.

In the two pictures below, I am conferring with some colleagues at UWC Faculty of Law.

There are two pictures below of one of the earlier cohorts of the LLM class in International Trade and Investment Law that I taught at UWC follows. Some students from this class have gone on to complete their PhDs and are now leading scholars and professors at esteemed centers of learning such as the University of Botswana. Also, from that same class, I can proudly say that I produced a Minister of Public Service and Administration as well as a Minister of Communications. The Honorable Ms Faith Muthambi held these two ministerial positions in the South African Government under President Jacob Zuma. Ms Muthambi can be seen in the second picture below wearing a black polo T-shirt with a green collar. I took the first picture below myself.

I have also previously served as Extraordinary Professor in the Mercantile Law Department at the Faculty of Law of another leading South African university, the University of Pretoria in Pretoria. Additionally, I served as Extraordinary Professor of Law at the University of Pretoria's Center for Human Rights. And I continue to teach as a visiting professor on the University of Pretoria LLM degree program in International Trade and Investment Law.

I am most grateful to Professor Daniel D. Bradlow, Professor Christof Heyns, Professor André Boraine, Professor Corlia van Heerden, and Professor Frans Viljoen, as well as many other faculty colleagues at the University of Pretoria for their edifying camaraderie, collegiality and support over the years. I have shared below a picture of the LLM in class in International Trade and Investment Law that I taught in 2023 at the University of Pretoria in South Africa.

Below is a picture I took of the 2013 LLM class in International Trade and Investment Law that I taught at the University of Pretoria. A number of the students from this class have gone on to complete their PhDs and are now leading scholars and professors at various universities. Others are working for leading international organizations and multinational firms such as TikTok in England and the Confederation of African Football (CAF) in Egypt. I appear in the second picture below with all of them.

Below is a picture of another LLM class in International Trade and Investment Law that I taught in South Africa.

Further, as noted above, I served in 2010 as Visiting Full Professor of Law at the Faculty of Law of the University of Cape Town (UCT). I am exceedingly grateful to Professor Pamela Jane (P.J.) Schwikkard, the then Dean of the Faculty of Law at UCT, and Professor Evance Kalula, a fellow Rhodes Scholar, who at the time was Professor of Law at Faculty of Law at UCT and is now an Emeritus Professor of Law at the said law school, for facilitating my Visiting Professorship. Since then, I have examined a number of PhD dissertations both at UCT Faculty of Law and at UCT

Graduate School of Business. In the picture below, I can be seen at a dinner event hosted for me by Dr Mundia Kabinga, a Senior Lecturer at UCT Graduate School of Business, and Professor Evance Kalula. Indeed, I am ever grateful to both of them for their kind and generous hospitality. I am also indebted to Professor Evance Kalula's dear wife, Professor Sebastiana Zimba-Kalula, who is now an Emeritus Professor in the Faculty of Health Sciences at UCT as well as to Dr Mundia Kabinga's sister, Ms Moonde Kabinga, who is a PhD scholar at UCT, for their warm welcome when I visited Cape Town.

In the picture below, I was enjoying some organic salmon caught from the wild in Cape Town, South Africa.

In the picture below, I can be seen with my good learned elder brother, Professor Evance Kalula in Cape Town, South Africa.

In the picture below, I am with Professors Evance and Sebastiana Kalula in Cape Town, South Africa.

Closely related to this, I continue to hold the academic position of Extraordinary Professor of Law at the University of Lusaka (UniLus) in Zambia, where Professor Evance Kalula has also served as Chair of the UniLus Council. Professor Evance Kalula, a Zambian national, has served additionally as a member of the International Labor Organization (ILO) Commission of Inquiry on Freedom of Association in Zimbabwe and has previously been the Chair of the South African Employment Conditions Commission (ECC), as well as a member of the Ministerial Advisory Panel of the South African Department of Economic Development (EDD). His other credentials include being a fellow of the African Academy of Sciences (AAS), an advisor to the Academy of Sciences of South Africa (ASSAf) Council, and a member of the Institute for African Alternatives (IFAA) Board and the Southern African Social Protection Experts Network (SASPEN) Board of Guarantors as well as serving as President of the International Labour and Employment Relations Association (ILERA).

In the early years after the founding of the University of Lusaka, I worked closely with the university's Vice-Chancellor, Professor Pinalo Chifwanakeni, in the development of the curricula for a number of degree programs at UniLus. Also, I was quite instrumental in recommending to Professor Chifwanakeni the appointment of some accomplished colleagues as Lecturers and Extraordinary Professors at UniLus. Notable among those appointed were Professor Samuel Munzele Maimbo, based at the World Bank in Washington DC, Professor Mumba Ngulube-Zulu, also based at the World Bank in Washington DC, and Professor Kazhila C. Chinsembu, then based at the University of Namibia, and my former graduate student at the University of Pretoria, Professor Mulenga Chipasha, who joined UniLus as a law lecturer and then rose through the ranks to become the Dean of the Law School and Associate Professor.

I have always been selfless in giving friends a chance. I am never intimidated or insecure. Rather, I am very secure in my own skin. I must also commend the UniLus Vice-Chancellor, Professor Chifwanakeni, for his trust in me. Professor Chifwanakeni has done a commendable job in developing UniLus into a worldclass university and making outstanding contributions to the development the higher education in Zambia. UniLus is now one of the leading Zambian private universities. In the diaspora, I have also played a key role in supporting the tertiary education stages that have led to the professional careers of many Zambians, including: Dr Sombo Muzata-Chunda, who is now teaching at James Madison University in Virginia, US; Ms Marjorie Mpundu, who is now a Chief Counsel in the Legal Vice-Presidency of the World Bank in Washington DC; Mr Arnold Kaluba, who got his graduate education at the University of Oxford; Mr Glory Chipoya, who got his graduate legal education at American University Washington College of Law in Washington DC; Ms Kate Mando Munuka, who now works for TikTok in London, England; Ms Misozi Masengu, who got her graduate legal education at the University of Durham in England; Mr Edward Kapili, who had a short stint at the International Monetary Fund (IMF) in Washington DC before returning to Bank of Zambia; and many others at Harvard University and other top universities. I often joke that my signature alone can get you into Oxford, Harvard, Yale, Stanford, Princeton, Cambridge, MIT, Cornell, Georgetown, Columbia, or Sorbonne. Indeed, I have not only mentored but also gotten many colleagues admitted to a number of these prestigious schools.

I remember a funny incident leading to the first visit my eldest sister, Catherine, made to the United Kingdom. I had already relocated from England to the US at the time. My sister was having trouble getting a friend of hers in London who had promised her that she would send her an invitation letter to get a British visa in Zambia to travel to England for vacation. My sister had been busy praising that friend of hers without realizing that she was just blowing hot air. When my sister was getting ready to apply for a British visa, the so-called friend of hers in London disappeared and stopped communicating. My sister was stuck. Then, a good friend of mine who was my sister's workmate in Lusaka asked her why she could not just ask me her young brother to write the invitation letter. When I heard the story from my friend, I simply smiled. I'd guess my sister was doubting the power of her young brother's signature, hoping instead that a less established signature in London could work. Talk of a prophet is not without honor, except among his own! Anyhow, I wrote the invitation letter for my sister's maiden visit to the UK, and to proceed to the US after a week or two in the UK. That one invitation letter I wrote got her both the British and US visas. My signature worked for both visas. It's as simple as that. My sister was then able to travel to the UK and stayed with a family friend of my wife and me before she proceeded later to the US. I wanted my sister to see the US as well. So, I got her the UK-US air ticket for a month's vacation in the US.

In giving back to Zambia, I have also served as a Visiting Full Professor of Law at the University of Zambia (UNZA) Law School under the Deanship of Dr Frederick Ng'andu. I served as Visiting Full Professor of Law at UNZA Law School in 2001. Also, in Zambia, I have supervised and examined several PhD dissertations both at UniLus and ZCAS university in Zambia. Currently,

I am also supervising a number of PhD dissertations at UNZA. In 2015, I was invited to give the 2015 Distinguished Lecture at the University of Nairobi School of Law in Nairobi, Kenya. These prestigious lecture series are only given by eminent and distinguished scholars of international repute who are invited by the School of Law. I have shared below some pictures taken at that event.

In the picture below, I can be seen with the then Dean of the University of Nairobi School of Law, Professor Patricia Kameri-Mbote, when she was presenting me with a gift of appreciation after the delivery of my 2015 Distinguished Lecture. Professor Kameri-Mbote holds a doctorate in law (JSD) from Stanford University in the US and is one of the few Higher Doctorate degree-holders in the field of law on the African continent. She was awarded the prestigious Higher Doctorate degree of Doctor of Laws (LLD) by the University of Nairobi in 2019. Currently, Professor Kameri-Mbote serves as the Director of the Law Division of the United Nations Environment Programme (UNEP).

Below is a picture of the poster announcing my 2015 Distinguished Lecture at the University of Nairobi School of Law.

UNIVERSITY OF NAIROBI
SCHOOL OF LAW
PARKLANDS CAMPUS

Distinguished lecture
Global Trends in Financial Services Regulation:
Lessons to share with Africa

Date: Thursday, November 5, 2015
Venue: Okoth Ogendo Boardroom, block A
Time: 5.30 pm

Kenneth K. Mwenda,
PhD, LLD, DSc(Econ)

Prof. Kenneth K. Mwenda serves as the Program Manager and Executive Head of the World Bank's Voice Secondment Program in Washington DC, USA. A Rhodes Scholar and Oxford law graduate, Prof. Mwenda taught law at the University of Warwick in the United Kingdom prior to joining the World Bank. He has also taught at several other leading universities in North America, Europe and Africa, and these include American University Washington College of Law (WCL) in Washington DC and the University of Miskolc in Hungary, as well as the University of Cape Town (UCT), the University of Pretoria, the University of Western Cape, the University of Zambia and the University of Lusaka.

A prolific writer, Prof. Mwenda's scholarly work has been widely cited not only in academia, but also by the courts of law and many international organizations. Prof. Mwenda is author of twenty-five (25) scholarly books and over ninety (90) articles in leading law reviews and academic journals. He holds, in addition to a PhD in Law from the University of Warwick, the rarely awarded Higher Doctorate degrees of Doctor of Science in Economics (University of Hull, DSc(Econ), 2014) and Doctor of Laws (Rhodes University, LLD, 2008). Also, Prof. Mwenda has been a recipient of several other scholarly awards, including a graduate fellowship from Yale University Law School. In addition, he served for many years as Senior Counsel in the Legal Vice-Presidency of the World Bank.

When I arrived at the University of Nairobi campus, I saw a number of posters and billboards inviting the public to my Distinguish Lecture. I took a picture of myself next to one of the posters. That is the picture that appears below.

I have also shared some pictures below where I can be seen interacting with faculty members and some students after delivering my 2015 Distinguished Lecture at the University of Nairobi School of Law in 2015.

In the three pictures below, I was paying a courtesy call on my good learned elder brother, the distinguished and eminent Kenyan Supreme Court Judge, Hon Professor Jackton Boma Ojwang, who is now a retired Justice of the Supreme Court of Kenya. Hon Professor Ojwang, who once served as the Dean of the University of Nairobi School of Law, holds a PhD in Law from the University of Cambridge in England. Also, he is one of the few Higher Doctorate degree-holders in the field of law on the Africa continent. In 2015, Hon Professor Ojwang was awarded the first Higher Doctorate degree of Doctor of Laws (LLD) to be awarded by the University of Nairobi.

In Kenya, I also spent some time with my good learned elder brother, the then Chief Justice of the Supreme Court for the Republic of Kenya, Hon Chief Justice (CJ) Dr Justice Willie Mutunga, who holds a PhD in Law from Osgoode Hall Law School at York University in Toronto, Canada, and is a distinguished thought leader and public intellectual. When I got to Kenya, the CJ had travelled for work to Latin America. He, however, sent me an email that he would be arriving the next day and would come straight to meet me at the hotel where I was staying. It was a very humbling experience to receive such honor from a man of such high office. And true to his word, the CJ arrived at the hotel to see me right on time. We spent a good two to three hours by the poolside at the hotel exploring contemporary issues of law, justice and development in Africa. It was another edifying intellectual fellowship with a great mind and a distinguished son of Africa. I have shared a picture below.

As a global thought leader, I have never wanted my thought leadership to be confined to or limited to Zambia or Africa only. Yes, I am a Zambian and an African, but I am also American. And I am proud to be both American and Zambian. Further, I have never denied my African heritage. But Zambia or Africa is not the only thing that I know. Even at the World Bank, my career has not been limited to Africa only, even though I am of African descent. At the World Bank, I have worked on almost all major regions of the world, including Europe, Central Asia, South Asia, Middle East, the Pacific islands, East Asia, the Caribbean Islands, Latin America, South America, West and Central Africa, North Africa and Southern and Eastern Africa. My academic life and experience too have not been limited to Africa only. As a global thought leader, I knew that I had to transcend my home continent, Africa, in my thought leadership, and not be boxed into one corner of knowing only about African issues.

For me, whether you are European, American, Asian, Australian, Canadian, a New Zealander, Caribbean, Latino, or Oriental, if you are to be a global thought leader, you must come out of your jurisdictional comfort zone and avoid being parochially confined to your home issues only. A global scholar or thought leader is never confined to insular issues of national or local appeal only. The concept of a 'globe' is bigger than the insular confines of national or continental pride. And so, for me, all in all, I have taught at leading universities in three different continents, namely, Europe, North America and Africa. That's my story and a part of my footprints in global thought leadership.

Over the years, I have often been a highly sought-after speaker, and have been interviewed and quoted by numerous print and broadcast media, including the *New York Times* (USA), the *Voice of America* (VOA, USA), *CCTV* (USA), the *Times* (UK), the *British Broadcasting Corporation* (BBC, UK), and Sky TV (UK). Some of my international broadcast media appearances on live television as well as some snippets of my print media appearances globally are highlighted on the following pages.

- Live TV interview from Washington DC on US Voice of America's *Africa 54* which broadcasts in many countries and on several continents (March 29, 2023, with hostess, Esther Githui-Ewart, on "African Peace Mission to Russia, Ukraine Examined").

- Live TV interview from Washington DC on US Voice of America's *Straight Talk Africa,* which broadcasts in many countries and on several continents (March 29, 2023, with hostess, Hayde Adams, on "US Vice President Visits Africa & Anti-LGBTQ Legislation in Uganda").

- Live TV interview from Washington DC on US Voice of America's *Straight Talk Africa* (March 29, 2023, with hostess, Hayde Adams, on "Queen Elizabeth's Legacy in Africa").

- Live TV interview from Washington DC on US Voice of America's *Straight Talk Africa* (May 4, 2022, with guest host, Peter Clottey, on "Yoweri Museveni: In His Own Words and A Discussion About Governance in Uganda").

- Live TV interview from Washington DC on US Voice of America's *Straight Talk Africa* (November 10, 2021, with guest hostess, Hayde Adams, on "Are military coups back in Africa?").

- Live TV interview from Washington DC on US Voice of America's *Straight Talk Africa* (August 28, 2019, with veteran US Voice of America broadcaster, Dr Shaka Ssali, on "A Report Card on Democracy in Africa - Straight Talk Africa.").

- Lead discussant on a live TV interview on CCTV's the Heat program, which broadcasts from Washington DC, USA, in many countries and on several continents (February 8, 2018), examining "The constitutional implications of South Africa's President Jacob Zuma refusing to step down on corruption charges before the end of his presidential term of office.").

- Live TV interview from Washington DC on US Voice of America's *Straight Talk Africa* (February 7, 2018, with veteran US Voice of America broadcaster, Dr Shaka Ssali, on "Constitutional implications of the mock presidential inauguration of Mr Raila Odinga in Kenya.").

- Live TV interview from Washington DC on US Voice of America's *Straight Talk Africa* (December 27, 2017, with veteran US Voice of America broadcaster, Dr Shaka Ssali, on "Populist leaders in Southern Africa.").

- Lead discussant on a live TV interview on CCTV's *The Heat* program, which broadcasts from Washington DC, USA, in many countries and on several continents (November 15, 2017), examining "The political crisis in Zimbabwe as the military forces President Robert Mugabe to resign.".

- Live TV interview with US Voice of America, which broadcasts from Washington DC, USA, in many countries and on several continents (July 10, 2017, interviewed by veteran US Voice of America broadcaster, Mariama Diallo, on "The threats of a public state of emergency in Zambia due to the political impasse between President Edgar Lungu and the main opposition leader, Mr Hakainde Hichilema.").

- Live TV interview from Washington DC on US Voice of America's *Straight Talk Africa* (April 13, 2016, with veteran US Voice of America broadcaster, Dr Shaka Ssali, on "The International Criminal Court and African Leaders.").

- Live TV interview from Washington DC on US Voice of America's *Straight Talk Africa* (December 18, 2014, with veteran US Voice of America broadcaster, Dr Shaka Ssali, on "Constitutional Reforms and the Term Limit for Presidents in Africa.").

■ Live TV interview from Washington DC on Sky News TV in the United Kingdom with veteran journalist Ms Lukwesa Burak (now with BBC), via skype (December 5, 2014), on "The International Criminal Court drops charges against Kenya's president, H.E. President Uhuru Kenyatta."

- Live TV interview from Washington DC on US Voice of America's *Straight Talk Africa* (June 18, 2014, with veteran US Voice of America broadcaster, Dr Shaka Ssali, on "The Controversy Surrounding the Election of the President of the United Nations General Assembly (UNGA) for the 69th Session.").

- Live TV interview from Washington DC on US Voice of America's *Straight Talk Africa* (January 1, 2014, with veteran US Voice of America broadcaster, Dr Shaka Ssali, on "Political Leadership, Civil Strife and Good Governance in Africa.").

- Live TV interview from Washington DC on US Voice of America's *Straight Talk Africa* (October 16, 2013, with US Voice of America broadcaster, Dr Shaka Ssali, on "The International Criminal Court (ICC): the prosecution of culpable African Heads of State, and the response from the African Union (AU)").

- Live TV interview from Washington DC on US Voice of America's *Straight Talk Africa* (April 11, 2012, with veteran US Voice of America broadcaster Dr Shaka Ssali, on "Challenges of Political Transition: Mali and Malawi.").

- Live TV interview from Washington DC on US Voice of America's *Straight Talk Africa* (October 12, 2011, with veteran US Voice of America broadcaster, Dr Shaka Ssali, on "Good Governance in Africa.").

I am ever grateful to colleagues in the broadcast and print media that I have collaborated with over the years for the great work that they do in the media arena. They provide invaluable platforms for many leading public intellectuals and pundits as well as global thought leaders to communicate their ideas to, and engage with, the rest of the world.

CHAPTER 15

Beyond the PhD

After earning my PhD at the University of Warwick, I felt there was something more that I could achieve. I was not content with ending with just a PhD. Getting a PhD did not feel as if I had 'arrived', especially since I was already a full-time law professor with an impressive publication record. Unlike many PhD students, I was never at any point a full-time PhD student but only pursued the PhD on the side while lecturing full-time at the University of Warwick. At the time, I was already an accomplished academic and was thus aiming beyond just getting a PhD. Generally, a PhD is the requisite qualification for newbies in academia, but I was already swimming in the deep end. Many people like to ask what qualification comes after you obtain a PhD. I have examined this question in greater detail in Chapter 4 of one of my books, titled, K.K. Mwenda, *Doctoral Degree Programs in Law: An International and Comparative Study of the English-speaking World*, (Heidelberg, Germany: Springer, 2022).

I would encourage the reader to pick up a copy of the book whose title I have provided above. Here, suffice it to say, whereas a freshly graduated PhD holder can pursue opportunities for a postdoctoral fellowship or get appointed as an Assistant Professor (or its equivalent, the post of 'Lecturer' in some British universities), such positions are simply academic appointments, not qualifications. Even a full professorship is only a senior academic appointment, not a qualification. So, what qualification then, or academic degree, is there beyond a PhD? Many people are not aware that in many common law jurisdictions, with the exception of North American jurisdictions, there is a very rarely awarded academic qualification that ranks substantially higher than a PhD. That qualification actually goes beyond the PhD. You can also find lighter versions of the same in some civil law jurisdictions. Pursuing a higher doctorate is, however, never the immediate step after a PhD. Let us take a more reasoned look.

First, it is important to stress that university academic appointments or promotions to such positions as lecturer, senior lecturer, reader, professor, vice-chancellor, rector or chancellor are not academic qualifications at all. Rather, they are simply appointments or promotions, as the case may be. You can even be removed from those positions or retire from the same, unlike an academic qualification, such as a PhD or Higher Doctorate, which is yours for life. Secondly, nobody ever studies for any qualification known as 'lecturer', 'reader', 'professor', 'rector' or 'chancellor', notwithstanding the variations in the nomenclature of academic and university administrative positions in the UK and the US, for example. And so, whether you are an academic in the UK or the US, at no time did you graduate from university with a degree called 'lecturer', 'assistant professor', 'associate professor', 'reader', 'professor', 'chair', 'vice-chancellor', 'rector' or 'chancellor'. These are just job titles.

Thirdly, the concept of an earned higher doctorate that is very significantly higher than a PhD is one that is rare in the US and Canada, but more established in the UK, Ireland and other Commonwealth countries.[10] Higher doctorates, it should be emphasized, are extremely prestigious and very rarely awarded. They are reserved for those senior scholars who have made exceedingly significant contributions to a science or body of knowledge through exceptionally insightful and distinctive scholarly publications, earning them recognition as international authorities in the field of research that forms the basis of the degree. In most cases, where a higher doctorate is conferred, the recipient, often a senior professor, is almost at the end of his or her academic career or is even retired. Even so, not many senior law professors ever receive a higher doctorate. As one senior law professor whispered to me when I was receiving my first higher doctorate: "The main reason why most of us don't apply for this degree is that if, as a senior professor, you submit the required substantial body of your published scholarly work for examination for a higher doctorate by a distinguished panel of examiners who, like you, are senior professors, and the examiners reject your

---

10 A higher doctorate should not be confused with an honorary doctorate, although both awards carry similar names of the degree actually awarded (e.g. Doctor of Laws, Doctor of Letters, Doctor of Science, Doctor of Civil Law, and so forth). A higher doctorate, it should be emphasized, is an earned award, but an honorary doctorate is not.

work or fail it, not only will the whole encounter be embarrassing and shameful, but it could also take away the credibility of your professorship."[11]

Fourthly, many senior law professors know the prestige of being awarded a higher doctorate in academia, but choose willfully to shut their eyes to the obvious, dreading the possible outcome that could ensue should they ever attempt it, especially if they have not built a credible portfolio of sole-authored scholarly work, as opposed to a collection of edited volumes of conference proceedings or books that are mainly co-authored.[12] Others have simply been compiling cases, statutes and other legal materials over the years into some form of compendium or books.[13]

Our children and grandchildren, especially those focused on legal scholarship or academia, must have a story to tell of where they come from. They should be able to point to a role model or two that they can easily relate to as one of their own, as opposed to just reading about foreign scholars that they may never even meet. It gives the young ones some self-reassurance that they too can be like the person standing in front of them.

On March 28, 2008, as I stepped forward to receive the Higher Doctorate Degree of Doctor of Laws (LLD) at Rhodes University in South Africa, awarded in recognition of my significant and substantial contribution to legal scholarship over the years, I could see the immense pride in the eyes of many African students and graduands at the ceremony. As noted earlier, it was the first and only time ever in the rich history of Rhodes University – arguably one of the top five universities in Africa – that a Higher Doctorate in Law was being awarded. It was also the first time ever in the rich history of Zambia that a Zambian was receiving such a coveted academic award. My Higher Doctorate degree from Rhodes University in South Africa came through almost ten years after my PhD at the University of Warwick in England. Let me share opposite a portrait picture of my Warwick PhD before I share that of my Rhodes University Higher Doctorate.

---

11 This view explains why there are extremely few higher doctorate degree holders in law in many Commonwealth countries. For example, entire English-speaking Africa has arguably not more than ten (10) higher doctorate degree holders in law.

12 See *Ibid*.

13 See *Ibid*.

As already established, there are only 8 to 10 individuals with a Higher Doctorate in Law in the entire African continent. When I walked up to receive this prestigious award at Rhodes University, I could see 'Zambia' written on the global intellectual map. History was being written for my native homeland. And the inspiring applause from the large audience that filled the entire graduation hall, the famous 1820 Settlers National Monument in Grahamstown, South Africa, continued long after the then Dean of the Faculty of Law at Rhodes University, Professor Rob Midgley, had finished reading the full citation for the conferment of Rhodes University's first-ever Higher Doctorate degree in Law, the degree of Doctor of Laws, on me. Hitherto, I know of no other scholar that has had conferred upon them the Higher (Senior) Doctorate degree of Doctor Laws (LLD) by Rhodes University. Only honorary LLDs have been conferred, but they are not the same thing as an earned Higher or Senior Doctorate. So, the conferment of the LLD on me by Rhodes University was a momentous occasion. All the people present, including several parents and other family members of the graduating students as well as professors, lecturers, other graduands, students and friends of those graduating, gave a standing ovation with thunderous applause. Proceedings stalled for a while as the crowd continued with the applause.

I have reproduced below the text of the citation delivered by Professor Midgley for my Higher Doctorate degree of Doctor of Laws (LLD) at Rhodes University.

Mr Chancellor,
This University does not often award a senior doctoral degree based on the examination of a person's published scholarly works. In fact, this is the first time ever that such a degree is conferred in the Faculty of Law.

The examiners commented that our graduand's books and articles show a remarkable broad and detailed knowledge of financial and supervisory systems all over the world - not only of legal issues, but also of economic structures and processes, especially in the financial industry.

Although he often concentrates on special structures in Southern Africa, especially his home country, Zambia, the candidate regularly raises issues of global importance. He is said to own a real treasure of experiences regarding developments in post-communist and post-colonial countries and his work evidences a blend of different legal cultures, statutory law and international law, which makes it unique in its field.

All the examiners had high praise for our graduand's work, which in their view, constitutes a distinguished contribution to the advancement of knowledge in the field of national, regional and international financial institutional and legal framework.

Mr Chancellor, I have the honour to request you to confer the degree Doctor of Laws on Kenneth Kaoma Mwenda.

After the graduation ceremony, as people trooped out of the graduation hall slowly, many kept asking me, "Where are you from to come and receive such an esteemed and prestigious award?"

And I replied calmly with a smile, "I am from Zambia!"

Below is the official portrait taken in my Rhodes University Higher Doctorate degree graduation attire. A number of South African universities have a similar red gown for their PhD graduates, but the difference between those gowns and a Higher Doctorate gown is that the latter has long sleeves whereas the former, that is, the PhD gowns, have short sleeves.

At a special post-graduation dinner hosted by the Faculty of Law of Rhodes University, I sat at the high table next to the then Chief Justice (CJ) of South Africa, the late Hon Mr Chief Justice Pius Langa. At one point, the CJ looked at me, smiled and asked me thoughtfully with some wit: "Are you still a lawyer?"

Only the CJ and I, out of everyone who had graduated from Rhodes University that day, were invited to the high table as VIP Guests to join the then Vice-Chancellor of Rhodes University, Dr Saleem Badat, the then Dean of Law, Professor Rob Midgley, who is now the Vice-Chancellor of Walter Sisulu University in South Africa, and a few other senior law faculty members. The nature and gravitas of the awards that Hon Mr Chief Justice Pius Langa and I received deserved special honor. And I recall with fondness the words of the CJ when he asked me if I was still a lawyer. He was a man of great insight. We had just come from a great ceremony where he was receiving the Honorary Doctor of Laws (LLD(Hon)) degree conferred by Rhodes University. I flew to South Africa from my base in Washington DC on March 25, 2008, to receive my Higher Doctorate degree of Doctor of Laws (LLD) from the same university. The earned LLD was conferred upon me while he (the CJ) received the honorary LLD. As noted above, it was the first time ever in the rich history of Rhodes University that such an esteemed award in law was conferred as an earned degree. So, maybe the CJ was right. At the time, I had not even turned 40 and was coming from outside academia to get the highest prize in academia. The lesson I drew from that experience is that you always have to believe in yourself as long as you are true to yourself. Nobody else knows your truth better than you.

When I boarded the plane at Dulles International Airport in Virginia, US, to fly to South Africa for my Higher Doctorate degree graduation at Rhodes University, I was travelling all alone. I flew to Port Elizabeth in South Africa, via Johannesburg. As noted above, I flew out on March 25, 2008. My wife offered to come along to render some support, but so much was going on in my mind that I did not want to subject her to my emotions. So, I said to her respectfully, "Let me finish this the way I started it. I have been alone in much of my academic battles. I had no family around at my University of Zambia (UNZA) LLB graduation ceremony. I had no family around at my Oxford

BCL graduation ceremony. Neither did I have family around at my Hull MBA graduation ceremony. Even at my Warwick PhD graduation I had no family around, but only a few friends present. For this Higher Doctorate, I would have loved my father to join me because he really understood and appreciated my academic journey more than anyone else. But he is not with us anymore. So, let me do this for him and I will be fine travelling alone, honey. Let me finish this the way I started it."

There were so many emotions going on inside of me. I knew the colossal magnitude of a Higher Doctorate in academia. It is not a small thing. In Zambia, I noticed the unmistakable envy and jealousy of some of my former colleagues in the Law Faculty at the University of Zambia. It was too obvious. They thought I was just too ambitious because they themselves had not achieved much internationally. My academic path was clearly different from theirs. Further, I was cruising at an international speed which is fiercely competitive, while most of them were working with a somewhat sluggish lackluster domestic speed. In highly competitive environments in the Global North, there are no speed limits on the road to success. By then, Zambia had not produced a single Higher Doctorate in any academic field or discipline, so I was breaking new ground and raising the bar to a scholarly height that no Zambian academic had ever reached.

In the first half of 2007, Rhodes University received my Higher Doctorate application and subjected it to internal scrutiny and evaluation, in accordance with the university guidelines, to determine if there was a *prima facie* case for my application to proceed to the next level of the university appointing examiners. My Higher Doctorate application contained six heavy boxes of several copies of my scholarly books for which I am the sole author, in addition to several binders containing several journal articles for which I am the sole author. Rhodes University made it clear that no coauthored works such as jointly authored monographs, edited volumes, cases and materials type of books or journal articles would be accepted. It had to be only my sole authored works. Fortunately, I was equal to the task, and thus complied with the guidance received from the university. A favorable determination was later reached by the university that there was indeed a *prima facie* case to proceed, and three distinguished and eminent law professors from the UK, Germany and South Africa were appointed by Rhodes University to examine the body of my published scholarly work for the Rhodes LLD degree.

I waited patiently for several months. After about six to eight months, I got word from Rhodes University that only one more report was being awaited. When all the three reports of the examiners were in, the decision was unanimous. All the three examiners recommended, without reservation, that I be admitted to the Higher Doctorate degree of Doctor of Laws (LLD) at Rhodes University. I received this great news with much delight from the Registrar of Rhodes University, Dr Steve Fourie, and was invited to start preparing to travel to Rhodes University for the formal conferment on March 28, 2008.

As noted above, I flew to Johannesburg en route to Port Elizabeth. From Port Elizabeth, I then connected to Grahamstown. As I journeyed from Port Elizabeth to Grahamstown in South Africa for the graduation ceremony, I could feel the presence of my father throughout. From Port Elizabeth, I took a small minibus to Grahamstown where Rhodes University is located. I arrived in Grahamstown around 7:00pm. I proceeded to get myself a guest room and then grabbed some dinner before showering and jumping into bed. I knew nobody at Rhodes University.

The next day, I went to pick up my Higher Doctorate graduation gown from a store in city center. I had paid for the full graduation attire before I started off from Washington DC. The store owner brought out my full graduation attire. I inspected it and everything was fine. I went back to my room and left it in the room before walking over to the Faculty of Law for a cocktail party that was being hosted a day before the graduation day for all the graduating postgraduate law students. Many law faculty members were pleasantly surprised to see that I was not as old as they had thought. At the cocktail party, I was introduced by the Dean of the Law School, Prof Rob Midgley, to many law faculty members at Rhodes University. They were all very impressed and happy to meet me in person.

The following day was graduation day. I dressed up and took a cab to the graduation hall which was a bit of a distance from the university campus of Rhodes University. During the proceedings, graduating (undergraduate) students from different faculties graduated first, followed by Masters degree recipients from different disciplines and then PhD recipients. Then, there was silence before the Dean of the Law School at Rhodes University stepped forward to read the citation. I was invited to stand next to him. I was the only candidate receiving a Higher Doctorate.

People wondered what was happening and the kind of degree that I was receiving. The Law Dean, Professor Rob Midgley, read out the citation, as provided above. My long scholarly journey to that moment had started from my earlier years as a budding scholar when I was a tutor and Staff Development Fellow (SDF) at UNZA in 1991/2. From a period of gaining knowledge to an epoch of adding to the existing body of knowledge and then passing down that knowledge, it had been a journey of courage and determination.

As I walked down the stairs of the graduation hall to the stage in front of the hall where the Vice-Chancellor and other professors were seated, I thought about my father so much. I thought about how proud he would have been to witness this moment. I could feel his presence throughout as if he was there. I remembered all the candid advice that he would give me. Everything came rushing through like he was talking to me right there in real-time. I almost broke down from the emotions and had to really hold myself steadily as I walked down the stairs to stand at the stage next to the Dean of the Law School. The Dean started reading out the citation of my Higher Doctorate, and when he was done there was what seemed like an endless standing ovation that filled the entire graduation hall, the 1820 Settlers' National Monument. I was walking to receive my Higher Doctorate degree from Rhodes University!

After the graduation ceremony, I took some pictures with a number of Zambian students who were so proud to see a fellow Zambian represent them so well at international level outside Zambia. They could not believe it because such achievements among Africans are often associated only with our West African brothers. But I am not from Nigeria or Ghana. I am from Zambia. Generally, I never let success get to my head. I have continued writing and publishing scholarly work.

In 2009, one of my mentors and good learned elder brothers, Governor Dr Caleb M Fundanga, and his gracious wife, Mrs Rosario Fundanga, hosted a major unprecedented celebratory event in my honor to recognize my distinguished scholarly accomplishments that remain unmatched in Zambia. At the time, I had also just been appointed as Extraordinary Professor of Law at the University of Pretoria in South Africa. It was the first of such an appointment for a Zambian legal academic at a leading South African university. Earlier in the book, I shared some pictures of that event.

Today, as I look back after receiving my second Higher Doctorate (DSc(Econ)) in 2014 – this time in Economics – from the University of Hull in England, I know that there is a God up there whose mercy endures forever and who sees and listens. Two world-class and highly renowned eminent professors were appointed by the University of Hull to examine my Higher Doctorate application for the DSc(Econ) degree based on the substantial body of my scholarly publications which were published after earning my first Higher Doctorate degree from Rhodes University. The decision of both distinguished examiners of my published works was, like the Rhodes University one, also unanimous. Both examiners recommended me unanimously for the award of the Higher Doctorate degree in Economic Sciences. And I knew there and then that I was making world history. I was breaking world records. It was unprecedented. As I stated earlier in this book, apart from myself, I am not aware of any other African or black person who holds an earned Higher Doctorate from the University of Hull. Among alumni and faculty, including former faculty, of the Business School at the University of Hull, I only knew of Professor Robert L. Flood, who taught me on the Hull MBA degree program in 1994/95, as having been awarded an earned Higher Doctorate in Economic Sciences by the University of Hull. Professor Flood, or 'Bob', as we often called him when I was studying for my MBA at Hull in 1994/5, received his DSc(Econ) from Hull in 1997. In my case, until 2019 when a distinguished Princeton University professor received his second Higher Doctorate (DLitt) degree from the University of Oxford after earning his first Higher Doctorate (DCL) from Oxford as well, I was the only known legal scholar in the entire English-speaking world with two Higher Doctorates in two different disciplines. I can only thank God for these blessings.

In their joint examiners' statement to the University of Hull, which report was later availed to me by the university, the two examiners of my Hull DSc(Econ) body of published work wrote as follows:

> The candidate's work reflects a broad knowledge of law, policy and economics which is required as demonstrable proof of a higher doctorate candidate. The candidate's published work which constitutes a coherent theme in international economic law. The candidate provides considerable contribution to the field and literature of international economic law. The candidate's work is, in most cases, consistent, coherent and logically presented. The published work is a distinction and constitutes a substantial, sustained and original contribution in the field. The candidate has adopted a very good methodology in most of his publications by inference to his wide experience in academia and in practice, in many jurisdictions, and many areas of law such as intellectual property law and public international law. The candidate's published work is well-researched and well-presented. The candidate provides a well-thought-out work with a wealth of information, very thoughtful and insightful contribution to the literature of international economic law.

Below is a portrait of me when I received my second Higher Doctorate degree in England. This second Higher Doctorate, as noted above, is the degree of Doctor of Science in Economics (DSc(Econ)) earned from the University of Hull where I took my MBA degree some two decades earlier. I would also like to mention that the University of Hull PhD graduation attire, unlike my Higher Doctorate degree attire for the DSc(Econ) degree, has a maroon color where the red color appears on my Higher Doctorate graduation attire.

When I flew to the UK for my second Higher Doctorate, I did not travel alone. I had promised my dearest wife, Dr J, and my beloved son, Jojo, that I would have them travel with me for my next milestone after I earned the Rhodes University Higher Doctorate. I kept my word and travelled with both my wife and son to the UK. They were both in attendance when I received my DSc(Econ) from the University of Hull. I had promised them that I was not done when going to South Africa for my first Higher Doctorate degree, and that I would take them along with me when I travelled to receive my next major degree or academic award. And I kept my word.

On this occasion, my family and I flew from Dulles International Airport in Virginia, US, to Manchester in England, enroute to Hull in Yorkshire. From Manchester, we took a train to Hull via Leeds. In Hull, I took my family around the city and the university, showing them where I studied and lived. It was so nice to be back in Kingston upon Hull after almost two decades. The hotel where my family and I stayed was right in the city center, making it convenient and manageable for us to move around. I have shared some photos of my family and me in Hull city center on the day of my Higher Doctorate graduation.

After the Hull graduation ceremony, my family and I travelled to Manchester and stopped over at the University of Manchester where my wife completed her Master of Public Health (MPH) degree program. I have shared below some pictures of my wife and son at the University of Manchester before we proceeded to London and Oxford, respectively.

That I had obtained my second Higher Doctorate was by no means a reason to become complacent and start thinking that I had now 'arrived'. Rather, I continued writing and publishing. To me, nothing much had changed. I had more work to do. In addition to my academic writing and teaching, I have also had my regular employment at the World Bank. In the picture below, I am being congratulated by the then President of the World Bank, Dr Jim Kim, MD, PhD, when I clocked twenty years at the World Bank in Washington DC, US.

If life were a spacecraft, I would say that the propulsion continued on all three engines, even after getting my second Higher Doctorate degree. Realizing that I had done most of my university education in England, where I earned four university degrees before moving to the US, and increasing to five after I got my University of Hull Higher Doctorate, it was time to get some exposure to the American higher education system now that I was living in the US. It is important to adapt to the environment where you are living instead of rigidly adhering to the norms or values of where you are coming from. So, as a mark of good measure, I decided to get some transatlantic exposure to the American higher education system.

However, I was not going to leave my full-time job to go back to school just for the sake of exposure to the American higher education system. Besides, I was already too qualified to attend full-time university like someone who is only getting to know higher education. All I needed was some modest exposure to the American higher education system to put some icing on the British cake that I had already baked when I went through the British higher education system.

To accomplish this, I decided to embark on some executive education programs in leadership and management at leading Business Schools in the US and outside the US. I also decided to get some university teaching experience in the US. So, in both the UK and the US, I have studied and taught at some of the best universities. To illustrate, in the UK I studied at Oxford, Warwick, London Business School, and Hull as well as taught at Warwick, whilst in the US I have studied at Harvard, Wharton, Yale, MIT, Stanford, Cornell, Georgetown and Northwestern as well as taught at American University and West Virginia University. I have shared below some pictures taken at Harvard Business School, MIT Sloan School of Management, Harvard Kennedy School, and Yale University School of Management.

Further, I have shared below a couple of pictures of myself at Wharton School at the University of Pennsylvania in Philadelphia, US, as well as my quote that appears on one of the institutional websites of Wharton School regarding the high quality of the Wharton Leadership and Management Program.

> "The Wharton *Leadership and Management Certificate* is an extremely valuable program. Since completing my MBA, so much has happened in terms of emerging best practices and new studies in management and leadership. The program was highly relevant for me in terms of enhancing and strengthening my skills as a manager, and it helped me build my career potential. The course content and delivery were excellent and well-structured, and the interaction with fellow students and faculty is another asset. I would definitely recommend this program."

Kenneth K. Mwenda

Program Manager, World Bank, Washington, D.C.

In continental Europe, I have studied at the Institut Européen d'Administration des Affaires (INSEAD) in France and taught at the University of Miskolc in Hungary. In addition, as stated earlier, I have studied and taught at several leading universities in Africa. All in all, I have studied and taught at major universities in three different continents, namely, Europe, North America and Africa. This broad and deep exposure to different higher educational systems in the Global South and the Global North provides me with enriched global perspectives that transcend limited, insular, and parochial or narrow knowledge bases. The future, I contend, is for those who are willing to embrace ambidexterity and to learn, unlearn and relearn what they know or what they ought to know so as to be able to generate continuously novel and creative ideas for today and tomorrow. Effective and authentic leaders never stop learning. Every moment or experience is a learning opportunity. For example, you will not understand fully the overt or covert racist tendencies of certain individuals from a certain part of the world or country until you interact with them or study their behavior. It will help you understand how they think, without making generalizations or stereotypes. I have come to learn to distinguish, for example, certain forms of American racism from certain forms of Russian racism or Arab racism. I would say the same thing for British racism, Greek racism, Latino racism, German racism, Chinese racism, Indian racism, Turkish racism, or any other form of racial or ethnic bigotry. Every experience is a learning opportunity. You learn.

The field out there is not a level-playing field. Issues such as white supremacy and white privilege often promote the exclusivity of whiteness for various socio-economic opportunities, making it difficult for a black man to get a seat at the table, unless and until he 'wears a blond wig' to be accepted by the white establishment. Otherwise, the black man has to prove himself three or four times more than his white counterparts for him to get a seat at the table.

It is even worse where the black man has to contend additionally with the Uncle Tom mindset of some fellow blacks who will schmooze and suck up to white folks, as they throw him under the bus just to get ahead. We have seen it all. These types of black folks will tell the white folks even what those white folks did not know about the black man just to dim his light. Also, some people can be calling you up or emailing you daily when they are desperately looking for a job at your workplace. You might even set aside time to attend to them, but the moment they get in, they start to behave and act as if they don't know you.

As part of my sustained commitment to continuous learning and professional development, I have also completed three professional soccer (football) coaching programs with FC Barcelona's Barça Coaching Academy in Barcelona, Spain. I completed both the Barça Coaches Academy I and the Barça Coaches Academy II football coaching programs as well as the Barça Professional Diploma in Football Coaching. So, yes, I have studied the science and art of soccer professionally as well as professional coaching for that beautiful game.

Now you might be wondering about the relevance of these football coaching credentials to my career. Let me push on. There is a strong nexus between matters of pedagogy in academia and sports or the music industry. For example, as a smooth jazz enthusiast, I follow techniques such as 'improvisation' in live jazz performances, and how that can be transported and applied to the context of, say, soccer, if a player is faced with a constrained situation during a game and has to come up with a creative solution. A good example here would be how to dribble past an opposition player to overcome a constrained stage-space during a game. This example shows that the concept of variable learning can help to develop transferable skills from one profession or discipline to another. By mixing up and switching around learning practices and exercises, or rather by promoting varied practice, you can enhance the creativity of the learner, enabling him or her to solve problems creatively with minimal or no supervision. Indeed, variable practice can help to promote higher levels of motor learning than constant, linear and traditional practice of the same thing over and over again. So, for me, my football coaching skills and my appreciation of smooth jazz, as a jazz enthusiast, both feed into my global thought-leadership. Besides, I would not want to watch a game of football from a point of ignorance. It helps if you can understand the science behind the sport to enable you to reach an enlightened viewpoint for making some informed and sensible comments.

A man who appreciates smooth jazz often has an eclectic taste for the finer things that life has to offer.

Although I was a smooth jazz enthusiast even before I left Africa, my many years of living in America have honed my appreciation of the rich tradition of smooth jazz.

In Chapter 1 of this book, I mentioned that based on my internationally recognized contributions as a global thought-leader who has published extensively and whose scholarship has won several coveted international and national academic awards, my alma mater, the University of Oxford, conferred on me the highest and rarest honor that any Oxford college can confer on a most eminently qualified and distinguished individual. That honor, which I describe more fully in the latter parts of this autobiography, speaks to my sustained commitment to global thought-leadership at the highest international levels.

CHAPTER 16

Father, husband and scholar

As a father, husband and scholar, my philosophical approach to the concept of family is that it starts with systems thinking, though it can be influenced at different recursive levels by various variables stemming from the external and internal environments that shape our thinking. At the outset, let me start by saying that a family is an open system, and not a closed system. Its subsystems, together with the main system itself, are interlinked to internal and external environments. For example, your spouse is a subsystem of your nuclear family, and he or she is connected to the children in the internal environment of the nuclear family as well as to his or her relatives in the external environment of the family. Even the type of institutions that you associate yourself with, such as churches, religious groupings, schools, workplaces, charity organizations, golf clubs, popular pubs, and all manner of associations, form the various subsystems of the external environment from which you can carry and bring into your nuclear family certain desirable or undesirable values.

As an individual, you are an open subsystem of your nuclear family and are therefore open to other subsystems in the internal and external environments as well. You are not insulated from the external environment of friends, workmates, neighbors, siblings or relatives. You talk to them often and exchange ideas. Some of those ideas from the external environment can influence you and end up in your family home or internal environment. A family is thus truly an open system. Norms can be transmitted between the external and internal environments of the family, and the transmission can flow in either or both directions, meaning that it can be from the external environment to the nuclear family or from the nuclear family to the external environment. That is why some marriages are disturbed by outsiders from the external environment, such as relatives, if the married couple is not careful. As noted above, a family is an open system, and your relatives are some of the subsystems from your external environment.

Also, this explains why sometimes a spouse can exhibit certain behaviors that mirror those of his father or mother. The values inculcated in your spouse in the environment where he or she grew up, that is, his or her parents' home, could manifest themselves when the two of you marry and form a nuclear home or family. So, what to do now?

Different people have a different understanding of family. To some, family does not mean much. To others, it is everything. My concept of family has been influenced by my Christian Catholic background and my conservative African traditional values. Sociologists and anthropologists have studied social institutions such as family and marriage as well as the cultural aspects of such institutions. It is not my intention here to revive those debates. Rather, suffice it to say that how you have been raised or socialized can affect how you view the institutions of marriage and family. Other factors that could affect your views include your personal experiences, especially if you either have been disappointed before or have benefited from such institutions. People sometimes project their personal frustrations or gain as the truth. Your level of exposure to other cultures and your level of education can also affect your views about marriage and family. In addition, the environments to which you have been exposed can shape your views. As we noted above, you are an open system that is malleable to ideas from the internal and external environments. All these nuances can be explained through systems thinking, as highlighted above.

I was raised on strong family values which stressed the importance of education, manners, respect, morals, ethics, charity, faith and love. My father was married to one wife, my mother, throughout his life. He never abandoned her at any time for any other woman. We would hear rumors of scandalous stories relating to some parents in the neighborhood. If there was anything of that sort about my father, I would have heard or known by now. There was nothing of the kind. Even some of my friends would admire my father's moral character, wondering why their fathers were not like him. As a child, you could not say much if a friend opened up to you on such a sensitive topic, as he questioned his own father's behavior or conduct.

My father was a devout Catholic Christian who, according to Catholic tradition and teaching, I consider a saint, not just because he was my father but because of how much he gave himself wholly to God throughout his life. I have travelled the world widely and met men and women, including several clerics and church enthusiasts, from all walks of life. Few of them can come close to my father in terms of moral integrity and character. We Catholics believe that saints are not only those canonized by the Vatican. In fact, some canonized saints have had interesting lives before they truly found God. Therefore, I am confident that men and women like my father are saints and that such men and women only come once in a century.

My father's upright moral character and edifying integrity stood out most of the time, even among his peers. There were no scandals concerning women, abusing alcohol, embezzling funds, engaging in corrupt practices or not paying debts. My father was not a priest, pastor, bishop or self-proclaimed prophet, yet his impeccable moral character and admirable ethical standing, as a truly devoted Christian, were way above that of many so-called men of God. You will know a good man when you come across one. You won't miss the fruits of that tree. And you don't have to scratch your head and think about it. My mother never had to worry about my father's moral or ethical conduct at any time. She herself would say it. Also, I had never heard my father insult anyone or use profanity, abusive language or other uncouth language towards anyone. Even when he was upset over something, my father always acted in a civilized and dignified manner. And you would never hear stories that my father owed people money, or that he had swindled people out of money and was trying to hide from them. Neither was my father involved in or associated with such disgraceful vices as embezzling public funds at the workplace, as is the case with some men. My father's moral and ethical character was simply edifying and beyond reproach. It made me very proud. He also never touched alcohol or cigarettes. Many of his peers actually looked up to him for moral leadership, guidance and wisdom. I was very proud of my father. He helped to shape my values. And I do not take anything for granted, because I saw how some of my friends who came from broken homes were affected by the mess in their parent's lives and homes.

I remember that my father gave his wife, my mother, a chance to get a good education and have a professional career at a time when most men just kept their wives at home as housewives. For that, and many other things, I salute him as a hero. I learned a lot from him. He was way ahead of his time.

When I got married, my wife was already a qualified medical doctor, but the lesson I had learned from my father to support your spouse in his or her career pursuits saw me put my wife in graduate school to enable her to pursue and obtain a Masters of Business Administration (MBA) degree from the University of Leicester in England. Some family relations started saying that I had a made a mistake to put my wife in graduate school and pay for her MBA degree studies because a woman can leave you once she gets an education. Also, because she was a medical doctor, others even wondered if she would manage to adapt to business studies and get the MBA degree. I would simply smile and tell them that if someone was going to leave you then they would leave, irrespective of what you did, and that if someone could finish seven tough years of intensive medical school at a reputable medical school in Zambia, what would be so difficult about getting an MBA?

People will sometimes give you misguided advice based on isolated conjectures and anecdotes of their own insecurities, as they try to generalize their own speculative fears. My father put my mother back in school, and she did not leave him. My wife and I have now been married for more than 20 years, and she has not left me. In fact, my lovely wife, Dr J, with our adorable son, Jojo, and I recently celebrated our 20th wedding and marriage anniversary in Nassau, the Bahamas. I have shared below some family pictures taken at a luxurious resort in the Bahamas in 2022.

Someone once asked my lovely wife, Dr J, and me: "Between the two of you, how many degrees do you have?" To that, I would say that what you see in the picture above are five prestigious degrees for my wife (BSc, MB ChB, MBA and MPH) and seven equally prestigious degrees for me (LLB, BCL, MPhil, MBA, PhD, LLD, DSc(Econ)). Together, as a married couple, we share twelve university degrees that include two Higher Doctorates, a PhD and a Doctor of Medicine degree. In terms of doctorates, we have four doctorate degrees in the family.

In the picture above, my adorable son, Jojo, and my lovely wife, Dr J, are settling in at the beach in the Bahamas. In the picture below, it's Versace baroque bathrobes at the beach.

In the picture above, my son, Jojo, is dressed in a Versace polo T-shirt while I am dressed in a Burberry polo T-shirt. That's how we roll in the Bahamas.

Her choice on that day was a Burberry T-shirt and some Burberry swim shorts while mine was a Burberry T-shirt and some Versace swim shorts. But our shoe game remained anchored in Versace.

Watching the dolphins spinning at close range in the air. A spectacular treat and experience.

Playing with the dolphins at close range in the water. Thank you, Bahamas.

The Bahamas are among the many Caribbean islands where my family and I have vacationed. I will share later in this chapter some pictures of the other Eastern Caribbean islands we often go to on vacation. For now, let me drop a few more pictures of the Bahamas treat.

As they say, if not a Versace robe, then what?

Aside from her MBA degree from the University of Leicester, my wife also earned a second Masters degree from the University of Manchester. I will explain the second Masters degree below. Here, suffice it to say that the following picture of my wife was taken in 2002 when she was studying for her MBA degree at the University of Leicester in Leicester city, England.

In the two pictures below, I was appreciating my lovely wife, Dr J, on Valentine's Day with the soulfulness of smooth jazz before taking her out on a dinner date.

My mother, Mrs Esther Mpande Mwenda, trained and worked initially as a nurse before she changed careers to train and work as a teacher. My father, Mr Joseph Toli Mwenda, did not discourage my mother from going to nursing school as a married woman. If anything, he supported her. He also supported her when she decided to switch careers and go to Chalimbana Teachers' Training College, now known as Chalimbana University, to train as a teacher. By the same token, I encouraged my wife to go to graduate school and get an MBA degree from the University of Leicester in England shortly after we got married. I did not stop her from going further with her education. If anything, I continued to support her when she later went for her second Masters degree, the Master of Public Health (MPH) degree from the University of Manchester in England. Indeed, I did not stop her or prevent her from obtaining both graduate degrees, the MBA and MPH degrees. I was there for her, encouraging her and providing her with financial support and an enabling environment to succeed. That is what I learned from my father.

Below is my wife's personalized business cardholder, with her credentials inscribed as described above. For lack of space, the credentials are abridged to fit her business cardholder.

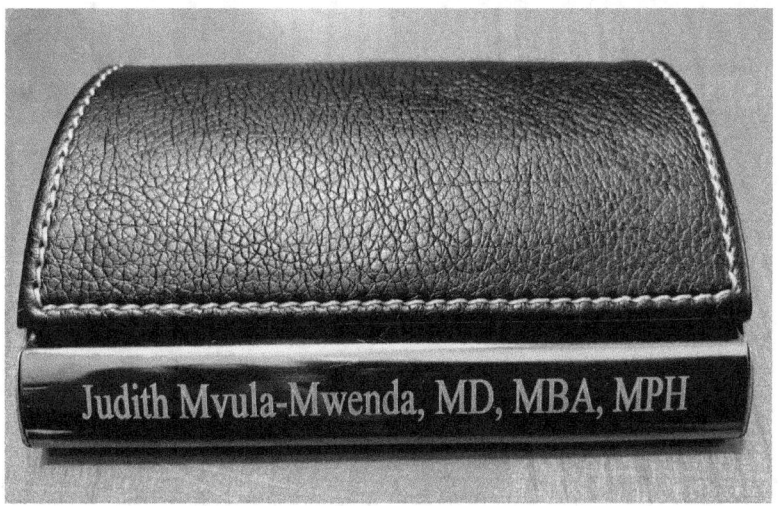

The idea behind that combination of postgraduate degrees for my wife was to ensure that, as a medical doctor, she not only got the skills to run a hospital or public health institution but also specialized as a technocrat in public health and preventive medicine. That way, one gets to grow professionally, not only in the field of medicine but also in leadership and managerial skills. My wife earned her Leicester MBA degree in July 2005 and her Manchester MPH degree in November 2008. I'd guess that if you are married to someone who values education highly, it encourages you to study further. Below is my own personalized business cardholder, with an inscription of my credentials.

Similarly, for lack of space, only my three doctorates are listed on my business cardholder, that is, the PhD and the two Higher Doctorates.

After completing her MBA and MPH degrees, my wife went on to pursue and complete postdoctoral training for physicians at two US Ivy League Schools, Harvard University Medical School and Cornell University. Again, I did not stop her or prevent her from pursuing her dreams but simply facilitated and supported her by providing her with an enabling environment to excel. Today, my dearest wife, Dr Judith Mvula-Mwenda, MD, MBA, MPH, is a Senior Director of a leading public health institution in the US, and is, undoubtedly, one of Zambia's most accomplished female physicians in the field of public health. The pictures below were taken in August 2024 when my son, JoJo, and I were seeing off his mother at the airport in Washington DC. As a corporate executive, my wife travels often, leading many corporate and business missions. Like me, she likes to travel light.

In general, my wife is a private person. I had to convince her to let me take the pictures above. She often keeps away from much of the public domain. You will not hear her making noise on social media or in associations or organizations of some professional women back home in Zambia or the diaspora. As a result, the Zambian nationals who know her know her mainly as my wife, though she is a highly accomplished professional in her own right and standing. In fact, my wife was one of the first Zambian doctors to earn both MBA and MPH degrees from top universities in the Global North. Prior to that, many Zambian medical doctors who ventured into public health would only get either an MSc degree or an MPH degree. A handful would push further to PhD-level, though the majority would only acquire local Zambian experience, with limited or no international experience beyond Africa.

In helping and supporting my beloved wife to build a powerful international career in public health, I learned a lot from my father. He empowered my mother to get an education the same way that I empowered my wife to go for graduate studies. In the US generally, it is not easy, even if you are a qualified medical doctor in your home country, to get a good job, especially if your degrees are, say, from Africa, some other part of the developing world or a transition economy. So, I made sure that my wife did not become a victim of such biases by using my experience in academia in the United Kingdom and guiding her strategically to land safely in the US job market. Indeed, I learned from my father the virtues of marriage and family. My father's life alone was a book from which you could learn if you cared to. He truly lived ahead of his time and was a man larger than life.

In the pictures below, taken in June 2024, my son Joseph, named after my father, can be seen graduating for his High School Diploma at the famous Constitutional Hall in Washington DC. My son graduated from Watkins Mill High School in Maryland, US. He is now pursuing his university education in the US.

In the picture above, with my son at the famous Constitution Hall in Washington DC.

In the picture above, my adorable son, Jojo, can be seen with his mum, Dr J. She is dressed up in an elegant Burberry outfit and a fine pair of Gucci shoes, while her son is dressed up in a fine grayish-blue suit and a black bowtie, with a matching pair of fine leather ceremonial shoes.

Growing up in Zambia, I learned so many things from my parents. I was actually at the United Nations (UN) in New York the week that my son was graduating from High School. I had travelled to New York from Washington DC for work. I was leading a 30-member World Bank team to the UN, but I knew that I could not afford to miss my son's graduation even though I had a busy schedule at the UN. We concluded our UN meetings on a Thursday evening and the next day, Friday, was my son's graduation ceremony. I had to be back in Washington DC that very night. I arrived there shortly after midnight and had to be up by 06:00am in readiness for the graduation ceremony. I slept for a few hours and was up by 05:00am. It is the discipline that I inherited from my parents.

I remember that when I was considering getting married, I wrote my father a letter, seeking his guidance and wisdom. From early childhood, I was never a rebel or a spoilt child who would just do things anyhow, or as and how they wished. I knew respect for elders. I knew our African culture. I grew up as an obedient child. My father often gave me as an example to my siblings, stressing how I would not just do things or make critical decisions about life without consulting my parents. That truth might not have sat well with some of my siblings, but my father was one man who never minced his words. My mother used to tell me that I am very much like my father, and that I too will tell someone facts to their face without mincing my words. That said, my father was one of the most humble and polite men you would ever meet. He was always polite, respectful, and diplomatic, but also frank and candid. If you are a person who tells the truth, you had nothing to worry about when you were in his presence. My father hated telling lies, just as I do. Telling lies is like insulting my intelligence, thinking that I cannot see past your shenanigans and lies. So maybe my mother was right after all.

When I was thinking of hanging up my jersey as an eligible bachelor, I went to my father and told him candidly what direction I was thinking of taking. In most of the disscissions I had with my father, he would never dictate the way forward. We would simply brainstorm, and he would then leave me to make the decision after highlighting some merits and demerits of each case. I still remember the two Bemba proverbs that he used when I sought his advice on getting married. He said to me, "Akoni ke kala umuti ka temenwe." (English translation: "A bird chooses for itself the branch of a tree it wishes to perch on. You cannot choose for it.")

Then he added: "Aka papa ka pa mu lomo mwine ako bula." (English translation: "Only you can remove the chapped or dry skin off your lip because only you can feel it. Somebody else can't do it for you.")

My father understood the journey that I had been through leading up to this moment when I turned to him for that critical piece of advice. At some point when I was at my lowest moment, broken and challenged with some personal issues that prevented me from getting married earlier, my father surprised me when he asked me to kneel down. He stood in front of me, while I was kneeling with my head bowed down, placed his hands on my head and prayed for me and blessed me. I had never seen him bless anyone else in the family or elsewhere. I was taken by surprise. I never saw it coming. I had read in the Bible how Isaac blessed his son Jacob (Gen. 27:27–29), and read elsewhere how in some African traditional cultures such parental blessings are part of their revered custom, but I did not know that this would also be possible for me. All I knew was that my father was a very prayerful man and that he also had deep knowledge of our African traditional customs and values.

As my father prayed, my mother sat nearby quietly. It was only the three of us in the living room at my sister Catherine's home. Somehow, I think my father could read what I was going through emotionally before he asked me to kneel down for prayers and blessings. I was going through so much pain and anguish. My father was a very prayerful man. I noticed at some point before the prayers and blessings started that he was silent, as if he was in a reflective, pensive and prayerful mood. Then he asked me to kneel down. He did not tell me why. He just asked me to kneel down. And I did not ask him why. I trusted him and did as he asked. My mother was quiet. It was as if she knew. She did not look surprised. I was wondering what was going on.

Then my father, now advanced in age, stood up and placed his hands on my head and started praying for me. I could feel from his parental voice, as he prayed over me, the deep love and care from both my parents. I never told or shared this story with anyone. I kept it to myself for 26 years. Both my parents crossed over without anyone of us saying a word about the incident. We never spoke about it. But deep down, I knew that it was a rare honor, privilege and blessing to be singled out for my father's final blessings, especially as I could see that he was now advanced in age and was having some health challenges.

I kept this whole incident a guarded secret from everyone for 26 years until 2024, when I was sponsoring my youngest brother, Joseph, for postgraduate studies at the University of Western Cape (UWC) in Cape Town, South Africa. It is tradition in the family that when you are going far away from home for school you get some wise words of counsel to encourage and strengthen you. My father gave me similar words of wisdom when I was going to England in 1992. I did not just take off from Zambia for Oxford like a hermit. My father sat me down and shared with me some words of wisdom and what I should expect where I was going. As I said earlier, I was raised in a decent home that had family values and manners.

On Saturday, September 14, 2002, my lovely wife, Dr Judith Mvula-Mwenda, and I got married in Washington DC, US. We had our marriage solemnized and blessed at a local Catholic parish in Washington DC, St. Stephen Martyr Catholic Church, where I used to go when I lived in downtown DC.

Prior to our wedding, my wife and I were invited by the church to attend some Catholic preparatory classes for marriage. We attended those classes in Takoma Park, Maryland, for about two months. In addition, one of the parish priests at St. Stephen Martyr Catholic Church asked us to get letters from our parents consenting to our marriage. I found this ridiculous, especially as my wife and I were both adults and, legally speaking, needed no parental consent to get married. Interestingly, when we are giving money to the church, say, through Sunday offertory or other forms of financial contributions to the church, the priest does not ask us to get parental consent before we can do so. The church folks just hurriedly take the money even if it is coming from a child. No parental consent is required. To that end, I humbly submit that the church can sometimes have double standards. And I am free to disagree with some of the practices or traditions of the Catholic Church, even though am Catholic. After all, it is not a sin to disagree. Things have to make sense. Religion without sense-making is nothing, but dogma. If you have difficulties disagreeing or not submitting to some of the controversial teachings or practices of your pastor, papa or prophet then you are lost. God gave you a mind to reason and think, not just to follow blindly. And for me, I believe that Catholicism itself welcomes intellectualism. I am an intellectual and remain so even within the Catholic church. I don't buy into anything that church folks say without subjecting it to critical thought and analysis. Logical arguments in matters of faith matter. After all, even priests study philosophy at the seminary for this same reason.

To that end, I could have asked the priest why he thought I needed to get parental consent in order to get married, but I chose not to cause any trouble. And if I was someone who is so sensitive about race issues, I would have asked the white priest if the parental consent requirement also applied to white couples, or was it just meant for black couples and foreigners of color? Maybe I was overthinking the whole thing and the priest was just abiding by the dictates of the church. I did not want to cause any drama and I just took it all in good part. I asked myself: what will it cost to me to get those parental consent letters? Nothing. So, why not just get the letters, as the church demands, and move on? Also, maybe the church could have a reason for asking for us to get written parental consent so as to avoid solemnizing a sham marriage of convenience. I am always open to different viewpoints. Obviously, the priest wouldn't have known or guessed that my wife and I had genuine, legitimate and bona fide intentions of getting married. So, on that score alone, I figured that I could excuse him. But then, there was also a risk that the requested letters of parental consent can be forged. So how does that help? How would the priest know if the letters were actually authentic and written by our parents or not?

Fortunately, both my wife and I are of high integrity. We did exactly as the church asked us to do and contacted our parents immediately, and both my parents and parents-in-law wrote their respective letters of parental consent, which we then took to the parish priest. A notable advantage of this bureaucracy, if I can give the church some credit, is that there is no room for shortcuts, that is, assuming that the rule applies to every couple across the board. You have to do things the right way, not trying to cut corners after discovering, say, that you have impregnated someone's daughter. Those maneuvers of trying to hide a pregnancy by rushing to marry someone so that it appears that she got pregnant after you married her don't often work in the Catholic Church. There is a period of about three months or so in which your intentions to get married will be announced in church every Sunday during Mass. You can't fast-track the wedding. It will not fly. Besides, in our case, the law in Washington DC law also requires you to take some medical tests before you can get married.

Everything went well. My wife and I are ever grateful to all the many friends, family members and colleagues who were present at our wedding. I have shared some pictures taken at the solemnization of our wedding at St. Stephen Martyr Catholic Church. The priest who married us was a different priest from the one who asked us for parental consent before we could get married. My wife and I were married off by Fr Tim who was actually younger than me. It was a bit funny, given that both my wife and I were used to seeing older priests at Catholic churches in Zambia. Yes, my wife has always been a Catholic, too. In fact, she attended a Catholic school for girls in Zambia, Ibenga Girls' Secondary School, before she proceeded to medical school at the University of Zambia. So, there were no issues between my wife and I concerning Christian denominations when we were getting married since we are both Catholics. By parity of reasoning, I did not have to do anything to convince my wife to join the Catholic Church since she was already a Catholic.

Matters of religion can be a thorny issue in many marriages, especially where the bride and the groom do not belong to the same religious or Christian denomination. You can end up with a clash of doctrinal, traditional and normative perspectives concerning matters of life and faith. It is not something to trivialize as many marrying or married couples do get stuck over competing interests concerning their divergent religious or Christian views.

I remember also receiving a lot of phone calls and various kinds of requests from some Zambian friends and colleagues in the US, especially those in the DMV area, asking to be invited to my wedding. Others would even ask me to invite their parents as well. It was overwhelming. That said, I don't believe in what I call 'poverty-sharing committees', as is common practice back home in Zambia, when preparing for a wedding. Such committees are basically fund-raising committees to fund or subsidize a couple's wedding, especially if the couple is struggling financially to host a wedding. Often times, the prospective bride or groom will set up a WhatsApp group, adding whoever they deem to be monied so that that person can pour in some resources, cash or get them some pre-identified 'expensive gift' to alleviate the couple's financial situation. This practice of 'poverty-sharing committees' seems to be part of the emerging culture in urban Zambia.

I, however, submit that it is not a part of our African tradition or custom in much of Zambian culture, but merely a 'poverty reduction strategy' adopted by many a desperate urban socialite. I believe that if you are going to get married, then you should be prepared to finance your wedding. Otherwise, do not hold a wedding and just go to church to have the marriage blessed. You cannot be inconveniencing people by adding them, with or without their consent, to poverty-sharing committees to finance your wedding. That's pathetic! Folks need to learn to live within their means. How can you plan for a big wedding when you don't have enough resources or savings? Some of these people plan for their weddings based on someone else's pockets. It's ridiculous. For me, when I was getting married, I footed the entire bill of my wedding. I did not bother anyone for money. And I made sure that I gave my wife and my guests a good wedding experience that they had never experienced before, with full catering and beverages all paid for aboard a luxury yacht on the Potomac River in Washington DC. There were no such things as wedding committees to prepare for my wedding. I paid for everything. And I took care of whatever needed to be taken care of. All my wedding guests just had to board the yacht and eat and drink as much they wanted.

The yacht that I had hired was appropriately called *Celebrity*. It was spacious, with all the right fittings befitting of a celebrity wedding. There was no question about who is going to serve the food or drinks, whether it would be relatives of the bride (aba ku cha nakashi) or the groom (aba ku chaume), because I had paid for everything, including full catering with professional waiters and waitresses. My guests just had to relax and enjoy themselves, while partying on any kind of drink and food that they wanted.

I had hired two limousines for the bridal party, one from church to the yacht and the other for the bride and groom exclusively from the yacht after the wedding reception to the bride and groom's private hotel. The yacht also had a nice musical system aboard, though a good Zambian friend and brother, Mr Kingfred Chisanga, volunteered to bring his full disco music system and to deejay at the wedding party, as we all wined, dined and partied aboard the *Celebrity* while sailing down the Potomac River. I am ever grateful to friends like that. It was like a wedding in the movies, as some showers started pouring while we sailed away.

The yacht had two decks. The lower deck had a dining room and lounge, with some private rooms for the bridal party, while the upper deck, the forecastle, had a dancing floor and some relaxing area. I have shared some pictures below of our wedding aboard the *Celebrity* in Washington DC. It was a memorable wedding that left a lasting impact among many a Zambian wedding held in the DMV.

My uncle, His Excellency Ambassador Professor Mwelwa Musambachime, who at the time was serving as Zambia's Permanent Representative to the United Nations (UN) in New York, was supposed to be the Guest of Honor at our wedding, but he could not travel at the last minute, as he was expecting the arrival of the Zambian president, His Excellency Dr Levy P Mwanawansa, and his delegation to the UN. My uncle, however, sent me a generous wedding gift to give me some moral encouragement and support. Earlier, I had written to him when I was preparing to get married, explaining my well-reasoned decision not to have my wedding in Zambia but in Washington DC. I had also informed my parents that I was doing this to avoid the pushing and shoving between families I had experienced when I first tried to get married in 1998. I needed no unnecessary egos to be flying all over the place from people who were not even putting money on the table. My uncle, Ambassador Professor Musambachime, gave me some sound advice, saying, "Ba Yama, nga uleupa, te bonse ba temwa. Sometimes you can find that even some family relations, friends and other people you consider to be close to you are not happy for you." ("My nephew, sometimes not everyone will be happy that you are planning on getting married. Sometimes you can find that even some family relations, friends and other people you consider to be close to you are not happy for you.)

Indeed, Ambassador Professor Musambachime was right. I had seen this type of jostling in 1998 when I first tried to get married in Zambia. Even in the US, I could hear some similar echoes, especially because my wife was not from the local community of Zambians in the DMV but came from outside the DMV with her own impressive professional credentials as a physician. I simply cut out all overzealousness and ruled that there would be no wedding committee for my wedding. Such committees are nothing but a source of gossip and confusion and a distraction when you are trying to get married. Some people were waiting to hear if there would be a wedding committee so that they could impose themselves on the committee, only to find that everything was being done by external professionals that I had hired.

The bridesmaid for our wedding, Reverend Mrs Catherine Bupe, flew in from Columbia, South Carolina, US, whilst the best man, Mr Chishimba B Yumbe, who was at the time working for the United Nations in New York joined us from his base in New York. The matron for our wedding was the ever elegant Ms Susan Sitemba, from Coventry, England. She flew in from England and did a fantastic job, The master of ceremonies was a distinguished academician in the US, Professor Gerry N Muuka, who at the time was a Professor of Management and Assistant Dean of the Business School at Murray State University in Kentucky. He flew in from Kentucky. Other eminent and distinguished guests included Professor Chola Chisunka and his dear wife, Mrs Chisunka, from upstate New York in Syracuse. Professor Chisunka was at the time serving as a Professor in the English Department at Fitchburg State University in Massachusetts, US. We also had in attendance for the solemnization of our marriage at church my World Bank Sector Director, Mr Paul Siegelbaum and my World Bank Sector Manager, Mr Alex Fleming, together with some friends from the World Bank.

I have shared a picture below taken when my wife and I went for our honeymoon in Europe shortly after wedding. This photo was taken in downtown Cardiff, Wales.

More than two decades after our wedding, my dearest wife, Dr J, still receives roses from her best friend and loving husband, Prof K.

For Dr J...

Family means a lot to me. I was raised on good family values. It is through the institution of family that God's idea of humanity was transmitted to us as a people. My son Joseph, or Jojo, was born in 2005 in the US, so he is an American. My wife and I took up US citizenship eventually, because family comes first, and we are now domiciled in the US. I invited over to the US my mother and mother-in-law when my wife and I were expecting Jojo. I have always been one who likes to honor and show love to others around me. Not everyone is generous enough to fly in their extended family members now and again. Some people, despite living abroad for many years and earning enough money, have never given their parents or in-laws such a treat. Put simply, we are not all the same. We are cut out differently. My mother visited both England and the US while she was still alive. My father too visited England when I lived in the UK though he had suffered a mild stroke by the time I moved to the US, thus limiting prospects for his international travel to the US. When I was a kid, my father traveled to Canada for his university studies, so both my parents were well-versed culturally. Also, from time to time, my mother would travel to neighboring Zimbabwe and Botswana in the late 1970s and early 1980s. As a result, I love taking my family on exotic vacations in various parts of the world.

I shared earlier some family photos taken in the Bahamas and in Cardiff, Wales as well as at such famed places of erudition as the University of Oxford, Harvard University, Yale University, MIT, the University of Warwick, the University of Manchester, the University of Leicester, and the University of Hull. Below are other pictures taken on family vacations elsewhere. In the picture below, I can be seen with my family on vacation in Cape Town, South Africa. Table Mountain appears in the background.

And, of course, I love trying out fine restaurants and good food when I am travelling. I have shared below some pictures of some lovely treats in Cape Town, South Africa.

In the next picture, I am with my family on summer vacation in Ocean City, Maryland, US.

In the picture below, I'm playing the saxophone over the waters at Dewey Beach in Delaware, US.

In the picture below, my family and I had just arrived for summer vacation at Virginia Beach in Virginia, US.

In the pictures below, I was with my family on summer vacation in Ocean City, Maryland, US.

The picture below is that of a young Jojo at the Great Wolf Lodge in Williamsburg, Virginia, US

Ever heard of Air Force 1? Well, check this out.

The following family pictures were taken in Orlando, Florida, while visiting Disney World.

In the picture below, I was back in Cape Town, South Africa, with family.

In this picture a young Jojo in Pretoria, South Africa, raises a friendly hand to President Nelson Mandela.

In the pictures below, I can be seen with my wife and son on a family vacation in the Caribbean Island of the Commonwealth of Dominica.

Office of The President

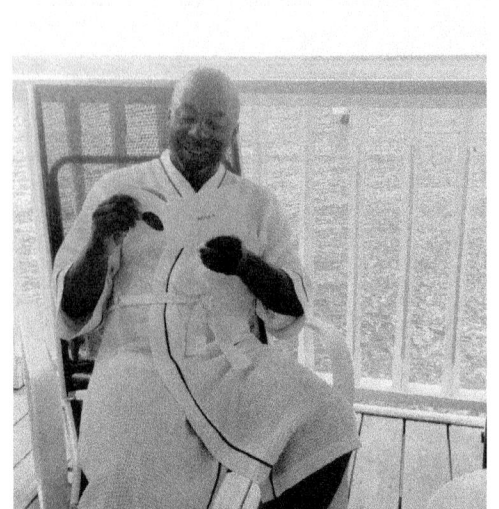

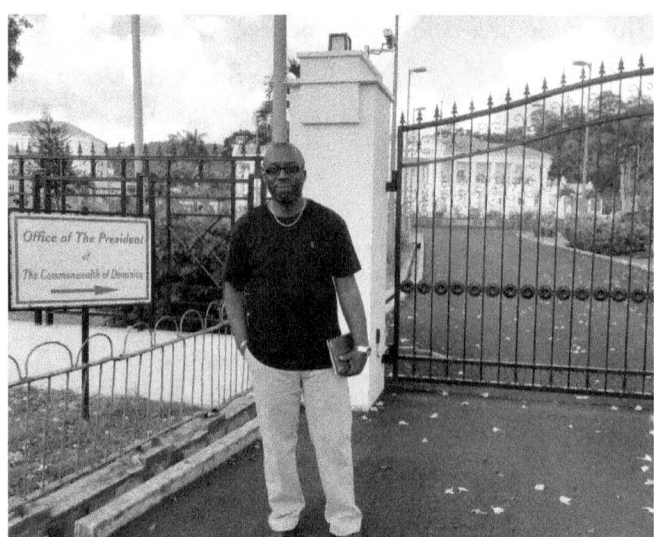

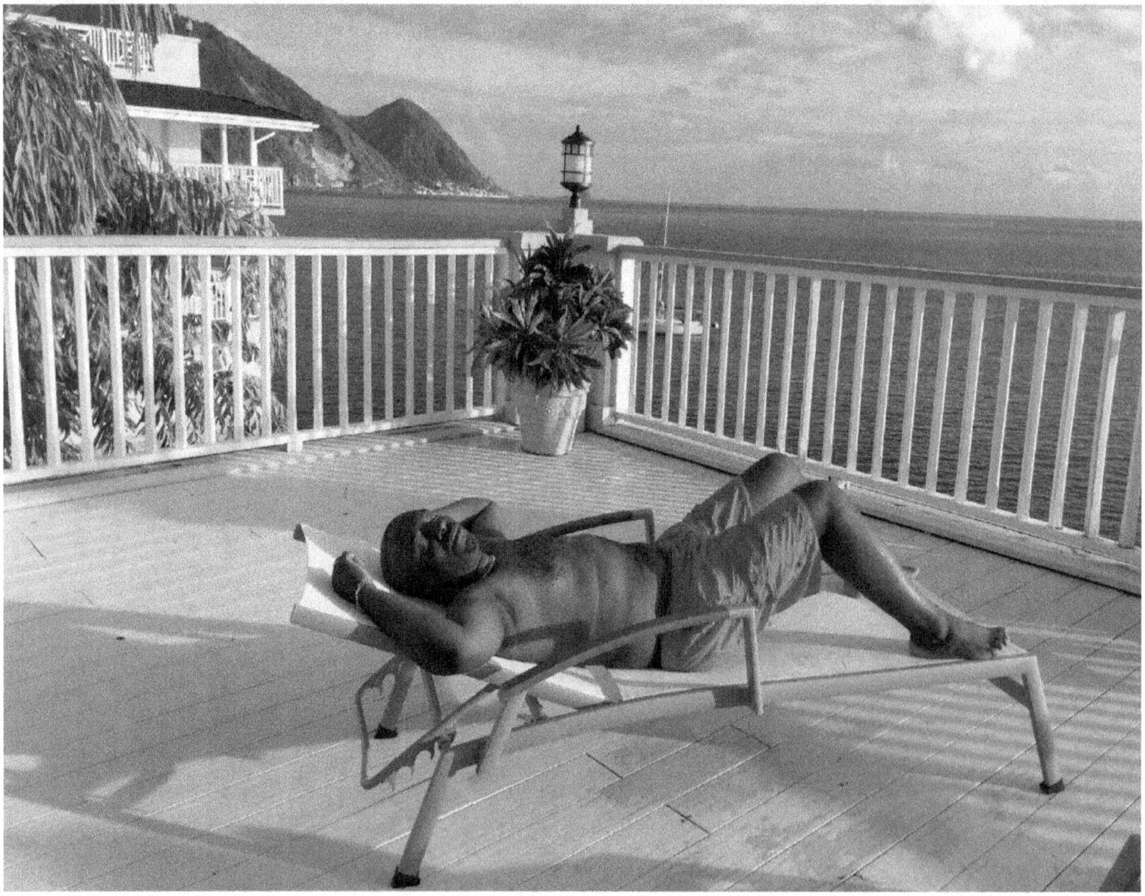

In the pictures below, I am with my wife and son on a family vacation on the Caribbean Island of Antigua.

Our footprints in the fine sand of Antigua beaches are captured by the three pairs of slides in the picture below. One pair is mine while the other two belong to my wife and son respectively.

In the pictures below, I can be seen with my wife and son on a family vacation in the Caribbean Island of St Vincent and the Grenadines.

In the following picture, I just needed to see the university campus on our way to Buccament Bay Resort, a luxurious vacation resort in St. Vincent and the Grenadines.

In the next picture, I am with my family on arrival at the airport in St Vincent and the Grenadines soon after checking through immigration.

In the pictures below, I can be seen with my wife and son on a family vacation in the Caribbean Island of Barbados. We had just gotten off the plane and were heading through to immigration clearance.

In this picture I was trying to do some light shopping at a popular shopping mall in Barbados after noticing that part of my luggage was missing. One of my suitcases was routed mistakenly to Jamaica by the airline folks, so I had to get some clothes while waiting for my missing bag to be delivered to me. It was finally delivered after two days.

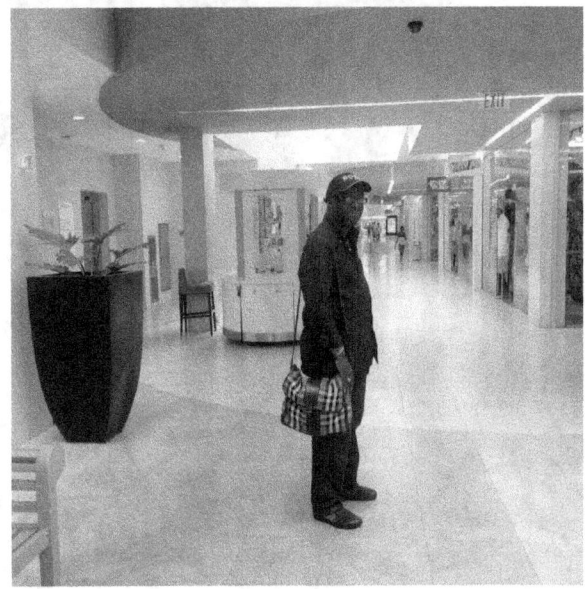

In these photos, I am with my family at the beach in Bridgetown, Barbados.

When I am on vacation with my family, I try to make the best out of every moment that we spend together. And I thank God for all the blessings. As can be seen from a few of the accessories below, when I am travelling, I often travel fully loaded though not too heavy.

At the beach, your sunglasses, slides, swimming attire and towel speak volumes about you before you even step in the water. There is no need to disrespect the beach by showing up in bad taste clothing. Even sharks can get offended. Every day at the beach deserves its own wardrobe.

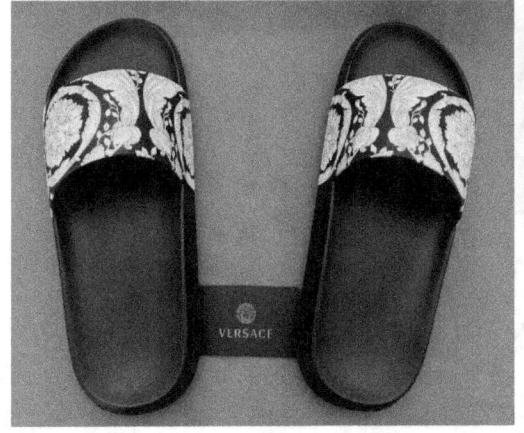

Indeed, cleanliness is next to godliness. Keeping your environment clean and tidy, including what you are wearing, is considered a virtuous and desirable quality.

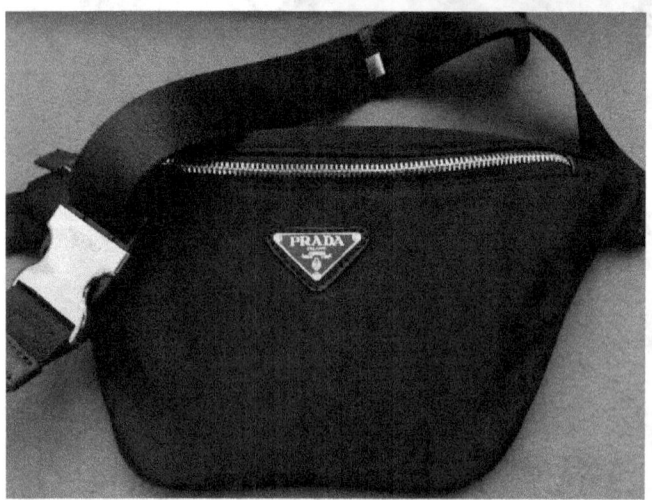

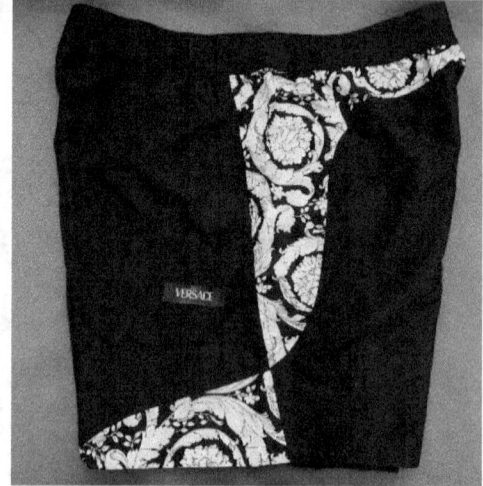

In the picture below, taken on Saturday, May 25, 2019, I can be seen with my wife and son in Lusaka, Zambia, when I was being honored at State House by His Excellency the then President of the Republic of Zambia, Dr Edgar C Lungu. I am ever grateful to President Lungu for this prestigious and highly coveted honor. Even before I received this honor, I always had a soft spot for President Lungu, especially for his sincerity and affable personality towards people from all walks of life. It was extremely humbling for my family and I to receive an invitation from the President to join him for an official ceremony at State House, especially that I was being conferred upon with what is arguably the most distinguished award that an eminent scholar of international stature and repute can receive from the Head of State.

In the picture below, taken a few days after the State House ceremony in 2019, as my family and I were about to fly back to the USA, my wife and son can be seen relaxing in the VIP lounge at Zambia's Kenneth Kaunda International Airport.

My lovely wife, Dr Judith Mwenda, and I, have been married now for more than two decades, and together, we have a wonderful son, Joseph (Jojo). Jojo reminds me so much of my father, especially for his love of school as well as for his exemplary and well-cultivated conduct. I am ever grateful to God our Heavenly Father, Jehovah Almighty, for the gifts of marriage and a wonderful family. These are gifts that we, as human beings, sometimes take for granted, yet not everyone receives such gifts. Therefore, gratitude is important in our everyday life. Never assume or feel entitled to anything. In the picture below, Jojo and I, enjoying some good summer weather, were out for lunch.

In the 2019 picture below, as my family and I were flying back to the US from Zambia via South Africa, my wife and son can be seen relaxing in the Business Class lounge at Oliver Tambo International Airport in Johannesburg, South Africa while waiting to board Business Class to Washington DC.

In the picture below, I am welcomed into the VIP lounge at Zambia's Kenneth Kaunda International Airport by my good learned brother, Hon Mr Mwamba Peni II, who served at some point as Permanent Secretary at Cabinet Office in the Government of the Republic of Zambia. I am ever grateful for his gracious and kind hospitality.

Over the years, I have come to realize that some people will always feel entitled to one thing or another. But I always tell myself that the world does not owe you anything. So, I often stop and look back to say 'thank you' to the people who have been there for me. We could all be better people if we were to realize that nobody owes us anything. That realization can help you and me to reduce our levels of jealousy and envy so that we can all clap for each other instead of thinking how to dim someone's light. People often hate others not because there is a genuine need to hate, but because of envy and jealousy. If they can't have what you have, or they can't reach the levels that you have reached, they start to hate. But how does hating someone help you?

There are no secrets to a happy life, marriage, family or home. Money is definitely not the only answer to your happiness. There are many folks out there who have a lot of money but are still lonely and miserable. Money often gives you only temporary relief. In fact, money is often the main source of a lot of problems. So, what to do now? In my humble view, a sustainable solution for a happy life, home, marriage and family is putting God first in everything you do, as you strive to make your money or do whatever is legit that you are working on. This means that between yourselves as a (married) couple you must not only become selfless to one another, but you must remain open with each other. Many professional marriage counsellors use terms such as 'communication', 'transparency', 'initiating', 'empathy', 'finances', 'trust', 'kindness' and so forth, because that is what it is called in psychology. In the Christian sense, it simply means a kind and supreme love that puts God first in everything you do as a family or married couple. Yes, as humans, none of us are perfect, but that does not mean we cannot put God first in whatever we do. At some point, you could stumble, but you must always hold steadfastly to the Cross of our Lord and Savior, Jesus Christ. Never leave the side of the Cross. For, the cross is your strength and fortress. If you are not a believer, or are an atheist or agnostic, then try to elevate love above all else. For, even with God, everything starts from the point of love. Otherwise, no alangizi, witchdoctor, ng'anga or sangoma can give you medicine for a happy marriage. Suspicious-looking herbs, powders, beads, body marks, tattoos, and all manner of concoctions are also not part of God's plan for a happy marriage.

CHAPTER 17

International and State Recognition of Global Thought-Leadership

In addition to receiving international recognition through various esteemed and highly regarded fellowships from such leading universities as the University of Oxford in England and Yale University in the US, I have received coveted international recognition for my global thought-leadership through, *inter alia*, various meritorious appointments to prestigious professorships at many leading universities in North America, Europe, and Africa. Further still, other international recognitions of my global thought-leadership include being invited by such esteemed international media as the *New York Times* (USA), the *Voice of America* (VOA, USA), *CCTV* (USA), the *Times* (UK), the British Broadcasting Corporation (BBC, UK), and *Sky TV* (UK) to offer my learned opinions and intellectual contributions. Also, the two widely revered and rarely awarded Higher Doctorate degrees of LLD and DSc (Econ) conferred on me by two leading world-class universities add to the list of my international accolades. I have already addressed a number of these milestones in the preceding chapters and will thus not repeat those discissions here. Suffice it to say, I have continued to advance the frontiers of thought-leadership both at the national and international levels, culminating in the national recognition of my scholarly work and global thought-leadership at the highest State levels. I highlighted, for example, in Chapter 3 of this book how the then Bank of Zambia Governor, Dr Caleb M Fundanga, as sitting central bank governor of Zambia, gave formal public recognition of my global thought-leadership when I made history in 2008 by becoming the first Zambian scholar to receive a Higher Doctorate in any academic discipline.

Furthermore, it is not a common feat for a scholar to be named and honored through the national gazette of a country for his or her outstanding scholarly accomplishments and contributions as well as receiving formal commendations from two Heads of State for such accomplishments and contributions. This rare honor, like that of a decorated military General, is different from, say, political appointments, where any Tom, Dick or Harry, through some spiritedly obsequious behavior and political connections, is able to lobby a cabal of cronies to have him or her appointed as Attorney-General, Solicitor-General or Minister of Justice. Of course, once elevated to such public office, the unscrupulous fella will then run with the ball and the law might not stop the Head of State from appointing him or her to the highly politicized statutory appellation of 'State Counsel'.

A number of undeserving and underqualified fellas have been able to wing it and gotten appointed as State Counsel in such an uninspiring manner. It's a charade. Even the so-called 'networking' that some people often parrot to justify their unethical behaviors of pleading for appointments and jobs from folks who are high up on the echelons of the political system or corporate ladder is nothing but cheap bootlicking and schmoozing. Indeed, if you don't have balls, you can easily become a star through what most corrupt people call 'networking'. Generally, political appointments and promotions are rarely done on merit and often follow patronage. By contrast, as a 'gazetted scholar', I am listed meritoriously in the prestigious Zambian national annals of the President's Honors and Awards. Until 2025, I was the only gazetted legal scholar in the entire history of the Republic of Zambia. Entry into such coveted State annals is a rare achievement amongst many a scholar and carries much more gravitas than, say, a mere political appointment. It is the closest you get to being declared a national treasure. The story of Pelé being declared, through the enactment of legislation, a national treasure of Brazil remains inspiring. One can draw some modest parallels from here.

I am exceedingly humbled by the exceptional gift that God has given me on the global and international stage as a leading pundit, global thought-leader and public intellectual. Hitherto, no other legal scholar from Zambia, whether alive or dead, has received the type of distinguished State honors that I have received from two successive Zambian Governments, the MMD Government and the PF Government. I highlighted these two honors in Chapter 1 of this book. The first national honor was conferred on me in June 2011 under President Rupiah Banda's MMD Government in Zambia when I was appointed as Honorary Tourism Ambassador for Zambia. I discussed this honor in Chapter 2 and will thus not repeat that discussion here. Suffice it to say that the second national honor conferred on me was in May 2019 when, pursuant to the Constitution of the Republic of Zambia, the Government of the Republic of Zambia issued Gazette Notice No. 586 of 2019, declaring me worthy and deserving to receive the coveted Presidential Honors for my distinguished and eminent global thought-leadership. The President's Insignia of Meritorious Achievement (PIMA) was conferred upon me on Africa Freedom in 2019. This 2019 distinguished Presidential Honor came after my unprecedented two Higher Doctorates as well as my many other academic and professional accomplishments. In the pictures below, I can be seen as the coveted PIMA award was being conferred upon me by the 6th President of the Republic of Zambia, His Excellency Dr Edgar Chagwa Lungu, at State House in Lusaka, Zambia.

I have often found myself setting the path for others to follow. This was a first for the Zambian legal academy. We only aspire to inspire. And much to the chagrin of the naysayers, I was honored not because of any partisan-political, tribal or regional affiliation, but purely on merit for my sustained and unparalleled intellectual prowess and academic achievements. Even the University of Oxford in England went ahead to honor me a few years later. Such accolades don't come easily. It is important to set the record straight.

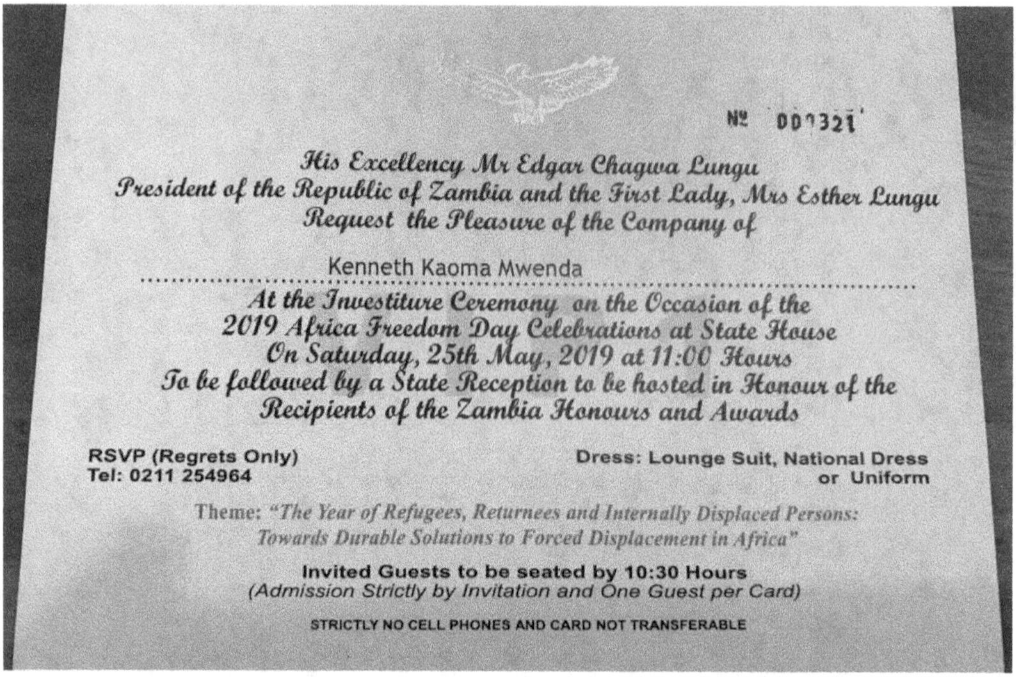

№ 000321

His Excellency Mr Edgar Chagwa Lungu
President of the Republic of Zambia and the First Lady, Mrs Esther Lungu
Request the Pleasure of the Company of

Kenneth Kaoma Mwenda

At the Investiture Ceremony on the Occasion of the
2019 Africa Freedom Day Celebrations at State House
On Saturday, 25th May, 2019 at 11:00 Hours
To be followed by a State Reception to be hosted in Honour of the
Recipients of the Zambia Honours and Awards

RSVP (Regrets Only)　　　　　　　　　　　Dress: Lounge Suit, National Dress
Tel: 0211 254964　　　　　　　　　　　　　　　　　　　　　　or Uniform

Theme: *"The Year of Refugees, Returnees and Internally Displaced Persons:*
Towards Durable Solutions to Forced Displacement in Africa"

Invited Guests to be seated by 10:30 Hours
(Admission Strictly by Invitation and One Guest per Card)

STRICTLY NO CELL PHONES AND CARD NOT TRANSFERABLE

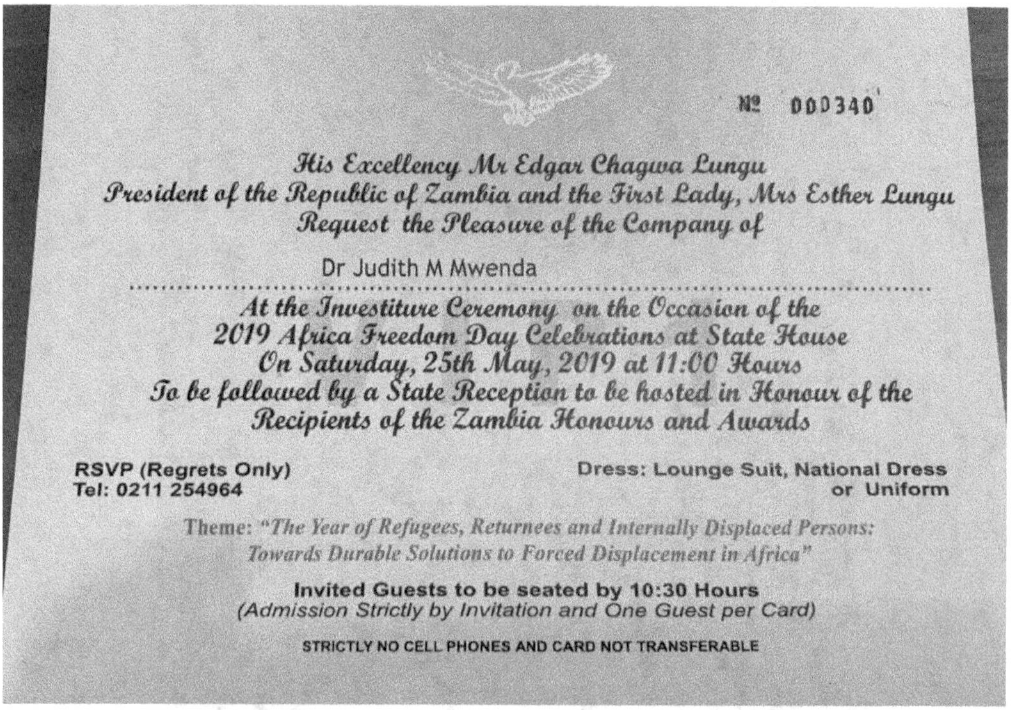

№ 000340

His Excellency Mr Edgar Chagwa Lungu
President of the Republic of Zambia and the First Lady, Mrs Esther Lungu
Request the Pleasure of the Company of

Dr Judith M Mwenda

At the Investiture Ceremony on the Occasion of the
2019 Africa Freedom Day Celebrations at State House
On Saturday, 25th May, 2019 at 11:00 Hours
To be followed by a State Reception to be hosted in Honour of the
Recipients of the Zambia Honours and Awards

RSVP (Regrets Only)　　　　　　　　　　　Dress: Lounge Suit, National Dress
Tel: 0211 254964　　　　　　　　　　　　　　　　　　　　　　or Uniform

Theme: *"The Year of Refugees, Returnees and Internally Displaced Persons:*
Towards Durable Solutions to Forced Displacement in Africa"

Invited Guests to be seated by 10:30 Hours
(Admission Strictly by Invitation and One Guest per Card)

STRICTLY NO CELL PHONES AND CARD NOT TRANSFERABLE

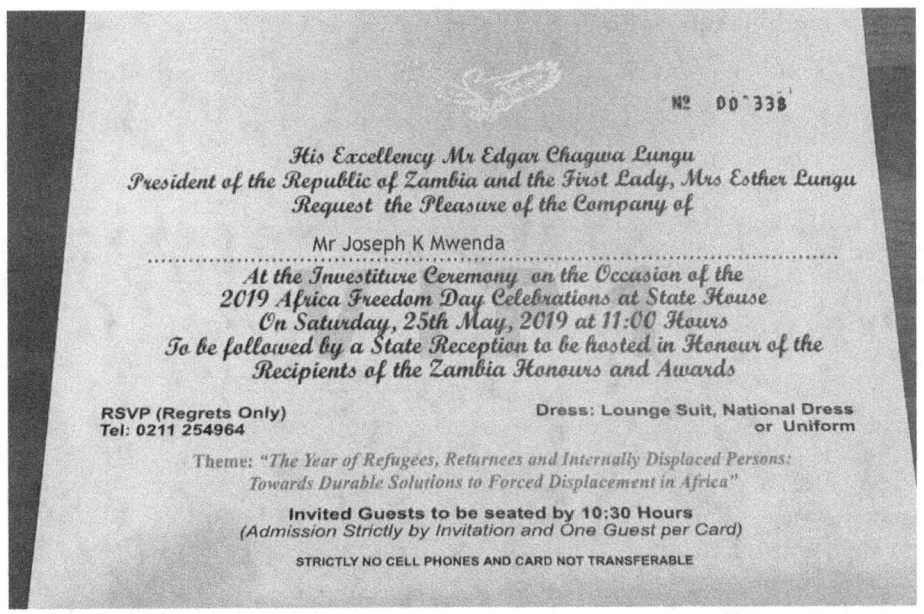

My lovely wife, Dr Judith Mwenda, and our son, Joseph, accompanied me from the US to Zambia to receive this prestigious President's Insignia of Meritorious Achievement (PIMA). I have shared some pictures below of my family and me at State House in Zambia when I was receiving the PIMA award.

Posing for presidential pictures with His Excellency President Dr Edgar Chagwa Lungu, the 6th President of the Republic of Zambia, shortly after he conferred on me the prestigious national honor of the President's Insignia of Meritorious Achievement (PIMA) at State House in Lusaka, Zambia, on May 25, 2019. Thank you, Your Excellency! You will forever be remembered and loved.

Below is a photo taken at the PIMA event at State House in Lusaka, Zambia, with my good brother Mr Bonaventure Mutale (on my right) and a colleague of ours (on my left).

On the page opposite is a press statement that I released in both Zambian State-owned print media, the *Times of Zambia* and the *Zambia Daily Mail*, soon after I returned to the US after receiving the PIMA award in Zambia. I believe in showing gratitude. That is how I was raised. And the Bible instructs us in Luke 17:11-19 as follows: "Now on his way to Jerusalem, Jesus traveled along the border between Samaria and Galilee. As he was going into a village, ten men who had leprosy met him. They stood at a distance and called out in a loud voice, 'Jesus, Master, have pity on us!' When he saw them, he said, 'Go, show yourselves to the priests.' And as they went, they were cleansed. One of them, when

SPECIAL THANKS TO HIS EXCELLENCY, THE PRESIDENT OF THE REPUBLIC OF ZAMBIA, MR EDGAR CHAGWA LUNGU, FOR THE PRESIDENTIAL INSIGNIA OF MERITORIOUS ACHIEVEMENT (PIMA)

I wish to express wholeheartedly my profound gratitude to His Excellency, the President of the Republic of Zambia, Mr Edgar Chagwa Lungu, for recognizing my sustained intellectual leadership as a thought leader that has done Zambia proud both at home and abroad.

This rare and honourable gesture by His Excellency, the President, is undoubtedly very humbling and much appreciated. It comes after many years of extensive scholarly writing and academic teaching on three (3) different continents, namely, Africa, Europe and North America. Some of my former students have gone on to become Judges at all levels of the judiciary, whereas others have served as Attorney-Generals, Cabinet Ministers, Law Professors and Deans of Law schools in their respective countries. The body of my extensive published work has earned me two (2) higher Doctorates, that is an LLD and a DSc (Econ), in two different disciplines from leading international universities.

My family and I cannot be any more grateful for the noble award from the President. This PIMA award serves as an indelible mark at the pinnacle of my scholarly heights. I am forever and eternally grateful to His Excellency, the President, for the honor. It is even more gratifying to be awarded the Presidential Insignia of meritorious achievement by such an accomplished Senior Lawyer as His Excellency, the President.

I am particularly humbled by this edifying gesture.

To God, our Father, Jehovah, thank you for watching over and ordering my steps. Your mercies endure forever. This journey would not have been possible without the work of your Hand, culminating in this prestigious award bestowed on me at State House, Lusaka, Zambia, during the commemoration of Africa Freedom Day on Saturday, May 25, 2019.

Finally, I take this opportunity to thank most sincerely my dear parents Mr Joseph T. Mwenda and Mrs Esther M. Mwenda, who taught me decency and human values of honesty, fairness, love, truthfulness and hard work. These values have sustained me in my erudite pursuit of knowledge. May their souls rest in eternal peace.

I would also like to thank my wife and son, as well as my fellow citizens, including friends who have given me their unwavering support. I salute you all, and may God bless mother Zambia.

Professor Kenneth K. Mwenda
PhD, LLD, DSc (Econ)
Rhodes Scholar
Website: http//kennethmwenda.com/about.htm

he saw he was healed, came back, praising God in a loud voice. He threw himself at Jesus' feet and thanked him—and he was a Samaritan. Jesus asked, 'Were not all ten cleansed? Where are the other nine? Has no one returned to give praise to God except this foreigner?' Then he said to him, 'Rise and go; your faith has made you well.'"

It is from the scriptures that we learn the grace of gratitude. For, what is written in the scriptures can only inspire us to uphold virtue, not to be self-conceited and behave as if we are entitled to be honored.

The news of my PIMA award spread like wildfire and was all over the various television channels in Zambia. I have shared below some screenshots sent to me by a number of people who watched on television the proceedings at State House.

Closely related to the foregoing, I am also listed in several elite international biographical publications of *Who's Who*. These listings speak to the international recognition of one's scholarly standing in the international community. I have provided below some pictures pertaining to the said biographical listings.

CHAPTER 18

Leadership and Lifelong Learning

Leadership and management are not the same thing. In many cases, you can manage without leading, but to lead, you must also be able to motivate others. There is a strong nexus between leadership and motivation. So, a leader is more than a manager.

A leader does three things essentially. First, he or she is able to lead the self through a conscious and enlightened sense of mindfulness, self-awareness, emotional intelligence and social intelligence. Secondly, a leader is one who can lead across and within teams authentically. Put simply, he or she motivates followers with a common or shared vision, and thus inspires trust and confidence. Thirdly, a leader manages effectively and efficiently tasks being carried out by his or her team. This third dimension of leadership is what preoccupies much of management. Tasks associated with, say, finance, business planning, budgeting and accounting, human resources management, information technology, marketing and operations management are intrinsic elements of management but do not necessarily speak to the broader spectrum of leadership. To lead, as opposed to managing, one must embrace also the first two dimensions of leadership outlined above. Otherwise, you will be able to manage a task, yet struggle to lead your followers or teammates. Task execution alone is not leadership. So, trying to manage people is often a poor way of leading. People are not tasks. They have emotions and other soft skills that require more than managing. Rather, you have to inspire and motivate people as you lead them, as opposed to just managing them.

Against this background, I submit that lifelong learning is an intrinsic part of authentic leadership. Every leader who aspires to be an effective and authentic leader must embrace a culture of lifelong learning. For how else can you lead if you cannot learn? You learn, for example, from your own mistakes as well as from those of others. You also learn from your successes as well as from those of others. Similarly, you also learn from reading, listening, observing and paying attention to what others are saying or doing, in addition to adapting to different constraints in the internal and external environments. So, a global thought-leader, I contend, is a lifelong learner. Every experience for him or her is a learning experience, for he or she continues to evolve daily. As a thought-leader, you cannot afford to be static because change is inevitable, and you must continue to learn, grow and adapt to change in order to survive. The environment around you is not static, but dynamic. It is continuously evolving and in constant motion. So, you too must evolve and remain in motion, as you learn, in order to adapt to changes in and around you.

In June 2021, I was elected as a Fellow of the Zambia Academy of Sciences, the highest scientific and academic national statutory body in Zambia for the advancement of science and knowledge. Election to the rank of Fellow is reserved for those individuals who have made substantial contribution to the advancement and improvement of knowledge. In 2005, I qualified as a Certified Anti-Money Laundering Specialist under the US-based Association of Certified Anti-Money Laundering Specialists (ACAMS), becoming the first Zambian to obtain this prestigious anti-money laundering qualification. This inspired many other Zambian professionals to get the ACAMS qualification as well. In 2004, I sat and passed exams for two prestigious qualifications offered jointly by the UK-based International Compliance Association and the University of Manchester, UK, namely, the International Diploma in Anti-Money Laundering and the International Diploma in Compliance. Again, I was a pioneer for my country. Prior to that, in 1999 and 2004, I completed two postgraduate certifications with the United Nations World Intellectual Property Organisation (WIPO Academy) in (a) Intellectual Property Law, and (b) Copyright and Electronic Commerce. Learning never comes to an end. There is no such thing as "Na li sambilila ukunya!" ("I am too highly educated to learn anything new.")

As a global thought-leader, you must keep evolving and adapting to the changing environment around you. For example, artificial intelligence is changing the way we work. Equally, the emergence of the COVID-19 pandemic showed that home-based work can at times be just as effective as working from the office. So, we must all evolve and adapt. In 2024, I was elected and appointed to the prestigious Archibald McDougall Visiting Professorship in International Law at the University of West Virginia Law School in Morgantown, West Virginia, US. And I travelled to Morgantown to take up that position. Let me share some pictures of my time as the Archibald McDougall Visiting Professor of International Law at the University of West Virginia Law School in the US.

Yes, I keep evolving and adapting. Change is constant. As the Greek philosopher Heraclitus of Ephesus, once said: 'The only constant in life is change.' We must all continue to adapt to the changes around us if we are to survive. Fo, tomorrow is for those who are willing to learn, unlearn and re-learn.

Lifelong learning as a mantra of thought-leadership invites one to learn from a variety of sources. It means going beyond and outside your comfort zones to learn or experience what is unknown to you. While you need not be an expert in everything, you must at least have a broad overview of contemporary issues in the global community. That is how you become a global citizen, as opposed to limiting your knowledge to parochial, insular or tribal issues.

Inspired by this philosophical outlook, I have been a smooth jazz enthusiast for many years now. And I love attending live smooth jazz performances. I have seen countless top smooth jazz and R&B artists performing live in the US. My choice of music, like my choices of fashion and art, speak to my aesthetic taste. As a fashionista, I continue to learn from the world of fashion in the same way that I learn from the world of jazz music. Every experience is a learning opportunity. Life is not monolithic. Neither is society confined to homogenous values. As an open system, a civilized human society embraces heterogeneity and is not driven by homogeneity.

It is from the perspective of heterogeneous value systems that variable learning is seen as an aid to strengthen our ability to abstract and draw lessons, including key takeaways, from an eclectic set of different experiences. Wine, for example, is not something that you just drink without smelling and savoring it. It is wise also to appreciate the vineyard and appellation of origin associated with certain wines. Your palate matters too. By parity of reasoning, transferable skills can come, say, from a metaphor or analogy that is outside the mainstream.

I have shared below some family pictures that highlight some of the experiences that have helped to inform my view of the world. In a number of these pictures, my dearest wife, Dr J, and my beloved son, Jojo, feature. What I can afford to wear, my wife and son also deserve. That is my concept of family. One must not be selfish at the expense of family. At the end of the day, as economists will tell you, *ceteris paribus*, an individual is a utility maximiser. We all want the best in a world of limited resources. I hasten to add, however, that the pictures shared in this book are in no way promotions or sponsored adverts. Rather, they are simply a reflection of my own aesthetics. After all, we all have tastes and preferences of one kind or another no matter how much we may try to pretend. For me, I don't pretend. I have no time to pretend. And I make no apologies. You can only apologize if you have done something wrong. Otherwise, if someone does not understand you, it does not mean you are wrong. Let them focus on their own. For we only aspire to inspire.

If not now, then when? Tomorrow is not guaranteed, my friend. Just enjoy your life and the blessings that God has placed in your life. If you keep worrying about what people will think or say, you will never be happy. Do not let people define your happiness. People will talk even if you are in the toilet minding your own business. Some will accuse you of staying in the toilet for too long whilst others will wonder what is keeping you busy. Then, there will also be those who will just be waiting for you to come out of the toilet so that they can see the look on your face. Whether you come out with a smile or serious face, people will still talk. Others will even accuse you of leaving behind a foul smell, yet you found it there when you entered the toilet. What to do now? You might as well just enjoy your life. You only have one life to live.

In the picture above, I was clad in Gucci sporty attire, with a matching Gucci cap and Gucci sunglasses, while sailing away aboard a luxury yacht and savoring a prodigious Petrus red wine. In the next picture, I am packing my Atelier Versace perfume to stay fresh on my trip.

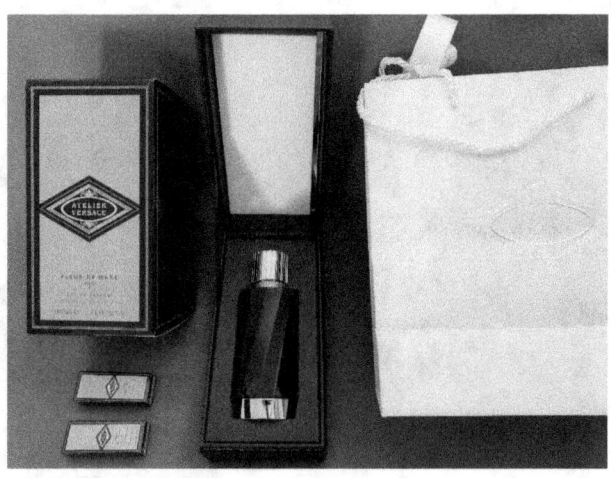

You are the architect of your dreams and the captain of your ship. Don't expect other people to do it for you. If you have to live your dreams or sail away on a romantic cruise, why not? What are you waiting for? Nobody will come around to grant you permission. You don't need their permission.

As honest as it can get, for we only aspire to inspire.

In life, you often have two choices. You can choose to be either amazing or amazed. There is just not enough room in the middle for one to sit on the fence.

Your garb represents your identity. It is not vanity but a part of your vanguard. It is about who you are. As an authentic leader at the frontiers of global thought-leadership, I have no time to pretend. Neither do I do things to please people or to gain their approval. My swag simply speaks to my persona and style.

Even your choice of fine wines and meals speaks to your personality. For, you are what you drink and eat.

You cannot divorce or separate 'cool' from 'school'. School must always be cool. To keep inspiring the young folks to go to school, it is wise not to make school look or sound boring. The pictures that I have shared herein are meant to motivate and inspire a child or two who could be doubting themselves on the value of going to school. I have made it simple by using pictorial presentations in order to communicate what young people can relate to. To that end, I have deliberately avoided delving into philosophical arguments on the value of education. Suffice it to say that school has style and fashion, as can be seen in the two photos below.

Below are some pictures of a Thanksgiving meal prepared by my dearest wife, Dr J. Thanksgiving in the US is a big thing. And the turkey, not a chicken, but turkey, must be nicely prepared.

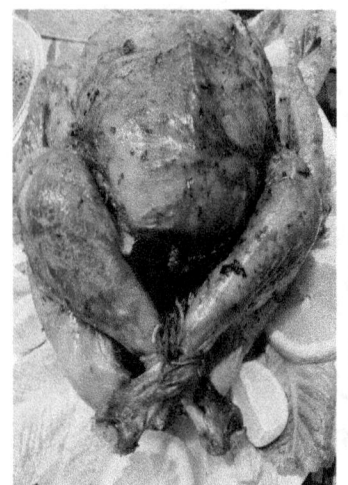

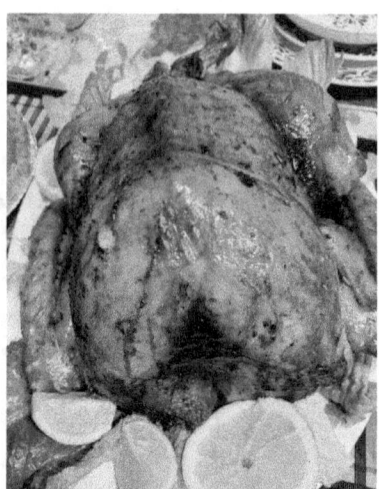

When you appreciate someone, you must show it. Don't expect them to guess. On International Women's Day 2024, I decided to gift my wife a Versace apron, a set of Versace gloves and a set of Versace grilling towels, given the lovely meals and barbecues that she often prepares for the family. They are pictured below after she unsealed the box.

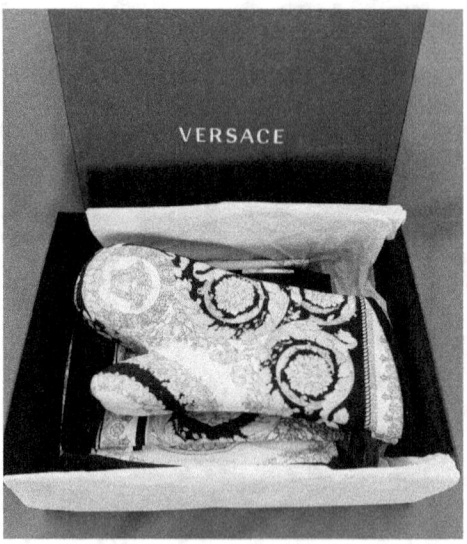

The picture below shows my eclectic taste in fine garb and fine dining places.

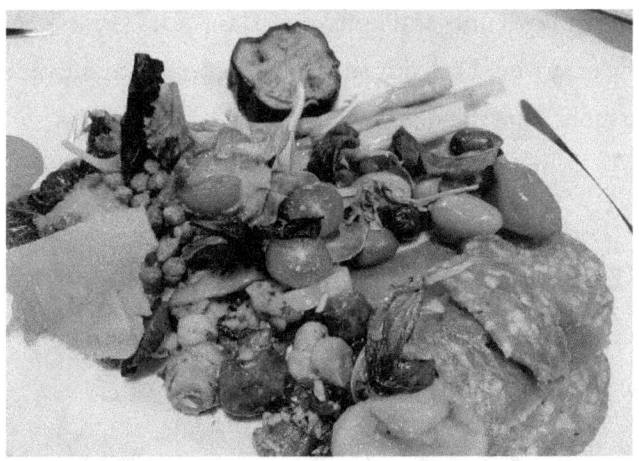

In the pictures below, my dearest wife, Dr J, our adorable son, Jojo, and I were dining out at Fogo de Chão in Baltimore, Maryland, US.

Another fine restaurant that my family and I often go to is Ruth's Chris Steak House. I have shared below a picture of my dearest wife, Dr J, our adorable son, Jojo, and me dining out at Ruth's Chris Steak House in Gaithersburg, Maryland, US.

If not dining out, we are either travelling or vacationing together as a family. In the next picture, I was treating my feet to some Balenciaga slides at the beach in Barbados.

Let me share some pictures of my family swag and our collective and individual fine taste for garb.

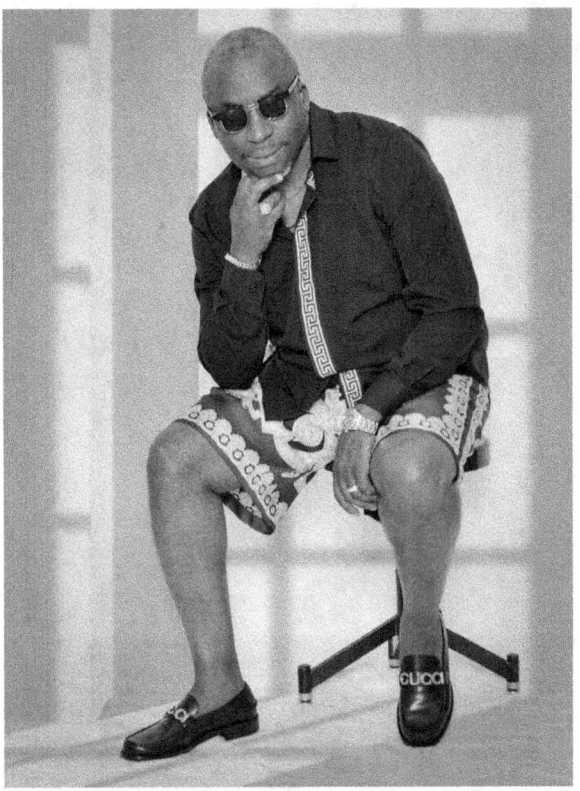

BEYOND THE PHD

It is always good to switch brands, depending on the occasion or event. Your loyalty should only be to your taste, not to a commercial brand, unless you are paid for it. Sometimes, when I am shopping for my dearest wife, Dr J, I try not to be too predictable with my choice of brands, and will get her anything from YSL, Louboutin, Hermes, Louis Vuitton, Gucci to Channel and others. Let me share a little touch of my own garb, switching to Burberry attire, Burberry coats and Burberry bags, in the next photos.

Different bags sit differently, depending on the occasion, the mood and the garb.

Cleanliness, as they say, is next to godliness.

I love to have some bottled spring water next to my red wine when I am relaxing in my hotel room.

My signature style is distinctively my own.

Nothing in the year feels as good as summertime at the beach.

Closely related to an eclectic taste of fashion and fine dining places is an appreciation of performing arts and such good music as smooth jazz.

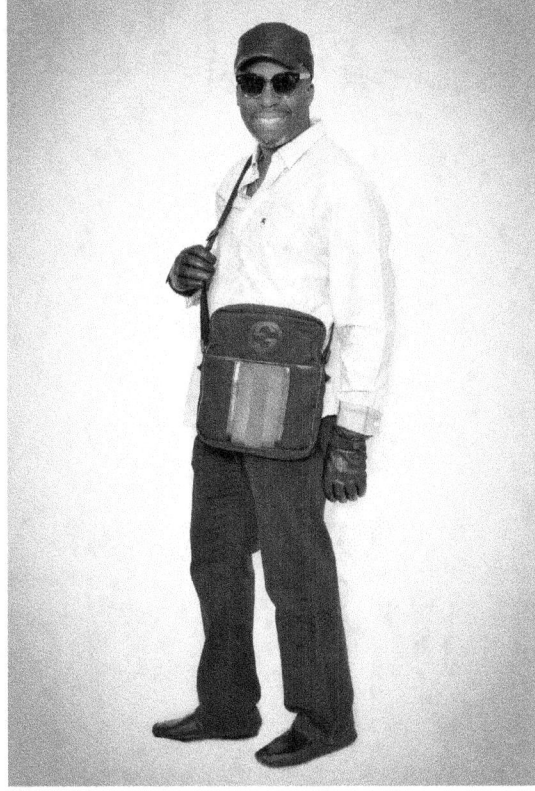

As a smooth jazz enthusiast, my style is never short of a jazzy touch.
I like jazzing it up, as in the pictures below.

In the pictures below, I was with my family in Manhattan, New York, US, spending some quality summer time together.

Sometimes, we go with the Gucci garb, as in the picture below. It all depends on the occasion and the mood. It's like that.

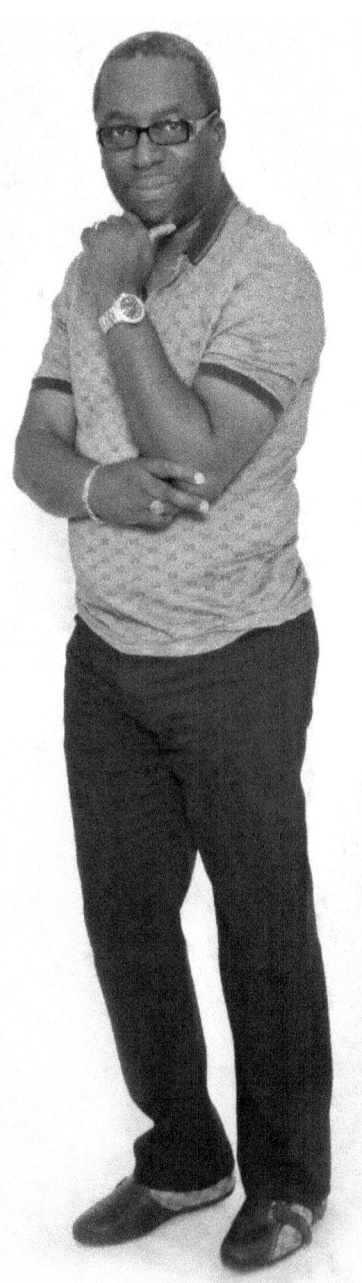

The apple does not fall far from the tree.

It is what it is. The favor of God rests on those who honor Him.

We do it for the people. We only aspire to inspire.

Show me the snow, and I will show you a man who can weather the snow without a winter coat but only the favor of God.

Following below are some pictures of my smart casual wear on some nice and sunny summer days, starting with a Gucci polo shirt and Gucci spectacles before switching to a Versace outfits.

The love of jazz is obvious from the two photos below, starting with the horn on a cold snowy day to a fine dinner with my lovely wife, Dr J, on the famed Odessey yacht in Washington DC.

Below are some pictures of my smart casual dress on a good weekend of spring or autumn weather.

My son knows my style. Together, we are a force.

Man cannot live by bread or ideas alone, for he lives in a material world from which he cannot escape.

In the picture below, his and hers at the airport in Miami, Florida, US, when transiting for vacation to the Bahamas.

In the picture below, with the then Minister of Finance of Zambia, Hon Ms Margaret Manakatwe, at the Zambia Trade Fair Show in Ndola, Zambia, before I gave my keynote presentation.

BEYOND THE PHD

We only aspire to inspire. The photo below is one of my favorites.

In closing this chapter, we end with fashion for the workplace, as an element of thought-leadership in the corporate world. Sometimes, you have to arrange your clothes and travel bags nicely when travelling to various parts of the world for business. How does that play out? Check this out.

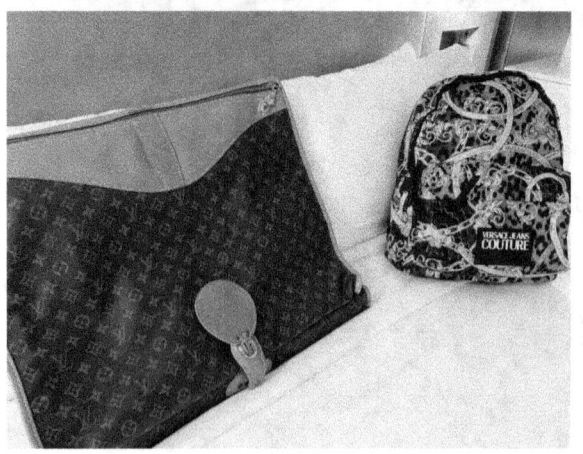
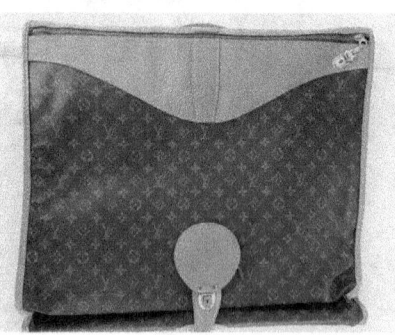

Cleanliness is next to godliness. You must always be prepared to look presentable for each and every occasion. For example, you cannot work out at the gym dressed in a white shirt, tie and suit.

Neither can you show up at a cocktail party dressed in jeans and a T-shirt. Even when attending office meetings, the type of pen you are carrying, the notebook you are writing in, the daily planner next to your smartphone and other related accessories around you all speak to your persona. They tell a story. They are not just decorations. But they help to define your taste and preferences.

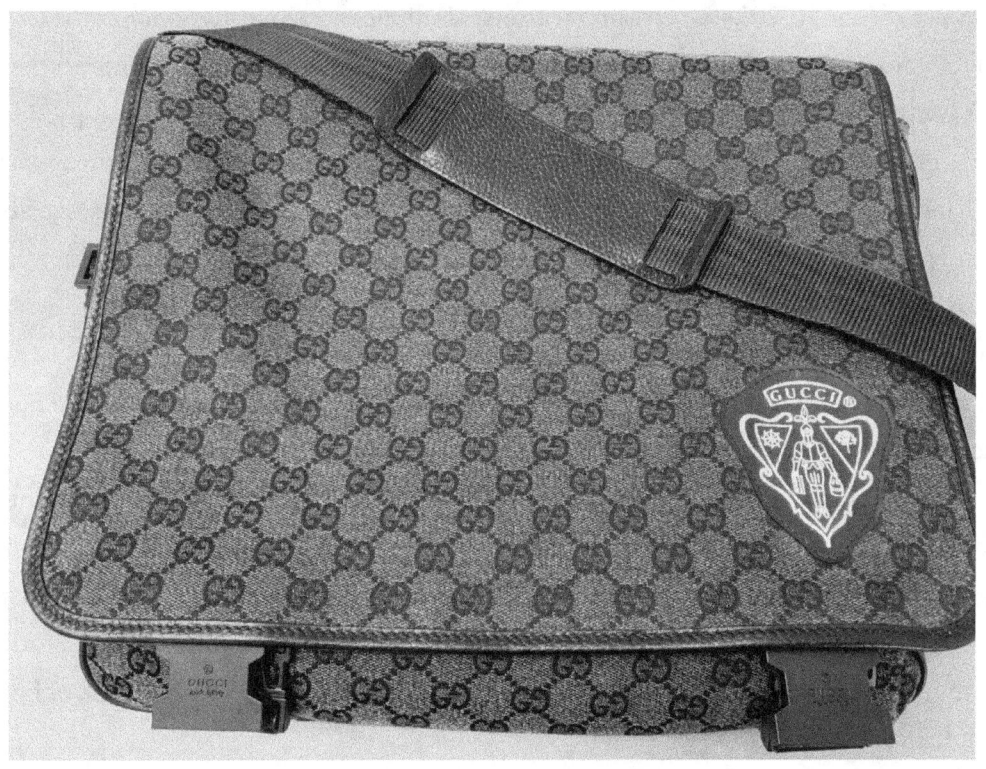

CHAPTER 19

The momentous Oxford gala dinner held in my honor

"I will restore to you the years that the locust has eaten."
– Joel 2:25

The week of June 16, 2024, when a momentous gala dinner hosted in my honor by the University of Oxford's Exeter College, in recognition of my getting elected as Honorary Fellow of Oxford's Exeter College, was scheduled to take place is the week when the Zambian president, Mr Hakainde Hichilema, was expected to be in Oxford to address a gathering of Zambians from the United Kingdom and elsewhere. The Zambian community's event was allegedly organized by some Zambian Rhodes Scholars who had previously studied at Oxford. Also in attendance were some Zambians based outside the UK who had flown in for the same event.

    I arrived in Oxford from my base in Washington DC on Friday, June 14, 2024. On arrival, I learned that the Zambian president's event was to be held at Exeter College, the same venue where I was scheduled to have my momentous gala dinner. It was an interesting coincidence. For some reason, Exeter College opted not to host the event for the Zambian president. That event had to be moved to another venue in the city. By contrast, Exeter College welcomed me respectfully and hosted the dinner held in my honor at the same venue that was being sought by the Zambian folks. Mine was not about politics or a political gathering. I was there to be celebrated for the formidable body of my scholarly works and for getting elected to the most rare and esteemed rank of Honorary Fellow at Oxford.

In life, there are doors that your inimitable geniality can open which not even politics or money can open, for the indisputable intellectual gravitas of your distinguished scholarly work precedes you. Even among the many pundits and intellectual luminaries that have attended or graduated from Oxford, not everyone reaches such levels. You can graduate from Oxford with a First Class, and even hold a teaching appointment there, but that does not mean that Oxford will celebrate you with a gala dinner dedicated or devoted solely to your honor. And it does not matter if, as an Oxford alumnus, you come from a wealthy elite or aristocratic family. To be honored at that level by Oxford, as I was, is an indelible mark of the highest academic respect that you command within and beyond Oxford. It is undisputably no mean achievement. It is testament not to be taken lightly. As I jokingly told my wife before flying out to Oxford:

"This is probably the most expensive dinner I have ever had. First, I had to spend quite some money to get myself a British visa. Secondly, it takes a plane, not a limousine or any other car, for me to get to the dinner venue. Yeah, I gotta fly, not drive. Ever been to a dinner where you have to fly? Thirdly, I have to get myself a First-Class seat on that plane befitting the purpose of my trip to England. You don't go to such dinners, especially if you are the one being honored, flying Economy-Class. Fourthly, the gala dinner is gonna be at the world's best university, the University of Oxford. It's history being written, honey! The haters and naysayers didn't believe in us, but God did. Fifthly, Oxford doesn't just throw a gala dinner in your honor if you have not earned their respect. Honey, this is it. It doesn't feel real even to me, but it is real. God did it, as DJ Khaled sings. Sixthly, I am going to Oxford just to dine and wine respectfully before flying back the next day to the US. I mean, who does that? I couldn't make this up. It's real. I am flying to another continent, not just another country, but another continent, to dine and wine in the company of profound intellectual aura and sophistication. And then I am back the next day in the US. This doesn't feel real, but it is. Not even Hollywood comes close. The feeling beats even the Oscars. I have never heard of any Hollywood celebrity fly to have dinner in Oxford and then fly back to the US the next day. This is it, honey. It's the highest elevation. As DJ Khaled sings on his song, 'God Did' featuring Rick Ross, Lil Wayne, JAY-Z, John Legend and Fridayy, 'You either win with us, or you watch us win.'"

On a more serious note, apart from His Excellency President John Kofi Agyekum Kufuor, the former President of Ghana, who is also an alumnus of the University of Oxford's Exeter College and graduated from Oxford in 1964, I am arguably the second black African to receive the rare and highly prestigious honor of being admitted as an Honorary Fellow to Exeter College since it was founded in 1314. Although some of my fellow countrymen and women from Zambia have also been through Oxford, say, as Rhodes Scholars, or on other scholarships, none of them have ever received the honor and recognition accorded to me by Oxford. And many other Africans have been through Oxford, but very few have had such an honor conferred on them. Oxford cannot honor you for nothing. You must be really worth the honor to be celebrated and honored at that level by Oxford. Even in Hollywood, Oscar awards for the main actor don't come easy. You can act in a movie, win a supporting role-award, but winning the Oscar as the main actor is at a whole different level. It is the same in the music industry. Grammy awards don't come easy either.

If, however, it were some university back home in Africa, and a Head of State showed up for a parallel event at the same venue and in the same week where I was about to be honored, I would probably have been asked by the university authorities to step aside and wait. But not at Oxford. Things are different there. Intellect and meritocracy reign. As my good learned friend Mr Kondanani Miti, a professional staff member at the Common Market for Eastern and Southern

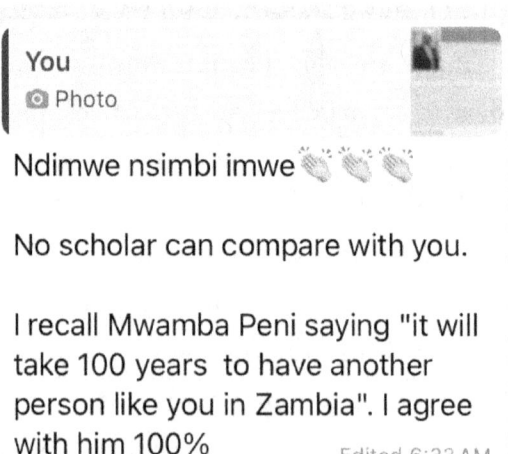

Africa (COMESA), wrote me in a WhatsApp message after I returned from my momentous Oxford gala dinner:

Below is a congratulatory message from my family, as published in the *Zambia Daily Mail* on Tuesday June 25, 2024, when news broke out that I was being celebrated and honored at Oxford.

Oxford celebrates Zambia's Professor Extraordinaire, Prof Kenneth K Mwenda, at a momentous dinner held in his honor!

On Sunday, June 16, 2024, the University of Oxford's Exeter College, established in 1314, and one of the four oldest colleges of the world's most prestigious university, celebrated Professor Kenneth K Mwenda, PhD, LLD, DSc (Econ), a Rhodes Scholar and Oxford alumnus, at a momentous dinner held in Oxford in his honor. As an Honorary Fellow at Oxford, Professor Mwenda has received the highest and rare honor that any University of Oxford college can confer on an eminently qualified person. From 1314 to date, Professor Mwenda is arguably the second black African after His Excellency President John Kufuor, former President of Ghana, who graduated from Oxford in 1964, to be elected as an Honorary Fellow of Oxford's Exeter College. This is no mean achievement. Honorary fellowships at Oxford are very rarely awarded. Professor Mwenda's distinguished scholarly work has received international acclaim in many parts of the world, including the US, the UK and South Africa, confirming the indisputable and immutable intellectual gravitas of his inspiring global thought-leadership. This is a first for Zambia. We, the Mwenda family of Luanshya, are therefore exceedingly humbled and proud to celebrate you, Professor Mwenda, as one of the most distinguished intellectual sons of Africa. May God continue to bless you. You are a true NATIONAL TREASURE!

As a distinguished and eminent global thought-leader, Professor Kenneth K Mwenda, you have been a formidable ambassador of Zambia and Africa at the highest international levels. Your name is a household name in many countries. You not only continue to share expert knowledge, as a public intellectual, through various international broadcast and print media, but have also made indelible and erudite intellectual contributions across the world. It is a truism that, through your edifying scholarly works, you not only have written 30 scholarly books and close to 100 scholarly articles in top-rated peer-reviewed journals but have also taught at leading universities in three continents, namely, Europe, North America and Africa. What a record! Until 2019, Prof Mwenda, you were the only known legal scholar in the entire world with two earned Higher Doctorates, in addition to a PhD, and all three doctorates earned from leading prestigious universities. Indeed, you have no equals at home and many other places. Two successive Zambian Governments under two different Heads of State have both honored you for your unparalleled intellectual contributions. Eminent societies of learned men and women too have honored you. Among your former students are Supreme Court judges and Constitutional Court judges, including a Chief Justice, as well as Attorneys-General and cabinet ministers. And you have advised several governments. Also, your multi-faceted career continues to chart the path for many Zambians and other Africans to emulate. Without doubt, you have inspired many. You are a trend-setter. And you continue to break new world records. Professor Mwenda, your scholarly eminence has also been published previously in the National Gazette of the Republic of Zambia. It's a rare feat. You are one of the very few gazetted scholars and are truly a national treasure.

The Joseph and Esther Mwenda
Family of Luanshya, Zambia.

The gala dinner held in my honor by the University of Oxford's Exeter College is one of those rare and distinguished honors from Oxford to celebrate an intellectual luminary of the highest standing. It was surreal. The event was exclusively in my honor. Unlike a university graduation ceremony where several students graduate, the Oxford gala dinner was dedicated exclusively to my honor. I was humbled, especially as I was the only person being honored at the dinner. It was a really touching experience to be honored by Oxford. You don't often witness the granting of such a coveted honor at that level in your lifetime. I even had to reschedule an appointment with the US federal government offices to be sworn in as an American citizen. Oxford was waiting. I just had to travel there.

I was later sworn in as a US citizen in November 2024.

I have always believed in hard work. I studied, lived and worked in the UK on a Zambian passport as a Zambian national when many African sisters and brothers as well as many other non-British folks would get into dubious 'marriages of convenience' by purporting to marry a British spouse just to get 'papers' (*i.e.* British permanent residency or citizenship) in order to live and work in the UK. I never did that. I refused to cheapen myself and my well-earned reputation. I kept my Zambian nationality even when I moved from the UK to the US. In life, we all have different blessings and talents. But the problem with some of our African brothers and sisters is that just because you are all from Africa (or from Zambia) and are in the United Kingdom or the United States, they think you are now at the same level and that they can start being too familiar with you or disrespecting you.

There is a difference between who you are, as a human being, and what you are, in terms of your station in life. The 'what' question is what separates the wheat from the chaff. It draws a distinction between social classes. We could all have boarded the same plane when leaving Africa, but what we are in England or America might not be the same. Levels differ. And the respect we each have earned is different. That is just how life is. You can't all be the same in terms of your station in life. Even if you are both from, say, the same country and work for the same organization in Britain or America, your credentials and qualifications differ, and thus you are not at the same level. So, it is wise to exercise some caution when you are dealing with someone who is not at your level and is way above your intellectual pedigree. That you are both from the same African country does not mean you should now start thinking you are at the same level. I have seen this unfortunate behavior in some of our people in the diaspora. Familiarity breeds contempt.

Despite all the prodding I was getting from some Zambians and other Africans to marry a British woman in the UK, or an American woman in the US, in order to get British or American 'papers', I chose to ignore such unsolicited and misguided advice. My professional and academic path was clearly different from theirs. Just because we were all from Africa or Zambia did not mean our experiences were the same. Besides, we were not cut from the same cloth, intellectually speaking.

One would be tempted to think that perhaps I was being too proud as an African man. Maybe I was, but for a good reason. At the time, Zambia did not allow for dual citizenship, so I chose not to give up my Zambian nationality. My philosophy was that if my British classmates at Oxford could teach at top British universities, what would stop me from teaching there as well? As I noted earlier, some of my Zambian brothers and sisters thought I was dreaming too much to think that I could get a white-collar job in the United Kingdom on a Zambian passport. They simply had no clue what I was bringing to the table. They were all shocked when I was hired to teach at one of the top ten

British universities, the University of Warwick, as a Zambian national, not a British national, and with a Zambian passport.

The same Zambian passport brought me to the US at the World Bank. I did not have get into any dubious marriage of convenience either in the US or the UK. I totally refused. And when I decided to become a US citizen, I used the powerhouse of my impeccable and strong educational credentials. I went for the highly competitive and prestigious Einstein visa to become a US Permanent Resident. And I was granted a Green Card. A few years later, I was sworn in as a US citizen. I have always believed in doing things the right way. And so, before becoming a US citizen, as I prepared to travel to England for the prestigious Oxford honor, I was confident that the US Oath Ceremony for my citizenship could wait until I was back from England. Indeed, I was granted permission by the US federal government offices to defer my US Oath Ceremony until I got back to the US.

At Oxford, when the then Rector of the University of Oxford's Exeter College, Professor Sir Rick Trainor, sent me an email to find a suitable date when I would be in Oxford so that Exeter College could arrange for the momentous gala dinner in my honor, I was in Cape Town, South Africa, giving lectures on a graduate degree program at the University of Western Cape where I have served as Extraordinary Professor of Law. I contacted the Rector in Oxford with a suitable date and started preparing for my UK trip as soon as I got back to Washington DC. I knew that this was going to be a major event.

Then, shortly before I started off for the UK, I got a US Federal Government Notice that I was to be sworn in as a US citizen at a US Federal Government Oath Ceremony just hours after my Oxford dinner. The Oath Ceremony for my US citizenship was scheduled to take place in the morning of the day when I was to return to the US from England. My flight was going to get me into Washington DC in the afternoon of that same day, meaning that I was going to miss the US Oath Ceremony. So I opted to reschedule it.

Once I had done that, I was ready to take off for England. I did not, however, realize the full depth, magnitude and significance of the Oxford honor until the day of the dinner. The event exceeded my expectations. It was simply splendid and full of Oxford tradition and aura. There I was, a simple African boy, receiving such a great honor at the world's most prestigious university. When my parents visited the UK in 1996, I did take them to Oxford and they visited my college, Exeter College, as well as the venue where I was now being honored. So, it felt as if they were both present at the gala dinner to witness the moment.

The Rector met me in the quad area of Oxford's Exeter College, as arranged earlier, at 7 pm. It was Fathers' Day, Sunday, June 16, 2024. We walked together to the Fellows Garden of Oxford's Exeter College. There, we found a sea of distinguished and eminent guests waiting for us. All the men, including myself, were dressed in tuxedo suits and black bowties. I had my signature Exeter College cufflinks nicely done on my cuffs. And my Balmain business cardholder and Balmain pen were both in place. I was ready.

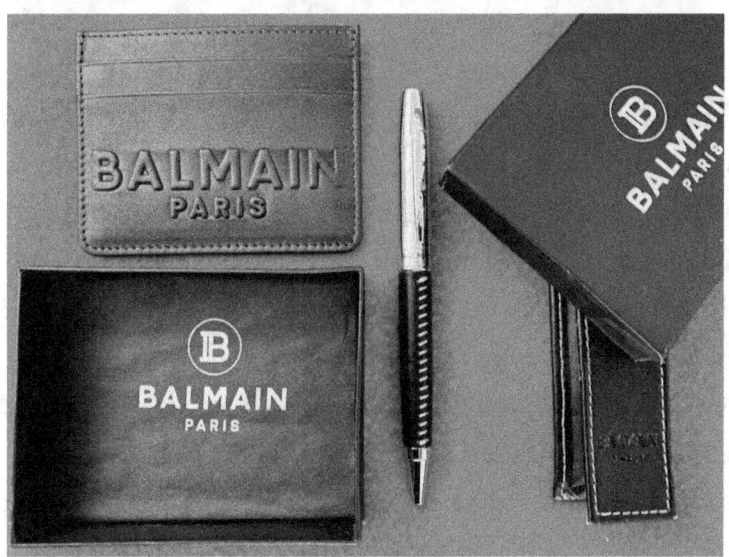

The proceedings of the Oxford gala dinner proceeded with polite but exhilarating Oxford tradition and formality. The aura at the event exceeded what you see at the Oscars or Grammys. Everyone was impeccably well-dressed, with a measured tone of decency and dignified conversation. There was nothing like uncontrollable laughter with folks throwing their feet in the air when laughing, or high fives and fist bumps. Rather, it was an edifying moment filled with decorum and etiquette throughout the evening.

I had to take it all in while processing the magnitude of this Oxford honor. It was surreal. It was not as if one were just graduating from Oxford. No, it was far more than that. It was at another level. I had already graduated from Oxford more than thirty years before that and was now back to receive the highest Oxford college honor. I remembered all the letters that my father used to write me when I was a graduate student at Oxford as well as his encouraging words. My parents never failed me. Although my mother did not write often, as she preferred hearing from me on the phone, I knew that both my parents were there for me. Back in the day, there were no social media for one to use to contact family members in Africa. The internet was just developing and had not yet been rolled out widely. Closely related to this, there were no smartphones either. To call Africa, one had to go to a public telephone booth to load the public phone with coins before dialing home. Three decades later, I was back in Oxford in an age when technology had evolved so much.

As we all prepared to proceed to the historical college dining hall that Sunday evening for the Oxford gala dinner, I was handed a black gown, similar to the one worn by the rector and other members of the Senior Common Room (SCR). I had to wear it on top of my tuxedo suit. It's part of the Oxford tradition. I could feel the elevation of my Oxford status from my previous Middle Common Room (MCR) station to becoming a member of the SCR. Given that the event was in my honor, I was understandably the center of attention. Also, I was the only African amongst the eminent persons present. Everyone wanted to greet me and offer their congratulations. It was a humbling experience. The intellectual gravitas and aura surrounding the event was such that one could not even entertain the thought of taking photos or selfies. Everyone around was well-behaved and elegantly classy. The conversations were of polite society, characterized by enlightened demeanor and intellectual sophistication.

Later, I saw a black guy walk in with two light-skinned black ladies who could pass for bi-racial ladies. I found out that he was a visiting fellow at Exeter College from Zimbabwe, and the two ladies he was with were African-Americans from Los Angeles in California, US. Among the guests, he was the only one who took out a smartphone for the two of us to take a selfie as soon as the rector finished reading out the citation of my biographical details while the rest of the gathering gave a thunderous applause at my impressive bio. When reading out the citation, the rector highlighted the various milestones and heights of my professional and academic career over several decades. I had never witnessed anything like this. I was so touched. Not everyone gets to be celebrated and honored at that level, especially at such a famed places as the world most prestigious university, the University of Oxford.

After the rector had read out the formal citation of my bio and introduced me to the distinguished gathering of learned men and women as the eminent person in whose honor the gala dinner was being held, he went on to state: "Professor Mwenda and I will now lead this gathering for some light drinks in the Senior Common Room (SCR) before we proceed to dinner."

It was my first time in the SCR. This is an intellectually sacred place that I could not even step into when I was a graduate student at Oxford. As a graduate student, I was confined to the MCR and would just hang out there. The SCR has always been for college fellows, tutors, lecturers and professors. As an Honorary Fellow of the college, I have now been elevated and admitted, by special honor, to membership of the SCR.

When the invited guests for the Oxford gala dinner got to the SCR, champagne and sherry were flowing as we all mingled and networked before the rector made the announcement that he and I would lead the distinguished guests to the vintage dining hall of Exeter College. My seat was reserved at the high table right next to that of the rector, so Africa had a seat at the high table. I was representing Africa, as a son of Africa I was being honored at Oxford.

The setting was impeccably well-arranged and the food was simply awesome. I had been asked ahead of time if I had any dietary restrictions. The menu was just as I had expressed in my response. It was all tailored respectfully to my taste. I was really humbled and touched. I was indeed being honored. And all eyes were on me, as people asked me where I was from originally, especially given my highly impressive credentials.

I have attended other high-level dinners in various exotic and expensive places, including at presidential palaces, but that Oxford dinner was out of this world. The sophisticated company of the erudite gentlemen and women, the high level of intellectually stimulating discussions, the impeccable etiquette across the board, the fine dinner table manners, and everything about the aura of Oxford dinners, were full of decorum as the rector gave grace in Latin before the meal.

The college chaplain was also present at the high table, as the college choir sang amazingly well before we all sat down to a sumptuous meal. That's Oxford. You don't just start eating like a vagabond or hermit. There are certain traditions of etiquette and fine manners that go with a fine meal and distinguished guests, and that is what you find at many an Oxford dinner that you don't find easily at other universities. It was simply an amazing and memorable evening.

On Sunday, June 30, 2024, not too long after I returned to the US from the momentous Oxford gala dinner, the *Sunday Mail of Zambia* published an informative article to capture my milestone achievement.

Closely related to this, I have shared below a photo taken in the Fellows Garden at Oxford's Exeter College before the proceedings of the Oxford gala dinner commenced. The Radcliffe Camera can be seen in the background.

A few hours before the Oxford gala dinner, I met up with some Zambian Rhodes Scholars studying at Oxford. We met for a networking and mentoring session over drinks. Below are some pictures taken with the said Rhodes Scholars.

It was so intellectually refreshing to be back in Oxford after graduating from there more than thirty years ago. Of course, I had been back several times for some intermittent visits since I graduated from there in 1994, but this particular visit was different. The visit had more deeper meaning. I was back at Oxford to receive the highest honor from my alma mater, Exeter College. I thought so much about the wise words of my parents and their visit to Oxford when they came to see me in the UK in summer of 1996. I replayed the history in my mind's eye. And I could feel their presence, as I was being honored with a fine dinner at Oxford. My parents left a strong foundation in me to excel to the greatest of all erudite heights.

When I arrived in Oxford from Washington DC, it was drizzling and the weather was quite grey. Luckily, I had my Versace umbrella to shelter me from the rain.

In Washington DC, I had left some good summer weather. I thought England would be like that too, though I took the precaution of carrying clothing for different seasons. British weather can give you three to four seasons in a day. It can be unpredictable.

I quickly settled in the suite reserved for me at Exeter College. In the picture below, I can be seen relaxing shortly after I checked into my suite and unpacked some of my accessories. I lay down wondering how I was going to cope with the unpredictable British weather.

British weather often requires you to be prepared for any season at any time of the day. So, I always carry an extra cap or two whenever I travel to England.

If temperatures were to drop, as was the case when I arrived in Oxford, I ready to change into a different set of headgear. I was fully prepared for any type of inclement weather conditions, as can be seen below.

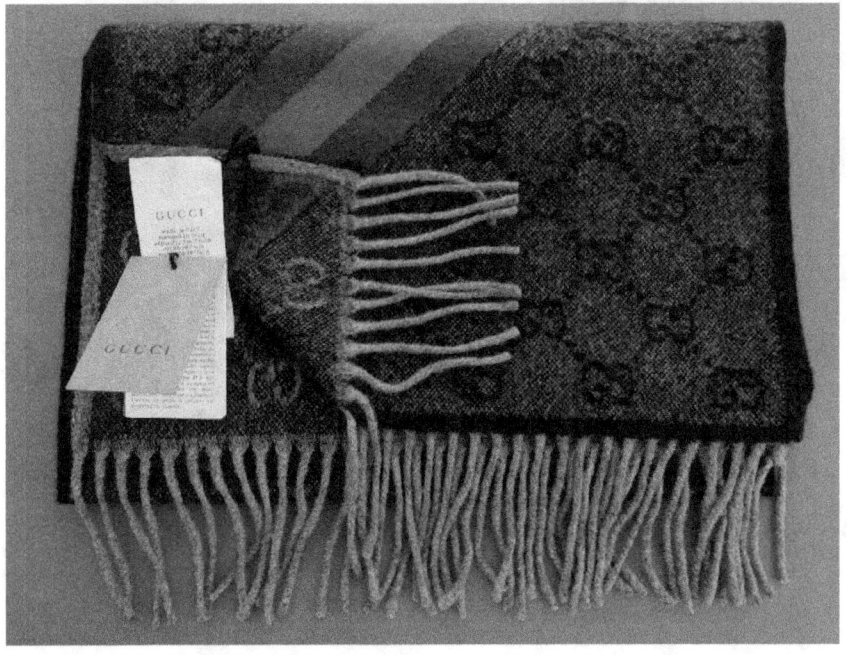

In the event that the weather in the UK got too hot and sunny, I knew that sunglasses, sports shorts and slides would do me good. Indeed, I was equal to the task, as can be seen in the pictures below.

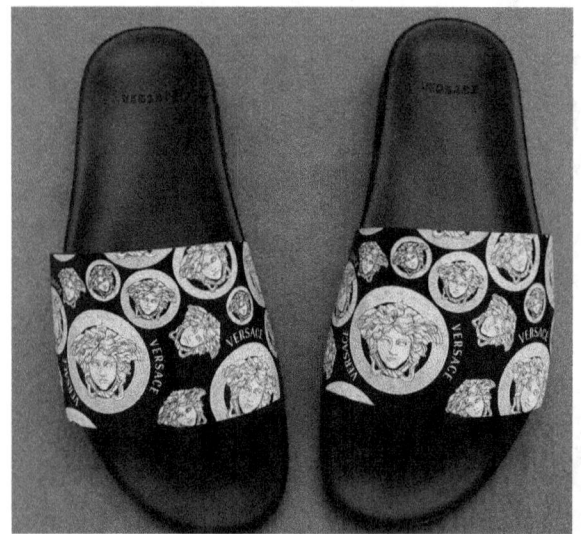

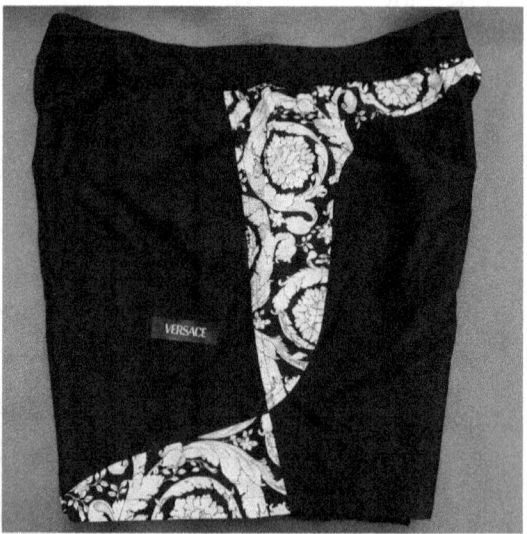

People often associate highly educated folks with looking unkempt, disheveled or shabby. Yet we don't hold church folks, such as pastors and other clerics, to the same standard, even though these folks are expected to live a pious and non-covetous or materialistic lifestyle. It is not uncommon, for example, to find a rich pastor who boasts of owning a jet and a wealthy estate or a portfolio of valuable assets bought mainly from moneys collected through the church. Instead of being a sanctuary of religious modesty, the church industry has now become a lucrative business for some folks. Yet academics and scholars are expected to remain poorly dressed, as they watch other folks dress up nicely and have a good time. We reject such thinking. People don't spend years in school only to end up looking like a scruffy nerd. Neither should the highly educated be precluded or ostracized from the world of style and fashion. They too can participate if they want to. It's a free world. There is nothing wrong with that.

In life, you have to be happy. Some people find joy in playing golf or tennis, for example. Others find joy in drinking beer or whisky. Then there are those who take joy in eating. It's a free world as long as you are not committing a crime or infringing someone's rights and liberties.

I love to treat myself to some fine garb. For life is not only about moral and ethical values, that is, the choice between right and wrong or good and bad. It is also about aesthetics, meaning that the beauty of life must be enjoyed too. If someone's taste for style and fashion is not a sin or crime and does not affect you, why should it be a bother to you? Are you a merchant of morals? The Bible tells us in Matthew 6:16-18:

"And when you fast, do not look gloomy like the hypocrites, for they disfigure their faces that their fasting may be seen by others. Truly, I say to you, they have received their reward. But when you fast, anoint your head and wash your face, that your fasting may not be seen by others but by your Father who is in secret. And your Father who sees in secret will reward you."

What this means is that you do not have to look impoverished to show or prove that you are a Christian. As long as you do not commit sin or profit materially from abusing or misusing the Word of God to acquire any of your material wealth or garb, you have not offended God. Christianity, I submit, is in our hearts and deeds. As the Bible provides in Matthew 6:5:

"When you pray, don't be like the hypocrites who love to pray publicly on street corners and in the synagogues where everyone can see them. I tell you the truth, that is all the reward they will ever get."

As human beings, we all have our own idiosyncratic values. Each person is made differently. And, as established already, society is not homogeneous, but heterogeneous. Therefore, our value systems cannot be monolithic. It explains why even among the faithful, there are different religions. Also, within Christianity itself, there are different denominations. Such is the value of diversity, equity and inclusion when it comes to the need for sensitive folks to be more tolerant of what they would want to have but can't have, or what they don't know or like. You cannot reason with an already biased or prejudiced person whose points of reference are different from yours. Acceptance is the beginning of the healing process.

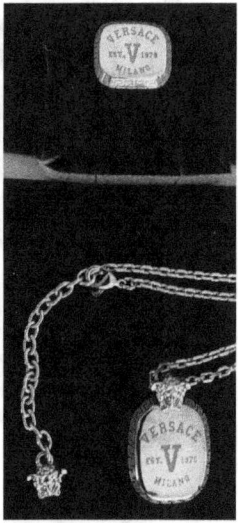

Even at home, I am equal to the task. Style, like charity, begins at home, as can be seen in the three pictures below, starting with the Balenciaga throw-on, taken in various parts of our home.

We must understand that intellectuals or the highly educated are just as human as any other person. They too have needs and wants. They too have feelings. So in this autobiography, I have tried to change the narrative that scholars and academics should look like a 'scruffy nerd' by steering away from that stereotype. To achieve that, I have used some pictorial images to marshal a paradigm shift that narrows the divide between the erudite and their apparent nonchalant attitude towards style and fashion.

To a large extent, dressing and fashion are a cultural expression. They are not just a mere statement. And culture often evolves with each generation. Culture is not static. In the photos below, I share a few pictures of one of my many custom designed suits.

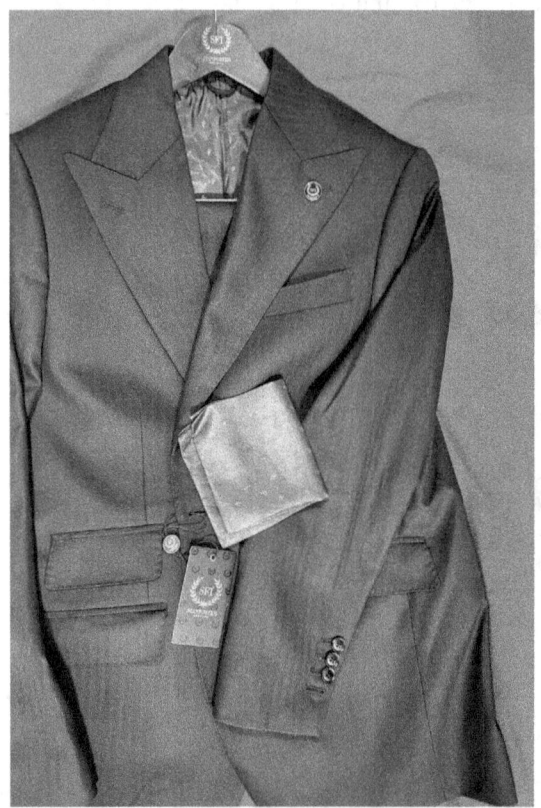

God gave each one of us life and we must appreciate it, as we enjoy what God has given us. We did not come into this world to be miserable. Life must be enjoyed and cherished. It must also be lived responsibly. Of course, not all days will be the same. Some days might be bad ones whilst others might be good ones. But that should not stop us from exuding a positive vibe.

As a scholar and public intellectual, I take the view that school must be made to look cool to the younger generation in order to inspire them to embrace the culture and values of knowledge and learning. It is from this perspective that I share some photos that the Gen Z and millennials can relate to because the photos speak to their narrative and culture. Indeed, you stand a better chance of winning the heart of a man or woman if you can speak his or her language. That is why we should never make school look boring. We gotta put some swag on academics before we lose the leaders of tomorrow.

Whatever talents and gifts God has given you, embrace them with your all. Every person has a special talent or talents that God has given him or her, but some folks don't just realize it. For me, fashion and dressing are some of my many talents. And I embrace them without apology or reservation.

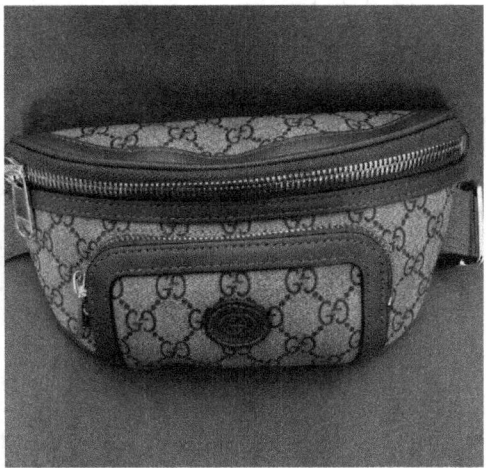

Indeed, my style is my own. I have never tried to be someone else. My signature is authentically mine.

In life, you can be inspired by an eclectic taste of assortments, but ultimately your style and signature should be your own. Put simply, be original. Don't just be anyone. Be someone. As a fashionista, fashion to me is a medium through which I express my appreciation of aesthetic values that life has to offer. Fashion is like a fine wine or a collection of fine art and poetry. Fashion is no different from a lovely bed of roses. It fulfils life and the aspirations of what life has to offer.

Let it be known that it is not unchristian to dress elegantly. Neither is it a sin. God does not worry about or concern Himself with the fine clothes that you wear, unless maybe where you are dressed in an erotic or sexually provocative manner. Dressing up in fine garb is about appreciating the good things that God has given us, especially if you can also stretch out a hand to help the needy. Even our Lord Jesus Christ's seamless tunic is reported in the Bible (John 19:23) to have been quite expensive and of such high quality that the soldiers did not want to cut it into pieces after crucifying Him. Indeed, cleanliness is next to godliness. Even the type of tie that you wear on your shirt matters.

And this includes the type of pen that you carry with you to important meetings as well as the one you use when signing important documents.

Your daily planner too, as noted already above, is no exception, especially for those of us who do not leave everything to digital or electronic calendar entries. Of course, when I am travelling, as was the case when I travelled to Oxford, England, for the momentous gala dinner in my honor, I also like to indulge in some shopping at the airport. It's therapy for what we call the 'feel good' effect. And a Burberry facemask and Burberry sunglasses come in handy. They help to protect you from air quality distortions and strong sunrays.

Overall, Oxford is such a lovely city. You easily fall in love with it. And I just love the vintage look of the architecture of many buildings at the colleges. I have shared below some pictures of breathtaking views of the quad and chapel of Exeter College, as seen through the windows of my suite. The pictures capture the uniqueness of the vintage inherent in Oxford architecture.

In the picture below, I can be seen at the Faculty of Law of the University of Oxford where I completed my two-year graduate studies in law.

The visit to the Oxford Faculty of Law evoked memories of my two years in Oxford as a Rhodes Scholar. I would get on a bike from my graduate students' residence, Exeter House, 239 Iffley Road, and brave the cold weather to cycle to the Faculty of Law to attend lectures and seminars. The lectures and seminars would be held at the Faculty of Law, whereas the tutorials would be held mainly in colleges.

CHAPTER 20

Conclusion

"But if serving the LORD seems undesirable to you, then choose for yourselves this day whom you will serve... But as for me and my household, we will serve the LORD."

– Joshua 24:15

As a scholar, global thought-leader and public intellectual, I have been influenced by many luminaries from different walks of life and at various stages of my professional and academic life. But my signature remains my own. I will list below a few luminaries that have been the best at what they do, especially those that have lived in my time. I have studied and followed, for example, such great men and women of unparalleled and unmatched excellence as: the balladeer of all balladeers, Mr Luther R Vandross, whose vocal range, musical genius, and eclectic taste in finesse (*i.e.* a well-cultivated brother who often donned Versace and Cartier) were simply out of this world; the greatest soccer player of all time who is considered by many as 'the King of Football', Mr Edson Arantes do Nascimento (known as Pelé), and who hardly ever struggled to live up to expectation in any major soccer game; Professor Albert Einstein, the renowned theoretical physicist who developed the theory of relativity, one of the two pillars of modern physics; Pope John Paul II, a well-grounded and renowned theologian and philosopher who was one of the greatest popes of the Catholic Church in modern times; Mother Theresa, an inspiring Albanian-Indian Roman Catholic nun who dedicated her life to serving the poor and sick in Calcutta, India; President

Nelson R Mandela, the iconic former President of South Africa who succeeded at uniting a multi-racial society at the end of apartheid, having himself served many years in prison at the hands of the white minority South African apartheid government; Mr Muhammad Ali, born Cassius Marcellus Clay Jr., who is considered by many to have been the 'king of the boxing ring' and the greatest boxing champion that the world has ever known; Mr Michael Jackson, the legendary King of Pop music, whose dancing and musical talent remains unmatched; Mr Robert 'Bob' Nesta Marley, the legendary King of Reggae music from Jamaica whose conscious reggae music inspired many revolutionaries; and, Mr Miles Davis, the legendary jazz musical genius, who played a pivotal role in the evolution of smooth jazz as we know it today. But, as stated at the outset, while I have been inspired by the best, my signature remains my own. As Luther Vandross once said, "I was never 'the new Teddy Pendergrass,' 'the new Sam Cooke,' 'the new Otis Redding,' 'the new Marvin Gaye.' I was Luther from Day One."

In life, as a scholar, you get to meet many scholars doing this and that, with some editing chapter contributions of other scholars into books. Others will be busy compiling compendiums of statutes and judicial rulings into books. Whatever they are doing, that is them, not me. And so, my signature as a global-thought leader has remained distinct and different from others in my field. For example, those who have followed my scholarly work know that I have written many groundbreaking scholarly books as a sole author, in addition to several articles in leading peer-reviewed scholarly journals. While it is acceptable to learn from others, in the end, you must be different. You cannot be a leader by just copying and imitating. That's not leadership. True leaders are creative, and they innovate.

Time and again, you will hear people talk about the Forbes List of the world's real-time billionaires. That list comprises names of some of the world's richest men and women. If I was all about making money, I would have wanted to be on such a list, especially as I do not believe in playing second fiddle. Indeed, why settle for less? But money does not move me. Rather, great ideas and deeds are what move me. Let us take a more reasoned look.

If I were to come up with a list of the top ten most influential Zambians with a significant global presence, based on the public perception of an individual's international standing and gravitas in the global community over the years as well as his or her outstanding accomplishments and distinguished awards, including the individual's visibility internationally over a sustained period of time, as opposed to mere isolated examples and anecdotal conjectures of someone holding a position of power at some point, I would, without hesitation, candidly start with the following three Zambian names as the indisputably mandatory names for the list:

1. His Excellency Dr Kenneth Kaunda, the founding President of the Republic of Zambia, and one of the most distinguished senior statesmen to have come out of Africa, whose unparalleled contribution to the liberation of Southern African from colonialism and apartheid remains unmatched. KK, or 'Super Ken', as he was fondly known, is a man who had the world wait on him as he tried to persuade Iraq President, Saddam Hussein, not to invade Kuwait. KK was at another level. The world does not wait on you like that unless you are a political heavyweight internationally.

2. Mr Kalusha Bwalya, one of Africa's greatest soccer legends, who played competitive professional soccer in four major regions of the world, namely Europe, the Americas, Middle East and Africa. He was voted the 1988 African Footballer of the Year by the magazine *France Football*, and nominated for the 1996 FIFA World Player of the Year as the 12th-best player in the world, becoming the first to be nominated after playing the entire year for a non-European club. Kalusha has also been a national team soccer coach of the Zambia National Football Team as well as served as the President of the Football Association of Zambia (FAZ), in addition to having served on a Fédération Internationale de Football Association (FIFA) Technical Study Group and on standing committees of FIFA and the Confederation of African Football (CAF). Kalusha, or 'Great Kalu', as he is fondly known, is the only Zambian to have been honored respectively by five sitting Heads of State of the Republic of Zambia, namely His Excellency President Dr Kenneth Kaunda, His Excellency President Mr Frederick T Chiluba, His Excellency President Dr Levy Mwanawasa, His Excellency President Mr Michael Sata and His Excellency President Dr Edgar C Lungu. Great Kalu remains one of Zambia's greatest ambassadors and the only professional footballer player from the entire Southern Africa to have been voted as the African Footballer of the Year. His outstanding football career inspired many other Zambian football players to go professional in Europe.

3. Professor Kenneth K Mwenda, the subject of this autobiography and whose outstanding accomplishments have been explored in the preceding chapters. A summary of those accomplishments is provided in the sections below. Professor Mwenda, whose distinguished professional and academic careers span three continents, namely, North America, Europe and Africa, remains the only Zambian scholar to have been honored by the world's best university, the University of Oxford, and is also the only African scholar to earn two Higher Doctorates in two different disciplines as well as the only Zambian scholar to have been honored by two successive Zambian Governments, namely the MMD Government and the PF Government.

After the three Zambian names highlighted above, the debate can begin on the remaining seven Zambian names that should follow on the list of the top 10 most influential Zambians globally. Indeed, there are many local champions, but few international or global icons. Therefore, the question of who should sit where only starts with the fourth person on the said list through to the tenth. An analogy can be drawn here with membership of the UN Security Council, which comprises five permanent members, namely, China, France, Russian Federation, the United Kingdom, and the United States, followed by ten non-permanent members elected for two-year terms by the General Assembly (with end of term year). To set the discussion in context, I am tempted to borrow the words of the Hon Chief Justice of the Supreme Court for the Republic of Zambia, Dr Chief Justice Mumba Malila SC, a University of Cambridge graduate and former academic, who averred on December 16, 2024, in his Call Day Address when admitting newly sworn-in Advocates of the High Court of Zambia as follows:

"Avoid the lure that has gripped some of the members of the legal profession who with modest, middle level law qualifications, call themselves experts in areas of the law where they, in truth, know bupkis about. It takes a lot to be an expert. Some of those that claim to be experts have done no notable in-depth study in those areas of law. They have no exposure and experience beyond their limited learning in local institutions. They have written virtually nothing that commands intellectual interest or attention. They are practically unknown beyond the borders of our country, yet they call themselves experts."

The Hon Dr Chief Justice Mumba Malila SC was on firm ground. I concur fully with his erudite exposition. There is a stark difference between a specialist and an expert. Even at PhD level, one is still not an expert until he or she hones and deepens their expertise to a reasonably acceptable height of being referred to by peers in the profession as an expert. A person who has just obtained a PhD is not expert, even if the PhD is from Oxford, Harvard, MIT or Sorbonne. He or she is simply a specialist, having specialized in a particular field. But, if you were to take, say, a full or distinguished professor at a leading research-intensive university, such an individual is more likely than not to command authority as an expert. Put simply, you can specialize in a particular field, but that feat alone does not make you an expert. To become an expert, you must travel beyond mere specialization and reach somewhere close to the horizon in your field. Otherwise, who knows you out there near the horizon? As we say in the Zambian language, Ichi-Copperbelt, that I referred to earlier in this autobiography:

"Umuntu ni ink, ba ka'amba! Noti ule sabaila fye, but ta wa sheta ne book. You can't know what you don't understand. Sonta epo wa bomba nefyo wa lemba tu mone nga uli mwaume sana. And sonta mu fyalo wa funda nemo wa soma." ("Knowledge is power. Don't just make noise without a deep understanding of issues. You will end up exposing your ignorance. Show us the body of your scholarly work and what you have written. And let us know the places of major repute where you have studied or where you have taught.")

In life, we are greater in giving than simply receiving and demanding. Great men and women recognize and acknowledge other great men and women. When God blesses you, you too must bless others instead of just waiting selfishly to receive more and more. On the evening of Friday, April 11, 2025, I organized and financed a momentous dinner at the Maslow Hotel in Sandton, Johannesburg, the heart of South Africa's business and financial center, to honor Zambia's internationally celebrated soccer legend, Mr. Kalusha Bwalya, fondly known as 'Great Kalu.'

Having lived, and worked as an accomplished professional, in three different continents, namely North America, Europe and Africa, I have come to learn that those who are secure in their own skin have no issue or problem with celebrating or honoring others. By contrast, it is insecure people who struggle with the idea of celebrating and honoring others. Personally, I have been celebrated at various distinguished fora by various eminent men and women. I have shared some of those rare moments in the earlier chapters of this book. So why can't I do the same and celebrate others? Why should it just be me receiving honor all the time? And why should I just wait for the government or Head of State to honor someone? Those of us who have already earned our respect internationally seek no additional validation. We simply strive to inspire others. Posterity will judge each one of us accordingly.

Some pictures taken at the momentous dinner to honor Zambia's internationally celebrated soccer legend, Mr. Kalusha Bwalya, follow below.

In organizing this wonderful dinner event, I sought the logistical support of my good brothers, Mr. Chishimba Brian Yumbe and Mr. Donny Mpande, who are based in South Africa to assist me with finding a decent and befitting venue for the event. I am grateful to them and everyone else involved. The evening was a gathering of distinguished and eminent persons who included some guests from such leading international organizations as the World Bank, the International Finance Corporation (IFC) and the African Development Bank Group as well as alumni of Harvard, Oxford and Cornell universities, in addition to engineers, lawyers, economists, academicians and other scholars. It was a night filled with honor, respect, joy, and laughter, punctuated by a recollection of great memories in the life of Zambia's soccer legend, Great Kalu, whose exceptional talent has left an indelible global mark and footprint on the beautiful game of football. Described by one Scottish international football coach, Ian Porterfield, who once coached the Zambian National Football Team, as the man with a left foot from Heaven, Great Kalu is a household in many parts of the world today. At the Johannesburg gala dinner, all the guests remained united in their admiration of the accomplishments of the soccer legend, Great Kalu, in the world of football.

In my opening remarks, I spoke about the importance of recognizing our national and African heroes, and said that I decided to honor the soccer legend for the remarkable contributions that he has made to Zambian football as well as to football across the world. One of my former postgraduate students from Burkina Faso, now a PhD student at the University of Pretoria, narrated how Zambia's football legend, Kalusha Bwalya, is even celebrated in a famous song in Burkina Faso. The dinner celebration was not only about the soccer legend's achievements on the pitch during his many years of an illustrious professional football career in various parts of the world, but also about the enduring impact of his enviable legacy as an outstanding ambassador of football in Zambia and many other parts of the world. The luxurious venue of the dinner, carefully selected by Mr. Chishimba Brian Yumbe and Mr. Donny Mpande, was befitting of the honor of a man of Great Kalu's international stature. The people present glowed with pride, reminiscing about momentous occasions such as when the soccer legend was awarded the coveted prize of African Football Player of the Year in 1988 as well as named the top scorer at the 1996 Africa Cup of Nations tournament, in addition, of course, to the solemn but victorious achievement when he spearheaded the rebuilding of the Zambia National Football Team after the 1993 Gabon air crash which took the lives of almost the entire national team.

The atmosphere at the dinner event in Sandton was euphoric and nostalgic, with the guests sharing a recollection of their memories from the early days of Kalusha Bwalya's soccer career. Many recollected memories of his remarkable achievements such as his unforgotten free kick goal in the 1996 Africa Cup of Nations (AFCON) match against Burkina Faso which ended in a 5-1 victory in favor of the Zambian 'Chipolopolo' Team. A guest from Burkina Faso shared his fond memories of the thrilling match, highlighting the respect that his fellow countrymen and women still have for the soccer legend and admitted to having supported the Zambian team during that match. Some guests from South Africa applauded Kalusha Bwalya for his valuable role as one of the very few carefully selected ambassadors who helped to secure South Africa's hosting of the first ever World Cup Football tournament on African soil. The soccer legend was presented with various valuable gifts at the dinner event. Everyone who was present expressed deep appreciation of Kalusha Bwalya as a true living legend and icon of the sport of football. They all highlighted the importance of giving him his flowers while he is still alive.

In the picture here, I asked a Zambian graduate student in the Masters degree class that I was teaching that week at the University of Pretoria to present the soccer legend, Great Kalu, with the various gifts that the guests got him.

Moved by the gesture of his friends, Great Kalu, expressed his gratitude, saying, 'This is the first time ever that such a dinner event has been held in my honor,' an emotional statement that touched the hearts of many guests, considering the numerous accomplishments and contributions that Great Kalu has made to the game of football throughout the time of his active years of playing football and afterwards.

As the night unfolded, the guests savored a delightful array of delicious food and refreshing drinks that were elegantly served. Conversations flowed effortlessly, filled with shared memories and admiration of the icon, enhancing the joy of the occasion. The room was filled with ambiance and cheer, as guests posed for pictures after dinner with the soccer legend and expressed kind words in his honor. Before the conclusion of the celebrations, the soccer legend Great Kalu extolled my exemplary and inspiring global thought leadership, highlighting my towering international academic achievements and accolades, as he presented me with a special gift of football memorabilia from the Zambia national football team's World Cup and Africa Cup campaigns.

As noted above, people who are secure have no issue or problem with celebrating or acknowledging others. Indeed, iron sharpens iron. In the picture below, I can be seen dressed in a FIFA-branded sports jacket and posing for a photo with one Great Kalu after the momentous dinner event held in his honor in Johannesburg.

At the dinner event, Great Kalu expressed his heartfelt gratitude to all the guests for their kind gesture in holding the rare momentous dinner in his honor. In particular, he thanked me for coming up with the idea and organizing the dinner event, together with my good brothers, Mr. Chishimba Brian Yumbe and Mr. Donny Mpande. The four of us posed for a historic photo that appears below.

One of the highlights of the night was Great Kalu's heartfelt speech where he reflected on his journey as a passionate and determined young man from Mufulira on the Copperbelt Province of Zambia. He highlighted how, with tenacity, he had had to overcome many adversities and challenges in his early football career as a youth in Zambia and later as a professional sportsman abroad, leading to his recognition as an international soccer legend. As the dinner event was coming to an end, there was a shared sense of fulfilment, pride and inspiration, with many people expressing their gratitude for being invited to this momentous and rare occasion where a Zambian hero was being honored.

In a world where heroes are often celebrated too late, the night of April 11, 2025, at the Maslow Hotel in Sandton stood as a testament to the power of timely recognition. Honoring Zambia's football legend Mr Kalusha Bwalya, the evening wove together joy, nostalgia, and inspiration, reminding us that resilience and dedication can transform a young boy from a humble beginning in Mufulira into a global icon. As guests departed, with their hearts full of pride, the story of Great Kalu remained a shining of example that when God blesses a man or woman, nobody can take away those blessings. Great Kalu's story is a shining example of what it means to rise above challenges and leave a legacy that unites nations and generations.

A few days before the momentous dinner hosted in Johannesburg, South Africa, to honor Zambia's internationally celebrated soccer legend, Mr Kalusha Bwalya, I attended a live concert of Gambia's musical icon, Ms Sona Jobarteh, at Strathmore Musical Hall in North Bethesda, Maryland, US. Sona's concert helped to psych me up for my trip to Africa. Sona is a multi-instrumentalist, singer, composer and the first female professional kora player to come from a griot family. In the picture here, I can be seen with Sona Jobarteh after her concert.

When I hosted the gala dinner for one Great Kalu, I was in South Africa giving lectures on the University of Pretoria Masters degree program in International Trade and Investment Law. I have shared below a group picture taken with my graduate students in Pretoria.

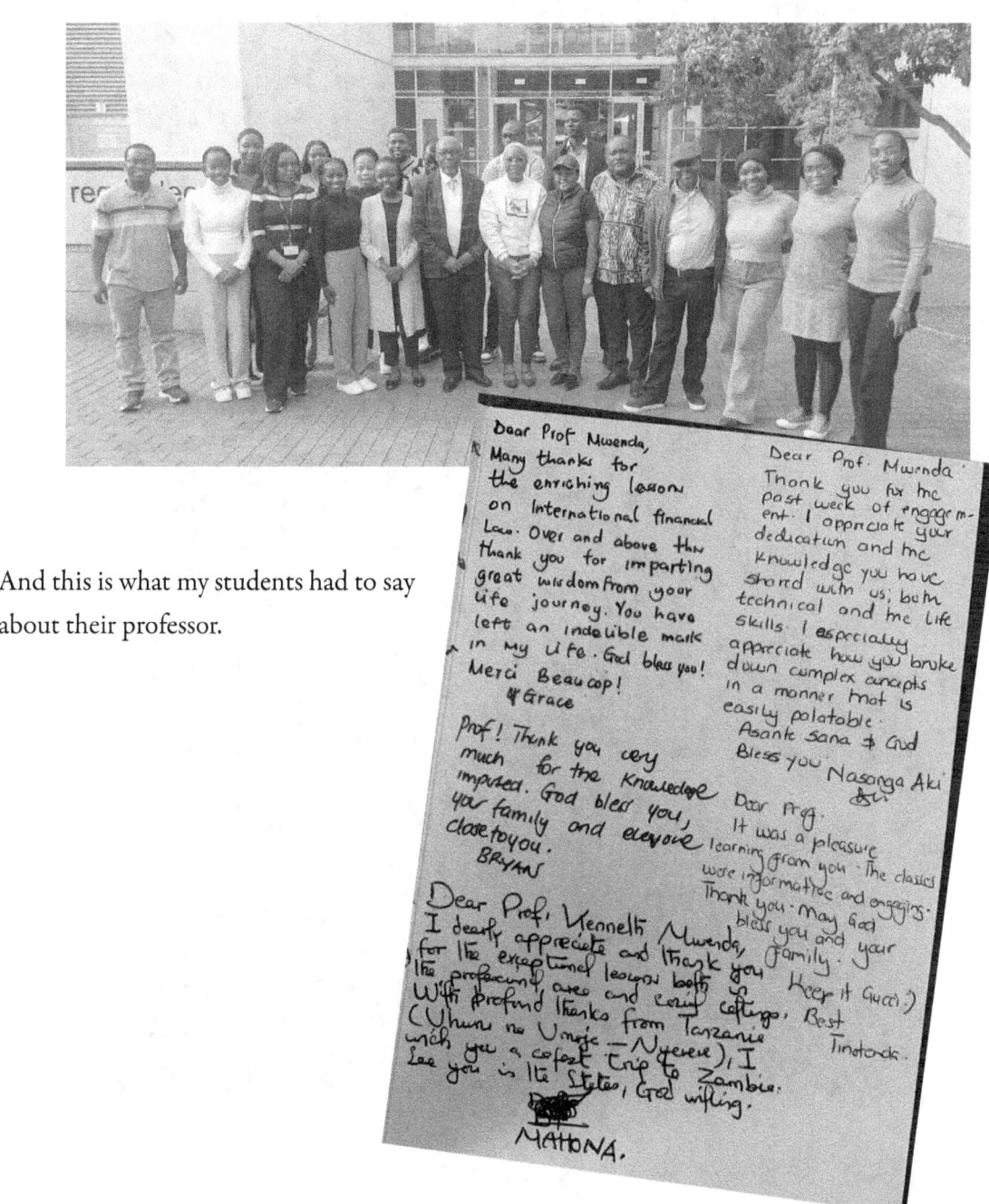

And this is what my students had to say about their professor.

Thank you Prof. Mwenda:
You have inspired me and I have got to appreciate the importance of investing in my career. May God richly bless you
— Faith Otuka

Dear Prof. Mwenda,
I am grateful that I have been able to learn from you, be inspired and empowered by you. May you prosper in all you do. Blessings!
— Faith Mukyala

Thank You so much for imparting so much knowledge with us. You have been truly inspirational. Wishing you Blessings upon Blessings
Bibi Makong.

Thank you Prof for the insightful week and especially shining a positive light on the Roman Catholic church.
Ashton

Dear Prof. K. Mwenda
I am deeply grateful for your engaging and insightful teaching in international financial law. I learned so much from your class, and I am thankful for the knowledge and skill I have gained.
Erole Bazil Najembe

Dear Prof,
Thank you for the knowledge and practical life lessons. It has been such a priviledge to receive your lectures from us and directing us to our roots.
Regards, Benard

Prof Mwenda, thank you for the amazing life lessons you have shared with us. You are truly truly inspirational. Regards Nosipho Makhanya

I am very humble to appreciate the mentorship, knowlege & life experience you shared with us. May God bless you.
Daniel from S.S

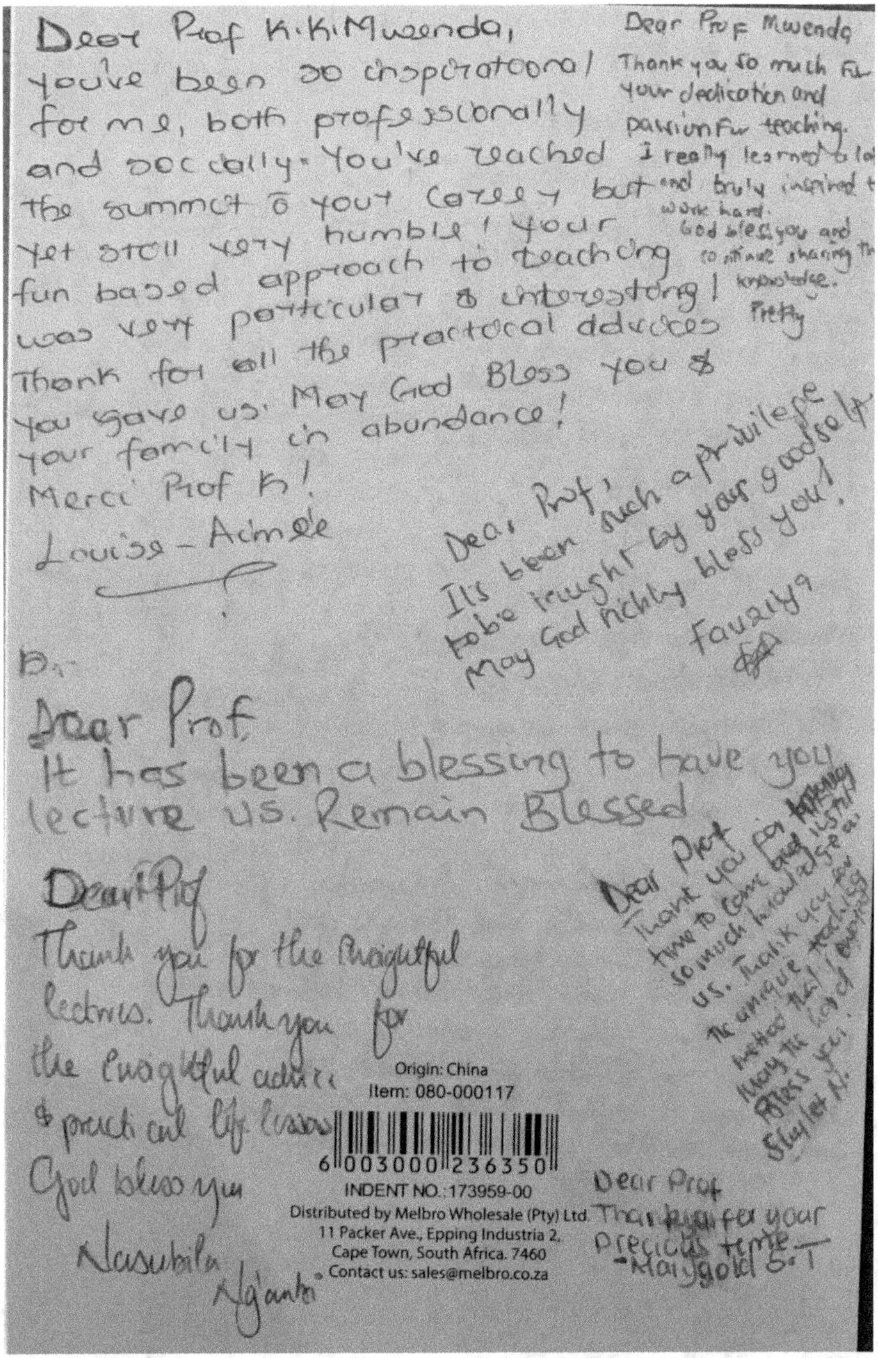

Dear Prof K.K.Mwenda,
you've been so inspirational for me, both professionally and socially. You've reached the summit of your career but yet still very humble! Your fun based approach to teaching was very particular & interesting! Thank for all the practical advices you gave us. May God Bless you & your family in abundance!
Merci Prof K!
Louise-Aimée

Dear Prof Mwenda
Thank you so much for your dedication and passion for teaching. I really learned a lot and truly inspired to work hard. God bless you and continue sharing the knowledge.
Pretty

Dear Prof,
It's been such a privilege to be taught by you. God bless you! May God richly bless you!
Fauziya

Dear Prof
It has been a blessing to have you lecture us. Remain Blessed

Dear Prof
Thank you for the insightful lectures. Thank you for the insightful advice & practical life lessons. God bless you
Nasubila Ng'ando

Dear Prof
Thank you for taking time to come and impart so much knowledge to us. Thank you for the unique teaching method that I enjoyed. May the Lord bless you.
Skyler N.

Dear Prof
Thank you for your precious time.
-Marigold S.T

Origin: China
Item: 080-000117
6 003000 236350
INDENT NO.: 173959-00
Distributed by Melbro Wholesale (Pty) Ltd.
11 Packer Ave., Epping Industria 2.
Cape Town, South Africa. 7460
Contact us: sales@melbro.co.za

From South Africa, I flew to Zambia to carry out some philanthropy commitments at Chawama Catholic parish in Lusaka, Zambia, before connecting to Zambia's Copperbelt Province for some wildlife safari.

In Zambia, good food and fine wines were in abundance as well.

In Africa, generally, one is easily spoilt for choice. You just have to know where to find what you want.

While on the Copperbelt, I visited my usual place of charity work and philanthropy in Luanshya, Dagama School for differently able-bodied children. On the flight from Lusaka to Ndola, I also met a colleague whose writing has been inspired by some of my public intellectual contributions. It was a humbling experience. We had never met in person before. I was traveling on vacation to enjoy some African safari. He was headed to another city, Chingola. He recognized me and asked one of the members of the airline cabin crew to hand me a copy of his book. So, I stood up and went to greet him. I also thanked him for the book. Prior to that, we had only interacted for a couple of years or so on social media through some of my posts on contemporary social-cultural and intellectual issues. His name is Mr Dominic Mufwinda Kapalu. A wonderful gentleman he is. I have shared below some photos of the book he gifted me.

Following below is a picture taken on my arrival in Zambia's Copperbelt region as well as some pictures of the wildlife at the game resort where I was staying in Luanshya.

In Luanshya, I ran into a childhood friend who I had not seen for a straight forty-five years! My good friend, Mr Osman Teladia, was my classmate in primary school at the then Catholic Convent School which was later renamed as Buteko Primary School after the Zambian Government took over a number of Catholic schools. It was a pleasant and nostalgic reunion, as we reminisced the indulgence of youth in the yesteryears when we were growing up in Luanshya. I had last seen Osman in 1980 shortly after we wrote our Grade 7 exams. For his high school education, Osman and his brother, Yusuf, moved to Zimbabwe.

Following below is a picture that Osman and I took outside the fancy white building that previously housed Barclays Bank in Luanshya, Zambia. It was good to be back where the story started forty-five years ago.

In life, not everyone can have a seat at the high table. Many are called but few are chosen. For example, some people will try to hide behind the language of work experience, especially if they lack strong academic credentials. They will tell you something like, 'A lawyer must appear in court', as if that, in and of itself, is the only thing that a lawyer can do. It is like saying a medical doctor should only work in a hospital, as if clinical work is the only thing that a medical doctor can do. Such narrow-mindedness is often found in people who not only lack depth in matters of erudition but also have limited global exposure and a poor understanding of issues. Their views are often myopically parochial and insular. We don't even know if that same work experience gained locally that they are trying to tout is worth writing home about.

Others just hate it when they come across someone who is far more educated or qualified than them because it makes them feel small due to their own insecurities. Such people will almost always want to steer away a conversation from topical issues of knowledge and learning to mundane social trivialities. They would rather talk about people and gossip than engage in edifying intellectual discourse. Indeed, that is what small minds do. They often talk about people, not ideas.

Every authentic leader knows that not everyone is going to like you, but if nobody talks about you for the right reasons then you are not an authentic leader. Leaders are visible because they lead and, thus, attract attention. Many leaders are lifelong learners. They are ever pushing themselves to do better and learn new and better ways of doing things. Leaders, however, must sometimes make tough decisions which might not sit well with some people. Leaders are not indecisive. They are often breaking new ground. Leaders also inspire and motivate. And they listen and show empathy. All these qualities and many more unavoidably attract conflict from, *inter alia*, those who might be envious of one's leadership signature. Sometimes such negativity comes from people close to you. For example, not everyone among your friends, workmates, neighbors, colleagues, extended family relations or immediate family members might value education as much as you do, even though they themselves might have a modest university education. Some people go to school not because they love school but because everyone else in their family is going or has gone to school. Others go to school simply because their parents or guardians insisted on it. If such folks were left to their own devices, without any intervention from, say, their parents or guardians, they would probably be illiterate today. They only got an education because everyone else in the family or their social circles was going to school. Yet such people often want to ascend to leadership roles and will have the nerve to tell you, with enthusiastic cynicism, that if rich people, loaded with money and little or no education, can hire university graduates to work for them, then you don't need education to make it in life and that education is not all there is in life.

Others will show you resentment out of their own racist or tribalist prejudices. You can't change them. A racist, like a tribalist, is quite shallow in terms of objectivity. Theirs is subjective value-laden perspectives steeped in pitifully unenlightened and thoughtless emotions. Sometimes, to understand a people, it is wise to look at their forefathers and how they lived. For example, in many societies in the Global North where slavery was practiced, racism is very much alive today. By parity of reasoning, in the Global South, in many societies where some Africans captured and sold fellow Africans to white slave traders during the Atlantic slave trade, you will find some vicissitudes of betrayal and aggression targeted at those who are considered outsiders or not to belong. The same is true in those cultures that provided middlemen from the Middle East during the notorious slave trade. History has a tendency of repeating itself, albeit in different forms. This submission here is not a stereotype. Rather, it is simply an appreciation of dialectics that, in the change from quantity to quality, the new often carries along with it some vicissitudes of the old. Admittedly, there can be some few exceptions where you find properties or characters in the new that are fundamentally different from the old.

Today, many folks want to lead, but they just don't have it, so jealousy creeps in against those gifted with authentic leadership skills. Jealousy is real. But, in life, if you are an effective leader, you yourself know your worth. A lot of people who don't know you might have opinions about you based on what they have heard from others without questioning the motives behind such gossip. Some people often pick up falsehoods in gossip circles and run with them as gospel truth. If folks don't have answers to a puzzle, they just fill in the blanks with whatever hallucinations they can dream of. You could have simply told off the person or people now spreading gossip and misleading others to stop being silly, but the badmouthing fella will never disclose his or her shenanigans or misconduct that was met with your rebuke.

Unfortunately, many folks don't take time to find out for themselves why certain people are telling them something about you. Later, when they get to meet you in person, they are pleasantly surprised to find that you are a totally different person from what they have heard or what they feared or expected. Their fears are disarmed upon realizing that you can even talk to them politely and respond to their messages on time, unlike the people that were misleading them.

With every experience, you learn something. And with that learning, you are no longer the same person you were yesterday. Your points of reference are not the same anymore. They are certainly different from those of folks you left behind in school or life. And quite often, you cannot reason with people whose points of reference are different from yours. Many folks will misunderstand you, not because there is anything wrong with you, but because you have been exposed to other cultures that they can only admire from afar and have not been exposed to. If, for example, you tell your ex-girlfriend who you had dated a while back in some small African town or city that, with your current British girlfriend at Oxford, you go out on dinner dates riding on bicycles, and that the Oxford lady never questions why you do not have a car and never asks you for money or a new cellphone, your African ex-girlfriend might think you are making it up. She might even think that you are being racist against a fellow black person. This is so because her limited exposure is confined parochially to the African context. Africa is all she knows. You can try this experiment in parallel societies outside Africa and the results are likely to be same. The truth is that you are no longer the same person you were yesterday and the person your ex-girlfriend knew back then.

For one reason or another, some people will choose willfully to shut their eyes to the obvious, pretending not to have noticed the change or transformation in you. But if God has chosen you for that seat or honor, nobody can take it away from you. If they try to deny you your rightful place, simply move to where you are appreciated and respected. Do not spend time with losers who are only hell-bent on disrespecting you or bringing you down. For theirs is far from healthy or constructive criticism but merely acts or omissions of evil. If you are going to sit with such people while waiting for them to recognize you, you will end up waiting for the rest of your life. You have to pivot, like a basketball player, and even dunk, before you can get a good shot at the basketball rim. Create value for yourself and claim it. Also, continue to be innovative while avoiding getting bogged down in daily mundane routines. You must aim to be different. That's what makes a world champion. Otherwise, folks are waiting to block your basketball shots if you can't dribble, pivot or dunk. Sometimes, you have to move around the basketball court to find some open spaces where you can create and claim value. Staying in one spot on the basketball court and expecting to be the most valuable player (MVP) just won't cut it.

As a young man in school and at university, I was always a confident guy. I believed, and continue to believe, in my God-given talents and capabilities. I have never doubted myself nor walked in the shadows of others. If anything, I am not easily impressed by what moves some people. My standards are too high for me to fall for any kind of mediocrity. I can see through superficiality, sophistry and mediocre charades. I knew many guys in school and at university who were so impressionable that they often ended up as henchmen of children of some local elites. These guys would spiritedly schmooze and ingratiate themselves with fellas from seemingly elite families. Others would even throw a colleague under a bus just to get ahead or close to the folks that they deemed the 'apa-mwambas' or the affluent. These pitiful fellas would also try by all means to marry into seemingly elite families. I have never been that kind of a person. I am about substance, not form. I am who I am. You take me as I am or leave me alone. I don't do things to gain the acceptance of others or to fit in. Neither do I suck up to anyone. I prostrate myself only before God, not fellow human mortals. You might call that being too proud if you are spineless and have no principles on which to stand, but I call it self-esteem and the confidence of believing in myself. As my former high school teacher, Mr James C. Malama, who taught me English at Luanshya Boys' Secondary School in Zambia in the 1980s, wrote to me on Wednesday, January 15, 2025, after watching a television interview of a distinguished Ghanian scholar who, with great admiration, mentioned my name and commended my global thought-leadership highly, "I couldn't resist sharing this. What an eminent scholar indeed! Your achievements speak for you."

These kind words are from someone who has not only known me from my early youthful days on the Copperbelt but who also taught me in high school and has followed my career path over the years. I have always believed that, as a global thought-leader, I must remain principled. It is important for a leader to have principles on which he or she stands instead of blowing with the wind. So, I refuse to be swayed by the wind or flava of the day. I am fine with being different than trying so hard to fit in by schmoozing and ingratiating myself with certain aspects of a popular culture that might not be appealing to me. I have seen some black folks who, lacking self-esteem, try so hard to gain the acceptance of white popular culture. These are hopeless poor souls who think that a white man is better than a black man. Some even take it that a biracial person ranks socially above a black person, referring to the biracial person admirably as 'umu colored'. What they forget is that if you mix coffee with milk, it does not acquire a new name but remains coffee. Indeed, that coffee does not cease to be coffee just because it has drops of white milk in it. Even some children of white slave masters who were born from black slave women were not considered during slavery any different from the black folks. They all worked together in the cotton fields, though a few would be given household chores within the slave master's residence.

That said, I am mindful that in South Africa the apartheid system created a middle racial classification of biracial folks, calling them 'coloreds', so as to place the black man further down the hierarchy of racial stratification. The coloreds would sit next to the Asians in the middle stratum. But the truth is that there is no such thing as a colored person if you visit or live in the Western world. There, you are either black or white. Period. As already established above, its either milk or coffee.

Against this background, black folks who lack self-esteem must understand that conformity has never been a hallmark of progress. Neither is docility. I once visited my native country, Zambia, and was staying at one of the fancy hotels in Lusaka. One busy Saturday afternoon, as I was returning to the hotel, I decided to check with the hotel concierge if there was any parcel for me since I had been expecting a parcel that day. There was a queue of about four to five people that I had to join before I could talk to the concierge. I joined the queue. Then a white South African guy showed up and jumped the queue to talk to the concierge. Nobody in the queue complained. They were all black folks. I found it strange. Even the hotel staff started to attend to the white guy.

I quickly interjected and asked the white guy to go to the back of the queue. He could not believe it. Somehow, it was evident that he felt entitled. I could see the shock on his face. The guy gave me an excuse that he had been in the queue earlier and just went to fetch something from his car. I looked him directly in the eye and could see the dishonesty. He thought he was being clever. So, I responded to him calmly, saying that I had been in that queue before he arrived in Zambia and I had just gone to fetch something in Europe and America but now I was back in the queue.

There was total silence. Everyone was now paying attention to the two of us. The white guy looked at me and smiled. He got the message that he was dealing with a different African, not the usual local docile ones that he could easily intimidate with his white skin. Reluctantly, he walked to the back of the queue. The next day, when I was having breakfast alone by the poolside, some of the Zambian local hotel staff who had witnessed the incident the previous day came to thank me for putting the white guy in his place. They informed me that the fella was rude and disrespectful to them but that they could not do anything because he was friends with Asian managers at the hotel. I smiled and told them that, whether white or Asian, it does not matter and that we all have to respect each other. I further explained to them that we are all human and that they should not be afraid of skin color. If anything, I continued, some of those fellas who try to push the notion of race superiority against black folks are nobodies in their home countries and that that is why they come to sub-Sahara Africa to make a living.

Throughout history, many great personalities, including Jesus Christ, have not been conformists. Maybe I was born a natural leader. I have a curious and authentic mind of my own. And I like to break new ground as well as to define my own path. I don't like walking in the shadow of others. Put simply, I only compare myself by my own goals, not by other folks' agendas. I have nothing to prove to anyone but myself. I compete only against my goals, not other people. Even what I eat or what I wear depends on my tastes. That is who I am.

One of my most trusted mentors at the World Bank, Dr Peter Larose, who held a PhD from a leading British university, the University of Birmingham, and served initially as a Senior Advisor to one of the Executive Directors at the World Bank before becoming an Alternate Executive Director and then subsequently an Executive Director at the World Bank, once said to me prophetically:

"Prof, I have followed your impressive professional and academic credentials closely. Man, you simply stand out. You have few equals, my brother. Your qualifications are so powerful that they can easily intimidate some people and make them feel jealous. But don't worry, my brother. You have my full support, and I will do everything possible to make sure that outstanding African brothers like yourself get rewarded accordingly."

Without doubt, Dr Larose was one of the most distinguished and decent people I have ever worked with. He was an honest man. He would stand by his word, advocating for your interests and mentioning your name to others in a room full of opportunities. Whenever he wrote a powerful endorsement of me to others within the institution, he would blind copy me on the email, so I can testify to the great man he was. There are very few good brothers like him. So I remain ever indebted to such a fine brother.

After Dr Larose's term as an Executive Director at the World Bank ended, he later became the Minister for Finance, Trade and Economic Planning of Seychelles. We remained in touch until his passing in 2022.

There is no dispute that individuals are utility maximisers. However, the world we live in usually offers us limited and sometimes scarce resources. This constraint limits our ability to optimize some of our choices. Otherwise, all factors being equal, almost everyone would go for optimal choices. That said, my goal has never been an obsession with making money. That is clearly not my choice. Rather, I have a healthy obsession with ideas. Indeed, that is where my optimal utility lies. I am a man of letters, ideas and learning, not a man of mere coins or notes. Anyone, including a criminal, can make money, but not everyone is endowed with the gift of great ideas. So, my professional and academic life is bigger than any occupation or a job title that I can hold at any given time. For, it is in the domain of ideas that I have earned my greatest respect. I have few equals there.

So, if people were to ask you who Professor Kenneth Kaoma Mwenda is, this autobiography has chronicled the story of my life. You could begin with a modest submission that he is the Zambian guy who, in three months only, studied on his own, sat for and passed the famous University of London 'A' Levels (Form 6) exams which would normally take Form 6 students two years of full-time study to complete. Much later, the guy turned down a fully funded graduate fellowship from the best law school in the US, Yale Law School, to join the World Bank. Indeed, if God blesses a man or woman with a unique gift or talent that not everyone has, it wise for that man or woman to embrace it with all their energy. No doubt, with hard work and God on your side, it eventually pays off, as offers keep coming. You then end up spoilt for choice.

If people were to ask you for the top ten legal minds to have come out of Africa in our time, one name should never escape your memory. For, whoever is reading this autobiography is a witness to the truth. When the history books are written and people were to ask you where else has Professor Kenneth Kaoma Mwenda worked apart from the World Bank, you can start by telling them that not only is he a Rhodes Scholar and he has studied at some of the most prestigious universities and business schools around the world, including Oxford, Harvard, Yale University School of Management, INSEAD, Stanford, MIT, Wharton, Cornell, Georgetown and Kellogg, he has also taught at many other leading universities around the world, including the University of Warwick Law School, University of Miskolc Law School, American University Washington College of Law (WCL), West Virginia University (WVU) College of Law, University of Cape Town (UCT)

Law Faculty, UCT Graduate School of Business, University of Western Cape (UWC) Law Faculty, University of Pretoria (UP) Law Faculty, University of Zimbabwe (UZ) Law Faculty, University of Zambia (UNZA) Law Faculty; and University of Lusaka (UNILUS) Law Faculty. He has also given distinguished lectures, keynote addresses and additional scholarly presentations at such other leading universities as Duke University Law School, University of South Florida Muma College of Business, George Washington University Law School, University of Nairobi Law School, University of Maryland Business School, and Howard University Law School. All in all, the man has taught at major universities in three different continents, namely, Europe, North America, and Africa. Professor Mwenda's distinguished academic career is, undoubtedly, without blemish.

And if people were to ask Professor Mwenda's former students, including many who have served or continue to serve as Supreme Court judges, Constitutional Court judges, Court of Appeal judges, High Court judges, cabinet ministers, Attorneys-General, ambassadors and others in diplomatic service, law professors and deans of law schools, as well as prominent lawyers at the World Bank, the International Finance Corporation (IFC), the African Development Bank (AfDB), the Southern

African Development Community (SADC), and the Common Market for Eastern and Southern Africa (COMESA), among many other leading international organizations, regarding their professor, here is what some have said:

A statement from the 2024 Masters of Law (LLM) degree class that Professor Mwenda taught at the University of Western Cape (UWC) in Cape Town, South Africa, in his capacity as Extraordinary Professor of Law at UWC

> **Dear Dr Mwenda**
>
> I hope this letter finds you in good spirits. On behalf of the LLM Trade '24 Group, I would like to thank you for taking time out of your busy schedule to teach the newest additions to the UWC LLM Trade legacy all about International Finance and Financial Regulation
>
> Your engaging teaching style and humorous character made every lecture interesting. From the very first class, it was evident that your approach to teaching was one-of-a-kind. You have a rare talent for breaking down complex concepts into understandable and relatable lessons, which not only made the material accessible but also sparked a bit of introspection in each of us.
>
> The lively and stimulating environment you created does not go unappreciated. You managed to turn a challenging subject into an enjoyable and interactive experience. The connections you built encouraged active participation and definitely kept us all on our toes.
>
> Moreover, your anecdotes and pearls of wisdom were invaluable. Each story and piece of advice you shared provided real-world context to the theoretical knowledge we were gaining. These moments were not only educational but also deeply inspiring, often leaving us with much to ponder long after the class had ended. Your ability to weave these insights seamlessly into your lectures added a layer of depth to our understanding and appreciation of finance.
>
> Thank you for your dedication, enthusiasm, and the positive atmosphere you cultivated. Your influence has undoubtedly shaped our academic journey and left a lasting impact on us all. We are truly grateful to have had the opportunity to learn from you and to benefit from your expertise and wisdom.
>
> We wish you all the best, and we hope to make you proud.
>
> Warmest regards,
> LLM Trade Class '24

A statement from one of the Juris Doctor (JD) students in the JD class that Professor Mwenda taught at West Virginia University (WVU) College of Law in Morgantown, West Virginia, USA, when he served as the 2024 Archibald McDougall Visiting Professor of International Law at WVU

> Professor Mwenda,
>
> Thank you so much for your teaching of our class this fall at the WVU College of Law. My goal in pursuing a law degree is to eventually become a diplomat with a specialty in International Law. Until your class, I had yet to explore that area of the law. I really enjoyed your hypo's and the deep dive into some of the financial institutions that make the world go round. My concentration in undergrad was Africa and the Middle East, so I was particularly interested in the stock market developments there.
>
> All in all, I'm just so thankful for your kindness and enthusiasm in teaching this subject. I hope you've enjoyed your time in the Mountain State, and I hope the country roads call you back sometime. On behalf of your West Virginian students, thank you!
>
> Sincerely,
> Ryan G. Maiden

Then, if people were to ask you that where else Professor Mwenda has worked within the World Bank apart from that institution's Legal Vice-Presidency (LEGVP), where he served as a prominent senior lawyer, you can educate them that he has also worked in six other World Bank Vice-Presidencies, namely, the Resource Mobilization and Co-financing Vice Presidency (RMCVP), the Poverty Reduction and Economic Management Vice-Presidency (PREMVP), the Europe and Central Asia Vice-Presidency (ECAVP), the Integrity Vice-Presidency (INTVP), the World Bank Group Human Resources Vice-Presidency (HRVP) and the World Bank Corporate Secretariat Vice-Presidency (SECVP). Furthermore, if they were to ask you, in the Legal Vice-Presidency of the

World Bank, what else did Professor Mwenda work on beyond drafting and negotiating complex World Bank legal agreements as well as providing sound policy operational advice to various World Bank project teams, you can inform them that he not only worked on World Bank projects and assignments in all major regions of the world, namely Sub-Sahara Africa, Middle East and North Africa, Europe and Central Asia, East Asia and the Pacific islands, South Asia, Latin America and the Caribbean islands, he also worked on providing impeccable and erudite technical legal advisory services pertaining to major World Bank projects in the field of private and financial sector development as well as led several notable knowledge management products. Indeed, striking a fine balance between global legal practice and global thought leadership is a rare gem in many a lawyer. You often have to be exceptionally gifted at what you do to maintain such a balance. In the latter years of Professor Mwenda's tenure in the World Bank's Legal Vice-Presidency, he was the only World Bank lawyer with a Higher Doctorate and was also the most published lawyer in that Vice-Presidency.

Further still, if people were to ask you where else Professor Mwenda has made notable contributions beyond the World Bank and academia, you are welcome to enlighten them that not only has he inspired and produced top-notch law graduates around the world who have gone on to become accomplished professors, law deans and scholars, he has also produced prominent senior judges, cabinet ministers, attorneys-general, and ambassadors as well as mentored and contributed to the career development of several leading government officials around the world. Some senior government officials who have worked under the stewardship of Professor Mwenda at the World Bank have gone on to occupy such key government positions as Minister of Finance or Deputy Minister of Finance. Others have returned to the World Bank as Senior Advisors and Advisors to some World Bank Executive Directors.

In the picture below, taken during the World Bank-International Monetary Fund 2024 Annual Meetings in Washington DC, Professor Mwenda can be seen in his element addressing a distinguished gathering of senior government officials from various regions and countries who have previously worked under his stewardship at the World Bank.

As a global thought-leader, Professor Mwenda's distinguished scholarly work has been cited by the courts of law. He is also listed in several elite biographical publications, including the Marquis Who's Who in the World, the Who's Who in America, Who's Who in American Law and Who's Who in American Education. Professor Mwenda's learned opinions are highly sought after by many leading international media houses. For example, he has appeared regularly on some of the most highly regarded international television programs and platforms such as the US Voice of America Straight Talk Africa live television program and the UK's Sky TV, examining contemporary global political-economic issues. Also, several governments have sought Professor Mwenda's policy advice on critical socio-economic development challenges. With such a rich professional and academic background, Professor Mwenda has not only been a prolific author of several dozen scholarly books and more than a hundred journal articles but has also won many prestigious and coveted international academic awards from various leading institutions around the world. In the picture below, not long after Professor Mwenda was elected as an Honorary Fellow at Oxford, he was invited, as one of the inspiring Rhodes Scholars in the Washington DC, Maryland and Virginia (DMV) area, to an exclusive business luncheon hosted by the then Warden and CEO of the Rhodes Trust (who is also a Professorial Fellow at the University of Oxford's Balliol College), Dr Elizabeth Kiss, at the Old Ebbitt Grill located near White House. Professor Mwenda is arguably the only Rhodes Scholar and staff of a Bretton Woods institution (*i.e.* the World Bank Group (including the International Finance Corporation (IFC)) and the International Monetary Fund (IMF)) who is currently an Honorary Fellow at Oxford. As he admits, the exclusive luncheon evoked some nostalgic memories of his Oxford years.

And so, when the history books are written, what else shall be told about Professor Mwenda? As noted at the beginning of this autobiography, until 2019, he was the only known legal scholar in the entire English-speaking world with two Higher Doctorates in two disciplines, in addition to a PhD in Law. Following several of Professor Mwenda's unparalleled scholarly accomplishments, a couple of Heads of State honored him for his outstanding and distinguished scholarly work. Professor Mwenda's name is now listed in Zambia's national parliamentary gazette, confirming the intellectual gravitas of the massive body of his scholarly work. More recently, Professor Mwenda was elected and celebrated as an Honorary Fellow at the University of Oxford, joining the esteemed ranks of his other eminently qualified peers who include several Nobel Laureates that, like him, also serve as Honorary Fellows at the world's premier university, the University of Oxford. So, not only did Professor Mwenda study at and graduate from the University of Oxford but he is also a recipient of the most prestigious and highest honor that any Oxford college can confer on a distinguished and eminent individual. A man of strong Christian values, Professor Mwenda believes in walking the talk of Christianity, as he continues to carry out his philanthropic work to assist vulnerable children in his native country, Zambia. He is also an avid football enthusiast and has completed three prestigious football coaching programs with Barça Coach Academy under FC Barcelona in Barcelona, Spain. So, this entire narrative, as presented herein, is how, at least, Professor Mwenda's name should be recorded when the history books are written.

The facts are there and there is no contest. Therefore, we shall not allow anyone to mute, distort or dim them. Facts are facts, and there is no exaggeration or embellishment here, but just straight facts. You can contest opinions, but not facts. As Thomas Paine once said, 'He who dares not offend cannot be honest.' Some folks get easily offended with the truth because they are either too sensitive or not just honest. Other folks are okay with the truth and facts because they are honest and realistic. But one who is not honest will always struggle with the truth and its irrefutable facts. I remember that my mother often used to tell me, 'If you hate a man, you are only blessing him for more success and prosperity.' She was right. For, the Bible tells us in Genesis 29:31: "When the Lord saw that Leah was not loved, He enabled her to conceive, but Rachel remained childless."

God is great. He will lift you up in the presence of your enemies and other haters. He will put them all to shame. In four different places in the Bible, God instructs us against hate. Psalm 110:1 provides: "The LORD says to my Lord: 'Sit at my right hand until I make your enemies a footstool for your feet.'" Similarly, Hebrews 1:13 repeats a similar message, referring to God's dictates as follows: "And to which of the angels has He ever said, 'Sit at my right hand until I make your enemies a footstool for your feet.'" In 1 Corinthians 15:25, the Bible tells us: "For he must reign until he has put all his enemies under his feet." Then, in Hebrews 10:13, the Bible instructs further that, "…waiting from that time until his enemies should be made a footstool for his feet." Yet there are those who choose to hate and not listen to God's command.

In this autobiography, I have stated facts not only as I have known them, but as they have been revealed to me. Yet someone out there, for reasons only known to themselves, might choose to be offended. That is not my fault. I know that there are some superficial cynics who, out of their own insecurities, envy and jealousy, are so obsessed and consumed with negativity that they will want to distort facts and water down the truth in order to dim or diminish someone's thunder, but nobody ever became great by trying to dim another person's light whilst they themselves are in the dark. It is difficult to clap if you are envious. Even if you try to pretend that you have not noticed someone's thunder, your pain won't go away. People can see the pitifulness of your pain. Not even your pretentious act of exaggerated clapping or a fake smile can hide such pain. People can still see the pain in your eyes and the absence of sincerity. Otherwise, bona fide support for a noble cause does not need to be explained.

We are, however, comforted by the fact that jealousy and envy are only a storm in a teacup. The truth will always prevail. Superficial cynics often try to shift the bar each time you meet a certain target just to make you feel small and not good enough. If you earn a Bachelors degree, they will tell you that a Masters degree is better. If you earn a Masters degree, and only had some certificates or a diploma with some work experience prior to that, but with no Bachelors degree, they will tell you that holding a Masters degree without Bachelors degree is not good enough and that you lack a strong academic foundation. If you had a Bachelors degree before earning your Masters degree, they will tell you that a PhD should be your next step. If you earn your PhD, they will tell you that you now need to publish, and that a PhD without publications does not mean much. There is no end to it. But if you look closely at the people saying all these things, they themselves are nowhere close to the targets that they are setting for you.

If you marry or get married, they will tell you that you now need to have a child. If you are blessed with a child, they will tell you that you now need to have another child to play with the first one. If you are blessed with a second child, and both children are girls, the same folks will now tell you that as a father, you need to have a son to inherit your name. People have issues. Many just can't stand your thunder, especially if you have done much better than them in life. So, they will look around for things to tell you that they think will make you feel inadequate, as they continue to shift the goalposts just to make you feel not good enough. Some will even come to you with gossip, informing you that XYZ said this and that about you without disclosing what they themselves said when XYZ was talking ill of you. They were probably even fueling the discussion but now want to play smart. Surely, if XYZ was saying this or that, why did they not stop him or her or, at least, correct the situation by setting the record straight? Probably XYZ could only say what he or she said because he or she was comfortable with you, the informer, meaning that you must have been a party to that malicious conversation. Otherwise you would have stopped him or her from badmouthing, or corrected them. People are not honest. Many folks try to play smart but aren't clever enough. For example, they will say that you should not have said this or that, or included this or that, in your autobiography, yet it is not their story but yours. You are the best person to tell your story. They themselves can't even write half a page. Look, if you have a better story to tell, then go ahead and tell your story instead of whining about someone else's life story.

If you travel to Cape Town, South Africa, they will tell you that Dubai is better than Cape Town. If you travel to Dubai, they will you that England is much better. And if you travel to London, they will tell you that there are better places to visit in Paris. If you travel to Paris, they will change and say that New York or Los Angeles offers more interesting things to do or see. Indeed, they will keep shifting the target. If you travel to New York or LA, they will tell you that summer vacations in Tahiti or Bahamas are so much better. At every stage, they will move the bar. And if you keep defying the odds and excelling at everything that they throw at you, they will say you are full of it. If they can't figure you out, they will say you are difficult. People are not honest. If they can't win against you, they will even start clapping for someone else just to make you feel bad. But do not be discouraged by such losers. That is why they are not in your winners' league. There will always be losers in life, and some of them are people close to you. They are envious and jealous of what you have achieved. Do not lose focus due to their shenanigans. They are frustrated people. There are always losers in the ecosystem of life. That is why such miserable folks rank way behind you while you are far ahead. They just can't stand to see you keep winning.

In the opening section of this chapter, I shared some insights into the window of my professional life. Those insights are all based on facts. Demonstrable and proven facts, unlike opinions, are not refutable. If anything, they are driven by empiricism and objectivity. By contrast, opinions, unlike facts, are often value-laden and subjective. For example, to say that Peter is a nice guy is subjective, for it is only an opinion, not a fact. Not everyone might see Peter as a nice guy. Put simply, never trust a man who tries to come out as a Mr Nice Guy. Some folks will be busy saying XYZ or ABC is a nice guy based solely on anecdotal conjectures, but not the true person that XYZ or ABC is. In life, an honest person will almost always unavoidably rub some people the wrong way with the truth. So not everyone is going to like him or her.

If folks keep saying you are a nice guy, especially folks that you have been trying to impress, then it is more likely than not that you pretend a lot by trying to impress those people. It also means that you are fake, not honest, and not true to yourself. For how else can you try to make the whole world believe that you are 'Mr Nice Guy' without offending anyone? Not even Jesus Christ was said to be a nice guy by those who were envious of Him. The former President of Mozambique, His Excellency Mr Samora Machel, agonizing over the challenges of colonialism and neo-colonialism, once said: "If one day you hear the Europeans praise me, know that I have betrayed you." Like Captain Thomas Sankara, the former Head of State of Burkina Faso, Samora Machel was an honest man. In the end, they also had him killed.

In life, as stated above, a person who is honest and does not pretend is likely to rub someone somewhere the wrong way. Even Jesus Christ rubbed many people who were not honest with themselves the 'wrong' way. He had many haters among the Pharisees, for example. People generally don't like the truth and some might not like you if you stand for the truth. A good number of folks are not just honest. Otherwise, if they were honest, they would have no litany of sins to confess before God every single day.

That said, a few folks, out of their pitiful ignorance of faith, can be excused from religious confession, for they simply lack the knowledge of God. Then there are other folks who are just too proud to confess. They remain with a troubled conscience, that is, if they even have one. Ultimately, it is the gravity of dishonesty, and the attendant shamefulness imprinted on one's conscience, that brings those who confess to confession.

Also, among some church congregants can be found some versions of the antichrist. Indeed, not everyone who stands at the pulpit articulating Biblical teachings impressively or purporting to perform miracles is of the Spirit of God. Even the evil one was once an angel, and he knows the Bible very well and can perform theatrics which look like miracles. You must pray not to fall prey to such trickery.

Even among the congregants, not everyone who attends church daily is a genuine Christian. Some use the church to hide their evildoing by pretending to be Christians. In some parts of world, Christians have been persecuted and continue to suffer martyrdom, but religious violence, like making money or accumulating wealth through the selfish use or misuse of the Word of God, is unacceptable. Nobody can think and decide for God. If anything, there are many ways to God. As such, we must all exercise tolerance and be magnanimous enough to appreciate diversity, equity and inclusion in matters of faith. And if you want to make money, you can make it but do not use the church to make money. There are things you just don't do if you have a moral conscience.

As we wrap up this book, let us take a more reasoned look at some examples of dishonesty. How many times do you see someone start acting or behaving as if they have forgotten that you helped them when nobody among their so-called friends, tribemates, racial cliques or 'holier than thou' folks were there for them in their critical moments? Some people even stop taking your phone calls if they think that they have now made it, pretending to be busy. There is nothing as nauseating as ungratefulness mixed with foolish pride and dishonesty. On a lighter note, the levels of dishonesty exhibited by some folks are not that acidulous. For example, if a European professional football team such as Manchester City, Arsenal, Barcelona FC, Real Madrid, Liverpool, PSG, Ajax, or Bayern Munich is playing a football game in Europe, how can you, watching the game on television in Africa, be saying 'We are playing tonight'. Who is 'we'? It is those folks in Europe who are playing, not you. You, the 'we', are just watching on television in Africa. You are nowhere close to playing anywhere in Europe. You are better off saying that the European team you support is playing in Europe, not that 'we are playing'. Who is 'we'?

A closely related example of dishonesty has to do with gossip. If, for example, you are going to gossip about someone, at least, mention also the good things that he or she has done for you or how he or she helped you out at some point. Do not try to be clever by only amplifying your own prejudices against the person. As noted earlier in this book, dishonest folks rarely acknowledge or mention how they were helped by the very person they are vilifying.

Another example of dishonesty relates to someone who claims to be a Christian but is busy dating or sleeping with a divorced man even though the man's wife never committed adultery for him to leave her. As long as you claim to be a Christian, you cannot run away from the fact that the Bible considers such a man to be still married, not divorced. It doesn't matter that the man has been divorced legally in a court of law. In Christianity, the Bible, not the statute known as a 'Marriage Act', is the main guide for an acceptable marriage. The Marriage Act, if anything, simply deals with the legal aspects of a marriage whereas the Bible deals with the moral aspects of a marriage. In fact, many dictates of the Marriage Act are inspired by what is contained in the Bible. The Marriage Act, on its own, cannot and does not inspire the Bible. Rather, it is the Bible that inspires the Marriage Act. Therefore, to try and comfort yourself that you can date or marry a supposedly divorced man even though he was the one who disappointed his wife is simply disingenuous. You cannot justify adultery through such self-serving argumentation. Adultery is adultery even if you try to make it look or sound amazing. In fact, your disingenuity in deliberately misinterpreting the relevant Christian teachings by advancing self-serving arguments in support of dating a supposedly divorced person, as explained above, only offends God more. Matthew 5:32 teaches us: "But I tell you that anyone who divorces his wife, except for sexual immorality, makes her the victim of adultery, and anyone who marries a divorced woman commits adultery."

Here it is unhelpful to take a narrow view of the gender involved, contending shrewdly that Matthew 5:32 refers to a man who marries a divorced woman, and not a single woman who marries a divorced man. Such dishonesty can't buy you Heaven. You cannot sanitize or cleanse adultery by using legalisms to make it look or appear acceptable.

Let us take a metaphor to explain this point more fully. You can be acquitted by a court of law on some technicality of, say, poorly managed forensic evidence for a crime you actually committed, but that does not mean you have satisfied the test of morality. People who often turn to legalistic arguments know that they fall short on moral grounds. Similarly, even if, say, the Supreme Court were to rule (legalistically) that abortion to terminate a pregnancy where there is no life-threatening condition to the expectant mother or the unborn child, or where the pregnancy did not result from any sexual abuse, is not a crime, morality might reason and hold otherwise. Legalistically, you are free to do as the law permits you, but before God the immorality of your sin will set in. Legalistic arguments just take you farther away from the morality imbedded in the Word of God.

This contrast between legalistic approaches and the morality imbedded in the Word of God is very much alive in the debate concerning adultery. Adultery is adultery even if the law does not criminalize it. Where adultery is not criminalized, as is the case is in many nations, it is a lawful yet pitifully immoral indulgence. In Matthew 19:9, Jesus Christ reiterates the Biblical teaching found in Matthew 5:32 on the immorality of the sin of adultery. Yet, some folks want to argue spiritedly and legalistically, with self-serving agendas, that it is okay for a single lady to date a 'legally' divorced man even though his wife never committed adultery in their marriage. But then, what is divorce in the Christian faith and how is it recognized by the Bible? Should we take a legalistic approach or a moral approach? This is a question that many Christian people try to avoid. Here, suffice it to say that the Bible talks about the adultery of a wife, not a husband, as the only ground of divorce, presumably because a man can be polygamous under some cultures and is therefore likely to date another woman as he converts his marital status to a polygamous one. Indeed, there are stories in the Bible of polygamous men, but none of polyandrous women. This is by no means misogyny or male chauvinism, but simply an articulation of socio-cultural norms reflected in the scriptures.

Other folks maintain that a 'legally' divorced man can date and marry a single lady by following the dictates of Exodus 21:10-11 in the Bible. That Bible verse, which speaks to emotional and physical neglect of a spouse, provides as follows:

"If he marries another woman, he must not deprive the first one of her food, clothing and marital rights. If he does not provide her with these three things, she is to go free, without any payment of money."

The words, 'She is to go free, without any payment of money', do not mean that she must now find herself a new husband or man. People like to justify their own shortcomings by twisting words to suit their situation. Even one who fails to complete his or her PhD studies will tell you that they do not need a PhD to make it in life. So, if a PhD is not necessary, why the hell did you register for one? People are not honest. Similarly, if someone goes through a nasty divorce, or fails to marry or get married, he or she is likely to tell you that marriage is not everything, and that it's something that some people simply over-glorify and exaggerate. But if marriage is not everything, as you claim, why did you get married in the first place before you went through that nasty divorce or breakup? And for those cynics who have been trying hard to get married, but without much success, why go through all that trouble of seeking marriage if it is just some exaggerated utopia, as you claim? People are not honest. We all want the best in life.

Economists will tell you that, *ceteris paribus*, individuals, acting rationally and endowed with relevant and timely information, and operating with minimal or no transaction and taxation costs, tend to be utility maximisers. Indeed, we all want the best in life and tend to utilize optimally the scarce resources available to us. It is this scarcity of resources that drives or motivates our optimal choices. That you could not afford to marry, or get married to, an educated spouse does not mean you should now start saying, 'A university degree is just a piece of paper. Degrees don't matter in marriage. We have seen educated people fail in their marriages.' Why are you being a prophet of doom, waiting anxiously for someone to fail, just because you yourself are married to a spouse who is not well educated? It is wise simply to accept your fate and the choices you made instead of hating others.

There are folks out there who will tell you, for example, that they too were brilliant students in university and could have taught at some top universities out there. But who stopped them from doing so? Nobody! Some people have issues, constantly trying to justify their own insecurities. Nobody asked them for an explanation, yet they are busy struggling to justify their shortcomings or what they lack. If you live and work in the diaspora, some folks back home will tell you that they too could have migrated to live and work abroad, but there is nothing out there that excites them. Yet you should see the excitement on their faces when they get a chance to visit Europe or America. Besides, nobody asked them if there is anything abroad that they admire or if they ever wished to migrate abroad. Some people just like to project their own insecurities through unsolicited justifications. Others try to put on some contrived British cockney accent or a fake New York accent allegedly picked up decades ago when they once visited or lived briefly in the UK or the US with their parents. These folks act as if they are the custodians of everything you need to know about Europe or America, yet they are just as African, Asian, Arab or Latino as any other African, Asian, Arab or Latino. The whole idea behind such facades is to try to create an impression that they are still relevant. But they are not. In fact, if it was up to them, a number of you out there in the diaspora would not be where you are and doing what you are good at doing. They would block all routes to Europe or America. But it is not up to them. It is up to God. It's between you and God. They have no say.

Many young people ask me what it takes to be successful. Some people look at the size of a crowd that is following someone, say, on social media, as a sign of success. Yet even pornography actors have heavy traffic of viewers on social media. Is that success? Other folks look at the money and material things 'owned' by or associated with a person for signs of success, yet much of that could be stuff accumulated on credit or as proceeds of crime. Can we call that success? Then there are those who focus on big job titles and high ranks as evidence of a person's success. Yet even a mediocre or average-qualified chap who is not very competent can be appointed or promoted to some high position or senior rank if he or she is constantly schmoozing with and sucking up to the bosses. Would you call that success?

One thing remains clear. Do not be misled by the kind of machinations highlighted above as evidence of success. By parity of reasoning, not everyone who befriends you or sucks up to you when you are at the top, trying so hard to make you feel successful, is your genuine friend. Most of these folks are just business associates or colleagues. You will get to know your true friends if or when you have nothing to offer them. A good number of them follow your 'success', that is, what you are, not who you are as a human being. For, they can only see your 'success', not the scars that led to it.

So, be wise enough to know the difference between 'who' you are as a human being and 'what' you are by virtue of your accomplishments, possessions, job title or finances. This will help you to understand the true meaning of success. For you must separate the 'what' from the 'who'. Because some opportunistic people like to gravitate more towards the 'what' than the 'who'. The sooner you figure this out the safer you are. Such an awareness will also help to keep you level-headed.

Otherwise, there are many good people out there who are inspired by other people's success stories. And that is how it should be. Unfortunately, there are bad folks, who, out of their own insecurities, fueled mainly by envy and jealousy, hate the successful. Some people just hate success.

Generally, many people's definition of success is often motivated by their own experiences or insecurities, regarding the threats or opportunities that they face. Hate, like witchcraft, is often driven by underlying resource limitations or constraints.

Without doubt, many folks like to project their own biases and insecurities on life issues. For example, someone can tell you that you don't need to have too many papers, that is, in reference to university education, to make it in life and that work experience is what matters most. If you look carefully, you will notice that most people who prioritize work experience don't have strong academic credentials themselves. But before prospective employers can even look at your work experience, they are likely to look first at your educational background or academic qualifications. Experience on its own, without any meaningful papers to back it up, is too risky to rely on. Another good example here is that of a person who desperately wanted to study, say, at the University of Oxford, but was turned down. This person could have ended up eventually at some Ivy League School in the US and will only be too quick to tell you that an Ivy League School is better than Oxford. But everyone knows that Oxford is Oxford. Even Americans themselves know that Oxford was there before the United States of America was even born. Other folks who could not make it to Oxford might end up loathing anything to do with it, even though it is arguably the best university in the world. There are even folks out there who can claim insanely that there is no difference between the degree that they got from some third-rate university and a degree from Oxford. For such people, cognitive dissonance often sets in. Let us take a more reasoned look.

Back in the days, Zambia only had one university, the University of Zambia (UNZA), until the Zambian Government converted the Ndola Campus of UNZA into Copperbelt University (CBU). So, CBU and UNZA became the only two universities in Zambia. I have touched on this point in the earlier chapters of this book. Some folks who did not make it to UNZA or CBU those days, but got their university degrees elsewhere at some foreign school, say, in Eastern Europe, China, India, or Cuba, as well as those who, by a stroke of luck, found themselves in the UK, the US, Australia, New Zealand or some other parts of Western (continental) Europe and managed to get themselves a university degree from there, often loathed UNZA with such a passion that it left you wondering if there was some underlying insecurity somewhere that fueled such hate. Others, however, did get admitted to UNZA but failed in First Year. You get to hear all sorts of stories and justifications from a number of these fellas. Some even claim that they chose not to go to UNZA or CBU because the two State institutions were often shut down by the government due to rampant student riots, and that the frequent university closures would delay the completion of university studies at UNZA and CBU. But until people see your Grade 12 or Form 5 High School exam results, it is not easy to sell them such a story. There are many folks out there who just never made it to UNZA or CBU, despite the fact that they redeemed themselves at some foreign university outside Zambia (or, lately, at some private university within Zambia). Thus, many UNZA and CBU alumni continue to ask, especially if you are making too much noise, what your Grade 12 or Form 5 High School exam results look like before you can even join them at the table for a drink, notwithstanding the fact that you returned to Zambia with a university degree from abroad. The UNZA and CBU alumni are not being snobbish. Neither are they questioning your degree from abroad. They just want to know what happened at Grade 12 or Form 5, and why you were not with them at UNZA or CBU. That's all they are asking. Is that too much to ask?

Speaking for myself, I am proud to say that both my wife and I are graduates of UNZA and that I graduated from UNZA Law School before I attended the University of Oxford and several other top universities in Europe and the US while my wife graduated from UNZA Medical School before she attended the University of Leicester and the University of Manchester in the UK as well as a number of top Ivy League schools in the US.

With the emergence of a plethora of private universities in many parts of Africa today, we have seen many people posturing and moonlighting as scholars and professors at these newly set-up private universities. Some of these institutions are not only poorly regulated but are not accredited by any internationally recognized accrediting body. Others are just diploma mills issuing phony degrees. Indeed, this development is not uncommon even in Zambia. As already established, in 1991, when I started teaching at UNZA, it was almost impossible for an individual to get hired as an academic there if you did not graduate with a merit or distinction for your first degree. And your first degree must have been earned at a decent and internationally recognized university, notwithstanding that you held a Masters degree or a PhD from a reputable university. The only exception to this hiring policy was if you had taught elsewhere at a comparably decent university and had some impressive scholarly publications.

Back in the day, entering academia was very prestigious and competitive. It was not a domain for wannabes or pretenders. Only the crème de la crème of intellectuals would be allowed in. This was a time when most of our public universities in Africa had such high international academic standards that no university or employer anywhere in the world would question a degree from any recognized university in Africa. It was a time when there were no computers, internet or artificial intelligence, but serious brick and mortar university libraries. We spent hours in the library as well as in our student rooms studying. There was no social media, not even smartphones or tablets. It was an age when one could only rely on his or her cognitive attributes but need also to have grit. There were no shortcuts. To get a merit or distinction in those days at UNZA was not a joke, unlike today when so many young students, including average ones, are coming out of university with a merit or distinction. Things have changed. Yesterday's merit is arguably not of the same value as a merit of today. Yesterday's distinction is also arguably not of the same value as a distinction of today. The same can be said of high school exam results in Zambia today. The six points of yesterday is arguably not of the same value as the six points of today.

Over the years, the rigor of academic standards seems to have been watered down. There has been some kind of inflation in how high grades are being awarded in some institutions of higher learning, with high grades being awarded quite easily. As a result, there is an apparent rise in the number of easily obtainable degrees that are being awarded every year. Some people might attribute this rise to technological changes, arguing that technology has now made it easier for students to access information. However, we often forget to look at the issue of quality assurance in the delivery of higher education, notwithstanding the argument of technological advancement. If, indeed, technological advancement is the reason for the ubiquity of high grades both in high schools and universities, then this trend should also be present in other parts of the world since technological changes are happening everywhere.

By parity of reasoning, we cannot oversimplify the need to ensure that all universities, whether public or private, are staffed with well-qualified academicians. While some individuals might hold out as scholars or academicians, clothing themselves with grandiose academic titles so as to appear as erudite learned men and women, a number of these folks would have struggled to make the cut under the rigorous faculty hiring practices of yesteryear. You cannot, for example, call yourself a professor when nobody has seen your published scholarly work. Worse still, you have never even taught at any leading and internationally recognized university, apart from moonlighting as an academic at some makeshift structure called a 'university'.

It must be noted that not everyone has the gift or talent of academic teaching or scholarly research. Teaching is a profession. Ideally, you must be trained as a university teacher, though we are mindful that in some parts of the world such training is not a requirement for one to be an academic. Be that as it may, when it comes to academic teaching, holding a Masters degree or a PhD alone is not enough. Your degree alone will not prepare you adequately for a serious academic career. In fact, we have so many people graduating today with all sorts of Masters degrees and doctorates from all sorts of schools. The first question, therefore, is: where did you obtain your education, and what is the full record of your academic performance, starting with your high school certificate through to your highest degree? The second question would follow logically: if you do not have any university teaching certification, where have you taught, what have you published and where has your scholarly work been published?

When I was in full-time academia in England in the mid to late 1990s, the British higher education authorities introduced a university teaching certification program for all academics in the United Kingdom, including professors. I had to complete that program even though I was already a full-time lecturer at the University of Warwick. When I moved to the US, I completed a similar university teaching certification program at Harvard University. So yes, I hold the highest university teaching credentials from both the United Kingdom and the US and have taught at leading universities in both countries and elsewhere.

Let me now recapitulate what I said in the introductory paragraph of Chapter 1 of this book. Some people, as I posited in that chapter, often settle for less whilst others are content with just being average. I did stress that you cannot glorify poverty and try to equate it with humility. Poverty is poverty. It is not humility. Folks who choose to live a low or average life when they can actually do better should not hate those who settle for better options and higher aspirations. Neither should the haters blame the high achievers for their suffering or expect those achievers to follow their frugal lifestyles. Each of us is free to choose his or her own destiny. It is a free world. And you do not need anyone's permission to dress nicely or look expensive. By parity of reasoning, you do not need anyone's permission to excel or succeed in life. If, for example, someone is envious of your habitual purchase of expensive T-bone steaks for your meals which he or she cannot afford eating on a daily basis, it is not your fault that he or she cannot afford to have such meals on a daily basis. If the person cannot afford what you can afford, they should not get upset with you but be inspired. Anger born out of envy never brought anyone success. In fact, if you look at the caliber of people trying to hate someone, they are nowhere close to half of what he or she has accomplished.

Also, if you look at, say, the differences between the local haters and those trying to honor someone legitimately at the global stage, you will see that there is simply no comparison between the two. Nobody knows the local haters anywhere, and nobody worth mentioning has ever heard of them. That is why haters are bitter people with small minds. But even if they were to aver spiritedly that, after all, genuinely wealthy people don't buy or eat T-bone steak daily like you do, and that people with serious money are actually vegetarians, it will not change a thing. Those haters still can't afford that T-bone steak on a daily basis as you can. And much to their chagrin, you are enjoying that T-bone steak as often as you want, while they can only watch and admire. It's as simple as that. Some people don't realize that you do not need their permission to be happy. They have no reason to be upset simply because you buy and wear expensive designer clothes that they can only dream of. That's your taste and your money. You have not asked the haters for money to buy your designer clothes. Rather, you used your own money, as you saw fit. Neither did you solicit an opinion from the haters on your purchases. So, why should they get upset and worked up, if it is not just out of jealousy and envy?

We must understand that some people enjoy shopping as a form of therapy after working hard in life. Such people deserve the best, especially if they have paid their dues through hard work. Let them enjoy their shopping and dressing. They do not owe you an apology for their success. As mentioned above, the folks you hate do not need your permission to be happy or to enjoy their life. How you feel is totally irrelevant to them or to any other normal human being.

For many people, the person they are hating is often not even aware of or responsible for the hardship that they are going through or went through when growing up. I mean, why bother with what someone owns or buys, as if he or she asked you for your money to buy whatever he or she owns or bought? Indeed, what is your *locus standi* in the matter? How does it affect you? Did the person even ask you for your opinion? If not, then why are you bothered or upset?

Haters are simply jealous and envious people. They are consumed with envy, spite, malice, and anger at the slightest mention of the success of a progressive person. To identify a hater, just pay attention to those who don't clap, or those who struggle to clap, when you are winning, because if it was up to them, you wouldn't win. But you keep winning. And everyone's hands stay up in the air, as you win again and again. Haters would rather be the ones in your shoes. If haters were to have just half of what you have, you would never hear the end of it. But because they do not want to see good in others, rarely does good come to them. That a hater endured severe hardship when growing up does not mean he or she should now be mad at those who come from privileged backgrounds or those who have worked hard and are now enjoying a better life than his or hers. Just work hard to improve your station in life. Some people think that the world owes them an apology for having faced abject poverty or severe hardship when growing up. No, it doesn't. The world does not owe you any apology. So, do not be angry at the world. Rather, find inspiration, not bitterness, in what you see around you so that you too can uplift yourself out of poverty. And this calls for humility and honesty on the part of the frustrated party, not bitterness, anger or malice.

One of my nieces reached out to me for advice when someone she thought was her good friend started posting subtle innuendo memes attacking her for the posts she would share on her own social media page. My niece wondered why someone would be so incensed by her posts when the posts had nothing to do with that person. I smiled and said, "Gal, people have issues. When that friend of yours and her husband bought a new car, did they not post pictures of their car on social media? What do you call that? Humility? I remember that you showed me those pictures. You were happy for them. But now they are not happy for you when you post pictures of your luxurious lifestyle. Why? What has changed?"

My niece went quiet, pondering and reflecting on my advice. I then went on to explain further. "People will tell you that rich people like Bill Gates don't do this or that, as if you said that you are competing with Bill Gates. Instead of speaking for themselves, people will try to fight you using someone else's name who is not even aware that they are using his or her name to fight their pitiful battles. Jealousy is the root cause of all this. If that friend of yours had the same opportunities as you, she would have made sure that you felt it. Look, every time she has had an achievement of one kind or another, hasn't she posted spiritedly on her social media page about such achievement? Did you ever tell her that highly educated people, such as Nobel Laureates, don't do that? You never did. Yet, she is busy attacking you. She has issues."

My niece responded calmly, saying, "Uncle, you are right. She is very competitive. She doesn't like it whenever I have something that she likes but can't afford. When she went on vacation with her husband, she splashed pictures of their vacation everywhere on her social media pages, but if I just post one picture of myself in a designer outfit, she starts throwing shade at me with subtle innuendo memes that I am boasting. Yet I have been there for her as a friend. I really don't understand her."

I smiled again and said to my niece, "Gal, do not expect everyone to like you. Some people will pretend to be nice to you, but their true colors will come out eventually. Not everyone will be happy for you. Even some folks who claim to be close to you, as Judas is said to have been close to Jesus Christ, can be envious of what you have. And they too can betray you. Such people would rather be the ones in your shoes. Life is like that. It is the same with some folks back home in Africa who say that there is nothing to be envious of in America or England. Many say these things out of sour grapes. Pay attention to the fact that they say these things without you prompting or asking them. It is a sign of insecurity and envy. Many have tried to migrate but were denied visas. Others succeeded but got deported later. People are not honest. They will rarely tell you the full truth. Even those who marry out of convenience rarely admit the real reason behind their marriage. They will simply say it is 'love'. Someone can go out of their way spiritedly to look for a white chick to date, yet he will be busy telling lies that even though he is African he does not see color in people when dating. But that same person is able to see color in your posts on social media. People are not honest.

In the opening paragraphs of this book, I explained that, notwithstanding any superficial cynicism, there are genuinely good people out there who want to be inspired with and by success stories of exceptionalism. Such individuals are not interested in low-life stories veiled with a fictitious sense of humility or modesty, but in real life issues of excellence. Indeed, you can be confident but humble. Confidence is not arrogance. Only an insecure person might view confidence as arrogance.

Let us take a more reasoned look at illustrations of confidence. When Billy Conn, the then light heavyweight champion, said he could dodge and outbox Joe Louis, the latter did not mince his words. He responded by saying, "He can run, but he can't hide."

Indeed, the ring became small, and Billy Conn could not hide. On June 19, 1946, Joe Louis actualized his words by knocking out Billy Conn. Now that is what I call confidence, not arrogance. The prophetic truth came to pass. Similarly, a few days before the January 22, 1989, World Cup qualifying football game in Lusaka between Zambia and the Democratic Republic of Congo

(DRC), Zambia's team captain, Kalusha Bwalya, known fondly as 'Great Kalu', was asked by a local television interviewer if he was worried that DRC had a star-studded team filled with such notable professional footballers as Kabongo Ngoyi and Santos Mutubile playing in top European leagues. Great Kalu, who at the time was also playing in a top European club, and had been crowned the previous year in 1988 as Africa Footballer of the Year, responded calmly but confidently, saying: "I play with them in Europe. They also know me."

Now that is what I call confidence. And when the game started at Independence Stadium in Lusaka, Zambia, Great Kalu stepped on the ball and signaled with his hands to two DRC players to approach him and try to get the ball from him. They both hesitated and froze in their tracks. You could see the psychology of the game that Great Kalu was imposing. The DRC players knew who he was and what they were dealing with. But one DRC players mastered some courage and tried to get the ball from Great Kalu. It was too late. The ball had already disappeared. Great Kalu was in motion with the ball progressing towards the DRC goalpost. Suffice it to say that Zambia won that game by 4-2, and Great Kalu truly lived up to his word that the DRC players knew who he was and what he was capable of. This, to me, is another a wonderful illustration of what confidence is.

I explained earlier that there are people out there who want to be inspired by those in high-flying careers as well as those with higher levels of education. There are also people who want to be inspired by fashionistas in modern trends of fashion and dressing, including those who are into worldly travels, fine wines, quality food and so forth. We should not hate such seemingly successful people just because our own lives are average or below par. Rather, we can, through observational learning, look for inspiration from various walks of life, as opposed to hating those who have done better than us. For, we can all choose to be amazing or amazed. So, my simple answer to the question posed in the opening paragraph above is that it depends on how you define success. Obviously, a loser and a winner will look at the meaning of success differently.

For me, success is not just about making money or gaining fame. Also, it is definitely not just about having power or influence. For example, when I look at some so-called intellectuals and African academics who are politically outspoken and vocal in my native country, Zambia, it is evident that a good number of them – with a few exceptions, of course – are just hungry and looking for jobs. They will support or condemn a political party not because they believe in any meaningful ideology, but because they are eyeing a position in government or are interested in some business opportunity associated with the government. If the party that they have been supporting comes to power but does not appoint them to a government position or give them any business contracts, they will start to attack the government. Then those with less political ambition will simply stay mute and won't criticize anything, even though things are no longer at ease. For them, as long as the ruling party is dominated by people from their regional base or tribal grouping, it is fine and there is no need to rock the boat. People are not honest. Put simply, if such fellas are cheering or clapping, just know that they are waiting for their next meal. But if they are insulting, just know that they have been ignored by the government and are now bitter. And when suddenly they become quiet, they still cannot be trusted. It is quite disheartening.

If, on the one hand, success to you means getting to the top of, say, the corporate ladder or the helm of leadership at all costs, then you would be well advised to focus on befriending the 'right' people in the corridors of power who can help you to get to the top. For even mediocre people do make it to the top, so you too might get away with it, though it might not last long because fakeness is not sustainable. It withers away quickly. As soon as those who helped you get to the top leave the organization or bureaucracy, you will become an 'orphan'. You will be exposed and there will be nobody to protect you from the attacks of your nemeses unless and until you find another godfather, godmother or sponsor, someone who wields power or influence within the system, to protect you. Otherwise, anyone and everyone who has been eyeing your position but could not get it will now come for you. They will resurrect their old bids and campaigns for your position. And they will come after you like rabid bulldogs to eat you alive, if you are not careful. Because they know that you are no longer protected and are exposed and vulnerable. It is even worse if they know that you have nowhere to run to.

In such situations, you will see someone suddenly put in a resignation, saying that he or she has decided to leave the organization to pursue other interests elsewhere. The person knows that he or she is vulnerable and that it is no longer safe to stay on since there is no one to protect him or her. You will just notice that, suddenly, the person is no longer being invited by his or her bosses to key management meetings or events and is hardly copied on important emails regarding critical management decisions. It is called 'constructive dismissal'. The person finds himself or herself in an intolerable work environment, compelling him or her to resign. It is a subtle way of effectively forcing someone out of a job. Sometimes, these subtle hostilities can leave you in a less respectful workplace once your sponsor, godfather or godmother leaves. On the surface, constructive dismissal often looks like a resignation or an early retirement. But it is not. The truth is that someone has been forced out. Now, if that is what you want, or what you call 'success', then you go ahead and give it a shot. However, just be mindful of the impending pitfalls on such a path. You might find yourself inheriting battles if you side with the wrong camp. Your godfather or godmother's adversaries will become your adversaries too, and those folks will just be waiting for your godfather or godmother to leave before they pounce on you.

On the other hand, if you remain professional, impartial and apolitical, choosing to leave an indelible legacy of professional excellence, irrespective of the politics and the culture of the environment around you, then the truth is your path, though you might not rise fast enough up the corporate ladder. The truth requires a great sense of patience, honesty, discipline, focus, hard work, determination, and respect for others. Dishonest people rarely take this path, for they are in a hurry to get to the top. Honesty, by contrast, is a long and painstakingly winding route which might take you longer to get to the top or to your desired goal. But if you stick to that path of truth, no cops will stop you on the way to check your driver's license, as they would if you were to take shortcuts on the highway of dishonesty, as you beat the red lights while cruising at a high speed to the top of the corporate ladder.

One who is on the path of truth hardly engages in corrupt or unethical dealings, unlike one who takes shortcuts and beats the red lights on the highway of dishonesty. You must remain transparent on the path of truth even if good people are rarely appreciated until they are gone. Be comforted in knowing that the one whose faith exceeds his or her social contacts or networks is stronger than the one whose social contacts and networks exceed his or her faith. For it is not by our networks or contacts with ordinary mortals that the fulfilment of our joy shall come, but by the Grace and Divine Power of God. Human beings come and go. You can't put all your hopes in them. Some folks can even betray you or let you down. For example, some so-called 'friends' and family members might not be there for you when you need them most.

In families, sibling rivalry, bordering on petty jealousy, envy and insecurity, can draw you apart. Some people don't like it when a sibling is doing much better than them or is not giving them money. They can even clap for the sibling's nemesis just to get back at him or her. People can be funny. Even among your friends, you can lose a friendship with someone over his or her political fanaticism and obsession with supporting a certain politician that he or she has never even met, just because they are from the same tribe or region. Such narrow-mindedness defies logic, especially if you have been there for that friend of yours. Such people would rather side with a politician who doesn't even know of their existence than appreciate a genuine friend who they interact with daily. As the old English saying goes, 'A bird in the hand is worth two in the bush.' How can you disrespect someone who has been there for you in preference to someone who doesn't even know you and has no idea of your existence? But the good part is that God will always be there for those who allow Him into their lives when mere mortals decide to leave. God will remain and stay with you as long as you allow Him into your life.

A person who dwells in the truth might appear to be a difficult individual to the less honest because the truth is often unkind. We must understand this basic principle of life. The truth can undress anyone who is not honest, irrespective of their rank, race, color, power, influence, creed, religion, ideology, education, finances, gender, age, social status or height. A truthful person does not wallow in twisting facts and compromising the truth. And he or she seeks no immediate gratification but remains loyal to the truth, no matter how bitter it tastes.

While some people's evil plots might appear to cast them as doing well in the short run, it is just a matter of time before reality sets in. There will be people that you have helped along the way to get them where they are who will go behind your back to gossip about you. Some will even try to compete with you. We have seen it. Others will be busy trying to undermine you and throw you under a bus when they are talking to your bosses at work so that they can secure their own promotion and get ahead of you. Come Sunday, these people will be holding the Bible in their hands at church as Born-Again Christians. You just wonder. But God has a way of humbling the dishonest. Sooner or later, someone will fail to complete his or her doctoral studies which they were pursuing secretly with the hope of surprising you that they also have earned a PhD. Some people can be competing with you when you are not even aware of it. They will tell you that they also graduated with a Distinction (First Class or summa cum laude) or a Merit (Upper Second Class or magna cum laude) when nobody asked them for their university degree classification. Others will tell you that they missed a Distinction by a point, as if that would change anything. Then there are those who will tell you that they have also published scholarly work, as if you asked them for their published work. Yet if you search for the names of these people in any library catalogue or on the internet, no scholarly work comes up under their name. You just wonder. Why can't people just accept their stations in life and be humble instead of trying to put themselves on a pedestal? The person they are fighting is miles ahead of them. You cannot win by trying to bring down a good man or woman. The truth always stays afloat.

As human beings, we sometimes question ourselves if there is something wrong with us, especially if we are faced with adversaries. We ask ourselves if we did something wrong, or if there is anything else that we could or should have done to ameliorate the situation. We never stop to think that we are fine and simply dealing with the wrong folks or knocking on the wrong door. People will tell you to wear certain types of clothes to help you to appeal to those in power or to a certain demographic audience. Others will tell you to speak and walk in a certain way for you to be accepted. There are also those who will ask you to tone down the truth for you to forge ahead. Some will even ask you to hide your strengths so that you are seen to be humble. In all that, we rarely stop to audit the environment that we are in or faced with and the type of people that we are dealing with. If you were to seek guidance from some of these people, they are likely to make you believe that the problem is with you, not them.

In life, there are mainly three scenarios that can help us to deal with the issues I have highlighted above. First, the problem could be you. We call that an internal issue. Secondly, the problem could be with the environment you are in or the people you are dealing with. We call that an external issue. because it is not your problem. Thirdly, the problem could be both an internal and an external issue. But some people only focus on the first of these three scenarios, insisting, for example, that you are the problem so as to guilt-trip you. Such critics often do not want to see you race ahead to victory. They will tell you, for example, that you cannot win because you are black or that you cannot reach certain heights because you are too young. Some will even question your networks or contacts, contending that you can only make it to a certain position if you know someone who can pull strings for you. Others will tell you that nobody came out alive. But the depth of your faith in God can make a difference. Human beings can talk all they want, but if God has you in His plans and favor, not even Goliath will stand in your way. At the right time, and in the right place, God's favor will be upon you. He will make it happen and open doors for you.

From the early stages of my academic career, I chose to go beyond a PhD. I knew that getting a PhD was not an end to itself, especially as, in relation to a Higher Doctorate, a PhD is a junior doctorate whereas a Higher Doctorate is a senior doctorate. Put simply, even earning two or more PhDs cannot be equated to one Higher Doctorate. I was convinced that there was something else beyond a PhD. One might be wondering why someone who already has an earned PhD would need to achieve something else beyond it. Don't we all know of people who keep purchasing mansions in different parts of the world, even though they already have a nice home where they live? Yet, a person can only sleep in one place at a time. You surely cannot sleep in all those mansions at the same time. It is also not uncommon for someone to have several luxury cars, even though he can't drive them all at the same time. We do not stop to ask ourselves, for example, why we need to have so many handbags, suits, ties, pairs of shoes, or expensive wristwatches when we cannot wear them all at the same time. Some men have several women that they date instead of just one. They can't explain to us convincingly why they are dating multiple women. The idiosyncratic factor is unique to each individual.

Looking back now, there were certain things that I thought I knew or understood when I was back home in Africa just because I had a university degree. However, the university degree that I and many of my colleagues earned in Zambia, valuable and rich as it was, gave us a false sense of intellectual gratification. We were just beginning a long journey of serious erudition. More scholarly work awaited us. When I arrived in Europe, I imagined everyone to think and act like back home in Africa. Like many first-time arrivals, I too lacked exposure. And this issue of lacking exposure applies also to many Europeans, Asians, and Americans who are first-time arrivals in Africa. They too experience it. There is some form of cultural shock. So, when I landed in Europe, I could not immediately appreciate the fact that cultures differ across the world. And I thought I had all the answers since I was a university graduate. It is called the indulgence of youth. It takes time to appreciate how other people live and do things differently elsewhere. The transformation or learning does not happen overnight. We might not even understand those people's culture until we have lived with them and their culture for a while. So, we should all be open-minded enough to learn, as opposed to holding rigidly on to our beliefs.

Before I conclude this autobiography, let me share a few anecdotes to sum up the story of my academic and professional journey. Growing up as a young law student in Africa, I never really fancied the idea of working as a legal practitioner, especially working in some small law firm whose culture of legal practice lacked much intellectual rigor and sophistication. Even when I went to study for the Bar and was attached to a law firm for my apprenticeship, I did not find litigation to be that intellectually challenging or stimulating. If anything, the lack of intellectual rigor and sophistication made legal practice quite unappealing and boring to me. I needed something more engaging intellectually, as opposed to just drafting basic legal agreements, affidavits, summons, notices and petitions or simply arguing facts and procedure in a court of law with little or no critical analysis of the relevant bulk of substantive case law.

Put simply, I think I was cut out to be a scholar, not to push paper in the court registry or to appear in chambers before a judge just for quick-win default judgements. Further, I was convinced that studying or teaching in Africa only, or writing only on African issues, was not the way to go. I needed to get international exposure both for my graduate studies and university teaching experience. If Europeans, Americans and Asians could travel to Africa and teach at our African universities, what was going to stop me from teaching at their universities in their home countries? I had to be a global scholar, I told myself. I was not going to be associated only with Africa and end there. If, as an African, all you do is research and write on Africa exclusively, you are likely to be labelled or boxed into a corner as knowing only about African things.

Indeed, why can't many more African scholars write, research or publish, say, on European or American matters, especially that many European and American scholars continue to write and publish on African issues? In this globalized world, as an African, I did not want to be perceived as knowing only African issues. I certainly had more to offer to the world. Yes, I am African and am proud of it, but Africa is not the only thing that I know. If Westerners have taken time to research and study Africa and her systems, why can't Africans do the same and find time to research and study Europe, America and Asia and their systems?

Generally, Africans have been slow to research and study Western cultures and systems. But if you do not understand a people's mindset and where they are coming from, it is hard for you to even negotiate with them, say, in a business deal. You have to study, research and understand, say, the business cultures and methods of various Asian peoples such as the Indians or Chinese for you to manage their craft effectively as you do business with them. Thus, some of my scholarly writing has deliberately and intentionally been on European, American and Asian institutions and systems. In addition, at the World Bank, I have worked extensively on European and Asian economies. Also, in academia, I have taught and given lectures at leading universities in countries and regions as diverse as England, Continental Europe, North America, South Africa, Kenya, Zambia, and Zimbabwe. Put simply, I am a global scholar and thought-leader whose experiences are shaped by an array of global experiences and are not confined parochially to insular African affairs.

Given the extensive global journey that I have travelled, I would be remiss if I did not extend my gratitude to the many individuals and institutions that have been a part of my life story. They are simply too many to mention and are in and from different parts of the world. I have mentioned some of them in the Foreword of this book as well as in the earlier chapters. Here, suffice it to say that I am truly grateful to each and every one of them. More importantly, I am eternally grateful to God Jehovah Almighty for the many blessings in my life. I do not take anything for granted. Many people only turn to God when they are in trouble or at their lowest in life. Indeed, very few people turn to God to thank Him when things are going well for them. For most folks, if things are well for them, they will even claim to be too busy to pray or go to church. But wait until they are faced with a major problem or are in the shadow of darkness deep down the valley of uncertainty, not knowing where their next meal will come from. That is when you will see them do almost anything to get God's attention. Even their arrogance will disappear.

Against this background, I want to step back with humility and thank God for all the blessings in my life and for giving me the wisdom and opportunity to thank Him even when things are going fine. I have no reason to be too busy or too arrogant to pray. And I have no reason to think that it is all about me as some kind of superman. My faith is more important to me than many things I have achieved or accomplished which might seem more important to others. My faith is the foundation of my gratitude to God for everything that He has done for me and continues to provide my family and me with.

It starts with God and then the family. Thereafter, the rest can follow. That's the order of precedence.

I am what I am, and who I am, because God knew me before I was even born. He prepared a path for me. It is not by my doing, but by God's Grace. God ordained and decreed my path. So, if I have led a truly extraordinary scholarly life, it is because God chose me for that. Equally, if I have been a monumental African figure in academia globally and broken world scholarly records as well as accomplished what many can only dream of, it is because God ordained that my path be as such. It is God, therefore, not me, who remains the greatest. And there is no other greater than God. It is He who deserves all the praise. For I am only a vessel of God. I am only His humble and unworthy servant who has gained favor from the abundance of His Mercy.

I reiterate this point about gratitude because some people have a weird sense of entitlement. They behave as if God owes them something. Many struggle to even say 'thank you' after they have received help. And even if we were to step down from the issue of gratitude to a deity to focus on our own human interactions, it remains a truism that gratitude is often elusive in the hearts of many.

I have shared below some pictures taken at our home in the US during our 2023 Thanksgiving family dinner. Thanksgiving is a time to say 'Thank you'. I remain ever grateful to my dearest wife, Dr J, for her impeccably impressive culinary skills. She makes it so difficult for me to eat or appreciate meals prepared in other people's homes and some hotels or restaurants because few can cook like her. Dr J is not only a highly educated woman but can prepare fine meals that even beat many 5-star hotel meals. I cannot ask God for more. Not every lady or wife out there knows how to prepare fine meals. I have been around the world and taken meals in various reputable hotels and restaurants, and I have seen meals and eaten in different homes around the world. I have also seen what some people post on social media, including pictures of poorly prepared Thanksgiving turkey which make you feel sick to the stomach. Thankfully, I don't have to eat such food. In the pictures below, you will see for yourself the exceptionally brilliant and remarkable culinary skills of Dr J.

A few years ago, I remember posting some pictures of one of our family's Thanksgiving meals on social media. Some Zambian lady based in Zambia spiritedly sprang to her feet, without my invitation or prompting, and decided to comment on how a 'chicken' should be prepared by Zambian cultural standards. Her ignorance was so obvious. In Bemba, we say 'Umwana ashenda atasha nyina uku naya ("A child that has never been anywhere beyond her mother's yard thinks her mother's style of cooking is the only way."). This lady could not even tell the difference between a turkey and a chicken. I asked her if she knew the difference, and if she had ever prepared a turkey before. She could not answer these questions but went instead into cognitive dissonance. She started arguing loudly with her misguided pride to defend her ignorance. It was clear that she had no idea how a turkey is prepared for Thanksgiving in America. It was also clear that she had never seen or eaten a Thanksgiving turkey before. All she knew was a Zambian chicken. As they say, a little knowledge is dangerous. Instead of admitting that you don't know something or are wrong, some people will start making noise just to defend their ignorance and pride. These are people who can't stay in their lane and want to comment on things that they don't even know or understand.

Below is a set of pictures taken at our home in the US for our 2024 Christmas family dinner, starting with some well-done steaks and oven-baked pork ribs.

A few days later, on New Year's Day, the menu was a most tender roast beef, the eye of round roast, accompanied by some organic salmon caught from the wild in New Brunswick, Canada, and an assortment of grilled organic tilapia and some extra steaks.

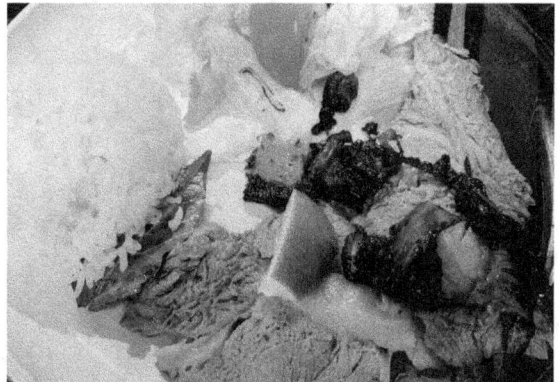

Putting in context the issue of gratitude that was explored above, I would candidly say that much of what is called 'old money' in Zambia today relates mainly to the old folks that the founding president of Zambia, Dr Kenneth Kaunda, offered jobs to on a silver platter after Zambia gained independence from Great Britain in 1964. Many of these African pioneers believed that because they fought for the country's independence as freedom fighters, they deserved to get the lucrative jobs that Dr Kaunda gave them. While we are thankful for their indelible contribution towards the liberation of Zambia, that argument alone should not make someone think that he or she was entitled to be rewarded with a lucrative job. Politics is about service, not rewards. Others whom Dr Kaunda left out of government or State institutions, together with those that he later dismissed from government, for one reason or another, resented or hated him with a passion. People have such a sense of entitlement. It's unbelievable. Be that as it may, we are thankful for the role that all these pioneers played in the development of Zambia, starting from the fight against slavery to that against colonialism, although, of course, not everyone from that generation was a freedom fighter. The truth is that most of these people walked into lucrative government and parastatal company jobs without competing for those jobs. Many never attended a single job interview for all the top executive jobs that they held in their lifetime. They would just be transferred around or appointed to different positions by Dr Kaunda. Put simply, Dr Kaunda 'made' most of those people into the elites and aristocrats that they became. But when Dr Kaunda was no longer in power, especially in his last days, how many of them were there for him?

In Zambia, every president that we have had, like the presidents of other nations, has brought with him some unknown characters and pretenders that are not known anywhere in the international community and who the Zambian nation has never heard of. Suddenly, some of these characters become bigheaded and start to entertain the thought of succeeding the presidency. You just wonder what goes on in the heads of some people. They have a weird way of showing gratitude. You were a nobody yesterday and now that someone has brought you to the high table to dine with him you start to entertain the thought of taking over his wife. What kind of nonsense is that, forgetting that you would not even be at that dinner table if it were not for his kindness?

In African politics, you can wake someone up from their sleep and offer him an opportunity to lead the nation, but tomorrow that same person will soon start behaving as if he got there on his own and will start to prosecute and persecute you on trumped-up charges of corruption. That is how some of our politicians repay each other when someone does them a favor to hand them power. They forget that there are other more deserving individuals out there who could have been handed that power. Similarly, you can appoint someone to a cabinet ministerial position who is unknown in political circles, but if later you decide to fire him or her from that cabinet position then he or she will start campaigning against you and will even join hands with the opposition to oust you from power. That is how ungrateful some of our people can be. Outside politics, it is the same. You can put a relative or friend on a plane for the first time in their life, and they will start behaving as if they are used to flying and it's not a big deal. Yet nobody, not even themselves, could put them on that plane. And all they have known their entire life is pedestrian walking, jumping on a bus, or driving some dilapidated 'auto-reconditioned' car that was dumped somewhere in Africa from some Asian country.

Such people have the guts to minimize your generosity to nothing. As one African brother once said: "You will be lucky if an African confesses to you by saying, 'Thank you for putting me on a plane for the first time in my life and taking me to places that I have never seen and which I could only dream of.' Even those who are drinking wine or whiskey for the first time in their lives want to behave as if they are used to such drinks until they begin to pour the drink in a glass not meant for wine or whiskey."

Put simply, before you celebrate your wins, learn to say 'thank you' to people who have helped to make things possible for you. Some people feel as if saying 'thank you' will water down what they have achieved, or it will steal their thunder. They would rather take all the credit selfishly, even if someone paved the way for them. In life, if you do not want to give credit to people who have helped you or to acknowledge their role in your life, then do not approach them for help. Just do everything on your own without involving other people. That is what principled people do. Otherwise, be humble and sit down.

To illustrate, as a young woman, you cannot go around asking married men secretly for one kind of favor of another, including financial favors or to be assisted with a job, yet claim to be a sanctimonious holier than thou Christian who cannot compromise her morals. The mere fact that you are asking secretly means you are capable of compromising your integrity. If the man starts to make advances to you, do not act surprised, trying to play innocent and claiming that you cannot sleep with a married man or someone's husband because it could hurt his wife. That is disingenuous. Even taking money from a married man can hurt his wife since that money belongs to the man and his family. Indeed, both what is inside the man's wallet and what is inside his pants belong to his wife. You cannot take either of the two without hurting her.

So, do not try to be clever by introducing double standards when it comes to money and illicit entanglements. People are not honest. Even men who live off women have similar issues. You cannot, as a healthy and fully able-bodied man, who, out of laziness, does nothing for a living apart from exploiting sexually and financially some desperate woman, insist that you are the man in her house, especially if you can't even provide for that home. You are simply a boy. The pants now belong to the woman, even if you are biologically the man. Just sit down and be humble.

In life, there are people who you can invite to break bread with you, but the day they will have bread they will not invite you. Instead, they will eat alone or invite other people who have not even been there for them. I am sure you have at some point come across such ungrateful folks. You can give opportunities to a man to sit with you at the table, but he will never give you similar opportunities when the time comes for him to extend you a seat. People are weird. You can share opportunities with someone, but when the time comes for him or her to share opportunities with you, the person will pretend not to know your situation. In fact, they will hide information from you. Folks who are guilty of such behavior know themselves. I do not have to mention names here. You can invite someone to your wedding, but he or she will not invite you when they are getting married. You can use your influence to get someone a place in university, but when he or she is graduating the person won't even bother to invite you to their graduation ceremony. Instead, he or she will surround themselves with people who were not even there when you were weighing in to support them.

People have issues. You can welcome someone to your home city when they move there. But as soon as the person knows where to buy bread and toothpaste, they start to act like they are veterans of the city and want to explain the city to you. Some people are just weird. If they have a family bereavement, they expect you to mourn with them, but when you have a family bereavement they are nowhere to be seen. They may even pretend that they were not aware, or had travelled out of town. People are not honest. Someone else's family loss cannot be more important than your family loss, yet some people expect you to attend their family funerals while they won't show up if you lose a loved one.

As humans, we all need to learn to respect each other better. No life is more important than another person's life. You can give a ride to someone in your car today, but tomorrow, if you no longer have a car and the same person finds you walking in the rain, he or she will act like they have not seen you and will drive past you. It happens. Some 'friends' can invite you to their bridal shower so that you buy them expensive gifts and then later pretend to have 'forgotten' to invite you to their wedding. The same people may even come back to you later to ask for a loan, as if nothing had happened.

Likewise, you can be buying beers for some people, but the moment you step out to go to the bathroom they will begin to badmouth you as if they were not drinking the beer you have just paid for. People can be ungrateful. Even those who started off life in the big city as dependents in your home will start to act like you never looked after them once they find their way around town. You can invite someone to your wedding, but when his daughter is getting married, he starts to act like he has forgotten and won't invite you. This world is full of weirdos. Such is life. Time reveals the true character of people. I must add here that it would be unwise for one to hide under the ubiquitous rubric of 'when you help do not expect anything in return' because such utterances are often nothing but a pitiful and disingenuous way of promoting docility. We pray because we want to go to Heaven. You can't say, 'When you pray, just pray and don't expect anything in return from God.'

Generally, people who are too narcistic feel as if saying 'thank you', or showing gratitude, will take away what they have achieved or diminish their accomplishments. Pride is a sin. It also signifies an inferiority complex of some kind. Lacking gratitude is simply a primitive, backward and uncultured sense of entitlement. The world does not owe you anything. Gratitude is not optional if you were well brought up and come from a home that had proper manners. Only someone from a home with no proper values, or an unscrupulous fella, will contest what I am saying here. Your attitude towards gratitude shows who you are, the type of values you espouse or ascribe to, and how you were raised. At no point can you say, 'I have already said, "thank you", what else do you want me to say?' Such an expression simply means that deep down your heart you would rather not be reminded of your ingratitude. Yet, when you wanted help, you were pretending to be humble and did not count how many times you kept calling and bothering someone for help. You did not count how many times you kept asking the person for help.

It is important to stress that a heart of gratitude does not count. That is why we say, 'I remain grateful' or 'I am eternally indebted', not because the person we are thanking always wants to be praised or thanked, but because the person delivered for us and, therefore, we cannot act like we have forgotten. It would be disingenuous for anyone to try to downplay the help that someone gave you, unless you are just not an honest person.

Some people have been known to borrow money, and when they fail to pay back, they start castigating the person who loaned them the money, contending that it is just a 'small amount' and that that person should not be making a noise or exaggerating the magnitude of the help rendered. People have a strange way of showing gratitude. Indeed, ungratefulness comes in many forms. The money you borrowed was 'so important' when you needed it, but now that you are required to pay it back, it has suddenly become 'small' or 'inconsequential'. People do not realize that by behaving like this, they are shutting the door on themselves for any future help from the creditor they have just disappointed. Your attitude determines your altitude.

For many people, telling their story is usually not an easy thing to do. There will always be some details that you might have forgotten or consider less important to delve into, not because you are hiding anything, but because the said information is either redundant or no longer useful. Some of it might not even relate to you directly and is therefore of less relevance for the purpose of telling your story. For example, it is a truism that some people that you grew up with who were frequent patrons of discos and nightclubs back then have either left this world or are now church elders. Others are even self-proclaimed prophets. But of what relevance would it be to chronicle their shenanigans in your autobiography? Your autobiography is about you, not about them. Similarly, there will be people who will want to take the credit where you did almost all the work alone and they just joined you at the last minute, as you finalized your project or assignment. Others will even say that you have only made it because they were praying for you, yet the person that put in a good word for you or wrote you that game-changer reference is someone else. Even where someone paid for your college or university fees, someone else will be busy trying to take credit that had it not been for his or her prayers you would not have made it. We see that every day. But hear me well on this one. Be grateful to the one who you know for a fact was the game-changer. Do not get misguided by the noise of attention-seekers. Some people like to steal the thunder of their friends. Even if someone claims to have been praying for you, thank especially the person who was the game-changer since God acted through that person, and arguably not through the supposedly prayerful hands.

When it comes to the stealing of someone's thunder, there are colleagues and bosses in many workplaces who disingenuously and dishonestly like to take credit for work that they have not done. For example, such people can add their name as sole author to a paper that they have not even written, while omitting your name, even though you wrote the paper. I know of someone, a black guy, who was asked by his white female boss, acting through her deputy, an African man, to prepare a paper for her to present at some conference. The paper was to be published later as part of the proceedings of the conference. It is possible that the white female boss could have asked her African deputy to write the paper himself, but the latter, knowing fully well that he could not produce serious scholarly writing, sought the help of the black junior who wrote the paper. Now, when commenting on the draft paper, the white female boss would only speak with her deputy, the African man, who would then convey the message to the junior writing the paper. For all we know, the African deputy could have created an impression to his white female boss that he was the one writing the paper, especially as he chose to block the black junior guy from meeting the white female boss and was only too eager to impress his white female boss as the main guy handling the assignment. The paper was published, and the white female boss had her name printed on it as the sole author, even though she had little or no input into the paper. The black junior guy who wrote the paper was not acknowledged anywhere in that paper, not even in the footnotes. Further, neither did the boss nor her African deputy bother to thank him for writing it. Rather, the white female boss simply took all the credit disingenuously as the sole author. Some people have no shame and will exploit you if they can.

Generally, racism operates like a caste system. It is not only about white supremacy or whites against blacks. You can also see it sometimes in the discrimination of some black folks by some brown and yellow folks such as Latinos, Arabs and other Middle Eastern folks as well as by some Indians, Chinese, and Filipinos who look down on people with darker skin as lower caste. Yet these brown and yellow folks rarely ever extend such discrimination to white folks just because whites have a lighter complexion than them and wield most of the economic power in the Western world. If anything, some brown and yellow folks try hard to assimilate themselves into white culture and to pass for a white person. Sadly, they not only try to act white, but also really want to be considered white, contrary to Dr Martin Luther King Jr's visionary dream where he said: "I have a dream that my four little children will one day live in a nation where they will not be judged by the color of their skin but by the content of their character."

I have also witnessed Greek, American, French, Belgian, German, English, Australian, Canadian and Russian racism, including versions of racisms from other parts of Eastern Europe, against some black folks. You can only deny that racism, especially institutional racism, exists if you yourself are a racist or demagogically attached to racism. Sometimes racism is fueled by white, brown or yellow folks feeling intimidated by a black person's powerful credentials. They will try to undermine or target him or her on racist grounds and even connive to give false testimony through collusion with some black folks who are ready to throw their own under a bus in order to get ahead. Indeed, you will be surprised that some blacks will be aiding the tormentors of a black person and will even be laughing and clapping until it is their turn to dance to the same music, the music of institutional racism.

Even amongst some black folks, there is discrimination based mainly on one's skin complexion, or one's nationality or tribe. Among some Africans, for example, the issue of tribalism is a major problem whether they are back in Africa or in the diaspora. Not even education has succeeded in detribalizing some African folks. For example, if you look at some African politicians, you will be shocked by how tribal they can be when it comes to pushing for their tribesmen and women to get lucrative international jobs abroad or when it comes to hiring locally into top jobs their tribesmen and women.

Other retrogressive prejudices that are common among some African natives have to do with discrimination on the basis of the religion that you follow or the kind of colonial masters' language that you speak. For example, some will want to know if you are Christian or Moslem before they can assist you. And within the Christian religion, for example, others might want to ask if you are Pentecostal, Evangelical, Jehovah's Witnesses (Watchtower), Seventh Day Adventist, Baptist, Anglican or Catholic. Closely related to this, discrimination based on the colonial masters' language spoken often points to differential treatment influenced by whether you are from a Francophone African country and speak French or from an Anglophone African country and can only speak English. Yet, the 'owners' of some of these colonial languages, that is, the white French and white English people, unlike some folks from their respective former colonies in lands afar, don't behave and treat each other that way. Also, in many black communities worldwide, the darker your skin complexion, the more likely you are to be ostracized by others. You will be marginalized by the lighter complexioned ones. But God has a way of punishing and humiliating the evil ones. Together with your tormentors, they will be tossed out by the system while you remain. If some of them remain, just know that they might not get some of what they were hoping to get in life such as finding a happy marriage or earning themselves a PhD. Somewhere along the line, life will catch up with them because God is a fair God. He protects His innocent children.

Further, when it comes to taking credit for work that someone has not done, if, say, a candidate for presidential elections were to win the elections, the same people who were doubting him or her and saying bad things behind his or her back will be the first to tell the newly elected President that they knew that he or she would win. People are not honest. They try to cash in on fame and success. Indeed, you will have more friends when you have money, power, fame or a high social status. Some people that you do not even know will claim to be your friends or related to you. Others who never used to talk to you will greet you with a bright smile and a hug, as if you have always been close friends. Yet, if you were to lose your fame, power or money, those same people will be the first to disappear and distance themselves from you as if you had a plague. As the old English adage goes: 'Success has many fathers, but failure is an orphan.' What is important, though, is for you to stick to the prophetic truth. But what is that prophetic truth?

I am awake to the fact that the truth often upsets or offends some people, especially if the offended person is too sensitive and not honest with himself or herself. Philosophically, we can try to debate the meaning of truth. There are many theories in philosophy about what constitutes the truth. I am awake to these theories. But it is not my intention here to delve into such philosophical debates. Suffice it to say that facts will drive much of what we consider the prophetic truth, not value judgements or theories.

Ideally, some people might like to see you place more emphasis in your autobiography on certain issues or a particular incident. You are, however, the best author of your life's story, not them. You know the facts best. Whichever way you turn the pen, you cannot satisfy everyone's preference because many people do not even have all the facts right. You know yourself best and better than anyone else, notwithstanding the arguments in psychology about blind spots and the implications of the Johari Window, a model used for understanding oneself. At the end of the day, you know yourself best and are in a better position to tell your story than anyone else.

In life, I have ten principles that I follow religiously. First, authenticity is key. You cannot afford to be a replica of someone else. Put simply, you have to work extra hard in order to differentiate yourself and your skills from your competitors and their skills so that you are not easily substitutable. Secondly, try to identify a niche where you can focus, so that you are not too general in what you do or have to offer. Thirdly, try to avoid pursuing costly strategies that bring you less benefit. One way of doing this is investing your time in forging valuable networks that you can leverage for your social capital.

Fourth, cultivate good people-skills to be able to get along with people. Fifth, try to hone both your social intelligence and emotional intelligence as part of your leadership signature. Sixth, do not be timid; do not mistake docility for humility. Rather, you should always remain confident, yet humble.

But how do you strike this delicate balance? Your ambition and assertiveness should be aligned with the context you are faced with, meaning to say that you should avoid overzealousness, overconfidence and celebrating your wins too early. And be nice to people, not arrogant.

Seventh, avoid getting entangled in organizational politics, and remain professional all the time. Eighth, avoid unconscious biases and treat everyone fairly and with respect. Ninth, be a good and active listener, showing empathy to others. Do not be quick to interject, or rule out people, when they are talking. Tenth, and equally important, be honest in your dealings. People will know if you are truthful or disingenuous.

In the early chapters of this autobiography, I stated that I was born and raised in Zambia up to the age of around 22, when I left Africa, as a Rhodes Scholar, to pursue postgraduate studies in the UK at the University of Oxford. I also mentioned that after completing my studies at Oxford, I settled in the UK as an academic and that I lived and worked in England for about a decade before

I moved to the US, where I have been for the last three decades. I added further that I have been a recipient of several international academic awards, including a competitive fellowship at the best law school in the US, Yale University Law School. All in all, I have been away from Zambia for a good four decades, though I do visit Zambia from time to time.

Closely related to the foregoing, I mentioned that I have been a recipient of the prestigious President's Insignia of Meritorious Achievement (PIMA), conferred on me in May 2019 for my distinguished scholarly achievements by the sixth (6th) President of the Republic of Zambia, H.E. President Edgar C. Lungu. In addition, as stated earlier, I am a recipient of another esteemed State award, a lifetime achievement award, where I was appointed in June 2011 as Honorary Ambassador of Tourism for the Republic of Zambia. The latter award, also bestowed for my distinguished scholarly accomplishments and contributions, was conferred on me by the fourth (4th) President of the Republic of Zambia, H.E. Mr Rupiah B Banda, acting through his Minister of Tourism. In July 2015, I was honored by the Institute of Directors of Zambia with an appointment as Honorary Fellow of the said institute. This distinction is the highest honor that the institute can confer on a distinguished and eminent person.

Then, in June 2021, I was elected by the Zambia Academy of Sciences, the highest scientific and academic national statutory body for the advancement of science and knowledge, as a Fellow of that academy. Again, the Fellow status is the highest honor. I have shared below some pictures of other coveted Zambian national honors that I have received, as a distinguished scholar, for my outstanding scholarly contributions to the international community.

Dr. Kenneth Mwenda
Washington DC, USA

Wednesday, August 7, 2024

Dear Dr. Mwenda,

Subject: "Shifting Mindsets: Empowering the Youth & Diaspora to Forge a Lasting Legacy" Education Award

Congratulations! We are thrilled to announce that you have been selected as the recipient of the Education Award at the upcoming Shifting Mindsets: Empowering the Youth & Diaspora to Forge a Lasting Legacy Gala. Hosted by Zambians Promoting Leadership in America (ZLA Foundation), this gala celebrates the remarkable achievements of individuals like yourself.

Your outstanding work as a scholar and academic in Zambia and around the world is truly inspiring. We are incredibly proud of your achievements, particularly your ability to publish research-based books that are widely utilized by others.

Congratulations once again on this well-deserved recognition. We look forward to celebrating your accomplishments with you and hundreds of others in the Diaspora.

If you have any questions, please feel free to contact me at freda@zlafoundation.com

Warm regards,

Dr. Freda Mwamba Brazle
Dr. Freda Mwamba Brazle
Founder, ZLA Foundation

Zambians Promoting Leadership in America
7527 Roswell Road, Suite 567601
Atlanta, GA 30350
zlafoundation.com

At international level, I have been an award-winning author, and my distinguished published scholarship has earned me two rarely awarded Higher Doctorates from two leading world-class universities. Also, I hold a third doctorate, a PhD, from another leading world-class university. Further, I have not only been a recipient of a highly prestigious and competitive fellowship from the best law school in the US, Yale University Law School, but have also been a recipient of what is arguably the most prestigious graduate scholarship in the world, that is, the Rhodes Scholarship tenable at the University of Oxford. More recently, as alluded to earlier, in 2023, I was elected by the Governing Council of the University of Oxford's Exeter College as Honorary Fellow of that esteemed Oxford college. Honorary Fellowships at Oxford, as already established, are awarded only to eminently qualified and most distinguished persons such as Nobel Prize laureates who have achieved the highest distinction in academia or public life.

As a believer in life-long learning, I have also studied at the prestigious Wharton Business School of the University of Pennsylvania, an Ivy League School, where I completed studies in Management and Leadership. Further, I hold additional qualifications in Management and Leadership from other leading business schools, including INSEAD (Institut Européen d'Administration des Affaires) in France, MIT (Massachusetts Institute of Technology) Sloan School of Management in the US, Stanford University Graduate School of Business in the US, London Business School in the UK, Northwestern University Kellogg School of Management in the US, Saïd Business School at the University of Oxford in the UK, Yale University School of Management in the US, Harvard University Business School in the US, Cornell University in the US, and Georgetown University in the US.

I am, however, awake to the fact that some people might be tempted ask how all this intellectual sophistication has benefitted or helped my native country, Zambia. It's a good question, and I won't dodge it. But before I respond, let me say something here that is equally important. I am not a politician and have never been one. We can't all be politicians. If I had wanted to be a politician, I would have striven to be among the top ten political leaders to have come out of Africa. The same standards of distinguished global thought-leadership that I apply to legal academia are what I would have applied to political leadership. There is no point in playing second fiddle. I am also not an entrepreneur or businessman and have never been one. Indeed, we all can't be entrepreneurs or businessmen. Like in the case of politics, if I had wanted to be one, I would have striven to be among the top 10 entrepreneurs or businessmen to have come out of Africa. My unparalleled and extraordinary achievements in the legal academy undoubtedly put me in the crème de la crème league of the top legal academics to have come out of Africa in our time. So, if you want to judge me, judge me by my scholarly contributions to the world, not by entrepreneurial zeal, partisan politics or the shenanigans of the corporate world.

As a family man, I had the honor in the earlier sections of this autobiography of introducing my family. To me, family is everything.

In the two pictures below, taken in December 2024, I can be seen with my dearest wife, Dr Judith Mvula-Mwenda, and our adorable son Jo-Jo, dining at a fine restaurant, Ruth's Chris Steakhouse, located in Gaithersburg, Maryland, US.

Another family picture follows below. It was taken at another restaurant that is one of our favorite family dinner outing places, Longhorn Steakhouse.

For me, as noted above, after God comes family, so I love treating my dearest wife, Dr J, and our adorable son, Jojo, to a deserving love that can only come from a loving husband and father. If it is a weekend lunch or dinner outing, it must be at a fine restaurant of their choice. If it is weekend shopping, it must be at some high-end or upscale shopping center of their choice. Because life must be enjoyed, though with a sense of responsibility. God gave us this world to enjoy it, not to be complaining, grumbling, whining, or nagging daily. Neither did God give us this world for us to hate, out of envy and jealousy, those who are doing better than us, or for us to start accusing them of boasting. There is enough room for everyone to enjoy this free world. And while saving money and investing it is good, you must also enjoy life as you go along. You cannot keep postponing happiness for a frugal lifestyle just because you want to save money, build a house somewhere in Africa, or be seen to be humble. Tomorrow is not guaranteed. Ambidexterity invites us to execute for the present while envisioning the future. So, you can be kind and generous whilst also saving and investing. The two ends are not mutually exclusive. You can do both concurrently. Why should I, for example, be eating chicken daily if I can afford some nicely done steak or some fine organic salmon? Or why should I deny my family a vacation, say, in the Bahamas, simply because we are building a mansion in Zambia? Being kind and generous is not the same thing as being extravagant or wasteful. But depriving yourself of happiness in the name of saving money is simply unacceptable. As you try to pivot between being generous and being frugal, just remember not to live beyond your means and not to be wasteful. For me, I believe in glorifying God, praising Him, worshipping Him, and thanking Him through the appreciation of everything that He has given us.

In the next picture, thanking God for my dearest wife, Dr J, with a gift to her of a Versace signature handbag.

In the next picture, relaxing at the Wharf in Washington DC before boarding and sailing away on a yacht for a yacht party I was hosting aboard the yacht on the Potomac River.

In the next picture, I was treating my dearest wife, Dr J, to a Ferragamo gift.

For my dearest wife, Dr J, an Yves Saint Lauren (YSL) signature handbag that appears in the next picture.

Another one! For my dearest wife, Dr J, a Prada signature handbag that appears in the next picture.

For my adorable son, Jojo, some fine D&G perfume set that appears in the next picture.

On Fathers' Day 2025 (in the next four pictures which include a full-grain leather Burberry business cardholder as well as a Louis Vuitton passport holder and a Louis Vuitton business cardholder), being gifted by my lovely wife, Dr J, and our adorable son, Jojo.

Gifting my dearest wife, Dr J, with a fine Burberry passport holder that appears in the next picture.

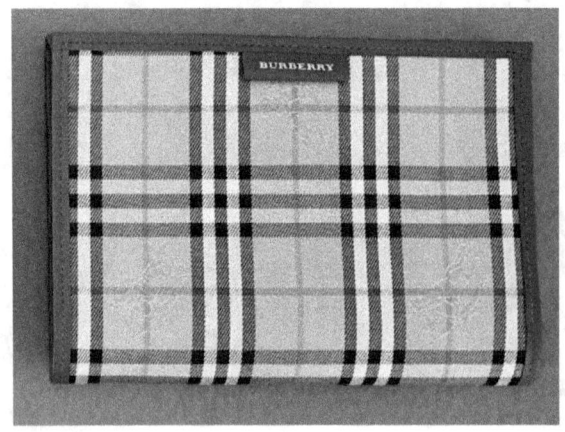

For my dearest wife, Dr J, some Moschino and Balenciaga sunglasses that appear in the next two pictures.

My wife, as established already, is a Zambian medical doctor who graduated from the University of Zambia School of Medicine (Ridgeway Campus) and holds postgraduate degrees from the University of Leicester and the University of Manchester in the UK. In addition, and as noted earlier, my wife completed postdoctoral programs at two US Ivy League schools, namely, Harvard University Medical School and Cornell University. Indeed, she is arguably the first Zambian medical doctor to obtain both MBA and MPH degrees from two leading British universities when it was not yet fashionable for many Zambian physicians to embark on that combination of postgraduate education, especially in the field of public health or preventive medicine. I am very proud of my dearest wife, as one of Zambia's most accomplished public health experts internationally. She now serves as Senior Director at a major public health institution in the US. Our lovely boy, Joseph (Jo-Jo), is currently pursuing university studies here in the US. I have provided another picture here of my family. This was taken when my family and I were visiting Yale University in New Haven, Connecticut, US.

I pointed out earlier that I left Zambia shortly after President Kenneth Kaunda lost elections to President Frederick Chiluba, and that before leaving I was teaching at the University of Zambia Law School. I also explained that in early 1992, while teaching at UNZA Law School, I won the prestigious Rhodes Scholarship to go to the University of Oxford for further studies. The idea was that I was going to come back to UNZA after my graduate studies in the UK. At the time, state funding of higher education across many African countries was becoming problematic, and I remember that in

Zambia, some senior academics had abandoned the UNZA academic cause and jumped onto the bandwagon of the wind of change for multiparty politics. They entered politics and were part of the newly elected government of the Movement for Multi-Party Democracy (MMD). I thought to myself, 'Am I also going to betray the academic cause and come back to enter politics or set up a small one-man law firm with all my postgraduate education from Oxford?' I was committed to my academic career. But the academic environment in Zambia was not conducive to a vibrant academic career. I had to think twice about returning to Zambia generally, and UNZA in particular, though I remained committed to giving back to Africa.

Another reason that made me stay on in the UK is that there was hardly any meaningful or impactful presence of Zambian legal academics holding full-time lectureships at top UK universities. I felt a need to make a difference. For the most part, many Zambian academics, either out of lack of confidence or other reasons known only to themselves, would just rush back to Zambia after earning their graduate degrees, leaving a number of other African academics to take up notable academic opportunities in the UK. So, I decided to change the narrative and make a difference, as opposed to being a mere spectator. No Zambian lawyer had ever served as a full-time law lecturer at a leading British university before my time. The most you would hear of was just some graduate teaching assistant or a tutorial fellow here and there.

In 1995, at the age of only 26, as I mentioned earlier, I became the first Zambian lawyer to hold a full-time law lectureship at one of the top 10 British universities, the University of Warwick. With this, I broke the record to pave way for other Zambian legal academics to become law lecturers in the UK. At the same time, I continued to collaborate and partner with many public institutions back home in Zambia as a way of giving back. This is only the beginning of my story of how I continue to give back to Zambia and mother Africa. That said, I am mindful that I can do more if only the local environment back home in Zambia were more welcoming and accommodating. As one of my Zambian mentees, Kasabo Mutale Kalusa, wrote in a WhatsApp message he sent me on November 30, 2024, after reading some excerpts of my book that is titled, 'The Recognition of Global Higher Education Qualifications in International Law': "I honestly feel that Zambia has let itself down by not fully and aggressively pursuing you, Prof. There is more that we needed to do. I can assure you that it will take us another 50 years to produce a Zambian national at your level."

Earlier, I pointed out that I joined the World Bank in 1998 on the highly competitive Young

Professionals Program (YPP). Again, I was a pioneer for my country as the first Zambian to join the World Bank on the YPP, paving the way for others to follow suit and start applying to the World Bank YPP.

My joining the World Bank at its headquarters in Washington DC helped to demystify the Bank to many Zambians who would not ordinarily have had the courage to apply to jobs at the World Bank. Many were inspired by my career path. If they are honest, they will tell you so. When I joined the World Bank, I only found one black Zambian professional there, and she was not many years from retirement. The rest came after me.

All in all, I have been with the World Bank for three decades now and have worked in all major regions of the world as well as covered all major sectors. Also, I have led many projects and worked as Senior Counsel in the Legal Vice-Presidency of the World Bank, in addition to working as Senior Counsel in the Integrity Vice-Presidency of the World Bank. Breaking new ground is something I am used to. I have been a pioneer throughout in my professional life. No Zambian lawyer had ever worked in the legal department of any Bretton Woods Institution until I paved the way for others to follow when I served as Senior Counsel in the Legal Vice-Presidency of the World Bank. Later, I moved on to take up a managerial role to lead both the World Bank Voice Secondment Program (VSP) and the World Bank Board of Executive Directors' Disclosure of Interests Program (DOI).

Concurrent with my work at the World Bank, I have continued to give back to academia in Africa and elsewhere as well as published extensively in leading peer-reviewed scholarly journals and with preeminent academic presses. I mentioned earlier that I have continued to hold professorial appointments as Extraordinary Professor and Honorary Professor at some leading universities worldwide. In fact, before any other Zambian legal academic was appointed as Extraordinary Professor in South Africa, I had already broken the ground in South Africa. In the US, I have taught at American University Washington College of Law in Washington DC. In 2024, I was also appointed to a distinguished Visiting Professorship at another leading US Law School. Further, I have been back at UNZA as Visiting Professor of Law and continue to serve as Extraordinary Professor of Law at the University of Lusaka (UNILUS). In a sense, I have not betrayed Zambia and Africa. They both still have me, notwithstanding the distance which can sometimes be bridged by the virtual world today.

I have highlighted above how I have broken new grounds, as a pioneering Zambian academic and professional, both locally in Zambia and elsewhere. I have inspired many Zambians as well as other nationals who have emulated and followed my career path both at the World Bank and in academia. Further, my teaching and research engagements at universities in Zambia and elsewhere in Africa cannot go unnoticed. For example, I continue to supervise and exam several PhD students in South Africa and Zambia. Also, I have helped a number of well-qualified Zambian mentees to obtain scholarships at various universities in South Africa, the UK and the US. A few of them have even ended up at the World Bank. And I continue to mentor many other Zambian professionals and academics, both at home and in the diaspora. It is a humbling experience, for example, when some prominent elite people that I knew in Zambia when I was growing up can ask their son, daughter, nephew or niece to reach out to me for mentoring and professional guidance. The elderly folks often know the difference between substance and form when it comes to a true beacon of hope for tomorrow's leaders.

When I look at, say, Muhammad Ali, he fought some of his notable fights in Zaire (DRC) and Manila (Philippines). And he travelled the world. Then, Pele played some of his professional soccer games in the USA. And he too travelled the world. Messi played in Spain and France. Now he plays in the USA. Put simply, whatever you do, I often tell folks to try to get some international and comparative exposure. It will serve you well. A parochial and insular approach to a professional life can be very limiting. When I lived and worked in Europe, my experiences were different from when I lived and worked in Africa. And living and working in North America too has taught me different things. Each experience offers me something new to learn from. Even as a scholar, my journey has never been confined to one country or continent. Go out there and see the world. There is a lot to learn. But if you don't travel, you will think you know it all or that you have all the answers.

In Zambia, I also continue to work closely with a Catholic school for children with different abilities where I lead some philanthropic work using my own financial resources. A few years after I started this initiative, some corporate donor jumped on the bandwagon, drumming up a lot of media publicity while imitating my charity work in the same space where I was operating. But that is fine with me. There is enough room for everyone to contribute. I don't do media publicity for such noble causes. Because I have no hidden political agenda or spirited marketing ambition. Rather, I have always been a Catholic Christian. I was raised as a Catholic. I have not forgotten those children. They are close to my Christian heart. Over the years, I have come to learn that although the Catholic Church, like any other Christian Church or denomination, is not perfect, many people who criticize it today were actually educated by Catholics. Indeed, many attended Catholic Schools.

Mindful of the unfortunate evils of child abuse at the hands of some irresponsible Catholic priests, for example, the church itself is a separate institution from those dark evils. So, one cannot say that he or she discovered something bad with the Catholic faith and have now found God elsewhere soon after exploiting and benefitting from a good Catholic education. That is disingenuous. With such folks, it is often their own dishonesty and disoriented spirit that drives them away from the Catholic faith. If you are dishonest or disingenuous, you can insult even people who educated you when they found you either semi-literate or almost illiterate. For me, it is hard to listen to people who show ingratitude or ungratefulness to those that have helped them because they can equally do the same to me. Consistency and loyalty are key in friendships and relationships. For example, I have often invited colleagues, who in their lowest and most difficult moments have come to me asking for some kind of help, to pray with me. But, for some of them, the moment God gives them what they had been looking for, that's it. You will never hear from them again. All you hear is people telling you how busy they are celebrating that they made it, got selected, or passed the job interview or university exam. They will not even give God any credit but will instead try to assign all the credit to themselves, as if they have never knelt down to ask God for His intervention. Suddenly things change and it becomes all about them, not God. Such people will only come back to ask you to pray with them if or when they are faced with another life crisis. But it is not in them to thank God properly for assisting them. In fact, once they have been delivered, you become irrelevant to them. They feel that they have gotten what they wanted and don't need you anymore. For such people, even thanking God is not a necessity or priority. Such is life. But gratitude is not just saying 'Thank you' and then running off. Rather, gratitude is how you behave after you have been helped. Because anyone can say 'Thank you', but few actually mean it.

I stated earlier in this autobiography that nobody in this world is perfect. We are all sinners. But the fact that nobody is perfect does not mean that we all have a license to be crooked or dishonest. When I pray, I pray not because am perfect. Also, I pray not because am holier than thou. Look, I am not of the gospel of prosperity. Rather, I pray to God because I am a sinner. And many a time, I feel unworthy before God. It is only by God's Grace and Mercy that my faith can be sustained to endure forever. And so, in my prayers and devotion, I ask God to look not on my sins, but on my faith. For I am a work-in-progress on this journey of faith. As Christians, many folks will be challenged at some point by the dark clouds that try to snuff out the light of God in you so as to dim God's candle of hope in you. But you must pray and continue to pray, as you ask for the Holy Spirit and God's Angels to protect and strengthen you in the battle. For, the battle is not yours, but God's.

In the three pictures below, I had driven with my family for about three hours and a half from Rockville, Maryland to West Chester, Pennsylvania, US, to attend a solemn Catholic Mass held at Saints Simon and Jude Parish for the veneration of a significant sacred relic of my patron saint, St. Jude Thaddeus, a first cousin of our Lord Jesus Christ and one of Jesus' twelve apostles. I could not miss that important Mass. In fact, when it was announced later that the said sacred relics would also be venerated in Maryland and Virginia, I attended two additional Masses in Maryland.

All three Masses were a lifetime experience, the closest that one can get to the physical incarnate being of our Lord Jesus Christ. In the Catholic faith,

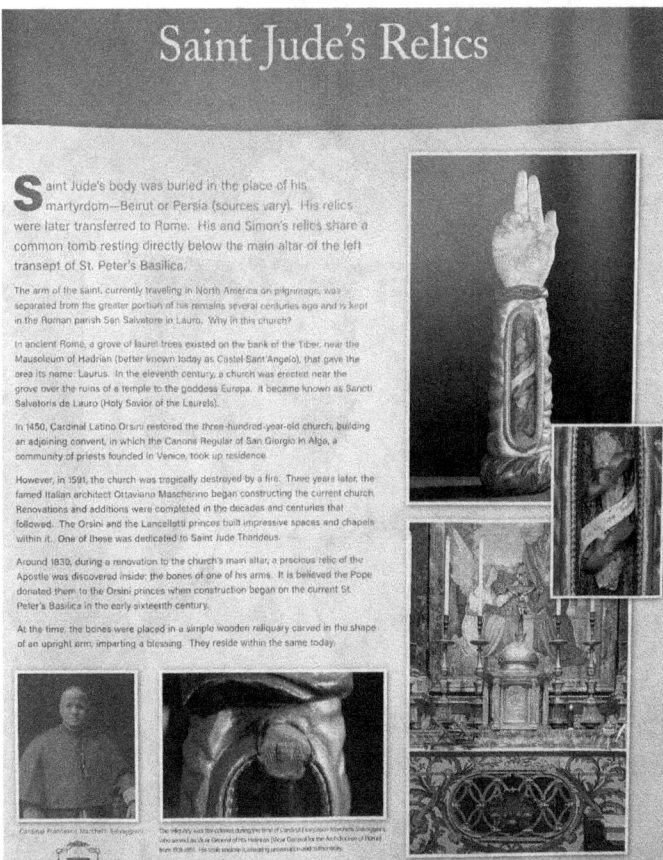

saints or the sacred relics of saints are not worshipped, because only God is worshipped. Instead, the saints and their sacred relics are venerated, while we worship God alone. The Catholic Church has two classifications of sacred relics, namely, significant (insigni) and non-significant. Examples of significant sacred relics relate mainly to the body, or significant parts of the body, of a saint, as well as the entire contents of the urn with the ashes preserved after cremation. Examples of non-significant sacred relics include small fragments of the body, as well as objects used by saints.

The picture below of the statue of the Blessed Virgin Mary was taken at the National Shrine Grotto of Our Lady of Lourdes at Mount St. Mary University in Emmitsburg, Maryland, US.

Wherever I travel to, I often try to look for a notable church or cathedral, especially a Catholic church, cathedral or basilica, since I am Catholic, to spend some time in prayer and meditation before I embark on my tours or business. And because I am not perfect, I must continue to renew and strengthen my faith in God every day. When I am in Cape Town, South Africa, for example, I often stay at hotels downtown near St George's Cathedral, the main Anglican cathedral in South Africa. I attend Mass at St George's Cathedral since it's a short walk from the nearby hotels. Generally, the Anglican Church liturgy is almost identical to that of the Catholic Church, so I can relate to that and am okay with it. There is no dramatic posturing or theatrical screaming and shouting. People simply worship quietly and respectfully.

In the pictures show here, my family and I took a road trip from Maryland to West Virginia one bright summer Saturday in 2024 to visit George Washington's Bathtub, a historic place in the town of Berkeley Springs, West Virginia. It was a long drive. It took us a couple of hours to get to the historic place where the first President of the United States of America, President George Washington, often visited for a spring water bath. When we got there, I was looking for parking and noticed a Catholic Church across the street. I drove over to the parking lot of the church. There was more than enough free parking space, so we parked there, and as soon as we all got out of the car, I invited my wife and son to join me for a moment of prayer at the church to thank God for the travelling mercies before we could go on with our tour. Gratitude is a must. And we must never forget to give thanks. For, as St. Padre Pio observed, "If people knew the value of the Mass, there would be policemen at the door to regulate access to the Church every time a Mass is celebrated."

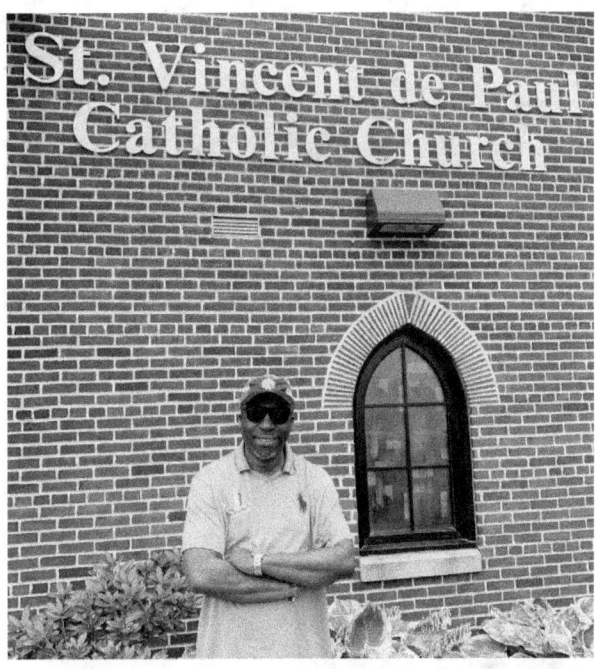

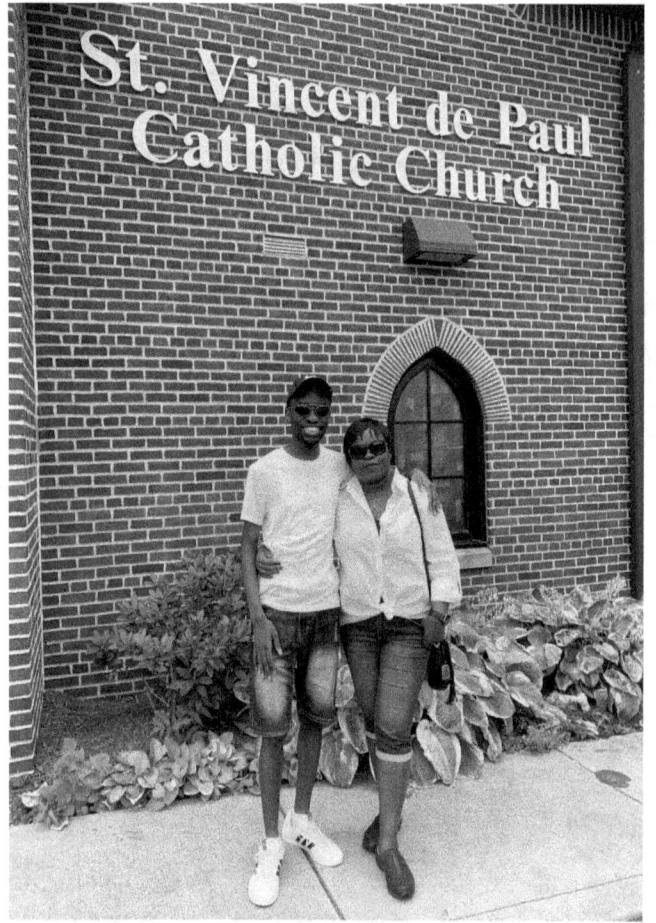

There comes a time when a man can no longer rely entirely on his mind to understand God. For, the mind has no heart. It might be gifted with sound intellect and a conscience, but it has no heart. But prayer can help us to see things through the eyes of the heart. It is through those eyes that we begin to discover the richness of God's divine mercy, allowing us to pray even for our close family members and friends who have gone before us so that they too can pray for us before God our Heavenly Father.

I have shared some pictures here of my dearest wife, Dr J, and my son, Jojo, in Berkeley Springs, West Virginia, US.

We grabbed some late lunch in Hagerstown, Maryland, on our way back from West Virginia.

The pictures below were taken in the summer of 2024 when I was vacationing with my family at the beach in Ocean City, Maryland, US.

Having lived not only in Africa, but also in the US and the UK, I can safely say there are some cultural attributes that I will not term 'generalizations', but which, for me, appear to be common in both the US and the UK, though somewhat different in Africa. I have adopted some of these cultural norms and practices while retaining my Afro-centric core values. First, generally speaking, the British are often more subtle, whilst the Americans are more direct. And money seems to matter more in America, while good manners are often emphasized in elite British society. In Zambia, the effect of British colonial rule still lingers on in the psyche of some of our people, though the indigenous native culture and practices seem to increasingly water down the British ethos.

Understanding the nuances of the cultural fabric and the different value systems of the place where you are operating from can help you to make better informed decisions. For example, effective time-management is critical in both the US and the UK. By contrast, in Zambia, someone can show up late and will be smiling as they walk in, without offering you an apology. Secondly, in the Western world, it is not common for people you help or assist to act with a sense of entitlement. Also, many people in the Western world hardly get upset if you tell them that you are not in a position to help or assist them. Neither do they go around asking their neighbors or friends for money. Someone can be homeless, but he will just beg on the streets instead of bothering a relative or friend. Otherwise, if you have no cash, you can either use your credit card or go to a bank to borrow money. You have to understand that nobody owes you anything for you to be mad at them for not giving you money.

To put things in perspective, people in the Western world hardly go around asking friends and relatives to buy them specific wedding gifts or asking for financial contributions towards the cost of holding their wedding. Even when someone gets pregnant out of wedlock or has too many children within the institution of marriage, do not expect other people to sort out your bills for raising that child or children. Sex is between two people only, unless it was a threesome. Those two people should be mindful that an orgasm is costly, irrespective of who experienced it between the two of them. Orgasms are not free. And nobody is going to subsidize your orgasms. That is why child support laws in the US are so strict. Why would someone be putting fuel in a car that he doesn't even drive, yet another man is busy skidding around in that same car for free at night? The guy who drives that car should be the one to put fuel in the car. By parity of reasoning, there is no need to pay rent for a house that you don't sleep in, unless you are doing it to help your children who are in college or university. Neither should we expect you to pay for a hotel room you are not occupying. You can only pay if, or, as and when, you are occupying that hotel room.

Likewise, someone who lent you money should not be giving you an explanation regarding why he needs his money back for you to return his money. Common sense dictates that you stop pretending that you have forgotten that you owe him a debt. Put simply, black-tax and dependency mindsets are an alien thing in much of contemporary American and British culture. Thirdly, in the US, it is not uncommon to see people celebrating their accomplishments openly whilst in much of our African societies such acts would be mistaken for bragging. Put simply, in Africa, you must hide your achievements under the bed and pretend to be humble even if you are not humble. Pretense is often misconstrued as humility in Africa. But nobody will see your star if it is hidden underneath the bed. Let it glow for people to appreciate it!

 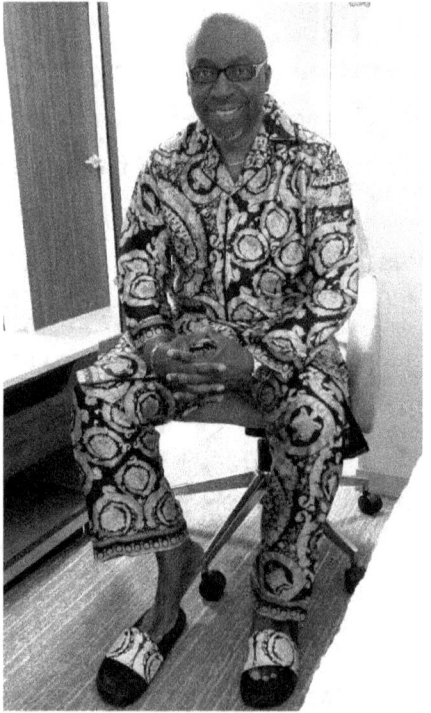

Indeed, what good is a star if you keep hiding it underneath your bed or pillow? It will not glow. And nobody will see it in order to appreciate its value. So, put it where it can shine and be appreciated.

Even a diamond hidden in the ground is of not much value until it is unearthed and polished for people to appreciate it.

In America, the concept of American exceptionalism encourages you to be exceptional. You can glow if you want. You are encouraged to speak up and be heard without feeling shy. You are also encouraged to get to the point instead of talking in circles and riddles or parables. Because time is money, many people in the West will tell you that they have other things to do instead of wasting their time listening to you beat about the bush. So, get to the point and stop waffling. What do you want? By contrast, in Africa we like to go into long, winding explanations and stories before we get to say what we want. Even when a visitor is invited to a meal, he or she will pretend they are not hungry while they wait for you to beg them again to join you for the meal. In the Western world, nobody has time for such procrastination.

I have lived in many places around the world and have travelled extensively. Quite often you will see differences between, say, an African brother or sister who has lived in Europe (as a professional or university student) before moving to the US, and one who comes straight out of Africa to

America, without spending some time, say, in Europe. The challenges are real. For example, if you live in America or Europe, it is wise to go out for a drink only when you can afford such an outing but not when you have no money. Don't expect other people to buy you beers, as is often the case back home in Africa. In fact, very few people in the Western world might even recognize you in the pub. Nobody knows you out there. People mind their own business. For the most part, you drink at home, unless you are dining out. Also, in the Western world, unlike back home in Africa, if your neighbors are starving or have family issues, it is their own problem, not yours. You can help them if they are okay with you helping them, but they should not feel entitled to your help nor come to bother you unless you are really close. Similarly, you can only attend a funeral by invitation, even if the deceased was your workmate or is a guy that you know from the neighborhood. People don't show up anyhow for funerals. Each to his or her own. You won't even find slay-queens or blessers in the Western world, unless maybe you go to some low-income neighborhood. That said, you will find several Marios and Ben 10s, especially among minorities in the US, because not every man has a clean criminal record or legal papers to allow them to work or has been to school to get a high paying job.

As I conclude this autobiography, I would like to share, among other things, some final remarks on the value of education. I will also share some cultural thoughts on the institutions of family and marriage from a Zambian cultural perspective. I will treat these two institutions, marriage and family, as one. In doing so, I first admit my own cultural and Christian biases. Why do I say so? Because the Christian and African values that I ascribe to often view a family ideally as a product of marriage, as opposed to a *sui generis* social construct that can exist outside the institution of marriage. In the secular world, you can have a family without a marriage. In my discussion below, I will also highlight the salient aspects of the Luapula-Bemba marriage tradition of 'amatebeto'.

As a general rule, when you are getting married or planning to get married, not everyone will be happy for you, including some people that might be present at your wedding. Human beings are strange. Let us assume in a hypothetical world that there was a requirement to get the permission of a jilted ex-lover, an envious friend, or a jealous relative or neighbor for you to get married. Do you think any of those people would grant you that permission? Put simply, much to the chagrin of such people, you are not under any legal or moral obligation to consult, notify or inform them that you are getting married. Their permission is simply not necessary. Neither do you owe them an explanation for your decision to get married. Marriage is between two people. If you do choose to explain yourself to them, it should be merely out of courtesy, not obligation. Otherwise, you are under no obligation to offer anyone any explanation. And as long as you are of sound mind and are of permissible age under the law to marry, the law does not require you to consult anyone over your intentions to marry or get married.

In life, any choice you make is likely to attract or involve some disappointment with someone somewhere. Each time someone is appointed or promoted, someone else will be disappointed or angry. That is just how life is. The superficial smiles of the disappointed or angry, no matter how disguised, are often not genuine. So, be wise. Such folks can pretend to be happy for you, but they are not. Some will even ask to be invited to your wedding so that they can pick up any gossip if anything goes wrong. You must remove all that noise that is in the way if you have to make progress in life. That is the starting point of progress. Otherwise, if you let the noise in, there will be noise in your marriage.

Now there is no such thing as a perfect marriage. Both parties to the marriage must not only be committed to the institution of marriage, but must also keep working at improving the marriage. But where does it start from? It starts with the choices you make at the beginning of courting. While there are no hard and fast rules about how to choose a partner for marriage, or which person to settle for, there are some obvious pitfalls that one can avoid. What I have highlighted below are simply my personal views. I respect the fact that others might have their own personal views as well. For me, the following are some pitfalls that one can avoid if or when considering to marry or get married:

- Do not confuse lust or infatuation with love, because lust and infatuation focus on a burning desire for immediate and short-term gratification whereas genuine love focuses on a selfless, sustainable and indefatigable longevity of the permanency of marital unity even in the midst of stormy weather. By contrast, lust and infatuation cannot withstand adverse or inclement weather conditions and often wane away soon after the release of passions.

- [ ] If you can, avoid marrying to impress people. The people you are trying to impress will not be there with you in your marriage. To impress people, some guys and ladies go for 'famous names', that is, marrying the son or daughter of some famous person or some so-called celebrity. Such marriages often come with a wedding full of pomp and splendor, as if it is a competition to outdo all other weddings. But soon after the wedding, the guests will retreat to their homes, and reality will slowly begin to set in for the newly married couple. Every day cannot be a wedding day, and that flamboyant wedding was only for that particular moment. Like lust and infatuation, many marriages predicated on the so-called 'famous names' don't last long. What happens if, say, the famous guy you marry can no longer play professional basketball or professional soccer due to an injury, and, thus has a significant loss of income? Also, what happens if the wealthy and famous parents of the lady you just married get convicted of drug-trafficking and their entire family empire descends into financial ruin? Think before you get excited about famous names.

- [ ] If you can, avoid marrying someone just because of their race, thinking that people of his or her race are better and wealthier than most people from your own race. Such inferiority complexes are common in some people of color who marry for the wrong reasons, until they discover that there are poor white people, as well as white people who have not been to any man's school. To assume, for example, that a white man is more loving and faithful than a black man, based purely on the television movies that you have been watching, is not only being naïve but reveals a pitiful sense of ignorance. Human beings are human beings wherever they are. It does not matter whether they are white, black, blue, green, brown or yellow, they are the same everywhere, except for some cultural differences. While men from some races, for example, like to have baby-mammas, without even hiding their shenanigans from the public, men from other races tend to be more discreet and often like to operate under the radar by going for call-girls, say, at a nearby hotel at lunch time, so as to avoid detection and getting entangled in public scrutiny. Yet, to the naïve person, the latter man is faithful simply because he goes straight home after work, pretending to be the most faithful husband the world has ever seen. Unfortunately, you don't know what he does at lunch or after the gym. Put simply, it is advisable to marry for love, not for whiteness. Otherwise 'jungle-fever' is not love as such. Rather, it is a psychological condition that requires treatment.

- If you can, avoid falling for stereotypes because some people will tell you that you cannot marry from certain tribes or nationalities. Admittedly, while cultures differ between or among various tribes, as well as between or among various nationalities, there is always an exception to the general rule. Even a rose garden has weeds and roses, and not everyone from a particular tribe or country is bad. You just have to find your rose and separate it from the weeds before it gets contaminated by them.

- If you can, avoid marrying someone just for their money. Money often does not last forever. Be prepared for that. Indeed, what happens if he or she runs out of money? Have you ever thought about it? The leading cause of marital problems or divorce worldwide today is not infidelity, as some people may think, but money! The absence or presence of money can lead to problems of their own. Be careful with money. Because the same thing that makes you smile if you have it is gonna make you cry one day. More money, while appearing like a solution in the short term, often ends up bringing you a new set of problems.

- If you can, avoid marrying someone just for their looks. Looks alone, like money, do not last forever. Looks often fade with age. The bootylicious derrière of a youthful lady, with all her enticing curves, will begin to lose shape with age. Likewise, the six-pack and the toned muscles of a youthful guy cannot last forever. Sooner or later, he will become a shell of himself, and you will even start doubting the virility of the parcel in his underpants. Be prepared for that.

- If you can, try to narrow the divide between your religious views and those of the person you want to marry. Otherwise, you will find yourself alone, with a stranger in your home. Religion, like issues of tribe and race, can be a thorny and divisive factor in many a marriage. It is always advisable to find a common ground between yourself and the person you are marrying. Otherwise, your partner may wake you up at midnight shouting in 'tongues' whilst you try to sleep.

- If you can, try to narrow the divide between your educational levels and that of the person you would like to marry. Otherwise, you will often be accused by your spouse of boasting, and might find yourself a stranger in your own home. Education, like religion, tribe and race, can be a thorny and divisive factor in a marriage. It is always advisable to find a common ground between yourself and the person you are marrying. That way, the children will not grow up wondering which of their parents to emulate academically.

- ☐ If you can, avoid a marriage where you have to inherit other people's problems, especially if you are young and have never been married before. Some people come with excess baggage into a marriage, seeking your sympathy as if you had been there when they accumulated those problems. You are not a messiah to solve other people's problems. Be real and avoid trying to be a hero for nothing. Some people can be ungrateful after you have welcomed them with open arms, notwithstanding the issues they came with. You might end up regretting it.

- ☐ If you can, avoid marrying someone just because you want him or her to take you with them abroad. Sooner or later, your true colors will show after you get there, as you are likely to disappoint the person that showed you the Western world for the first time. It can get ugly, if you are not careful. These are the kinds of calamities that can be avoided by just being honest with yourself, without trying to exploit someone.

- ☐ If you can, avoid marrying a rich old person who has not much time to live so that you can inherit his or her wealth soon after he or she dies. Such maneuvers are pure evil. They will catch up with you.

Generally, marriage is a beautiful thing. In fact, in the Catholic Christian faith, marriage is a sacrament. It is considered a sacred covenant that God ordains between one man and one woman. But if you look around you today, you will notice that a number of people have not lasted long in the institution of marriage, especially those living in or coming from laissez-faire and less conservative cultures. Many don't even last a year or two. Others just hang on in there. Then there are those who enjoy and thrive in a happy lifelong marriage, growing together in old age.

Some marriages start off with some rough patches. Things get better or begin to stabilize with time. It's like turbulence on a flight soon after take-off. The turbulence will dissipate fairly quickly as you pick up altitude, and the flight begins to stabilize. Other marriages start off on a high note and end up on the rocks. There is no single formula for a happy marriage or family. Every situation is different and unique. We can, however, draw some lessons of experience from certain team-dynamics, especially since married couples are often seen as a team. I have been married for more than two decades. And so, I have some valuable experience that could allow me to share some wisdom here.

In the picture below, a little Versace gift for her while out at the beach.

The following pictures speak to how, collectively, my lovely wife, Dr J, our adorable son, Jojo, and I roll as a family.

Now, let me turn to the discussion on the amatebeto tradition in Zambia. Amatebeto is a ceremony where the bride's family host a feast for the husband and his family some years after the marriage. It is a cultural tradition among the Luba-Lunda diasporas who migrated from the Democratic Republic of Congo and have now settled in modern-day Zambia's Northern, Muchinga and Luapula Provinces. Among these diasporans, however, there are some subtle and minor distinctions in their traditions, as some of these migrants assimilated the local traditions and customs of the local people that they found wherever they settled. For example, the tradition of 'uku lasa imbusa', which is practiced mainly among the Bembas when a young man is getting married, is found among the Bembas, and less among the Luapulans. Some tribes from Luapula hardly subscribe to 'ilayshi lya mbusa' (*i.e.* rituals relating to the 'imbusa' tradition of the Bembas).

That said, the 'amatebeto' tradition, by contrast, is somewhat universally accepted by many Luba-Lunda diasporans from Zambia's Northern, Muchinga and Luapula Provinces. Closely related to the foregoing, there is also the tradition of 'ichi-langa mulilo' among the Luba-Lunda diasporans which is often confused with amatebeto by many people. Interestingly, many other Zambian tribes now try to copy the tradition of 'ici-langa mulilo' from the Luba-Lunda diasporans in Zambia, though they often label it incorrectly as 'amatebeto'. Amatebeto, among Zambia's Luba-Lunda diasporans found in Northern, Muchinga and Luapula Provinces, is different from 'ici langa mulilo'.

Whereas ici langa mulilo is a pre-marital traditional ceremony of the Luba-Lunda diasporans which the bride does not attend, and only her aunties and other relatives are in attendance, amatebeto is a post-marital ceremony that only occurs after many years in marriage. At the ici langa mulilo ceremony, the bride's aunties and relatives will take various dishes of traditional food that they have prepared to the home where the groom and his relatives are waiting for the groom to taste and sample the food, as the bride's relatives pay close attention to study the groom's food preferences. The ceremony is somewhat akin to a wine-tasting event where the bride's aunties pay attention to the type of wine that the groom enjoys most so that they can relay the message to the bride about his favorite wine. In my case, I had to travel to Zambia with my wife for my 'ici langa mulilo', as an imitation of the real 'ici langa mulilo' done, say, in North America or Europe, often tends to be quite superficial, diluted and distorted.

A day after the wedding, the newly married couple is then introduced to the 'uku lula' ceremony, another Luba-Lunda diaspora tradition that stresses to the newly-wed the importance of keeping or maintaining a happy home. Thereafter, and many years after you have been married, you could be presented by your in-laws, if you are lucky, with the much revered 'amatebeto' ceremony. Using a metaphor, I would say that amatebeto is like a PhD whereas ichi langa mulilo is like an associate or university first degree.

Of course, there are other traditional Bemba ceremonies such as 'ukwingisha mu ng'anda' that are best described as being awarded a professorship by your in-laws, as they accept you into their home just like their own biological son. Now many chaps in Zambia or from Zambia do go through ici langa mulilo before they get married, but few of them get honored with amatebeto. And among those few, some are not even matebeto material but only get presented with amatebeto simply because the wife and her relatives had to quickly organize the amatebeto to make it appear as if she has had a blissful and enriching marriage. People sometimes pretend and try to cover up mediocrity just to avoid shame and embarrassment, especially where their daughter or female relative is married to an irresponsible and hopeless fella.

Culturally, however, amatebeto was only extended to a son-in-law who had demonstrated substantial works to show that he has been taking care of his in-laws and wife in a respectful, dignified, kind and generous manner. For example, in the picture below, I surprised my wife with a good treat at a Burberry store before treating her and my son to an assortment of some fine perfumes. That is who I am. And I do this regularly for my family as well as for others that are close to me.

And the assortments follow.

Below is a picture I took in 2024 of my dearest wife, Dr J, at Ronald Reagan Washington National Airport in Arlington County, Virginia, US, when my son, Jojo, and I were seeing her off and before she checked-into the First Class lounge in readiness for an executive trip to St. Louis, Missouri, US.

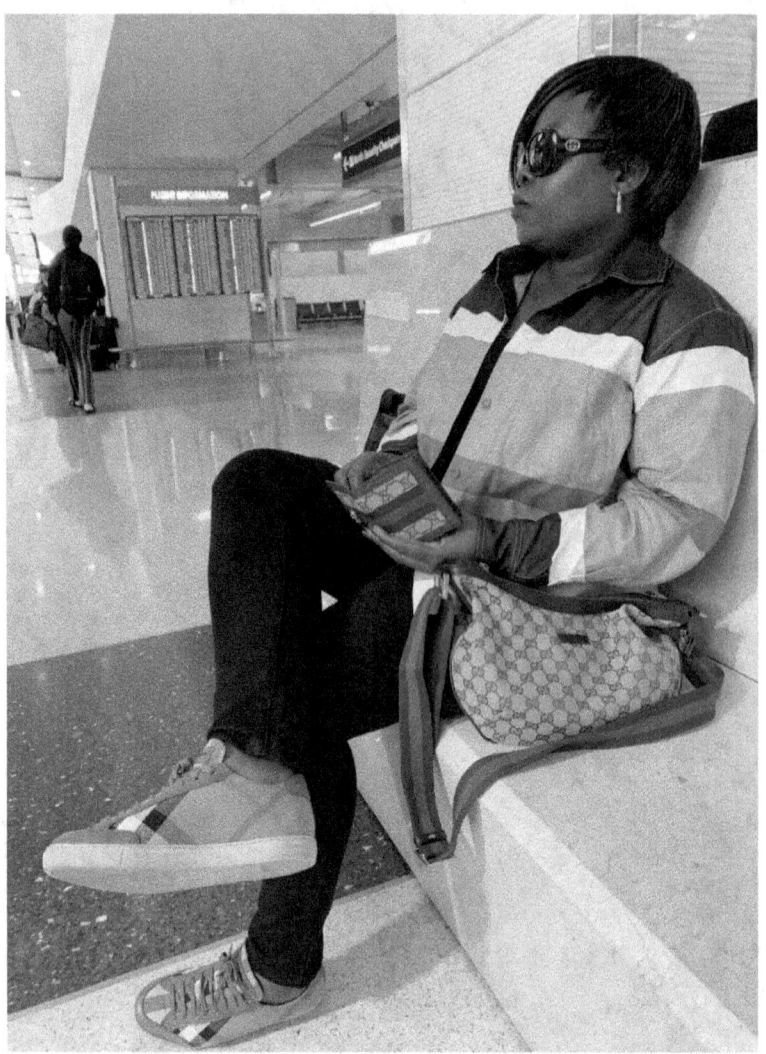

Closely related to the foregoing, a man must also take care of himself as he cares for others.

As I have said before, my style is my own. I have always stayed original and never tried to imitate anyone else. I refuse to be, and can never be, an inferior imitation of someone. Rather, I am who I am. There can only be one me. It's not only about confidence and self-assurance, but it is also about authenticity. I am true to myself.

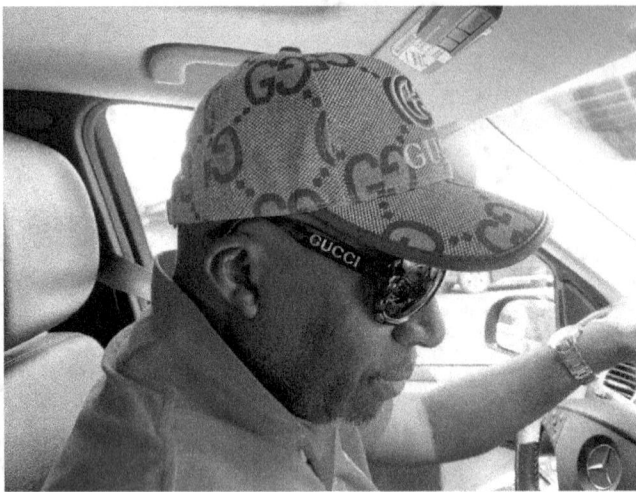

Always remember – if not now, then when? In life, you can choose to be amazing or amazed. That's a choice you will have to make at some point, whether consciously or unconsciously. Otherwise, it sucks being a spectator all the time. If God has given you a gift, then embrace it with both hands instead of living an apologetic life.

Without doubt, how you plan your day at the office and at home really matters. A fine assortment of decent daily planners helps me to arrange things in order. It makes a whole lot of difference.

Today, in many an urban Zambian setting, the level of expectation of what it takes for a man to be honored by his in-laws with the amatebeto ceremony has somewhat been compromised and watered down. Even those who are married to some unscrupulous fella known to everyone as a conman try to put up a show that they too are happily married and push for their irresponsible husband to be honored with amatebeto. I know this view might not sit well with some people, but I speak only the truth. If you are not guilty, there is no need to panic.

In the picture below, I surprised my boy, Jojo, with some Burberry gifts. I bought these gifts at a Burberry store at one of the airports in Europe while my family and I were on a family vacation. This is who I am.

You will know a man not just by how he takes care of himself, but also by how he takes care of his family and those around him.

In general, the amatebeto tradition, as a badge of honor for a married man whose generosity and kindness are appreciated by his in-laws, is often carried out after you have been married for many years. This tradition is celebrated with a grand ceremony after your wife's parents and relatives, having noticed that you have been a good son in-law who has been there for them, throw you some kind of big cookout party. Put simply, you cannot throw amatebeto for some lazy ass who is being looked after by his wife. And we have many such characters the world over. Some call themselves 'businessmen' while others are self-styled 'consultants' of one sort or another. A number of them are just conmen trying to survive off women. Amatebeto was never meant for such fellas. They can attend someone's amatebeto and pick up some trash or litter, but they are not to be 'tebetad'.

When we talk of the amatebeto tradition, even how you conduct yourself as a husband and father matters. It is not a tradition for a man of straw such as a thug, an unscrupulous fella or some vagabond. Below are three pictures taken with my family on one of our usual family prayer and retreat visits at the National Shrine Grotto of Our Lady of Lourdes, in Emmitsburg, Maryland, US.

In the picture that follows below, I can be seen standing next to a mosaic image of Saint Jude Thaddeus. This picture was taken in Washington DC at Our Lady of Lourdes Grotto at the Franciscan Monastery of the Holy Land in America.

I pray not because I am at a low point in my life or facing any kind of life challenges. I don't have to wait to be in a crisis before I can turn to God. And I will not deny God because I think I am now too educated to believe in things that science cannot prove. Neither will I deny God just to keep a portion of my fan-base or followers that does not believe in God. Rather, I pray because I am grateful to God for everything that He has done for me and continues to do. So, my faith is an act of love and gratitude, not one of desperation. I choose to normalize love and gratitude.

Closely related to the foregoing, I have shared below some pictures of my dearest mother, Mrs Esther Mpande Mwenda, a strong woman of Christian faith, when she was receiving my 'amatebeto' on my behalf in Luanshya, Zambia, from my wife's parents and relatives (*i.e.* my in-laws) more than a decade after my wife and I got married.

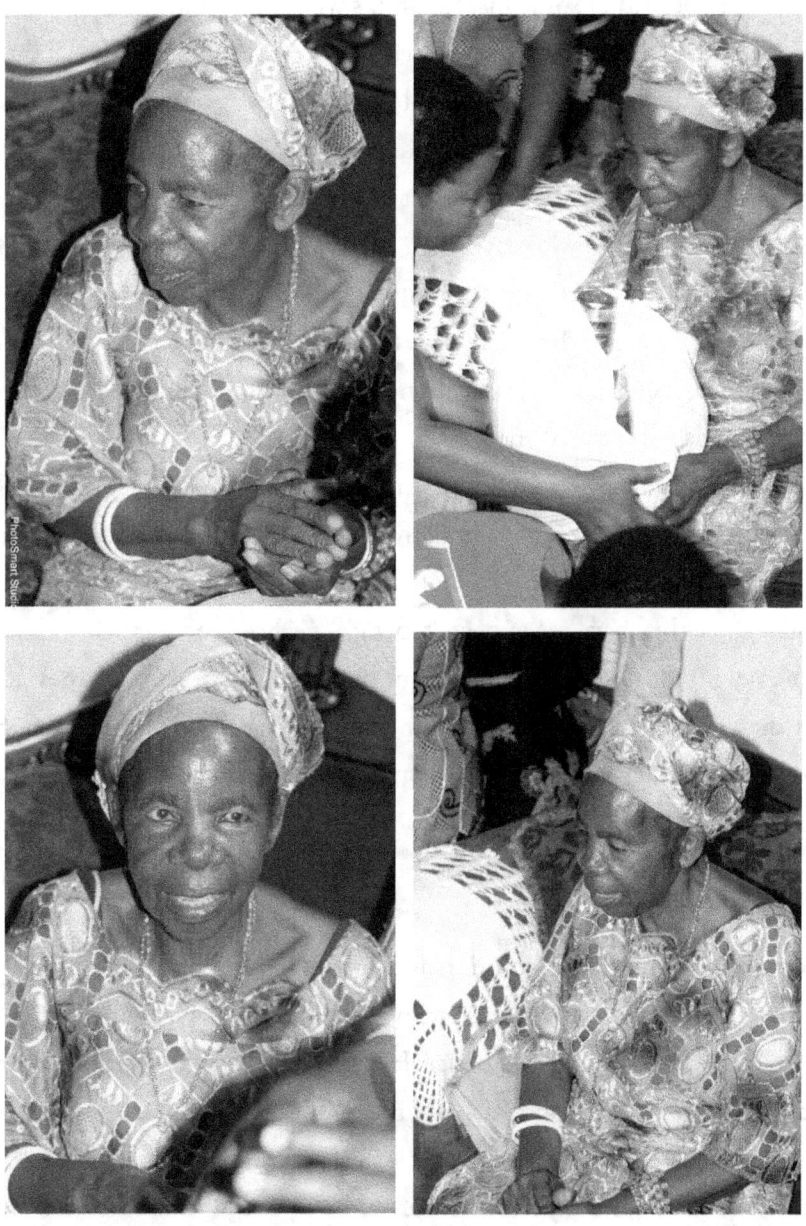

As you can see, amatebeto is not for small boys or men of straw. Many married fellas roaming the streets of Zambia have never been honored with amatebeto by their in-laws. Such fellas often try to justify, downplay and console themselves by saying that you don't need such archaic traditions in today's modern world, and that all you need is a happy marriage and money to build yourself a big mansion. The same can be said of some insecure folks who, having struggled and not succeeded at getting a good education, will tell you that school is not everything. They often argue spiritedly but ignorantly that, at the end of the day, money is all that matters. People are not honest. If you fail to get something, it does not mean that that thing does not matter. It matters, but you just failed. Be honest and admit that you wanted something but failed to achieve it.

Life is interesting. Some people who have never been 'tebetad' before despite having been married for several years, when invited to a friend or family member's matebeto, might, out of jealousy and envy, opt to stay away, while pretending to be very busy on the day of the amatebeto ceremony. They will do everything and anything just to avoid attending a colleague's amatebeto ceremony since they themselves have never been accorded such a dignified honor by their in-laws. Even some insecure family relations will act that way. For example, some ladies, if their spouse has not been accorded amatebeto by her family, especially if the family has little regard for the guy she is married to, will avoid attending her sibling's amatebeto. For some guys too. it's the same. They will stay away and pretend to be busy since they have never been 'tebetad' (*i.e.* honored by their in-laws). People have issues. Even some neighbors and workmates might behave like that as well. They all don't want to be reminded of their failures. The success of someone is a painful experience for them instead of getting inspired by such achievements. Some people are just weird.

I learned a lot from my parents and continued to learn from them up until they passed on. On the one hand, my father was a reserved man who often spoke only when it mattered most. Every conversation with him was a learning experience. He was quite pedagogical in his approach, but also empowering and encouraging. He was a man of great wisdom. My father used to read a lot.

When I was leaving Zambia for graduate studies at Oxford in 1992, my father sat me down for some wise words. The incident took me by surprise. I was caught unawares. I wondered what he wanted to say to me. I did not expect him to address the issue of youthful indulgence in pre-marital sex where one is going away to a foreign country, but my father did so. He decided to address the elephant in the room boldly and courageously, without mincing his words. I was a bit embarrassed since such topics are often shied away from and are viewed as taboo in our African culture, especially if guidance is coming from a parent. But my father knew that I was a grown guy and was going abroad for the first time with nobody to watch over me. He knew that if he did not talk to me about this sensitive topic, nobody else in the family would. So, he confronted the painful truth that often besieges many a youth in their indulgence of youthful indiscretion.

I listened quietly and attentively. I never said a word. Throughout, my eyes were gazing at the floor, hoping that the discussion would end sooner than later. In my African culture, silence is a sign of respect, and you do not look the elders in the eye when they are talking to you. You must look down. Looking down, however, should not be confused with guilt, as is often the case in many cultures in the Global North. Rather, in much of African culture, it is a sign of respect to the elders.

As Africans, we do not ask our elders funny questions when they are talking to us and sharing wisdom. We simply listen quietly and attentively, and only speak when we are invited to ask questions or are allowed to speak. Even so, we do not ask questions to challenge the elders. Rather, we can only speak politely, not aggressively, to provide the elders with some context or valuable information for them to reach a more helpful decision. Those who are not very familiar with African traditions and cultures should understand that we can have our own African version of democracy in the midst of discipline. Democracy for us in African culture is not anarchy. What others in the Global North perceive as pertinent aspects of their democracy is viewed in some African circles as a mere dispensation of anarchy.

In much of Africa, as in other parts of the Global South, our philosophical discourse places more emphasis on responsibilities and moral obligations than individual rights and entitlements. We believe generally that there has to be order and structure in any democracy. We also take a view that society must have structures and hierarchies at which certain decisions are made and that these structural hierarchies must be respected in order for peace and tranquility to prevail. In Africa, you do not just utter words carelessly in the presence of or while you are before the elders. That's chaos and anarchy, not democracy.

While my father often stressed Christian values, educational enlightenment, personal discipline and focus, my mother, on the other hand, was more pragmatic and helped me to understand the intricacies and ramifications of certain forms of African indigenous knowledge, a topic that my father showed very little interest in. My mother knew that, as a loving and caring mother, she could not leave me in this world, as her son, with ignorance of the unspoken ways of mankind. I needed to be both book-smart and street-smart in order to navigate around this world.

As an African, it is important to understand how Africa and some Africans operate. Because, after all, we are Africans. Being a Christian does not mean that you should now be naïve enough to start thinking that everything and everyone in this world are good. Even the Bible recognizes that some people are evil. There is a big difference between discerning evil and believing in or practicing evil. The former is within the realm of Christianity and Christian faith, whilst the latter two are not. Put simply, naivety is not a thing that Christians should entertain. You must know what you are dealing with as a Christian. This world is certainly not full of good people singing 'kumbaya' night and day. That is not how the world operates. There are many bad people out there. It is written in the Bible.

Also, philosophy teaches us that for every force in a particular direction there is a countervailing force in the opposite direction, meaning to say that, if there is light, then there is also darkness. For how else are we to know that light exists if we have no idea what darkness looks like? Darkness is the antithesis of light. In the Bible, Jesus Christ represented good and was thus constantly confronted by forces of evil. That is the real world we live in. Even within the church, you will find some concealed elements of evil masquerading as the faithful. You must have the ability to discern. Not everyone will be happy for you. Even some of those who smile at you do not mean it. Read them carefully and in totality, not just by their smile, for there are many wolves in sheep's clothing. Recognizing the negativity inherent in certain phenomena and distancing yourself from such malevolence is far better than believing in it. That awareness can help to shield you from the costly ignorance of naivety. Because ignorance is costly. Africa as understood by the Africans themselves is different from Africa as understood by the whites from the Global North. But in all this, God is the alpha and the omega.

People often ask me what has driven me to the heights that I have reached as a global scholar and thought-leader. There are many reasons that drive my motivation and I have highlighted 10 of them above. Closely related to the outlined 10 principles of life, if you know who you truly are, there will be no room for jealousy, pettiness, envy and unnecessary competition each time you see someone excelling. Clap for others, as you wait for your turn. You only become bitter when others succeed if you have nothing to show for it and are, thus, envious.

Also, learn to be kind and generous. Do not be selfish and self-centered, or try to fake what you do not have or who and what you are not. Just be yourself. Telling lies or embellishing your credentials won't take you anywhere, no matter how well you try to fake it. Eventually, the truth will come out, and you will have nowhere to run to or hide. Remember that there is no substitute for hard work. You just have to put in the hours. You have to prepare in order to succeed or excel. It's like appreciating a good meal. You need to focus on the intricate culinary details before you can even savor the food.

In the picture below, I was preparing a family meal on Memorial Day holiday in the US.

In the first of the pictures below, my son Jojo is holding a basketball as he prepares to shoot for the basket. It starts with preparation before you can execute the throw or leap into the air. Each picture shows a different phase or stage in the cycle of implementing a task.

Phase I – Scanning the environment and contemplating the next move.

Phase II – Pivoting, positioning yourself, finding your fit and going for it.

Phase III – Taking a good shot while you keep your eyes on the ball for a possible rebound.

Through variable learning, we can pick some lessons from the game of basketball and apply those transferable skills to whatever task we are working on.

In most cases, it is wise to go to school before you can think of opening your mouth to challenge a learned person. Otherwise, you will just end up embarrassing yourself. Ignorance can be quite costly. It is better to prepare against ignorance.

Closely related to this, one must try to cultivate both emotional and social intelligence to be able to lead authentically in an ever-changing environment. It is helpful, indeed, to read about things such as emotional intelligence and social intelligence, as well as mindfulness, in order to understand what they mean.

Also, do not be afraid of, or get intimidated by, the pretentious posturing or talk of men of straw. A number of these folks are nothing but mere façades. Always look for substance over form. Also, look for sustainability, consistency and longevity over a mere flava of the day. Many flavas change quickly and you won't even remember them.

In addition, do not be swayed by naysayers. Close your ears to the noise. Skeptics are there for a reason, especially if they can't be where you are or in your shoes. That's why they have remained behind. Your job is to lead, while theirs is to follow. They remain behind to hate, while your job is to continue soaring and making a difference and mark. Their bitterness will, however, not change a thing.

And remember that every opportunity is a learning opportunity. You must try to learn even from the least regarded and the neglected. It is wise to embrace variable learning and to learn even from unconventional sources that many people do not often pay attention to. For example, you can stop on the streets to ask the homeless how things are going. It will help you get a pulse on the economy.

Finally, do not forget to say 'thank you' to those who have made it possible for you. For us Christians, God comes first and then our families, followed by all the game-changers who have been there for us. Your gratitude and attitude will determine your altitude. In the picture immediately below, I am with my son, Jojo, on a family vacation in Yorkshire, England. My wife took this photo.

In the next picture, taken in New York, US, at a dinner outing, I was dressed in a tuxedo suit the Oxford way.

Some will tell you that education is not everything. Others will tell you that you can't eat books, and that money is what counts at the end of the day. But why are they talking when nobody has asked them? If you look carefully at these naysayers, you will notice that a good number of them are people who tried their hands at education but failed or struggled with school. Some people, if they hear that you are planning to embark on a PhD, will tell you that a PhD is not necessary. Don't be fooled. They just don't want you to get ahead and obtain what they have failed to get. If you were to succeed, they would feel defeated and outdone, so they would rather derail you from your dreams and ambitions.

I once overhead a group of young and overzealous aspiring academics obsess about the H-Index on Google Scholar as the basis of determining one's scholarly impact. What the young rookies did not understand is that the H-Index is driven by many factors and some of them are not even academic or scholarly. For example, if you would like to generate a higher H-Index you can simply co-author a peer-reviewed scholarly journal article with a dozen or so co-authors. Then you can agree amongst yourselves as co-authors to each prepare an article and list each other as co-authors. In essence, out of, say, eleven co-authors, and for the work for each author of just one journal article, you will each appear on the eleven journal articles as co-authors. In addition, you can agree to ensure that you all keep citing your co-authored journal articles and recommend them to your students and other academic audiences for more citations. This dishonest way of manipulating the H-Index is not uncommon. Suddenly, you find that the same authors appear as co-authors on several papers. In the process, their co-authored 'work' gets wide visibility and attracts a higher H-Index. It's that simple.

Another way of manipulating the H-Index is to write on a topical or sexy theme, especially one that has the interests of the Western world. Even if that work is simply a 'working paper' which has not even been peer-reviewed, it can generate high citations as long as it is out in the public domain, especially if it was published by a notable think-tank institution or university. The name of the publishing institution alone will help to sell the working paper widely. And that can generate a high H-Index for the author or co-authors, as their working paper might end up getting cited extensively. Now contrast this with, say, some excellent scientific research work written on obscure and less known African traditions or customs. Do you think such scholarly work will be widely cited in the west to produce a high H-Index rating? That is why we maintain that the H-Index is a highly misleading indicator of scholarly impact. Only naïve scholars obsess with it.

In many cases, if, from your lofty position as an African scholar, you decide to condemn Africa and write all sorts of disparaging things about it, your work might attract a higher H-Index, as some scholars in the West might reference your work widely to justify their cynical views of Africa, maintaining that, 'After all, one of their own has spoken.'

A third way of manipulating the H-Index is where a head of department of a research institution or department insists that his or her name should be added as co-author to any publication that has to come out of the department before they can authorize the publication of that research work. This makes the head of department appear to be a prolific researcher, with his or her name spewed everywhere on other people's publications as co-author. Obviously, the broad citation of those publications will generate a higher H-Index for that head of department. That said, the more difficult route which many scholars try to avoid is writing scholarly work as a sole author. This is a path I have chosen for the greater part of my scholarly writing. I do not do books such as 'Cases and Materials', and I seldom do collected volumes of chapter contributions written by other authors or a compendium of statutes and other legal materials. Most of my sole-authored scholarly work appears in peer-reviewed academic publications, and they include peer-reviewed monographs and scholarly articles published by such leading and high-impact publishing houses as Oxford University Press (OUP), Cambridge University Press (CUP), the University of Oxford Law Faculty (UK), the World Bank (US), Columbia University (US), Carolina Academic Press (US, Routledge-Cavendish Publishing (UK), Springer (US and Continental Europe), George Washington University (US), Michigan State University (US), Rutgers University (US), Gonzaga University (US), Richmond University (US), California State University-Fresno (US), University of Idaho (US), University of Toledo (US), Pretoria University Law Press (South Africa), Cambridge Scholars Publishing (UK), Murray State University (US), Whittier Law School (US), Cambria Press (US), Ashgate Publishing (UK), Commonwealth Legal Education Association (UK), Abersytwyth University (UK), Murdoch University (Australia), the University of Miskolc (Hungary) , University of Tilburg (Netherlands), Institut für Wirtschaftsrecht Johann Wolfgang Goethe–Universität (Germany), University of Hong Kong (China), National Law School of India University (India), University of Zambia (Zambia), University of South Africa (South Africa), University of Stellenbosch (South Africa), University of Nairobi (Kenya), University of Ghana (Ghana), University of Dar-es-Salaam (Tanzania), University of Lesotho (Lesotho), University of the Orange Free State (South Africa), and the University of Zimbabwe (Zimbabwe).

Coming back to the issue of cynics who dismiss the value of a PhD, in the field of law, for example, I have met many people who have only gone as far as a Master of Laws (LLM) degree. Now there is nothing wrong with that, but let me push a bit further to make my point. Some have LLMs, say, from some Ivy League school, and feel somewhat invincible about that, but we know that all LLM degree programs in the US, unlike most American Juris Doctor (JD) degree programs, are not even professionally accredited by the American Bar Association (ABA). In many cases, if you have a PhD and find yourself before such an LLM degree-holder, you will notice the uneasiness of the person. The PhD causes them a lot of discomfort. They feel threatened and will label anyone with a PhD or JSD/SJD degree as 'too academic'. I have seen how such LLM folks will not give a chance to a well-qualified candidate at a job interview because the candidate has a PhD, while they themselves do not. People have issues.

It is worse if the candidate has even published scholarly work. The superficial cynics will be quick to label the candidate as 'too academic', yet their sentiments are simply a reflection of their own insecurities. That you yourself lack a PhD does not mean you are more 'practical'. It could simply be that you are wanting in education or are underqualified. For there is no correlation between having inadequate, insufficient, insignificant or modest qualifications and being practical. It might actually be that you should consider going back to school to upgrade your skills and résumé instead of frustrating people who are more qualified and educated than you are. Indeed, there is nothing as practical as a good theory.

If you look carefully at a number of these cynics, most of them failed to get a competitive PhD scholarship or were rejected in their PhD applications. Others just don't have what it takes academically to attempt a PhD. There are also those who failed to finish their PhD studies, or abandoned their doctoral studies, for one reason or another. Today, a good number of all these people will tell you that a PhD is not necessary until you find them clamoring about some phony honorary doctorate purchased from some diploma mill or online unaccredited school. People are not honest.

The same can be said of many PhD holders who feel that they have arrived after earning their PhD from a top-ranked school, only to realize that there is also a concept of a Higher Doctorate that ranks substantially higher than a PhD. Some PhD-holders could even be teaching as professors at various colleges or universities. Instead of simply admitting that, notwithstanding the fact that they have a well-respected earned PhD, they do not have what it takes to earn a Higher Doctorate, they will tell you that they have no need for a Higher Doctorate because they already have a PhD or have served as an examiner of a Higher Doctorate before. People are not honest. Why would you start to explain yourself before someone even asks for your comment? I mean, why are you talking when nobody asked you? Just say you don't have what it takes to get the highly revered and coveted senior academic award, the Higher Doctorate degree.

Naysayers, cynics, haters and malicious skeptics all belong to the same category of insecure people. More often than not, you will find that their achievements or accomplishments are nowhere close to those of the person that they are attacking. Instead of getting inspired, they become envious. Jealousy consumes them. If it was up to them, you would not graduate. If it was up to them, you would have no college or university degree. If it was up to them, you would not receive all the honor that you have received. If it was up to them, you would be ignored and rejected everywhere you go. If it was up to them, your name would never be mentioned at the table of opportunities. If it was up to them, nobody would clap for you when you are winning. But the truth is that it is not up to them. It is up to God and you. So, those cynics who scoff at education and the educated often speak from a point of insecurity.

In their scornfulness, there is often an underlying envy and insecurity that they try to mask or hide through unwarranted sarcasm, positing that 'we need entrepreneurs, not just getting degrees and degrees'. They point at prominent CEOs and billionaires who only have a modest education, saying you don't need to get a lot of education to make it in life. While it is true that some top jobs don't go to the most qualified or most educated people, you must continue to celebrate your victories no matter how small or big they are. You don't have to apologize to anyone over your achievements. Much to the chagrin of the naysayers, do not shy away from celebrating your victories. Celebrating your successes is simply stating a fact that could inspire others. More often than not, the fact will inspire someone somewhere. And that fact is what you have earned or achieved. Do not, however, throw caution to the wind. Be mindful not to celebrate too early because haters can conspire to derail you. That said, whoever is in denial of facts can go to hell. You don't owe him or her anything.

Admittedly, there will be instances where you might be far better qualified than some of the people that you report to. But then, should that bother you or should it become an issue? Not at all. You do not go to school just to get a promotion at work. So, be happy with whatever excellence you have achieved, because not even your haters or some people that appear to be ahead of you come anywhere close to what you have accomplished. Life is like that. Nobody has it all. And so, much to the chagrin of the cynics and haters, let it be said again that there is nothing as costly as ignorance. Not even money can rescue an ignorant person from the shackles of their ignorance.

Claiming to be rich while dismissing the value of erudition, for example, is nothing but a red herring of ignorance. Because even an entrepreneur needs to have some kind of education or knowledge in order to succeed. But the unenlightened cynics are misguided by a lack of education or through indoctrination, misinformation and miseducation. Using ichi-Copperbelt, one would say it as follows: "Mona iwe, wa filwa isukulu ati 'Iyo, kano entrepreneurship'! Bu entrepreneur nabo ubwa nsala. Umu nobe ali soma ukunya, iwe nobu tutu bobe, ati: 'Education is not everything'. Elo chibe shani?" ("Entrepreneurship is not a substitute for education. You need to get some vital knowledge about business. What do you gain or benefit from saying that education is not everything?")

True wealth comes with the edification of the self. You might try to think of yourself as doing well in life, but doing well alone is not enough. You must also do good. Doing good is different from doing well. The latter act is often driven by quantitative variables whereas the former is driven by both quantitative and qualitative variables. Doing good, more than doing well, is what makes each one of us into a responsible and good citizen of this world. The goodness in us is what makes the world a better place to live in. And such goodness will help to save our planet from climate change, environmental degradation and all the atrocities of war, hunger, poverty, disease, famine and man-made disasters.

Embracing exceptionalism is something I have always subscribed to. You cannot create value for yourself if you do not differentiate yourself from your competitors, rivals or new entrants in the market. And if you cannot create value, how do you expect to survive to claim any value? From whom will you claim it? For, you must create value in order to claim it. So, work to differentiate your strengths and capabilities from those of your competitors, rivals or new market entrants. Put simply, try to be different from others, as you strive for exceptionality. Do not just sit there as an 'average Joe', carrying on with life as if all is well and safe.

In the pictures below, I am being interviewed in my home in Maryland, US, by a team from the elite Ivy League business school, the University of Pennsylvania Wharton School. The Wharton team drove all the way from Pennsylvania to interview me at my house in Maryland. It is does not happen that easily that folks from such a prestigious school as Wharton can come to your home instead of you going to them. You have to earn their respect to attract such honor.

It is important to add that creating value for yourself by being innovative and differentiating yourself in the market or industry helps with branding yourself strategically. Otherwise, you can be replaced or substituted easily if you have nothing different or exceptional to offer, especially if you are a minority. In this world, as long as we are not in Heaven, there are limited seats for minorities. Not even arguments in favor of meritocracy over mediocrity can sometimes redress the imbalance. Generally, mediocrity abounds. That said, as a global thought-leader, I have chosen to take the path of meritocracy. There are few on that path. My scholarly works can be found in many parts of the world. Many people around the world and from different walks of life have access to and have benefitted from my ideas. In August 2024, for example, a good colleague, Dr Dennis Lembani, who is an academic at the University of Zambia (UNZA), sent me the message below after he returned from a visit to some rural parts of Zambia in Eastern Province.

Paid a visit to a friend's house in Chipata this week..checked the bookshelf..only to find my Professor's books 👆🏻👆🏻😁😁

Like Michael Jackson's music, or Pele or Messi's soccer prowess, as well as Muhammed Ali or Mike Tyson's legendary boxing, my intellectual ideas have permeated those rural areas. It is important to add that the extent to which some sections of the public expect you to be exceptional is sometimes dependent on your race or gender. Just try to ask a minority person who is a professional soccer player and has played under a coach or team-manager who has a soft heart for players from a certain ethnic or racial background if he would get enough playing time. And if you happen to be in the starting lineup, do not be shocked if you are substituted early. Sometimes, even your team-mates who, unlike you, are not minorities, can be part of the racist cabal by choosing not to pass the ball to you often so that you look ineffective.

We cannot pretend that there are no racial or gender prejudices out there. Yes, there are some good people in this world, but there are also bad people. We cannot be blind to that truth. So, we have to remain mindful of what is on either side of the aisle. I know that many business schools shy away from including topics on racial bigotry in the curriculum for a course such as organizational behavior yet, racial prejudice is there in society and industry. Indeed, such topics should be covered in the curriculum of courses relating to organizational behavior. Very few management or leadership professors will tell you about, say, 'white privilege' in the job market or at a workplace. Yes, they can talk about 'unconscious bias', or 'blind spots', but they will not be direct enough to mention a term such as 'white privilege'. Yet, it's there. You can graduate from an MBA degree program thinking you will have the same job opportunities as your white colleagues until you begin to see how quickly they are being hired and promoted while you keep getting turned down or overlooked. These are the kinds of things that they don't teach you in business school because such topics make many people feel uncomfortable.

You could have attended the same Ivy League university as your Caucasian friend, but he will be given a chance on the basis that, having graduated from an Ivy League school, he must have the potential to excel, whereas you will be required to show that you not only graduated from that Ivy League school but also have the requisite experience, not just the potential, to perform. It's called 'white privilege'. Your Caucasian friend will be considered on the basis of 'potential' while you will be assessed on the basis of 'actual evidence of work experience'.

And so, the race issue remains the elephant in the room, as discussions on race are often set aside or taken off the diversity, inclusion and equity agenda and replaced by issues of sexual orientation and gender empowerment. To hedge against the risks of racial discrimination, some minorities end up marrying into the dominant white race just to get the so-called 'passport' of being accepted among members of that dominant race. It's rough out there. These aspirants or people of color try as much as possible to assimilate themselves into white culture. There is an unspoken belief that if you are from a minority race and marry one of their (white) sisters or brothers, maybe they will look after you nicely so that you too can look after their white sister or white brother nicely. Life can be quite stressful for some people of color who try so hard to fit into the dominant white culture. They often even have to resort to code-switching by dropping their native African, Asian or ghetto accent and picking up a seemingly 'acceptable' American or European accent. Some end up throwing a fellow minority under a bus so that they can remain looking good in the eyes of their white boss and be favored over the minority gasping for air under the bus. It can get dirty and ugly out there. Indeed, a number of minority folks are constantly struggling to get the white man's attention and approval. So, it is not uncommon to see some Uncle Tom-type black folks, Latinos and Asians among minorities. They will even go to the extent of inviting their white bosses and workmates to their homes for dinner on weekends, but will never invite a black person unless he or she is a boss who can help them move up the corporate ladder. To impress their white guests, they will make sure to cook a fine meal that they have only read about in a cookbook or seen in a movie. They will even order expensive wines that they themselves have never drunk before. That is the real world out there, not the stuff that is presented to you in textbooks.

By contrast, in much of the developing world where race issues hardly matter, a parallel of the elephant in the room is tribalism and religious prejudice. Similarly, many business schools in the developing world will not teach you about how tribalism or religious prejudices affect organizational behavior. Folks would rather pretend that the world out there is a level playing field. It's not. In the workplace, a number of issues relating to career development have nothing to do with the quality of your work performance or the strength of your qualifications. Even experience can get overlooked sometimes. Careers often depend on whether you 'belong' or someone likes you. It is as simple as that.

The battle between meritocracy and mediocrity is real. As long as we are not in Heaven, mediocrity abounds and there are limited seats available for meritocracy. Most seats are taken up by mediocrity. This explains why it is not uncommon to find folks joining a popular golf club or charity organization not because they love to play golf or believe in the goals of that charity organization, but just to improve prospects for their own career progression on the corporate ladder. Others join dark secret societies where some seemingly powerful guys in the corporate world congregate just to move up the corporate ladder or gain some business opportunities. Then there are those who schmooze constantly or flirt around, while others even sleep with their bosses, just to bolster their career prospects. Everything is concealed under the umbrella term 'networking'. Many people are not honest. They just don't want to say it as it is because they don't want to rock the boat.

It's up to you to figure things out.

www.ingramcontent.com/pod-product-compliance
Lightning Source LLC
Chambersburg PA
CBHW051358070526
44584CB00023B/3201